ST**A**TE
OF THE NATION
South Africa 2003–2004

Edited by John Daniel,
Adam Habib & Roger Southall

HSRC
PRESS

Compiled by the Democracy & Governance Research Programme,
Human Sciences Research Council

Published by HSRC Press
Private Bag X9182, Cape Town, 8000, South Africa

HSRC Press is an imprint of the Human Sciences Research Council

ISBN 0 7969 2024 9

Cover photograph by Yassir Booley

Production by comPress

Printed by Creda Communications

Distributed in South Africa by Blue Weaver Marketing and Distribution,
PO Box 30370, Tokai, Cape Town, South Africa, 7966. Tel/Fax: (021) 701-7302,
email: booksales@mweb.co.za.

Contents

List of tables

List of figures

Acronyms

ABET	Adult Basic Education and Training
AGOA	Africa Growth and Opportunity Act
AIDS	Acquired Immune Deficiency Syndrome
ANC	African National Congress
ANCYL	African National Congress Youth League
APLA	Azanian Peoples Liberation Army
ASAHDI	Association of Vice Chancellors of Historically-Disadvantaged Institutions
AU	African Union
BCM	Black Consciousnesss Movement
BER	Bureau for Economic Research
BIG	Basic Income Grant
C2005	Curriculum 2005
CBD	Central Business District
CBO	Community-based organisation
CD	Conference on Disarmament
CEPPWAWU	Chemical, Energy, Paper, Printing, Wood and Allied Workers' Union
CHE	Council on Higher Education
COSATU	Congress of South African Trade Unions
CSO	Civil Society Organisation
CSSDCA	Conference on Security, Stability, Development and Co-operation in Africa
CWIU	Chemical Workers' Industrial Union
CWU	Communication Workers' Union
DA	Democratic Alliance
DENOSA	Democratic Nurses' Organisation of South Africa
DITSELA	Development Institute for Training, Support and Education for Labour
DLA	Department of Land Affairs
DoE	Department of Education
DoH	Department of Health
DoL	Department of Labour
DP	Democratic Party
DPLG	Department of Provincial and Local Government
DRC	Democratic Republic of Congo
DTI	Department of Trade and Industry
EEA	Employment Equity Act
EMIS	Education Management Information System
EU	European Union
FASSET	Financial, Accounting, Management Consulting and other Financial Services

FAWU	Food and Allied Workers' Union
FEDUSA	Federation of Democratic Unions of South African
FMG	Financial Management Grant
FDI	Foreign Direct Investment
FET	Further Education and Training
FTE	Full-time Teaching Equivalent
GDP	Gross Domestic Product
GNP	Gross National Product
GEAR	Growth, Employment and Redistribution
GET	General Education and Training
GNU	Government of National Unity
HAART	Highly Active Anti-Retroviral Therapy
HCT	High Commission Territory
HIV	Human Immunodeficiency Virus
HRD	Human Resource Development
HRV	Human Rights Violations
HSRC	Human Sciences Research Council
IDASA	Institute for Democracy in South Africa
IDC	Industrial Development Corporation
IDP	Integrated Development Plan
IFP	Inkatha Freedom Party
IMF	International Monetary Fund
IPILRA	Interim Protection of Informal Land Rights Act
IPS	Institute of Public Servants
ITB	Industry Training Board
JET	Joint Education Trust
LED	Local Economic Development
LFS	Labour Force Survey
LPM	Landless People's Movement
LRAD	Land Redistribution for Agricultural Development
MCC	Medicines Control Council
MDC	Movement for Democratic Change
MDM	Mass Democratic Movement
MEC	Member of the Executive Committee
MERG	Macroeconomic Research Group
MK	Umkhonto we Sizwe
MLA	Monitoring Learning Achievement
MP	Member of Parliament
MPL	Member of Provincial Legislature
MSP	Municipal Support Programme
MTCT	Mother to Child Transmission
NACTU	National Council of Trade Unions
NAFTA	North American Free Trade Area
NALEDI	National Labour and Economic Development Institute

NAM	Non-Aligned Movement
NAPWA	National Association of People Living with HIV/AIDS
NCACC	National Conventional Arms Control Committee
NCHE	National Commission on Higher Education
NCOP	National Council of Provinces
NDA	National Development Agency
NDPP	National Directorate of Public Prosecutions
NDR	National Democratic Revolution
NEC	National Executive Committee
NEDLAC	National Economic Development and Labour Council
NEHAWU	National Education, Health and Allied Workers' Union
NEPAD	New Partnership for Africa's Development
NGK	Nederduitse Gereformeerde Kerk
NGO	Non-governmental Organisation
NNP	New National Party
NP	National Party
NPT	Non-Proliferation Treaty
NQF	National Qualifications Framework
NSA	National Skills Authority
NSDS	National Skills Development Strategy
NUM	National Union of Mineworkers
NUMSA	National Union of Metalworkers of South Africa
NUSAS	National Union of South African Students
NWG	National Working Group
OAU	Organisation of African Unity
OBE	Outcomes-based Education
OHS	October Household Survey
PAAB	Public Accountants' and Auditors' Board
PAC	Pan Africanist Congress
PAWE	Performing Arts Workers' Equity
PMA	Pharmaceutical Manufacturers' Association
POPCRU	Police and Prisons Civil Rights Union
PEI	President's Education Initiative
PMG	Parliamentary Monitoring Group
RAPWU	Retail and Agricultural Processing Workers' Union
RDP	Reconstruction and Development Programme
RENAMO	Mozambique National Resistance
SAAPAWU	South African Agriculture and Plantation and Allied Workers' Union
SACCAWU	South African Commercial, Catering and Allied Workers' Union
SACOL	South African College for Open Learning
SACP	South African Communist Party
SACTE	South African College for Teacher Education
SACTU	South African Congress of Trade Unions
SACTWU	Southern African Clothing and Textile Workers' Union

SACU	Southern African Customs and Monetary Union
SADC	Southern African Development Community
SADF	South African Defence Force
SADNU	South African Democratic Nurses' Union
SADTU	South African Democratic Teachers' Union
SAF	South African Foundation
SAFPU	South African Football Players Union
SAHRC	South African Human Rights Commission
SAICA	South African Institute of Chartered Accountants
SAIIA	South African Institute of International Affairs
SAMA	South African Medical Association
SAMWU	South African Municipal Workers' Union
SANCO	South African National Civic Organisation
SANDF	South African National Defence Force
SAPS	South African Police Service
SAQA	South African Qualifications Act
SARHWU	South African Railway and Harbours Workers' Union
SARS	South African Research Services
SASAWU	South African State and Allied Workers' Union
SASBO	South African Society of Bank Officials
SATAWU	South African Transport and Allied Workers' Union
SAUVCA	South African University Vice Chancellors Association
SDA	Skills Development Act
SETA	Sectoral Education and Training Authorities
SLAG	Settlement and Land Acquisition Grant
Stats SA	Statistics South Africa
TAC	Treatment Action Campaign
TGWU	Transport and General Workers' Union
TIMMS-R	Third International Mathematics and Science Repeat Study
TLC	Transitional Local Council
TUCSA	Trades Union Council of South Africa
TRC	Truth and Reconciliation Commission
UDF	United Democratic Front
UDM	United Democratic Movement
UN	United Nations
UNCTAD	United Nations Conference on Trade and Development
UNITA	National Union for the Total Independence of Angola
USAID	United States Agency for International Development
WITS	University of the Witwatersrand
WTO	World Trade Organisation
ZANU-PF	Zimbabwe African National Union/Patriotic Front

Preface
From the South African Review to the State of the Nation

From inception in 1983 to final issue in 1995, *South African Review* was guided by a set of consistent intentions and themes. It was conceptualised as a 'review which broadly and thematically tried to make some sense of what was happening in South Africa'; and which would include 'historical and background information, contemporary analysis and interpretation', and projections of likely 'future trends and developments' (Preface, *South African Review* 1, 1983).

Contributions were 'primarily concerned with the dynamics and forces at play in South Africa, not with individuals or events. For it is organised and powerful social forces – rather than individuals and their intentions – that are reshaping South Africa both internally and in relation to the rest of the world' (Introduction, *South African Review* 1, 1983: 1).

South African Review was a project of the Southern African Research Service, a small agency which also published *Work in Progress (WIP)* magazine from its inception in 1977 to closure in the mid-1990s. The relationship between *WIP* and the *Review* involved an important symbiosis, with contemporary material presented in the bi-monthly magazine often influencing and structuring the more measured and interpretive contributions to the book. A constructive continuity between those writing for *WIP* and the *Review*, the editors and publishers, developed and endured over a decade, and this was a key factor in the success and influence of both projects.

This first issue of *The State of the Nation* displays strong consistencies with progressive writing and publishing of the 1980s. There are even consistencies in the author profile, with some half a dozen authors in this volume having been regular contributors to the *Review*. Even the broad subject areas identified for analysis show similarity, despite the seismographic changes in society over the 20 years since the *Review* was first published. The first *Review* grouped articles under the broad categories of:

○ South Africa and Southern Africa
○ Politics

- The economy
- Labour
- Education, health and housing
- Women (by which the editors meant gender relations).

The State of the Nation presents its contributions under the categories of
- South Africa in Africa
- Politics
- The economy
- Society in transition.

The continuity in traditions could hardly be clearer.

Of course, the environment has changed radically since a group of over 50 potential contributors met in Johannesburg in February 1983 to debate whether there was value to the *Review* initiative and, if so, to give it form and structure. Georgina Jaffee, who put together this first contributors' meeting, had driven the length and breadth of the country to canvass the idea, and obtain 'buy-in' from who we would now call 'stakeholders'. Her journey provoked suspicions, and not only from the security police who often followed her from city to town, meeting to meeting. New initiatives also provoked concern amongst some of the organised forces of opposition and progressive politics of the time. What was the agenda? Did it support 'workerists' or 'populists' in the union movement, 'Charterists', black consciousness adherents or the small socialist-left formations of the Western Cape?

Discussions sometimes had to be held in conditions of secrecy. Some participants were subject to banning or house arrest orders, were ex-political prisoners, union organisers or community activists. There was no well-equipped conference centre for the pioneers of the *Review* to meet with potential contributors!

Gerhard Maré, who has contributed a piece on the nature of the state to this volume, was a founding editor of the *Review*. With a group of volunteers, we undertook the daunting task of content and copy-editing the first contributions, many of which were handwritten. Computer editing and digital desk-top publishing were still a few years away, and hard-copy editing and retyping, reading of typeset galley proofs against original copy, and manual correcting of word breaks are continuities which happily have not been maintained between the first *Review* and the first *State of the Nation*.

Publishing ventures such as *The State of the Nation* – and, indeed, the *Review* in its time – contribute in a range of ways to the intellectual life of a society. One of the less visible manners in which this occurs involves creation of 'sufficient consensus' around the issues and areas which are central to critical analysis, debate and research. Media in general, and print publications in particular, can never succeed in telling people what to think (the dreams of successive generations of propagandists and apologists notwithstanding!). However, credible, consistent and coherent writings which successfully reach target audiences do have the effect of creating agreement on what is central and fundamental, and what is secondary or peripheral, in the analysis of society.

This process of putting a sufficient number of people on 'the same page' to have a meaningful dialogue, based on a reasonably common information base, is vital to the development of a political and intellectual culture of progressive analysis, interpretation and research. Without it, the strengths of an intellectual pluralism and openness easily degenerate into an atomised relativism, in which every interpretation has identical import, and in which no social explanation or analysis is deemed to have greater credence than any other.

A hidden consequence of the *Review's* success was the development – within a small, but influential community – of a sufficiently shared understanding and common information base to facilitate dialogue, debate and analysis. The publication of this first *State of the Nation*, co-ordinated and structured from within the increasingly intellectually credible Human Sciences Research Council (HSRC), holds out this same possibility to the various audiences which it will reach.

The State of the Nation is an exciting project which recaptures the critical focus of the most progressive writing of the 1980s. Borrowing from the tradition of the *South African Review*, it takes its focus from the annual presidential speeches on that topic, seeking to review where we are and where we are going as a nation. Its appearance is welcome, perhaps even overdue, and it deserves to become a regular port of call for everyone who wants to keep abreast of the key developments taking place in South Africa.

Glenn Moss, September 2003

Glenn Moss was a founding editor of the *South African Review*, retaining editorial responsibility for it throughout its existence. Currently a long-term consultant attached to Statistics South Africa, he was also previously managing director of Ravan Press, and editor of *Work in Progress*.

Introduction

Adam Habib, John Daniel and Roger Southall

The State of the Nation project

This book is the first in an intended series of regular, hopefully annual, volumes which will seek to address the state of the South African nation. It has two sources of inspiration.

First, it is quite deliberately modeled on the *South African Review*, edited by Glenn Moss and others during the 1980s and 1990s, which appeared seven times and provided a thematic examination of the then state of South African politics, economics, labour, education, society, foreign affairs and so on. *South African Review* adopted a perspective which, whilst never uniform, was politically progressive and obviously stridently anti-apartheid. It brought together academics and activists within the covers of its issues, and was intended to provide popular yet informed analyses. As such, it was as much an instrument for shaping strategy and tactics as it was a valuable tool for lecturers and students. It rapidly established itself as essential reading for all those who were concerned to understand South Africa through some of those darkest of years, and to its credit, it became a thorn in the side of the then government.

The second source of inspiration is the annual 'State of the Nation' address to Parliament in which the government presents its own perspective on South Africa's present status, and reviews achievements and problems encountered over the last year. This tradition is one apartheid legacy which has been carried over into the new dispensation. These speeches are important occasions, a regular report back by the government to the South African people, and a manifest guide as to how the country's rulers see and wish to present themselves. Inevitably, any government in such a situation is likely to present a favourable gloss on its performance, and its opponents are equally likely to focus upon such presentations as exaggerating successes and minimising failures. Away from the immediate arena of party politics, this series of volumes will use the annual presidential speeches far less for attack than as frameworks for interrogation, query and debate.

In contrast to the *South African Review*, which appeared during the 'struggle years', *The State of the Nation* will be appearing in a very different era, a time of 'democracy' and of hoped for 'development and delivery'. Like its predecessor, it will seek to provide overviews of the state of politics, government performance, the economy and so on. Equally, it will try to draw together the reflections of activists and journalists, as much as academics, in a way which will provide the ordinary reader with an easy-to-read guide to contemporary South Africa. Likewise, the intention is that the series will be politically progressive in tone, attempting to judge the condition of South Africa by what is desirable rather than simply by how much it has moved beyond the undesirable. Yet, because in a democracy there are never easy answers to the dilemmas that are thrown up, there can rarely be agreement: consequently, ideological diversity will not simply be encouraged, it will be inevitable. At the same time, although authors will be encouraged to offer critical judgements, the emphasis will also be upon measured and balanced assessments, in recognition of the far more complex era that South Africa has embarked upon. Overall, taking their cues from the annual presidential speeches, the volumes will attempt to provide regular benchmarks of 'where South Africa is and where it is going'. Their purpose will be to provoke debate, stir controversy, celebrate and irritate; and if they achieve anything approaching the impact of the *South African Review* of yesteryear, they should be judged to have served their purpose.

The state of the nation after ten years of democracy

What is the state of the South African nation as we approach the tenth year of democratic rule? This is the question we posed to all of the contributors to this volume. Each was requested to reflect on their particular sector with a view to addressing this question. Obviously a decade is not sufficient time to unravel the disparities bequeathed by 300 years of white domination and more than 40 years of apartheid rule. But it is sufficient time to at least start offering preliminary judgements about our socio-economic progress and the political and development trajectory chosen by our elites.

The first decade of democratic rule will have been overseen by two presidencies, the first led by Nelson Mandela between 1994 and 1999, and the second by Thabo Mbeki from 1999 to 2004. Commentators often reflect on how different these two presidential terms have been. Not only do they reflect on the personalities of the two presidents, lamenting the aloofness of Mbeki and comparing it to the amiableness of Mandela, but they often also suggest that Mandela's presidency was marked by reconciliation, which Mbeki is said to have abandoned for empowerment and narrow African nationalism (*Mail & Guardian* 4–11 July 1997, 30 April–6 May 1999 and 21–28 December 2002). Mandela is thus seen as the reconciler and democrat, while Mbeki is perceived as the ultimate technocrat, busy centralising power in an 'imperial presidency'.

But is this a fair description of the two presidencies? After all, a careful look at the annual 'State of the Nation' addresses of both presidents, delivered at the opening of parliament in February of each year, will reveal that they have covered much the same issues and reflected on the same concerns. Mandela did indeed engage in reconciliation. His first presidential address began with a poem from Afrikaner poet, Ingrid Jonker, stressing the compatibility of simultaneously holding an Afrikaner and an African identity (Mandela 1994). Moreover, throughout his administration, he undertook high-profile symbolic reconciliation initiatives in an effort to convince whites and other minority racial groups that they had a place in the post-apartheid South Africa.[1] But this theme was also carried in Mbeki's 'State of the Nation' addresses. In his 2002 address, for instance, he approvingly quoted a study by the University of Stellenbosch, which validated his administration's delivery record. He praised this bastion of the Afrikaner establishment for the constructive role it was playing in the reconstruction of post-apartheid South Africa (Mbeki 2002). Similarly, Mbeki's overtures to the New National Party (NNP) to form an electoral alliance in the aftermath of the break-up of the Democratic Alliance (DA), was partly inspired by the desire to provide Afrikaners with a stake in the post-apartheid political establishment (Habib & Nadvi 2002).

There was also a high degree of consistency between the presidencies on the economic front. The shift to neoliberal economics, as reflected in the adoption of the Growth, Employment and Redistribution Strategy (Gear), occurred early in the Mandela presidency and was consistently defended by both presidents in their 'State of the Nation' addresses. Even Mbeki's much vaunted Black Empowerment Initiative predates his presidency, having its roots in the Reconstruction and Development programme (RDP) that served as the African National Congress's (ANC) electoral manifesto in the 1994 elections. In addition, the tensions within the Tripartite Alliance and the ANC leadership's stringent approach to dealing with criticism from the Congress of South African Trade Unions (Cosatu) and the South African Communist Party

(SACP) have spanned both presidencies. Indeed, it was Mandela who first publicly chastised the Alliance partners for their criticisms of the government's macroeconomic policy, and asked them to leave the movement should they be uncomfortable with its direction.

The overlap and consistency, in both positive and negative terms, between the two presidencies is thus significant. Nonetheless, a careful read of the underlying overtones of both presidents' speeches, conduct and behaviour also suggests some differences. This has been reflected in the foci and emphases of the two presidents. The former did stress the reconciliation theme far more effectively than he did either the empowerment or redress ones. The result was that midway through his term concern emerged within the ANC and amongst large segments of the populace that too much was being done to appease the beneficiaries of apartheid and too little to address the concerns of the victims of racial oppression. This concern reflected itself in the controversy accompanying the release in October 1998 of the first five volumes of the final report of the Truth and Reconciliation (TRC) Commission, when a significant component of the leadership of the ANC rejected the report for what it incorrectly saw as the equation of the crime of apartheid with some of the human rights abuses conducted in the course of the liberation struggle.[2]

The philosophy and ethos of the Mbeki presidency is best captured in his 'Two Nations' address on the occasion of the parliamentary debate on reconciliation and nation building held in May 1998. In an often moving and even poetic treatise, Mbeki described two nations, one white and the other black. The former's citizens, he argued, exhibited the lifestyles of the developed world, and were 'relatively prosperous with access to developed economic, physical, educational, communication and other infrastructure'. (Mbeki 1998). The latter's inhabitants were subjected to the poverty and immiseration resulting largely from the condition of underdevelopment typical of the most marginalised and disempowered communities in the world. This dichotomy between privilege and disadvantage, which is racially defined, had to be transcended, Mbeki argued, if South Africa was to have an even chance at reconciliation and nation building. Was South Africa on the path to transcending this divide? Mbeki answered in the negative, lamenting the fact that the beneficiaries of our past refused to underwrite the upliftment of the poor. Comparing South Africans to the Germans who poured enormous resources into their nation-building project, Mbeki made a passionate plea for a greater magnanimity on the part of South Africa's privileged citizens

(Mbeki 1998). It is their generosity, he declared, that is required for a reconciliation project that has at its core the principle of social justice. Without such justice, neither racial reconciliation nor nation building would be possible in South Africa.

Assessments of the state of the nation need to be made against the backdrop of this presidential address. Supporters of government are correct to maintain that the disparities we have inherited from 350 years of white domination cannot be eradicated in a mere decade. But it must be also borne in mind that we should not use apartheid, declared by the international community a crime against humanity, as the sole yardstick to measure our progress. That progress needs to be measured against the goals of the anti-apartheid struggle and the historic possibilities of our time so well captured in Mbeki's 'Two Nations' address. Is progress thus being made to transcend the two-nation dichotomy that has characterised our society for so long? Is the principle of justice enshrined at the core of our nation-building project? It is these questions that the various chapters in this particular collection are dedicated to addressing – as a precursor to later volumes which will deepen and extend assessments of the 'state of the nation'.

Reconciliation and nation building

Reconciliation and nation building can take different forms. They can be a minority project designed to incorporate previously oppositional elites into the dominant political and economic structures, or they can be founded on justice so that the whole of society is transformed in ways that benefit its entire citizenry. Almost all chapters in this volume lend themselves to addressing this issue.

The volume is divided into four thematic areas: political, economic, social, and international. Chapters in each of these areas speak to a specific aspect of our transition. The political chapters, for instance, reflect on our progress in entrenching democracy through analyses of institution building and race relations; the economic ones speak to key issues concerning the transformation of the South African economy, or the lack thereof, with a view to determining its beneficiaries and victims; the social chapters investigate the implementation and effects of service delivery in various sectors; and the international chapters explore South Africa's contribution to the region in order to assess its implications for democracy, peace and stability on the continent.

As editors, we are deeply conscious of large gaps. Our political overviews tend to be top-down, rather than looking at 'politics on the ground floor', and we recognise, for instance, the huge need in the future to take a hard look at the role of the provinces or what is going on in both the larger metropoles and the most far-flung, rural areas of our country. In our economics section, we make no apology at all for focusing overwhelmingly upon the growing crisis of unemployment, its causes and its impact upon trade unions, for this is the key issue which confronts the mass of ordinary South Africans who looked to democracy and ANC rule to bring them material 'liberation'. Yet we are conscious of our lack of detailed treatment of the government's economic restructuring and its achievements as much as its failures. Equally, for all the Mbeki government's stress on black empowerment, study of the success or otherwise of its strategies remains in its infancy, and we will need to address this in detail in our second volume covering 2004–2005. Likewise, so much more could have been included in our review of South African society in transition: neither sport nor religion gain a mention, yet both contribute so much to our societal fabric. And whilst Maxi Schoeman offers us a fascinating study of South Africa as an emergent middle power, we carry nothing on an absolutely key aspect of the democratic transition, that is, the transformation of the Defence Force. This volume constitutes an imperfect start for our longer vision. Yet a start it is and, if nothing else, it enables us to set an agenda for the future.

Democracy and institution building

This opening section is comprised of five contrasting and wide-ranging chapters. The first, authored by Gerhard Maré, focuses on 'the state' itself and investigates its essential character. Full of nuance and rich description of the contradictions of the post-apartheid state, Maré seems to conclude on one single note: the post-apartheid state, while having broken free in important respects from its racialised past, nevertheless has remained imprisoned by the shackles of its capitalist origins. This then establishes the parameters, which both defines its potential for incorporating new social groups into the post-apartheid order, and simultaneously limits its capacity to address the extreme levels of poverty and inequality in South African society.

Whilst accepting the undoubted capitalist character of the state, Southall's investigation into the party system tends to arrive at a cautious conclusion concerning the nature of class power and dominance. Analysing the state of parties (including the Tripartite Alliance and opposition parties) through an exploration of the controversy surrounding Jeremy Cronin's interview with Helena Sheehan, he reasserts the SACP leadership's view that, while the centre-right is ascendant within the ANC hierarchy, the state of play in the party is too fluid to arrive at any definitive conclusions about the class character of the ANC. In addition, Southall is critical of many political commentators from both the left and right who express concern that the decline of opposition parties and the increasing dominance of the ANC leads, inexorably, to the weakening of the 'quality and depth of democracy'. Instead, like Cronin, he maintains that the continuation of 'the Tripartite Alliance as a site of struggle' constrains the rightward shift of the ANC and holds the party at least partially accountable to its left-wing allies.

What Southall does not address, of course, is the enormously complex issue hinted at, but not addressed explicitly in Maré's chapter, of whether there is such a phenomenon in South Africa today as a 'ruling class'. Clearly, explorations of the relations between political and economic power, between the ANC and corporate capital, and how this determines the class character of the state, should be amongst the most pressing questions confronting social analysts today. During the 1970s and 1980s such issues were paramount. With the arrival of 'democracy' during the 1990s they tended to be forgotten in the search for a common nation. Yet they have an unruly habit of forcing themselves back on to the agenda, often at what are strikingly uncomfortable moments for dominant forces in society, precisely because they seek to lay bare the power relations which determine 'who gets what, how and when' – especially in societies like South Africa, which are riven with inequality. Most certainly, as Maré has pointed out, examining the continuities between the apartheid and post-apartheid states is easily as important as addressing the discontinuities. This series will make no apology for insisting upon bringing such questions of power, state, class and inequality back on the agenda.

These questions are highlighted by the chapter on the TRC authored by two former TRC researchers, Madeleine Fullard and Nicky Rousseau. This offers a hugely sobering analysis of how a lack of political will and compromises borne of negotiated transitions can inhibit the potential for realising a just reconciliation. Conceiving the TRC as the flagship of a fleet of institutions established in the mid-1990's tasked with the responsibility of addressing past injustices and building a human rights culture in the country, they provide a historical excursion of this institution's genesis, its operations, its evolution, and ultimately its slow disbandment. While arguing that the TRC's achievements were substantial, Fullard and Rousseau nevertheless argue that the non-payment of reparations to victims, the failure to prosecute individuals who were not granted amnesty or who snubbed the process, the political initiative to grant a general amnesty, and the failure to complete its tasks, all compromise the institution's legacy and leave an aftertaste of bitterness and injustice, which cannot but inhibit the establishment of a human rights culture in the country.

On a closely related theme, Xolela Mangcu analyses the state of race relations in post-apartheid South Africa. Distinguishing between Mandela's 'racial reconciliation' and Mbeki's 'transformative reconciliation', he argues that the former was necessary for its time. Mandela's assurances to whites, which he sees as being rooted in the dominant motif of ANC politics, were crucial for averting a backlash at the dawn of the transition and for focusing the attention of the international community on South Africa. Mbeki's more transformative agenda, which requires a greater responsibility on the part of the white community, is equally necessary and legitimate, Mangcu argues, yet is compromised by his administration's tendency to resort to racial labeling when confronted by critique. In the end, the challenge confronting the country, he argues, is to return to the project of racial transformation without burdening it with crude racism from ruling party and oppositional politicians.

Doreen Atkinson's chapter is of a qualitatively different kind, focusing upon her particular passion: establishing systems and modes of 'delivery' of resources to the poor and establishing 'capacity' for 'development' in the search for the 'human rights culture' that Fullard and Rousseau would like to see. Located at the local level, it first provides an historical overview of the initiatives to transform this tier of government, and then proceeds to analyse the obstacles to its efficient functioning. Atkinson recognises the paradox that at the time when most see local government 'as the primary implementation agent for development programmes', its capacity is most compromised. The result is increasing public dissatisfaction with local government. As a result, Atkinson concludes her chapter by calling for 'a concerted inter-departmental approach to building municipal capacity (which) will unblock the obstacles to developmental local government.'

The political chapters of this volume clearly suggest that progress toward the entrenchment of democracy and institution building has been mixed. On the more positive side, we have a number of institutions at both the party and state level that constitute a break with our racial past. In addition, we have transcended the symbolic reconciliation of the early years and adopted a transformative initiative that is necessary for a just reconciliation in this country. But, on the negative side, four systemic deficiencies continue to plague nation building. First, the post-apartheid state remains a prisoner of narrow class interests, thereby limiting its transformative potential. Second, the lack of a viable opposition in the party political system weakens democracy, even if, according to Southall, this in part is compensated for by the existence of oppositional elements within the Tripartite Alliance. Third, managerial capacity is limited in some state institutions, particularly at the local level, which hampers the processes of service delivery. Finally, the potential for transcending the racial divisions of our past is compromised by both the failures of apartheid's beneficiaries to acknowledge their complicity in the imposition of that racial order, and contemporary state and political (including opposition) elites' continuous resort to the race card for narrow political gain. Unless these systemic weaknesses are addressed, just reconciliation and nation building are unlikely to be realised in South Africa.

Economic transformation

The demise of apartheid and the arrival of democracy have seen South Africa's re-entry into the global economy as a full member of the international community, without the constraint of sanctions and other obstacles to trade. It is now commonly acknowledged that the government's early shift from the RDP to Gear was, in part, a recognition of the need to move South Africa from an inward-looking, heavily protected economy to one that is able to compete efficiently in rapidly globalising markets. Taking on board many of the mantras of the International Monetary Fund (IMF) and the World Bank, and brazening accusations that it has opted for 'neoliberalism' rather than social justice, the ANC-led government of former radical political prisoners, activists and guerrilla fighters – whilst seeking to achieve greater equity between the races in the allocation of resources and transfer payments (such as pensions and disability grants) – has sought to achieve a 'lean and hungry' state capable of steering an increasingly aggressive economy. It claims not inconsiderable achievements. Economic growth, albeit far lower than hoped for, has been consistently achieved, year by year, since 1994. Business has been challenged to become more efficient by the relaxation, if not abolition, of protection. Revenue-raising capacity has improved markedly. Black entry into the corporate sector has been fostered, and black empowerment set firmly upon the agenda. South Africa's international credit rating has improved steadily and its reputation for sound economic management has increased by leaps and bounds. Indeed, few members of the stock exchange would do serious battle with the assertion that the South African economy is now more competently steered than at any time during the last 40 to 50 years. Yet despite all this, the rate of inflow of international investment and re-investment of domestic capital has been disappointing. Combined with the impact of the re-structuring of industry, and the effect of volatile conditions upon South Africa's primary export staples, South Africa's experiment with democracy has been accompanied by the politically and morally disconcerting rise in unemployment. It is this particular development which informs our two related overviews of the economy.

The first, authored by Nicoli Nattrass, investigates the state of the South African economy through a focus on trends in unemployment, employment earnings and job creation. Recognising that unemployment is the single most important challenge confronting our young democracy, and that government's existing economic trajectory has aggravated the problem and is unlikely to make a significant dent in unemployment, she champions the case for a universal Basic Income Grant (BIG) that is underwritten by a consumption tax. Arguing that this need not threaten foreign and domestic investment in the economy, and indeed suggesting that the increased demand resulting from the implementation of BIG might even prompt such investment, Nattrass makes a persuasive case for why government ought to adopt a more energetic response to the challenge. But she is not optimistic, and correctly so, for, as she notes, government is opposed to such a social-democratic response primarily on ideological grounds.

Miriam Altman offers a related analysis, which focuses upon the South African economy's experience of 'jobless growth'. She notes a shift from formal to informal employment, with fewer returns to education, few contractual obligations and benefits, and lower wages. This could have its compensations, she argues, if the informal sector was drawing in the unemployed. Yet, she argues the converse, with the households of South Africa's poorer citizens being drawn into a vicious downward cycle. In this she seems to echo a recent report of the South African Human Rights Commission (2003) which, whilst focusing more upon the government's delivery of service record than upon its management of the economy as such, suggests that many ordinary people are getting poorer. Indeed, a recent report by Statistics South Africa (2002) charted the alarming spectre that – whilst there is a growing black middle class – the economic divide between white and black is not narrowing, and in some respects is getting wider.

Rather than pinning blame upon the government's alleged ill-intentions or incompetence, Altman focuses upon the unenviable dilemmas faced by a minerals-oriented economy. Whilst Gear was premised on the manufacturing export-oriented development paths pursued by high-growth states in South East Asia, South African growth has been slowed by a 'resource curse', that is, that high-value exports (such as gold) provide perverse incentives to invest in high capital-using industries, creating vested interests in these resources, and thereby limiting broader participation. Whilst growth rates of around eight per cent have been required in rather more labour-absorbing countries to even stabilise unemployment, South Africa's growth rates have been considerably less, and employment has increased dramatically. Whilst Gear has understandably emphasised employment creation via labour-intensive export growth, the government could secure better job growth by more forcefully promoting the expansion of industries serving unmet basic needs, expanding entry into the market by small enterprises, promoting linkages based on procurement opportunities, and more active labour market policies. All these elements are present in Gear, but need greater emphasis.

Another aspect of the employment: unemployment equation is examined in Percy Moleke's article on the level of skills in the labour market. In particular, it focuses on the impact of two key post-apartheid pieces of legislation (the *Employment Equity Act* and the *Skills Development Act*) designed to redress the skewed pattern of human resource development bequeathed by the apartheid system. That inheritance was one characterised by vast race and gender inequalities in occupational structures and by educational and training systems which perpetuated these inequities; by huge income disparities; a shortage of skills in critical areas and an over-abundance of unproductive skills; and, finally, by high un-and under-employment levels amongst Africans.

While noting that the period since 1994 is too short a one to expect a dramatic turnaround in this situation, Moleke suggests, however, that the results of nine years of occupational and on-the-job training, as well as the two pieces of redress legislation, have been disappointing. While not denying some advances by a statistically small number of African males, Moleke observes that the basic apartheid fact of white domination of the upper echelons of the economy remains essentially unchanged. However, within this phenomenon Moleke points out that one group is advancing up the management ladder faster than others, and that is white females. What this suggests is that employers faced with a lack of skilled African managers are resorting more and more to the gender dimension as the means to meeting their equity obligations.

Moleke is also critical of on-the-job-training which she suggests limits redress and reinforces inequalities because it tends to take the form of upgrading the skills of those at higher occupational levels and they are overwhelmingly white. This form of training also tends to be biased against those who lack numeracy and literacy and they happen to be overwhelmingly black workers. It is this high level of black illiteracy and poor numeric skills which Moleke suggests lies at the root of South Africa's human resource development crisis. Overcoming it will take decades and solutions will have to be sought from both inside and outside of the labour market, and, particularly in regard to the latter, in the classroom. There is only a limited amount, in Moleke's view, which equity legislation and affirmative action policies can achieve.

The data upon which Moleke based her observations and findings is some three to four years old. At the time of writing, the HSRC's Human Resource Development (HRD) research programme is evaluating the findings of the largest national survey of HRD skills undertaken since 1994. Moleke's hoped-for contribution to the next *State of the Nation* volume will make for interesting reading. It will reveal if democratic South Africa is gradually beginning to overcome probably the most crippling of apartheid's legacies. The consequences of failing to do so will be dire in the extreme.

The increasingly bleak employment situation is reflected in Sakhela Buhlungu's exploration into the state of trade unionism in contemporary South Africa. This focuses principally on the largest trade union federation, Cosatu. It investigates the impact of the political transition, and South Africa's integration into the global community, on union membership figures, and on the federation's power, alliances and capacity to influence the trajectory of our transition. Buhlungu's principal argument is that political and economic transitions have weakened the union movement politically and organisationally, and this has negative consequences for the consolidation of democracy in the country. He concludes on a pessimistic note, recognising that Cosatu's current strategies and alliances are unlikely to address its crisis, yet he does not hold much hope for a change in its political orientation.

The prognosis on the economic front emanating from these chapters is thus bleak. Government's ideological prejudices compromise its ability to address unemployment, the single biggest challenge confronting our democratic transition. Furthermore, many argue that its flagship programme of black economic empowerment is likely to continue serving the interests of a small elite, even with further regulation and financial support from the public and corporate sector. These defiencies are unlikely to be addressed especially since the one agency – Cosatu – capable of compelling the adoption of a set of policies that could service the broader citizenry, is unable to do so due to having been weakened and compromised by its strategic alliance with the ruling party. If democracy was to have been a path to a better life for all, then this does not seem to be borne out by the empirical data and qualitative analyses contained in these chapters tasked with investigating our economic transformation.

Societal reconstitution and service delivery

This section is comprised of six chapters, two on societal reconstitution and four on service delivery. The first of these, authored by Adam Habib, investigates the impact of the democratic transition and globalisation on civic life in South Africa. It argues that civil society, the largest constituency of which represents and organises black civic life, has been reconfigured in important ways by these processes. Civil society is now divided into three distinct components. First, service-related and research-oriented non-governmental organisations (NGOs) are increasingly involved in work subcontracted to them by the state and/or international organisations. Second, social movements have over the last few years begun to emerge to organise and manage resistance to one or other aspect of political and socio-economic life. And third, the largest component of civil society is informal community-based organisations, which are simply involved in surviving the ravages of the neoliberal environment. Not consciously political, these organisations represent the informal sector of civil society. This plurality of civic life, which in many ways represents the normalisation of South African society, results, Habib argues, in a plural set of state-civic relations that span a continuum defined by adversarialism on the one end and partnership and co-operation on the other. He concludes on the note that this plurality both in civic life and state-civil society relations is beneficial for democracy for it enables the diversity of representation and contestation that is required for the institutionalisation of democratic institutions and the entrenchment of democratic practice in South African society.

Acheampong Yau Amoateng and Linda Richter's intellectual exploration has a narrower focus, the state of the family in post-apartheid South Africa. Through a secondary analysis of the 1996 population census data, they investigate four elements of the family: household structure, marriage, child-bearing and divorce. Their first finding is that there are a multiplicity of family forms in South Africa with two predominating – the nuclear unit and the extended family. The former is more identifiable with the white community, whereas the latter is typical of the African community. Coloureds and Indians tend to reflect a mixture of these two family patterns. In addition, Amoateng and Richter demonstrate that marriage, divorce and fertility rates are falling, while non-marital cohabitation is becoming more popular. Their conclusion is that:

> the family in all its diversity, appears to be alive and well in South Africa. While such forces of modernisation as industrialism and urbanisation have brought about certain obvious changes, its resilience is demonstrated by the persistence and continuity of certain elements which have been and continue to be vital in ensuring its viability in the face of the onslaught of globalisation.

The four chapters on service delivery provide a review of education, health and land redistribution in post-apartheid South Africa. The educational chapters, authored by Linda Chisholm and Jonathan Jansen, focus on schooling and higher education respectively. Chisholm's investigation into Curriculum 2005, the most significant curriculum-reform initiative in South African educational history, provides both an excursion of the events that culminated in the Revised National Curriculum Statement, and an analysis of the actual changes that this statement heralded. Her overall assessment of the state of the schooling arena is captured in her concluding words:

> There have been achievements, but challenges remain … Spending on education has improved, infrastructural provision has expanded, pupil:teacher ratios have narrowed and enrolments and participation of children in schooling have increased … And yet much still remains to be done: resources remain unequally spread, the quality of education remains compromised by intractable legacies of the past and learning achievements remain poor, especially amongst the poor in those provinces that have incorporated the former bantustans.

Jansen's chapter on higher education concludes on a more optimistic note. Investigating the shift in higher education policy from massification to mergers, and the reasons that informed it, he argues that 'the restructuring of higher education has been driven by the twin goals of global competitiveness and national development'. The strategy of massification was abandoned in favour of mergers as a result of two related phenomena: the dramatic decline in student enrolments in higher education, and the significant incline in institutional instability in black universities and technikons. The positive effect of this policy shift to mergers, Jansen argues, will be a more deracialised higher education system with a better quality, but smaller number of institutions. However, he recognises that this would come at the cost of rural students unless 'meaningful alternatives are instituted, nurtured and sustained' for them.

Mandisa Mbali's chapter on health is an investigation into the state of AIDS policy making in South Africa. The chapter provides a chilling historical overview of the policy contestations between the Mbeki administration on the one hand, and the Treatment Action Campaign (TAC) and the mainstream scientific establishment on the other. She indicates how the Mbeki presidency – influenced by denialist views, a desire to respond to racial stigmatisation, and financial considerations – refuses to provide adequate health care for those living with HIV/AIDS. However, it is a story that is not entirely depressing. For Mbali also demonstrates how the innovative use of mass protest and legal instruments by the TAC has forced the state to retreat, and enshrine in official policy, many of the demands advanced by medical scientists and civil society. Although she recognises the devastating effect this policy-making paralysis has had for those living with HIV/AIDS, she is cautiously optimistic that the government may be just at the point of transcending its apprehension of anti-retroviral drugs, and that this may lead to the rolling out of a comprehensive programme to address the AIDS crisis in South Africa.

Finally, Michael Aliber and Reuben Mokoena's chapter on the state of the land question investigates the progress of the post-1994 programme of land reform. Arguing that the first phase of the reform programme had not achieved its target of redistributing 30 per cent of the land in five years because of being burdened by over-ambitious targets, programmatic mistakes, and unrealistic goals and objectives, they reflect on the government's subsequent restructuring of the programme into three sub-programmes: land redistribution for farming or settlement, land restitution, involving the restoration of land or cash compensation to victims of forced removals under apartheid; and tenure reform, which seeks to improve the clarity and robustness of tenure rights, mainly for residents of former homeland areas. They conclude that overall, South Africa's land reform efforts constitute a mixed story. There has been new and important legislation put in place, and lessons learnt. Yet land reform is far from being a major government priority, not least because there is no national consensus as to whether and why it is important. They argue that whilst South Africa's far more responsible leadership is unlikely to follow the land-grabbing example provided by its counterpart in Zimbabwe, and that even if South Africa's land question does not represent a ticking time-bomb, it does remain highly problematic. The most crucial problem, they opine, is that of the government enunciating a clear vision about what land reform can and should achieve with regard to both redressing past wrongs and promoting the economic empowerment of the historically disadvantaged.

On balance, the chapters in this section tend to be more optimistic than those of the former two. Two factors underscore this optimism. First, as Habib and Amoateng and Richter demonstrate, society and its institutional expressions are being reconfigured in important ways that benefit democracy. Indeed, contemporary political and economic processes are engendering a plurality and diversity in society, which serve as some of the founding blocks for democracy. Second, as almost all of the chapters on service delivery indicate, the first few years of the post-apartheid regime was a period of missed opportunities, bureaucratic bungle-ups, and strategic miscalculations. But it was also a decade of learning. To their credit, the officials and leaders of the post-apartheid regime learnt from their mistakes and revised their policies, programmes, and implementation plans. This then enables almost all of the authors, without exception, to conclude on a cautiously optimistic note about the prospects of delivery in education, health care and land reform.

South Africa in Africa

There have been few changes brought about by the transition from apartheid to democracy more dramatic than South Africa's international position. Apartheid South Africa was pilloried as the polecat of the world. It had long been expelled or excluded from the large majority of international organisations; it was subject to a multitude of sanctions; and even its best friends, such as the United Kingdom and the United States, needed to keep it at arms length. Following the move to democracy, however, South Africa has not only rejoined the international state system as a full member, but it has in many ways become celebrated as a model for other states to follow.

In her rich chapter on the country as an 'emerging middle power', Maxi Schoeman explores the demands imposed upon, and the dilemmas faced by, the newly-democratic South Africa. Traditionally, she argues, the term 'middle power' has referred to states located at some mid-point in the international hierarchy of states (in terms of size, power and rank), which have accepted a role of exerting a moral influence on the international system. This they seek to do through international organisations as they provide a comparatively stable and orderly environment. By contrast in this new post-Cold War era, which has seen an eruption of conflicts in the 'second' and 'third' worlds, there seems to be a changing of the definition, role and functions of so-called 'middle powers' like Brazil and India located in the developing world.

What she terms 'emerging middle powers' are countries which play, or are expected to play, the role of regional peacemakers and police, promoting acceptable rules of international behaviour, and sometimes exerting influence in situations where big powers cannot. 'Emerging middle powers' are therefore located in an ambiguous position. They are variously supported and encouraged as regional powers by big powers and regional weaker states alike, yet simultaneously they are often resented, criticised and sanctioned by both, precisely because that role demands that, at times, they tread on the toes of both those above and below them in the international hierarchy.

Schoeman sees South Africa as growing steadily, if sometimes rather uncertainly, into this status of an 'emerging middle power'. On the one hand, South Africa, via its promotion of the African Union (AU) and the New Partnership for Africa's Development (Nepad), has begun to display the confidence needed for it to become a 'regional power', whilst simultaneously it has valued participation in international organisations and agreements as routes towards the promotion of international peace and security. It has also played an important mediating role between the interests of the North and the South, for instance with regard to the issues of nuclear non-proliferation and arms control. On the other hand, mindful of the country's apartheid past, South Africa has proved extremely cautious about assuming the role of regional power within Africa. For instance, it has proved reluctant to play a decisive intervening role in Zimbabwe, or a major role in continental peace-keeping operations, whilst simultaneously, it has proved sensitive to African perceptions that it is too pro-Western and too keen to impose 'un-African' values upon a continent with a deeply flawed history of respect for democratic pluralism and human rights. Schoeman views as possible solutions to these dilemmas the government placing greater emphasis both upon continental multilateralism and its position as a moral exemplar, that is, its becoming a good global citizen by being seen to uphold values of peace and democracy.

The final chapter in this volume, by John Daniel, Varusha Naidoo and Sanusha Naidu, examines aspects of South Africa's emerging foreign policy towards Africa through the lens of South Africa's fast-growing economic relations with Africa. Based on empirical data detailing South Africa's growing trade with Africa and its investment in, and acquisitions on, the continent, the chapter investigates whether this phenomenal corporate expansion (in which parastatals like Transnet and Eskom are to the fore) is serving in political terms to perpetuate and intensify the hegemonic and interventionist attitudes of the former apartheid state towards Africa. Daniel et al. argue that a collective of factors – excess amounts of investible capital held by South African corporates as a result of sanctions under apartheid, the paradox of the local business community's regional strength and international weakness, the desire by international banks to have an African investment partner for financing on the continent, the forces of globalisation and neoliberalism which have prised open the formerly closed markets of Africa – have conspired to direct South Africa's interest and financial resources into Africa.

While noting that South Africa's corporates pursue their narrow economic interests in their operations on the continent, the authors argue that this is not being translated into additional political muscle by a once-hegemonically inclined South African state. Instead, they argue that the 'leopard' of the South African state has changed its spots and now self-consciously eschews hegemonism in favour of 'quiet diplomacy' and multilateralism. Its favoured approach now is to act in partnership with other African states, like Nigeria, or through multilateral fora like the Commonwealth, the AU and the Southern African Development Community (SADC). Its promotion of the Nepad ideal is consistent with this low-key and collaborative approach to African affairs. While this stance is generally favoured by the authors, they are, however, critical of the Mbeki government's approach to Zimbabwe, where they argue it has failed to take even a moral position in regard to the fascist excesses of a neighbour and important trading partner. Non-interventionism should not also include keeping silent in the face of tyranny. Humble hege-monism, in their view, has its limits and can in certain circumstances be seen as an abdication of leadership.

The two international chapters raise troubling questions about South Africa's engagement in Africa. It needs to be borne in mind that the development and establishment of peace and stability in Africa is not simply a moral responsi-bility, nor a payback for support to the liberation movements during the long years of apartheid. Rather it must be conceived as in the long-term interests of South Africa itself. For without peace, stability and development on the conti-nent, Africa and South Africa are unlikely to be the recipients of large quantities of foreign direct investment. Moreover, Africa's market will continue to remain limited, stunting the capacity of South Africa's corporates and its parastatals to exploit their regional advantage to the full. The broad conclusion to be drawn from these two chapters, when they are set alongside, is that whatever South Africa's short-term interests, it cannot escape assuming greater regional responsibilities, with all the costs (as well as opportunities) this incurs.

Defining the post-apartheid political project

How then should we define the state of the nation as we approach the tenth anniversary of its democracy? The chapters in this volume clearly suggest that the answer to this question has to be a nuanced one. There has been marked progress made in some areas, whereas in others there are troubling features that remain or are even developing. On the positive side, there has been deliv-ery, or at least there is now the prospect that such delivery might happen. On the negative side, there is the dominant party syndrome, the lack of managerial capacity within public institutions, the policy limitations placed on the state by its neoliberal ideological underpinnings, an alarming level of unemployment, the elite nature of black empowerment, and the increasing weakness of the labour movement. Our assessment of the state of the nation has to be holistic, capturing both the advances made and the setbacks experienced.

But if our assessment of the state of the nation is mixed, does that mean that we cannot define the essential characteristics of the post-apartheid political project or determine its implications? Not at all. All political and socio-eco-nomic projects have contradictory elements. This is simply the nature of human existence. Analysts need to see beyond the contradictions to come to terms with the essential characteristics of the phenomena under investigation. Moreover, analysts need to go beyond the rhetorical statements of leaders or even their intentions.[3] In the real world, outcomes are often unintended ones. This is even more the case when grand political projects and social engineering exercises are undertaken.[4] Thus analysts interested in understanding the long-term implications of political projects need to go beyond their contradictory elements and the intentions and rhetorical statements of their leaders.

Our conclusion at this point in the life of the 'new' South Africa is that the post-apartheid political project is defined by two essential characteristics. First, it is a democratic project of deracialisation in which racial groups previously disadvantaged are systemically incorporated, empowered and affirmed. Second, a rigid, restrictive macroeconomic policy, neoliberal as some would describe it (Habib & Padayachee 2000; Marais 2001, especially chapter 5), lies at the heart of this political project. Whatever the rhetoric or intentions of political leaders, the net effect of this coupling of economic neoliberalism with political democracy is the deracialisation of the apex of the class structure. Not the entire class structure. Rather deracialisation is confined to the upper echelons and strata of South African society.

President Mbeki, as was indicated earlier in this chapter, spoke of South Africa being comprised of two nations. His intention, outlined in his address to the national legislature on the occasion of the parliamentary debate on reconciliation and nation building, was to transcend the binary national divide and integrate our citizenry. But this noble goal is not the likely outcome of the political project which he leads. Instead, his political project is likely to result in the entrenchment of the national divide.[5] The first nation, the more privileged one, is likely to be deracialised with the incorporation of black entrepreneurs, professionals and the middle classes. But the second nation, the marginalised and disempowered, is likely to remain as it is presently constituted. And even though some whites, Indians, and coloureds might be pushed into the marginalised category, the second nation will remain largely black. This is because it currently takes a racial form and since market-oriented projects simply reproduce social divisions, the racial form of the class character of the second nation will most likely continue into the future (Alexander 2002).

At the beginning of his term, President Mbeki spoke about the need for a 'just reconciliation'. Five years later, as we approach the end of his first term of office, one has to conclude that a 'just reconciliation' still eludes South Africa.

And as he himself recognised, so long as that is the case, the political project of nation building is itself compromised. In a twist of irony, it is President Mbeki's own words that capture the conundrum of our contemporary political reality:

> To refer to the reality that our past determines the present is to invite protests and ridicule even as it is perfectly clear that no solution to many current problems can be found unless we understand their historical origins …. By this means, it comes about that those who were responsible for or were beneficiaries of the past, absolve themselves from any obligation to help do away with an unacceptable legacy …. This … is producing rage among millions of people … to which we must respond seriously. In a speech again in this House, we quoted the African-American poet, Langston Hughes when he wrote – 'What happens to a dream deferred?' His conclusion was that it explodes. (Mbeki 1998)

Notes

1 Note his visit to and tea with Mrs Betsy Verwoed, wife of the apartheid Prime Minister, Hendrik Verwoed, and his donning of the Springbok jersey when South Africa hosted the Rugby World Cup in 1995. For a discussion of these reconciliation initiatives, see Xolela Mangcu's chapter in this volume.

2 For a critical discussion of this, see Madeleine Fullard and Nicky Rousseau's chapter in this volume.

3 This is one of the weaknesses of Saul's earlier writings on the South African transition. In these he took the rhetoric of ANC leaders and consultants at face value (Saul 1991). In recent years, however, he has been quite critical of the nature of this transition provoking as a result, a fair degree of controversy (Saul 2000).

4 Look, for instance, at the outcomes of the grand political projects of communism and social democracy.

5 In a widely read and referenced article in *Work in Progress*, Morris argued in early 1993 that a 50 per cent solution was one of the possible outcomes of the South African transition (Morris 1993). His fear of that time now seems to have been borne out.

References

Alexander, N (2002) *An ordinary country: Issues in the transition from apartheid to democracy in South Africa*. Pietermaritzburg: University of Natal Press.

Habib, A & Nadvi, L (2002) Party disintegrations and re-alignments in post-apartheid South Africa, *Review of African Political Economy* 29 (92): 331–338.

Habib, A & Padayachee, V (2000) Economic policy and power relations in South Africa's transition to democracy, *World Development*, 28(2): 245–263.

Mandela, N (1994) *State of the Nation Address by President of South Africa, Nelson Mandela.* Parliament, Cape Town, 24 May.

Marais, H (2001) *South Africa: Limits to change: The political economy of transition.* Cape Town: University of Cape Town Press.

Mbeki, T (1998) *Statement of Deputy President Thabo Mbeki at the Opening of the Debate on 'Reconciliation and Nation Building'.* National Legislature, Cape Town, 29 May.

Mbeki, T (2002) *State of the Nation Address of the President of South Africa, Thabo Mbeki.* Parliament, Cape Town, 8 February.

Morris, M (1993) Who's out? Trying to side-step a 50% solution, *Work in Progress* 87: 6–9.

Saul, J (1991) South Africa: Between barbarism and structural reform, *New Left Review* 188: 3–44.

Saul, J (1991) Structural reform: A model for the revolutionary transformation of South Africa?, *Transformation* 20: 1–16.

SAHRC (South African Human Rights Commission) (2003) *4th Annual Economic and Social Rights Report: 2000–2002.* Johannesburg: SAHRC.

Statistics South Africa (2002) *Emerging and spending in South Africa: Selected findings and comparisons from the income and expenditure surveys of October 1995 and October 2000.* Statistics South Africa: Pretoria.

Part 1: Politics

The state of the state: Contestation and race re-assertion in a neoliberal terrain

Gerhard Maré

Introduction

How should we assess the state of the state in South Africa? Let me begin by affirming that discussions of the post-apartheid state are fraught with contradictions, and it could not be otherwise during a prolonged period of flux. While, in general, the most intense theoretical debates about the state are currently located in writing on globalisation, most would agree that examining the case of South Africa needs to proceed from local specificities. In the first instance this means addressing the transition from the apartheid state to the post-apartheid state (for an overview, see, for example, Habib 1995). There are indeed several broad positions taken on the nature of this political transition: a first position sees the new state as having arisen out of the ashes of the old, defeated state;[1] a second suggests that the post-apartheid state has been constructed on the foundations of the previous political structure and that the essentials of the state were given; at another extreme, a third perspective asks whether post-apartheid South Africa has simply changed (or is busy changing) the complexion and the political allegiance of the occupants of the same edifice.[2]

The African post-colonial state has often shown itself to be a vehicle for theft and illegal accumulation, for repression and massacre, and for inter-state warfare. During the liberation struggle in South Africa, the state was seen as that which had to be captured and utilised towards various noble and developmental ends. In its existing form, the state was accepted as the logical starting point in a world consisting of states.[3] There was little need to think carefully and critically beyond many of the apparently common-sense elements of statehood.

It is not often that the opportunity arises when a people can self-consciously be called upon to construct a state, or at least be said to have a direct say in such construction, rather than have it surreptitiously or violently thrust upon them. In Africa, the process of decolonisation provided that historical moment several times in the late 1950s and early 1960s, stimulating much academic interest in the processes of state formation. Yet, the results of these processes have been far from auspicious (Freund 1984; Kapuściński 2001; Mamdani 1976; Saul 1979; Shivji 1976). Events around the division between India and Pakistan similarly provoked interest (for example, Alavi 1972). More recently, the collapse of the Soviet Union provided opportunities – such as in the cases of Georgia or Czechoslovakia and Yugoslavia – for examining the growth of new institutions and practices, as well as the intended or unintended continuation of old political patterns.

South Africans, through decades of struggle, opened up new political possibilities for themselves – from meek beginnings of requests for recognition and incorporation during the early twentieth century, to calls for a radical rejection of the political and economic order that had been created through western capitalist expansion. In the 1990s, South Africa's people appeared finally to have achieved the opportunity to decide on what moral order, what economic system, what gender relations, what kind of political representation, what institutions of social control, justice, welfare, punishment, and education, in short, what state would serve them best.

It proved a tall order. To an extent that should not be underestimated in its implications for democratic claims and assertion of a culture of involvement, the oppressed grasped this opportunity, people who had for so long been excluded from participation in political decision-making or who had been granted a peripheral, twisted notion of democracy. They did so in the most down-to-earth way, by standing all day in the blazing sun on 27 April 1994, and voting to approve what they believed had been done in their name and to elect representatives to a government which would give form to a newly inclusive state. Prior to this, however, they had to all intents and purposes been sidelined and excluded, not only in the formal process of negotiations from 1990, but also through the very circumstances that had been the result of their previous social segregation under apartheid – illiteracy, poverty, rural isolation, and oppression of various kinds (race, gender, class, and political; also, most strongly in the case of rural women, under traditional authority structures).

Instead of exploring innovative ways to involve those who would be newly incorporated into a shared society, the new state became the product of negotiation and compromise between elites, namely, between leaderships representing the militarily and economically undefeated apartheid state, and those of the opposition – primarily what had been known as the 'Mass Democratic Movement'. The vibrant organisations of civil society and popular uprisings that characterised the struggle years were eclipsed from their roles as direct participants, their power abstracted to use as a bargaining tool during negotiations.

So, is a new form of state order in the process of creation in this new South Africa? If so, is the new form an adaptation to conditions of imprisonment within the processes and institutions of globalisation, and/or within the legacy of apartheid? Is this state formation something within which, in the view of President Mbeki, 'the overwhelming majority of our people consider themselves as actors …' (2002: 1)?

Such an assessment of the post-apartheid state needs to be considered in terms of four broad issues, even if a final verdict is far from possible. First, we must affirm that analysis of the state in South Africa is inevitably obligated by its descriptive prefix, 'post'-apartheid. The post-apartheid state should be measured by the manner in which it came into existence, as reflecting a commitment by people attempting to redress an oppressive past and create a humane society. Such commitment to a multi-faceted rupture gave rise to the Constitution, a checks-and-balances document both for the state as an institution and for individual state agents within it. At the heart of this redress is the question of what the state has inherited in terms of social inequalities, and how it has confronted that legacy.

The second issue is to assess the sources of the political legitimacy of the current state, to assess the extent to which it reflects a durable relationship between citizens and state. The (non-)transformation of the ANC from liberation movement to ruling party raises important questions about the nature of its hegemony. As a formal representative of a people the modern state is about ideas of what is supposed to be and what exists; it is about notions of nation; about a moral order in which expression is given to the values of the society, both internally between citizens, and in its relations to the rest of a world consisting of states; it is about belief and trust in the impartiality and the efficiency of the practices of civil servants, especially those charged with delivery in welfare services, security, justice; in the efficacy of each vote in shaping society; in the strength and durability of democracy, and its continual adaptation to new conditions.

Third, the state may be assessed in terms of its effectiveness as a delivery mechanism to the people it represents, the actual structures and institutions that have been retained or created to suit the needs of the new inclusiveness that characterises the country at a political level. The state is about structures, institutions and practices, and about the individual agents that fulfil the many tasks required of the ideal of an impersonal and efficient bureaucracy that Weber characterised as the essence of the modernising and modern state. This demands that we also assess the abilities and shortcomings of the state and the causes, as well as the effects, of failure and of successes.

Finally, the state should be considered as a site of struggle between competing interests, most especially between class interests. This means addressing the state as existing within a capitalist system with struggles over the resources, benefits and rights that the state has the power to ensure or mediate. The state has a monopoly over the legitimate use of powers of social order and repression, but also those of allocating important benefits to citizens. Who gains and on what basis are they fighting for what?

While these four considerations do not formally structure the discussion that follows, they form the basis of my investigation into the state of the post-apartheid state.

This paper, exploratory and suggestive as an introduction, is presented in two broadly-defined sections, framed by the four questions above: first, thinking about the apartheid state and the nature of the transition and, second, locating a discussion of the post-apartheid state within its own local specificity. This, the first chapter in this volume, sets out to suggest ways both of theorising the state and of assessing its mode of operation as we move towards the third post-apartheid elections in 2004. The chapters that follow are more concretely located.

The apartheid state: What was it?

If the new state is indeed 'post-apartheid', then we need to examine the way in which the apartheid state was conceptualised. Central to ways of understanding that state were arguments around race and class, categories that organised a system of economic exploitation and political domination and discrimination (amongst many, see Adam 1971). The gendered nature of the apartheid state was discussed far less often (see Manicom 1992). These arguments of the importance of race and/or class have diminished notably more recently, for a range of reasons (certainly including the suppression by the ANC itself of such debates as aligned with 'unrealistic' social visions and representing 'ultra-leftist' tendencies). However, debates around class formation and interests are slowly coming to the fore once again, not specifically in relation to the continuation of inequality.

Pre-1994 debates on the apartheid state were at times heated, but there was general consensus on its essential elements. In the first place, it was a state form based on notions of race that demanded and justified the exclusion of the majority from any involvement in the central institutions of power. The racialised native population was further fragmented into ethnic 'nations'. The way in which race categorisation was achieved and firmed under apartheid has been the subject of scrutiny (for example, Dubow 1995; Posel 2001a, 2001b). Posel notes that rather than engaging in the 'uneconomical waste of time and money' to try and determine race 'with precision', the National Party (NP) government instead engaged in a 'deliberately more flexible, elastic approach to the definition of race categories' (2001b: 55). The 'confidence in the authority of everyday experience as the site of racial judgement' (Posel 2001b: 56) that characterised this approach, unfortunately lives on – something to which I will return.

Second, the apartheid state was also analysed as a peripheral capitalist state that relied on a migrant labour system, which allowed a form of cheap labour that was required especially by the mining industry. The migrant labour system itself rested on the maintenance of a spatially and socially separate society of subjects (to be distinguished from the citizens that formed part of the modern democratic state), and, therefore, also a specific gendered order (where a migrant system of single males relied on the continued subsistence production of women in spatially-separate areas) and reliance on traditional authority for control over and legitimation of distinct social relations (Mamdani 1996). One reason for the defeat of the Boer Republics was that British imperialism needed a more efficient and centralised form of control over labour for the mining industry, perceived to be the engine of growth in what was to become the Union of South Africa in 1910, while continuing with and establishing extreme forms of segregation. From its inception, therefore, the state was tied into a global system of markets, based on its raw materials extraction, where diamonds and gold played a central role from the second half of the nineteenth century.

The apartheid state upheld and regulated an existing economic system that was, therefore, most often characterised as racial-capitalism. Freund has, however, questioned the value of such a slogan in terms that remain appropriate: He questions the extent to which 'one can simply so marry racism and capitalism. Moreover, it can lead to a fancy way of talking about racism without taking the problem of capitalist values and forms seriously' (1986: 127–8). The class system followed lines that approximated the racialised divisions of the country: an overwhelmingly (but not exclusively) white bourgeoisie; largely skilled and supervisory workers, drawn from the white population, and supplemented by Indian and coloured workers where legal or *de facto* preference areas were created (Western Cape and Natal). The proletariat (urban and rural) and non-commercially active rural population was overwhelmingly black African.

The segregationist and apartheid state was a site of contestation between different class interests. O'Meara, for example, argues that from 1933 to 1939 the 'struggle between the national and metropolitan-oriented fractions of the bourgeoisie eased slightly …' (1977: 186), illustrating this approach. The structures of the state illustrated the struggles for control and direction, especially at the level of advantage to fractions of capital. Policies relating to migrant labour and urbanisation most clearly reflected the contest between different fractions of the bourgeoisie – such as between agricultural and mining capitals. O'Meara notes that the NP benefited from the apparent ambivalence of the United Party on the issue of labour stabilisation through a relaxed policy on urbanisation, and came to power when Afrikaans-speaking workers, farmers and petty bourgeoisie combined to take control in 1948 (1977, 1983). O'Meara (1996) displays this analytical approach with greater complexity in his analysis of the 40 years of apartheid domination of the state. Hudson and Sarakinsky (1986) added the role of an urban African bourgeoisie as a factor in relation to struggles over the direction of the apartheid state in the mid-1980s.

Third, the apartheid state inherited the Westminster model of parliamentary representative democracy established in 1910. The issue of the apartheid state as also a democratic state was often overlooked in the literature – serious and polemical – in favour of simple condemnation. The fact is, however, that by the time of the transition, institutions of democratic representation had long been in existence in South Africa, attendant with a long undeniable tradition of democratic participation and representation of interests – even if applied to a specified margin of the population. It was thus why some analysts described South Africa as an '*herrenvolk* democracy' (Adam 1971), while it is that very democratic participation by the *herrenvolk* that adds, in the eyes of some, to the culpability of white voters (see Alexander 2002).

In addition, the apartheid state was also a repressive state, employing the range of institutions at its disposal to maintain both the racial order – against all those deemed not to be white – and the capitalist – acting against trade unions and trade unionists. Here too, the state was partnered internationally in a range of issues – from training in torture procedures to development of nuclear and biological and chemical weapons. South Africa was also a successful exporter of arms in this highly competitive market (and contentiously continues with this lucrative trade to this day).

During the PW Botha era (1978–1989), the form of South Africa's race-exclusive democracy was eroded. Parliament and the Cabinet were peripheralised during this period, as Botha created a parallel state system of security structures, and centralised control into his office through a National Security Management System. The Office of the State President was characterised by Swilling and Phillips as:

> the lynchpin of key strategic thinking and action. By 1988 this
> office and its incumbent had become the most decisive decision-
> maker in the state – a level of power centralisation not uncommon
> in societies going through a violent interregnum. (1989: 80)

It was these structures that FW de Klerk attempted to dismantle before the period of transition.

While there was general agreement in the apartheid-state literature about the central characteristics of the apartheid state, there was much less consensus in debates about the relative weight to be given to class and race elements in their explanatory power – as separate or in their articulation. This meant that the resolution of the problems created by class and race dynamics in the construction of an alternative future society was not agreed upon generally. Some held that the racist or racialised state placed a massive hindrance in the way of unfettered capitalist development. This position was best reflected in what became known as the 'O'Dowd thesis' (see O'Dowd 1974, 1978). Its logic was thus – the market would in time do away with the racist order and do so without the need for revolutionary struggle; in its place, capitalism would flourish and the country would join the ranks of the developed world.

A second analytical position theorised a relationship of mutual (but, importantly, non-essential) effect between class and race. Racism had allowed the very rapid growth of capitalism in South Africa, and along with the mineral wealth and the ability to attract skills during the nineteenth century, infrastructural development and a measure of industrialisation had taken place. This was in contradistinction to other settler-colonial states in Africa. South Africa had, therefore, managed to escape from total dependence on mineral extraction. Lipton best articulated this position from a liberal perspective. She argued that 'the standard question in the debate about South Africa – whether economic growth shores up or erodes apartheid – is too crude and needs reformulation. The first question is: what kind of economic growth?' (1986: 9).

A more radical take on this same position was that while it was possible to support the National Democratic Revolution (NDR) (that is, the creation of a normal, non-racial and democratic capitalist society), this would not lead inevitably to socialism. Where the successful NDR would lead would depend on struggle – in which the working class would play the leading role – towards a society that must be rid of capitalist exploitation, one that would at the very least have to redefine itself away from the existing racialised cheap labour system. For radicals who saw race and class as mutually interacting variables, the revolution would require two stages – the second driven, as Freund pointed out, by the working-class organisations, the only elements that 'have an interest in pressing forward with socialist demands meaningfully' (1986: 124).

Third, an argument was advanced for an essential link between capitalism and racism in South Africa. In this view, to destroy racism (apartheid) was to destroy class oppression (capitalism). It was, therefore, possible, and made sense, to support a broad, multi-class struggle against apartheid, even if your support was aimed at the demise of capitalism (see, for example, Cronin & Suttner 1986: 129; Hudson 1987: 57).

While the 1980s was marked largely by popular struggles, some analysis focused on the class nature of society. The apartheid state was in obvious and growing trouble, brought about by both visible and extreme forms of protest within a multitude of sites (from townships to the workplace, from religion to sport), as well as by structural problems in the economy (both internal and international). This crisis had to be addressed. Thus, some contributors to the *South African Review* (SARS 1983) described politics in South Africa as being in a process of restructuring designed to conserve the system of racial capitalism. The state was characterised as reflecting an alliance between the government, big business and the military. Apartheid was seen as setting the limits to the unfolding of the tension between, on the one hand, repression, and, on the other, reform and restructuring; the link between race and capitalism demanded the continued exclusion of the racialised majority – contributing to the general tension (SARS 1983).[4]

These debates are central to the task of understanding the dynamics of the transition and the restructuring of the state it entailed. They marked the points of active contestation over the shaping of the new state. For, if the dominant perception during the struggle against apartheid was that the state was essentially racially exclusive and only secondarily, economically exploitative, then the restructuring aimed to make the new state reflect the racialised demographics of South African society. It therefore would enable a new aspirant and racialised bourgeoisie to emerge as the prime beneficiaries of new state policy, in odd echo of the previously powerful who benefited from the struggle for *volkskapitalisme* 60 years earlier (O'Meara 1983, 1996).

To be sure, the inclusion of the majority of South Africans into a new franchise system had to alter the balance of forces to include new, now legitimate, demands for welfare, infrastructure development, education, health benefits and so on – something that was notably absent from the apartheid society. And it was to be expected that in the new order it would shift such demands off the street and into the terrain mediated by political representation – that is, into parliament, policy-making and elections. Potentially, these new agents would then be involved in structuring society. In other words, it could be expected that the poor and oppressed, overwhelmingly women, would be given greater leeway in struggles over state form and direction. However, as O'Meara reminds us, '… there are real structural limits to the efficacy of agency' and what he terms the 'boundaries of the possible' (1996: 482) are set in ways that are not necessarily directly reflected in the notion of majority rule.

If, on the other hand, the dominant interpretation of the past had been that the system was capitalist, within which racism and racialised exclusion served to bolster a particular form of exploitation, then for this position to carry the day the working class and those sympathisers located within the liberation movement would have strongly advanced an alternative, amounting to a rupture with the apartheid state and the dominant interests within it.

However, as indicated above, this position was neither dominant nor homogeneous – the two-stage revolution would immediately dilute demands for the inclusion of radical demands within transitional negotiations.

The state in transition: 1990–1994

Inheriting the apartheid state?

The government that came to power in 1994 operated with a commitment to alter the social landscape within an absurdly short time – and hence with possibly the wrong tools. The worst of the calamitous social inheritances were inequality and exploitation, racism and race thinking, and the relegation of women to a peripheral role – within a context that had not been experienced before: the horror of the HIV/AIDS epidemic with its cumulative decimation of society.

Moreover, the country's full global integration occurred immediately after the political change measured by the seismic event of the fall of the Berlin Wall – a condition that affected the previous regime in immeasurably different ways from those that shaped the new state, or that set new parameters of possibility in its actions. I have already mentioned that South Africa, since Union in 1910, owed its growth to integration into primary commodity markets. If two broad periods characterised the pre-transition period (British domination and then the post-World War II integration into a world shaped by the Cold War), the world in which the ANC, the apartheid state, and national and international pressure groups during the negotiations found themselves was that of turmoil after the fall of the communist alternative.

Both in terms of practical support and an ideological alternative to capitalism, the collapse of the Soviet Union affected the confidence of both main parties to the negotiations process; it strengthened, however, the neoliberalism of the new world order and the apartheid negotiators wishing to minimise disturbance of the essence of the old order; and it provided ammunition for those who were all too willing to argue that there is no alternative to competing for a place in global production and consumption.

The ANC's negotiating position was also severely constrained because conservative forces to the right of it had not been defeated effectively, and during negotiations the threat of a far-right and military counter-offensive remained. Structurally, too, there were demands on the state form that had to be acknowledged. The legacy of apartheid is not only to be found in social conditions. At most levels, the state was inherited. This meant that state structures themselves had to be reformed to meet the demands both for the extension of functions (where quantitatively more and qualitatively more diverse people had to be serviced by a central state) and the extension of access (to people – black people and women particularly – previously excluded from participation at the higher levels). It should hardly surprise that the political transition to democracy in South Africa has been condemned by some as an incomplete transformation. Alexander, for example, notes that '… since its inception in 1912 and throughout its history, the ANC has never been a revolutionary organisation. Its leadership was not even rhetorically committed to the overthrow of the South African state' (2002: 46; also Marais 2001). Alexander notes as well that the international legality of the apartheid state was not questioned.

To be sure, some state departments restructured their functions and some structures were completely abolished (for example, the bantustan authorities and the tricameral parliamentary system to cite the most obvious). Yet mechanisms for change, other than market forces, have been left up to policies of affirmative action, the handing out of rewards for decades of loyal service in the struggle against apartheid, and the need to ensure a new social commitment beyond the narrow confines of the exclusivist apartheid state (see, for example, Hugo 1990, discussing affirmative action in the public service).

The Mandela presidency and the state 1994–1999

Ensuring loyalty

The uncertainty of the transition provided Nelson Mandela with the greatest challenge of his presidency, namely, to ensure a balance between the clear need to effect rapid change to meet the demands of a majority that had been excluded from state benefits, and the need to achieve loyalty to the state from dominant or threatening elements within society. The former, it was believed, would be loyal as long as service delivery and steps towards a state that reflected their aspirations were rapidly addressed; the latter if it could be seen that neither lifestyle nor opportunities in the longer term were under threat. The focus from Mandela was, therefore, on changing the face of government, and engaging in gaining the symbolic capital that would ensure national loyalty, even while restructuring took place. Events such as the Rugby World Cup, tea with Betsie Verwoerd, the notions of the 'miracle transition' and the 'rainbow nation', were examples of this shallow and symbolic, but also effective, exercise. Similarly, the 'sunset clause' ensured that too rapid a change of personnel in the state structures did not occur due to the pressures for redress through affirmative action.

But this attempt at legitimising the new state, through both looking backwards and forwards to meeting the needs of the newly enfranchised, was bound to be an uneven process. Continued reliance on many of the agents of the previous state, both black and white, left certain departments and activities vulnerable to heel dragging and even to sabotage. Positive signs, however, were the Constitution (of which more below) with a left-leaning Constitutional Court; emphasis on getting into place affirmative action legislation (although the *Employment Equity Act* was some years off); speeding up of black economic empowerment – that had already started during apartheid; a commitment to gender equality and affirmation of women; and restitution and redistribution of land.

At the same time, however, there were signs of disappointing continuities as well as unexpectedly rapid breaks. A continuity that promises to continue to create disturbances in the social landscape was that of accepting the racialised past, with its view of the population represented in the four spokes of the national wheel. The population continued to be addressed in race terms, and individuals were expected to behave in terms of race solidarities, and events were often in the first instance interpreted in racialised terms (see Maré 2001, Posel 2001b). Mandela was also guilty of this, such as his reprimand to dark-skinned journalists, pointing out clearly where he saw their loyalties properly lying, and where criticism was seen as traitorous behaviour.

An example of the unexpectedly rapid change was the departure from the RDP, a programme that had provided continuity with the rhetorical commitment to the Freedom Charter in the ANC's first election campaign. Two years after these first elections, the RDP with its 'growth through redistribution' approach was superseded by the 'distribution through growth' mantra that has since driven macroeconomic policy (see Padayachee 1998 for a discussion of policy formulation before and during the transition).

Whatever else may be said in retrospective evaluation of Mandela's presidency, the overwhelming evaluation will always be in terms of the transition to democracy and his iconic role within that. That role also left the state with the imprint of an organ of power with a human face.

The Mbeki presidency and the state 1999–2003

Freezing the 'National Democratic Revolution'

Ideological contestation for hegemony within the state has been both open and vicious, as well as diplomatic and cloaked in the language of struggle solidarity (that is, as a question of location within the 'movement'[5]). Mbeki's repeated reiteration of the NDR as the hegemonic project of the post-apartheid state has been a pointed reminder to the ANC's Alliance partners of the limits of state restructuring and of government policy. But now, in distinction from the struggle past, the NDR is being presented as an end in itself and not as the first of a two-stage process. The near total disappearance even of a mention of the Freedom Charter, (never mind debates over the tenuous socialist content of the clauses of this document which was so central to mobilisation during the struggle against apartheid), is a pertinent measure of the extent to which Mbeki's ANC no longer feels it necessary to cast the ideological net wide. Instead the NDR, expressed through black economic empowerment and employment equity policies at higher levels of the state, serves to direct state policy. The employment of race categories and racialised justifications by the ANC ring increasingly hollow as the dynamics of multiracial capitalism unfold and the poor and the sick are still left behind.

While economic space within a capitalist framework has opened up visibly under Mbeki, the liberal space created in the immediate aftermath of 1994 and during Mandela's presidency is closing down. An intolerance of dissent marks Mbeki's style, with pressure on the media more consistent than was the case with Mandela's occasional outbursts. The government has even had to take on the Constitutional Court as that state organ is called upon to enforce service delivery. It is difficult not to see repeated calls for the transformation of the judiciary as anything other than a cry for a more conservative and pliable high court system.

While the continued assertion of the total relevance of race in understanding and acting on society has never been in question at the level of government, the Constitution did prohibit the inappropriate racialisation of post-apartheid South Africa. However, inside Mbeki's ANC, notions of race are used more and more as a tool of explanation – and to justify certain actions (or inactions). Thus, for example, the DA is written-off as 'white' and ignored; in Zimbabwe, the Movement for Democratic Change is conceptualised not as representing the interests of flesh-and-blood (black) Zimbabweans, but as a 'puppet' of the (white) British. The Zimbabwe African National Union-Patriotic Front (Zanu-PF), however, (while perhaps guilty of some mistakes) is seen as representing the real aspirations of black Africa. Across a spectrum of issues – inequality, capitalism, the HIV/AIDS epidemic, criticism – one sees a degeneration of the national debate to a level of race populism.

Simultaneous with this intolerance of dissent, commentators have remarked on the centralisation of power under Mbeki. This is reflected in the growth of the Office of the Presidency, and the peripheralisation of Parliament as a forum for debate – non-attendance by Cabinet members and by the President; a very low level of debate; a lowering of ethical standards (not to be measured against apartheid standards but against those set by the movement itself), and instead, a preference for political solidarity (Daniel 2001/2).

A 'post'-apartheid state?

So, is there a new state in this new South Africa? At an obvious level, and no less important for that, the answer is an emphatic 'yes' with the new state reflecting in subtle and fundamental ways the momentous changes that have occurred in the country since 1990. It does, after all, reflect the victory of the majority for inclusion in democratic practices, and the Constitution stands as symbol of, and tool for, realising that victory. But the specifics of the victory, the special benefactors amongst the victors, the short- and long-terms gains, these and many more aspects can only be judged over a longer period, and not in the flux that continues to characterise the 'new' South Africa. It is not avoiding the issues to say this. The turmoil of transition cannot settle, to the extent that it ever settles, so soon.

The centrality of gender issues and gender equality is one such ongoing issue. Govender can note that: 'In contrast (to the United States of America), in the last five years South Africa has developed one of the best constitutions in the world in terms of its commitment to building substantive gender equality ...' (1999: 3), but qualify it by referring to the legacies of apartheid, to attitudes that need to change, to the operation of state departments, and to budget decisions that do not give substance to such praiseworthy commitments. The *Women's Budget* series offers one indicator of practical implementation, or of failure to do so, of constitutional commitments. Others are to be measured against the actions of the Commission on Gender Equality and the Office on the Status of Women, and against the efficacy of the extension of citizenship to all South African women in alleviating inequalities (see Hassim 1999).

The analysis of a gendered state is not to be achieved through measures that focus only on the position of women, but, as Manicom has argued writing on the apartheid state, 'gender does not feature in the race-class debate … and it is certainly far from conventional to refer to the masculinist state, the patriarchal state – along with the colonial/segregationist/apartheid/capitalist/reformist state in South African history' (1992: 444). And it certainly still is not 'conventional' to do so.

Earlier, I identified four issues that would allow us at least to make some temporary evaluations, and to indicate positive and negative measures against which to analyse: first, the rupture from apartheid; second, sources of legitimacy for the new state; third, and related to the second, the success of the state as service deliverer; and, finally, the state as site of continuing struggle.

The rupture with apartheid

The break with apartheid is, as already indicated, complete in certain respects. In others, however, the modern state at the end of the twentieth century is a given in terms of its functions. The state continues to ensure the relations of private property, now even more so in terms of intellectual property; it continues to maintain the conditions for profitable investment, and the free circulation of commodities; it ensures territorial integrity, with the increasingly important concomitant of control over the movement of people; it negotiates in the global forums for the most favourable deals for the 'commanding heights of the economy'; it acts as the representative of a state in dealings with other states; and it controls the legitimate use of force and the major institutions of socialisation.

As such, the post-apartheid state has never questioned the external boundaries of the new state. As a member of the Organisation of African Unity (OAU), now the African Union, it has internalised the mantra of not contesting inherited colonial boundaries, even though these are to the detriment of some of South Africa's neighbours, notably Lesotho. While internal remapping removed apartheid's bantustan borders, more significant was the move away from the social content of those spaces (as ones of extreme discrimination: labour reserves, locations of the 'surplus people', places of overt bias in allocation of welfare, infrastructure, services, or whatever other measure one employs), as well as the reasons for their existence (a clear and violently enforced alternative to political and social inclusiveness). But even in the abolition of the bantustans, limits to transformation have been acceded to. The Inkatha Freedom Party (IFP) has been allowed to ensure that the issue of the powers and status of traditional leaders remains on a burner, even if not consistently at the front, and it has found increasing support from across the country for the maintenance and even extension of such authorities. Along with the ANC's far from resolved position on the symbolic or administrative place of such agents and institutions, political manipulation of these distorted remnants of pre-capitalist society continue.

There are other areas where there might have been choices, although some would argue that 'realistically' there were none: South Africa is locked into dependence on international investment – including patents and copyrights, technology, and acquisition of sophisticated equipment, such as in the arms industry; and the country is tied to the organs of regulation of international capitalism, such as the World Bank and the IMF – although here the argument is that 'change from within' is quite feasible. But most centrally, South Africa has remained a capitalist state, an issue to which we have to return time and again, with its obvious and ever increasing displays of private wealth amidst the existence of public squalor. The frequent denials over the last few years that the ANC, rather than the SACP and labour, ever offered a socialist alternative bespeaks of at least a modicum of embarrassment at the rebuttal of suggestions of alternatives.

In summary then, the post-apartheid state is the state of capitalism. While there remains a very genuine commitment amongst many to the general upliftment of all, it is contradicted by countervailing tendencies and by the choices actually made.

Legitimacy of the state

The Constitution that established an inclusive democratic order in South Africa is also the major source of its legitimacy. It has been seen to provide recourse for citizens, individually and as movements in civil society, to call the government to book. The Constitution of the Republic of South Africa commits the new state to non-sexism, non-racism and to act against all forms of discrimination. It has also been found that while it is accepted that the society was skewed before the transition to democracy, constitutionally the new state is committed to redress and social transformation (see Govender n.d.: 14, quoting a 1997 Constitutional Court finding). To enable redress it qualifies the prohibition against unfair discrimination with a rider: 'unless it is established that the discrimination is fair' (RSA 1996: 7). Govender writes that: 'It was imperative that a constitution drafted for South Africa responded to this reality [of discrimination and inequality] and imposed obligations and established structural imperatives which sought to ameliorate this crisis' (n.d.: 15). The state is obliged to realise the socio-economic rights mentioned by the Constitution.

What this means is that the citizens have recourse to redress from the state other than during elections. The Constitution allows demands for the provision of rights to basic education, health care, and so on, to be enforced. Govender notes, however, that the Constitutional Court has found that there are times when the state can argue that the general provision of services outweighs the demands of individuals to these services, eg. expensive health care, as in the case of Soobramoney (n.d.: 16). However, elsewhere it was found that the state had to provide a minimum (and progressively increasing) level of services. The Constitution has created 'a right to social assistance', which was enforced by the Constitutional Court in the case of *Grootboom v. Oostenberg Municipality and Others* in regard to shelter for children (see, for example, de Vos 2001; Liebenberg 2001; Sloth-Nielsen 2001).

De Vos argues that the Constitutional Court has accepted that the state has a transformative function that can be legally enforced. The Bill of Rights 'requires the state not only to respect the various rights, but also to protect, promote and fulfil them.' This means that the status quo of immense inequality cannot be accepted as given, but that the state must 'take steps to reach the rights-based goals that might at present seem difficult or even impossible to attain' (de Vos 2001: 261). It would be interesting to see if such legislation could be used to dispute the state's allocation of money through the budget, such as in the contentious arms purchases.

The TAC has also called upon the Constitution to achieve the goal of forcing the state to provide nevirapine to HIV-positive women giving birth in state hospitals. Judge Botha ruled that the state had a duty to undertake measures to 'prevent or reduce the mother-to-child transmission of HIV' (*Treatment Action Campaign and Others v. Minister of Health and Others 2002*). Here, however, the TAC has resorted to a public campaign of defiance to force implementation.

The Constitution has also created innovative institutions to give citizens greater direct or indirect call on the state for protection, access to information, representation, and so on. To mention some of these: the South African Human Rights Commission (SAHRC); the Public Protector; the National Council of Provinces (NCOP), each add another dimension to the new state form. The SAHRC, for example, has not only taken up the issue of racism in the media, albeit under a cloud of criticism and even ridicule, but also monitors the transparency required of businesses in South Africa under new legislation – such as the *Promotion of Access to Information Act* (2000) and the *Electronic Communications and Transactions Act* (2002).

However, the Constitution has also become a site of struggle in itself. This has occurred not just between the state and citizens (as indicated above), but because of the amendments to allow floor crossing between elections. The events surrounding this issue during 2002 – to strengthen, of all things, an ANC-NNP alliance, and to allow the ANC to take control of KwaZulu-Natal, the very province that provided the scene for a decade of killing fields, and where compromises were justified on the basis of the need to achieve peace – cannot but have harmed the legitimacy of the state, as reflected in the much lauded Constitution and in the democratic process.

As with most nationalist movements, the ANC presents itself as fulfilling a mission. That mission was entrusted to the ANC by 'history', but personalised by specific individuals who could give expression to it. This mission was defined in wider terms than the mission claimed by the ANC's rival, Inkatha, during the years of struggle, but it mobilised its support in a similar way. While Inkatha was conveyed by its leaders as the vehicle of an ethnic mission to give voice to the Zulu nation, the ANC was entrusted with the broader task of 'founding the African nation'. In the recent words of ANC Youth League (ANCYL) President Malusi Gigaba: 'the founding of the ANC in 1912 was a culmination of this process [of resistance against colonial conquest] and was to fulfil the historic mission that earlier forms of organisation and struggle had failed to accomplish. Its historic mission was to unite Africans for national liberation' (*Daily News* 03.02.03). Mbeki also makes a claim that there is an 'historic goal' to be realised 'step by step' by an undefined 'we', of 'eradication of a centuries-old legacy of colonialism, racism and apartheid' (2002:1).

Some sociologists argue that what distinguishes the modern nation from its pre-modern prototype is the obliteration of kinship as the principal means of transmitting political status and its replacement with 'free' rational individuals under state bureaucracy and secular law, the implementation of a socialisation system of universal education to replace loyalty to clan with loyalty to a state (see Gellner 1983). In the case of South Africa, I would argue, to the contrary, that the idea of a 'mission' referred to by Gigaba (and others) creates a system of 'moral kinship' that is defined not by pre-capitalist kinship relations, but by selective inclusion in the 'historic mission' defined by the ANC. This is not a unique process, but is a feature of the modern quest for political control that has been shared by similar organisations (the rhetoric of both the NP and Inkatha is replete with examples). The mission creates loyalties, responsibilities and protection that fall outside the notion of an impersonal, rule-bound state and its meritocratic bureaucratic institutions. The effect is that the ANC's historical mission demands conflation of the movement with the state, argues for the collapse of civil society into the state, and arrogates the dispensation of political morality to those who hold power within the 'national liberation movement'.

This would seem to be the only way to understand the loyalties towards members (the cases of Alan Boesak and Tony Yengeni come to mind), a loyalty displayed as morally sanctioned through membership or participation in the historic mission (within which the abstraction, 'the struggle', was central). Furthermore, the sensitivity and extreme reactions to criticism (see Daniel 2001/2: 2) and to critical questioning of the basis of authority with which servants of the state operate might also be located in such an explanation. Loyalty becomes a means of controlling critical debate, especially serious in the ANC in its transition from political movement to ruling party, and a hazard that greatly limits the ideally even-handed and efficient functioning of the state.

Delivery

Service delivery is essential in maintaining the legitimacy of the state, and not just of the government in power. This is especially the case in a society with such gross inequality (not just poverty), as is the case in South Africa. Liebenberg (2001: 234–5), quoting United Nations Development Programme figures, notes that the country is placed third from the bottom of all countries on the inequality scale – only Brazil and Guatemala are lower. Posing the issue like this immediately confronts us again with the debate on race, gender and class, particularly the questions of whether we address inherited social inequality through race-based or through class-based policies of redress, and of how gender is sidelined in both class and race discussions?

Inequality indicates discrimination, exploitation and accumulation, as well as the misallocation of the profits made from such exploitation. This applies also to the choices made and pressures applied on decisions on the allocation of taxes gathered by the state. Inequality relates, as well, to power relations that allow certain social groups to ensure the allocation of resources to themselves, or to effectively engage in capitalist accumulation. It also indicates a failure of effective priorities to address the situation. If inequality grows it would seem to be an indication of continuities in the system of economic exploitation, even if democratic reform has guaranteed a greater number of political participants. Political participation, if democracy is effective, does provide the potential that such power be translated in a more even distribution of welfare. This reality is a sore point of embarrassment, explaining the vehement and personalised reaction of the ANC in government to arguments (such as were recently levelled by Professor Sampie Terreblanche (2003) in *A History of Inequality*, and through the publicity that preceded its publication) that inequality is worsening, not unexpectedly accompanied by the creation of a small but growing group of black beneficiaries – the black economic empowerment participants whose lobbying powers ensure effective use of the state as site of struggle. The issue of poverty and inequality is indeed desperate and compounded by the effects of AIDS. While certainly not medically discriminating, it is amongst the poor that HIV/AIDS cuts its swathe of destruction most swiftly.

The new state did not create capitalism, did not actually ensure the spread of property relations, did not separate people from direct access to and control over the means of production – what Marx called 'primitive accumulation'. That founding process had occurred under colonialism, and had been extended and maintained since 1910 through the policies of various governments. Instead, unless the capitalist route was to be abandoned in the short or medium term, the post-apartheid state was required to liberalise the boundaries of capitalist control and ownership by deracialising it. Of course there were many black capitalists before 1990, but they were largely located in the bantustans and operated under extremely restrictive conditions (see Hudson & Sarakinsky 1986).

Yet, more to the point than actual participation in class exploitation – which is limited to a small proportion of the population – it is the growing ethos of entitlement to disproportionate reward that permeates the new South African society, including the state, that affects both inequality and the ruthlessness with which wealth is sought. This is evident not simply in the corruption that is evident in political parties – ruling and opposition – but in the civil service and public control facilities, corporations and the like. It is also evident in the salary figures and justifications of university vice-chancellors and chairs of councils, of chief executive officers and directors of companies, of the discrepancies between entry-level police men and women and their senior officers. My point here, however, is not about the level of corruption (which may well have been more extreme under apartheid, especially in the arms and fuel industries, and around services and facilities delivered to voteless black people), but about the social location of so many cases that have come to court or may still do so, and the manner in which accusations and even convictions are handled. In the numerous cases, of which Tony Yengeni, Winnie Madikizela-Mandela, Joe Modise, the Shaik brothers, and even the Deputy President, Jacob Zuma, are but a small sample, it seems that principle of service counts for less than political solidarity.

This cannot but undermine the legitimacy of the state. Inequality and rampant consumerism must have an effect on the way a society thinks of itself and of the state. It will affect those who benefit or who realistically expect to benefit very differently from the mass of excluded people. French sociologist, Alain Touraine, writing about Algerian urban youth and their availability for Islamic fundamentalism, noted: 'Their anger was directed against a Western producer-consumer society that was at once so close and so inaccessible' (2000: 115). The forms that such anger take will, of course, vary from one historical context to the next, but the signs are here too.

Inequality, therefore, demands redress and efficient service delivery. The Constitution commits the state to such delivery, making some of the recent rulings appropriate to mention in this context. The commentators on the Grootboom case referred to above, draw attention to the Constitutional Court's emphasis on the 'reasonable implementation of policy' and not just formulation of policy (Liebenberg 2001: 242). Liebenberg concludes her case study of state social assistance by stressing that there are two 'key implications' of the Grootboom case: first, that 'any policy development must include as an integral component the need to ensure the effective implementation of the relevant social assistance programme'; and, second, 'the state is obliged to expand, and not reduce, access to social assistance rights by those who are unable to support themselves and their dependants' (2001: 250).

This point is raised here not just because it reflects the functioning of the state and its abilities and efficiencies, but also because it reflects on the relationship of citizens (and in this case especially the poor, rural people, women, and so on) to the state at a level of trust and of its legitimacy.

A recent case in KwaZulu-Natal highlights what I am referring to. In early 2003 a massacre took place in KwaMaye, about 20 kilometers from Bergville in the northern Drakensberg region. Galina Xaba (64), her daughter and five children were shot and then burned in their hut. Local people, and the mayor of the uThukela municipal district, link this regrettable and horrifying incident directly to the inability of the local police to curb stock theft, and bring the culprits to book. Instead a vigilante group, calling itself the 'Black Scorpions' has recovered 80 per cent of stolen cattle since its formation, as against the two per cent recovery rate of the South African Police Service (SAPS). The success of the Black Scorpions is clearly related to extreme tactics, with several people dead after questioning (*Mail & Guardian* 07.02.03). This is simply one example of vigilante activity attributed to the failure of the police. On 9 February 2003 it was reported in news telecasts that the Minister of Safety and Security, Charles Nqakula, had admitted that the SAPS did not have the resources to fight crime effectively in South Africa – an astonishing statement, if not the first such statement.

In addition, the police are deliberately targeted by criminals, undermining morale even more than low salaries and unequal remuneration. While the situation has not yet reached the level of Colombia where, as the drug cartels' assault on the Colombian state increased (from 1985 to the early 1990s), 200 judges, 1 200 police and more than 150 journalists were killed (Adelman 2002), the levels are much higher than in comparable countries.

Corruption, too, is widely linked to inefficient policing, while members of the public have come to expect corrupt behaviour as well as the inability to enforce laws. Legislation is passed to enforce the use of hands-free cellphone systems, but it is soon said by the Commissioner of Police that it will not be enforceable; the Minister of Transport responds to the holiday-time carnage in 2002/2003 by saying that there are simply not enough officers, and that corrupt officials make it impossible adequately to apply laws. The University of Natal's Accident Research Centre notes that in a study that it undertook, 82 per cent of the 80 traffic officers interviewed said that they knew of another officer who had taken bribes, while similar percentages of both drivers and pedestrians believed that bribes were regularly offered and accepted.

It is becoming acknowledged in an increasing number of areas that even if legislation is passed, the ability to act on it – and to enforce it if required – remains beyond the reach of state organs, or open to abuse and non-compliance because of corruption. In the area of pollution control and environmental protection generally, corruption is extensive – with the most recent high-profile case being the allegations against senior politicians in the Western Cape (Peter Marais, former Western Cape Premier, and David Malatsi,[6] deputy Social Services Minister in the national government). National conservation director of the Wildlife and Environment Society of South Africa, Cathy Kay, notes that: 'We have the best environmental laws in the world, but there's no political will to implement them' (*Sunday Times* 26.01.03). Here, as in so many other instances of the public good, it is the poor who suffer most under the consequences of environmental neglect, as they do directly in the area of social welfare.

It goes beyond whether the state is actually inefficient or corrupt and has to include the general perception by citizens of the functioning of the state. This investigation is, after all, directed at the form of state, of which perceptions shape the overall ethos within which the state is perceived.

Site of struggle

O'Meara concludes his analysis of the domination of the NP over apartheid South Africa with the note that:

> analysis of state politics requires a complex and necessarily fluid understanding of the competing power bases within the state, the various (and competing) political and bureaucratic cultures through which actors understand their places in the broader scheme of things, the issue-areas at the heart of state politics and the personalities of the individual actors concerned. (1996: 485)

Such an investigation and analysis cannot be undertaken here. It does, however, need to be highlighted as necessary for further theorising and empirical investigation. I have indicated the areas within which such an investigation of the state as site of struggle needs to be located: class, gender, race, ethnicity (if by that we refer to claims for particularist recognition on the basis of ethnic social identities – such as recognition of traditional leaders, claims to land, language rights, and so on). Struggle is certainly not to be seen as undesirable. On the contrary, the absence of struggle and the closing down of space within which it can occur is to be guarded against. What it demands is a focus on the issue of power, and how that is mobilised and where it is located.

There are institutions that serve as locations of struggle: constitutionally-created bodies such as the National Economic and Labour Council (Nedlac), the SAHRC, the Commission on Gender Equality, the Pan South African Language Board serve as examples. Nedlac especially, with its representation of labour, business, the government, and civil society, has shown strong disagreements on policy, and not only in strictly economic matters, such as the case of anti-retroviral policy early in 2003.

The struggles are not only about policy formulation, but also about the ideo-logical justifications and approach that dominates within the state. If the working class is to contest the meaning of the NDR, specifically away from it being seen as essentially a victory of the aspirant capitalist class, then it would seem that it also rejects a racialised post-apartheid. With the re-racialisation of politics and the economy, a victory for a black bourgeoisie meets the ideo-logical requirements of both international capital and conservative states, and can be proclaimed a victory for black people – much as Buthelezi had done in his racialised and ethnic populist mobilisation during the 1970s and 1980s, 'every successful businessman a brick in the wall of black nationalism', to para-phrase him somewhat.

To perceive the state as site of struggle between competing interests is only half the battle, and this returns me to the starting point: the state reflects changing power locations, and it reflects this in many sites, including 'non-state sites' as Manicom has pointed out in relation to 'gender regulation' through 'churches, familial relations, indigenous social organization' and so on (1992: 457). Such an approach presents social scientists with fascinating studies of the state as a new form, reflecting both old and new social agents.

Conclusion

In opposition to theorists who saw the South African social formation as a 'special type' of colonialism, Freund wrote in 1984 that to see the struggle against apartheid as an anti-colonial struggle 'misses the mark in a country which, despite its colonial roots in history, has been effectively independent for decades'. He concludes by contrasting an Africanist and a Marxist perspec-tive on change in South Africa. The former would see it as the last of a 'long trail of victories for nationalism'; whereas the latter would see a revolution which would 'provid(e) Africa with its first industrialised socialist economy and bring about a storm that would be likely to sweep aside crisis-ridden regimes over half a continent!' (1984: 288; also see Freund 1986). Instead of this appealing vision we have a South Africa that is propping up the crisis-ridden neighbour Zimbabwe from anything but a socialist base. Does this mean that we have to place the South African transition and state within the long line of African transitions that utilised the state for enrichment of a bureaucracy and rapid class formation into a dependent bourgeoisie? Or do we instead have a complex set of (complexly articulated class, gender and race) contestations, occurring under conditions, internally and globally, vastly different from those that applied during the wave of decolonisation?

Most immediately, the transition in South Africa demanded that at the level of political structures and of political representation of interests, the tension between reform and repression that characterised the transitional apartheid period be resolved through the democratic incorporation of all South Africans under equal citizenship rights; but it did not demand that capitalism, as a system, be abandoned or even altered to the extent that the phrases in the Freedom Charter expressed the crafted expression of 1950s 'popular will'. Rather, the transition demanded that measures ensure the continuation of the capitalist system, and to maintain South Africa's specific location in terms of global capitalism. The NDR was a call for extension and for incorporation – extension of social and political rights and obligations, and incorporation (for some) into the ruling class.

Notes

1   Mathatha Tsedu (now editor of the *Sunday Times*) recently used the phrase: 'Rebuilding a nation from the ashes of a past like ours is a daunting task' in an editorial (*Sunday Times* 26.01.03).

2   There is an awkward contradiction in politicians and commentators wanting both to claim the defeat of the apartheid system (and hence of the state form that gave it continuity – the 'ashes' argument), while simultaneously to hold on to a selection of 'legacies' that continue to bedevil the post-apartheid social formation (the foundations of the inherited-house argument).

3   See Marais (2001: 2) for the application of this idea as characterising the liberation movement's approach in South Africa.

4   It would be an interesting exercise to look at the vocabulary used to analyse from a critical perspective the apartheid social reality, as against the predominant concepts employed post-1990: then it was 'classes', 'monopolies', 'black petty bourgeoisie', 'racial capitalism', etc.

5   The governing party sees itself as a 'movement' which raises interesting questions about the separation of a state – seen as the fulfilment of a mission of a 'movement' – and the existence of the ANC as a governing 'party' – protector of a multi-party democracy for which it had fought.

6   David Malatsi could serve as an illustration of several other continuities, serving as he does in a government that now includes not only the IFP, the Pan African Congress (PAC), but also the NNP. Malatsi is also one of many examples where the old apartheid, tri-cameral and bantustan political and economic elites have seemingly effortlessly become part of the new order – and this transitionary migration goes far beyond the necessary compromises to maintain stability, as might have been the argument with high officers within the South African National Defence Force (SANDF) and SAPS, and includes perpetrators of crimes, security police, and individuals against whom questions of murder and assassination hang.

References

Adam, H (1971) *Modernizing racial domination: the dynamics of South African politics.* Berkeley: University of California Press.

Adelman, J (2002) Andean impasses, *New Left Review* 18: 41–72.

Alavi, H (1972) The state in post-colonial societies – Pakistan and Bangladesh, *New Left Review* 74: 59–81.

Alexander, N (2002) *An ordinary country: Issues in the transition from apartheid to democracy in South Africa.* Scottsville: University of Natal Press.

Cronin, J & Suttner, R (1986) *30 Years of the Freedom Charter.* Johannesburg: Ravan.

Daniel, J (2001/2) The Mbeki presidency: Lusaka wins, in *SA Yearbook of International Affairs.* Johannesburg: South African Institute of International Affairs.

De Vos, P (2001) Grootboom, the right of access to housing and substantive equality as contextual fairness, *SA Journal of Human Rights* 17: 258–276.

Dubow, S (1995) *Illicit union: scientific racism in modern South Africa.* Johannesburg: Witwatersrand University Press.

Freund, B (1984) *The making of contemporary Africa.* London: Macmillan.

Freund, Bill (1986) Some unasked questions on politics: South African slogans and debates, *Transformation* 1: 118–129.

Gellner, E (1983) *Nations and nationalism.* Oxford: Basil Blackwell.

Govender, K (n.d.) *Attempting to achieve substantive equality in one of the most unequal societies in the world.* Johannesburg: SAHRC.

Govender, P (1999) Preface, in D Budlender (ed.) *The Fourth Women's Budget.* Cape Town: Institute for Democratic Action in South Africa (IDASA).

Habib, A (1995) The transition to democracy in South Africa: Developing a dynamic model, *Transformation* 27: 50–73.

Hassim, S (1999) From presence to power: Women's citizenship in a new democracy, *Agenda* 40: 6–17.

Hudson, P (1987) On national-democratic revolution: A reply to Cronin, *Transformation* 4: 54–59.

Hudson, P & Sarakinsky, M (1986) Class interests and politics: the case of the urban African bourgeoisie, in SARS (ed.) *South African Review 3*. Johannesburg: Ravan.

Hugo, P (1990) Affirmative action in the civil service, in R Schrire (ed.) *Critical choices for South Africa: An agenda for the 1990s*. Cape Town: OUP.

Kaplan, D (1980) The South African state: The origins of a racially exclusive democracy, *The Insurgent Sociologist*, 10(2): 85–96.

Kapuściński, Ryszard (2001) *The shadow of the sun: My African life*. London: Penguin.

Liebenberg, S (2001) The right to social assistance: The implications of Grootboom for policy reform in South Africa, *SA Journal of Human Rights* 17.

Lipton, M (1986) *Capitalism and apartheid South Africa, 1910–1986*. Aldershot: Wildwood House.

Mamdani, M (1976) *Politics and class formation in Uganda*. New York & London: Monthly Review Press.

Mamdani, M (1996) *Citizen and subject: Contemporary Africa and the legacy of late colonialism*. Princeton: Princeton University Press.

Manicom, L (1992) Ruling relations: Rethinking state and gender in South African history, *Journal of African History* 33: 441–465.

Marais, H (2001) *South Africa: Limits to change: The political economy of transition*. London: Zed Books.

Maré, G (2001) Race counts in contemporary South Africa: 'An illusion of ordinariness', *Transformation* 47: 75–93

Mbeki, T (2002) *State of the Nation Address by the President of South Africa, Thabo Mbeki*. Parliament, 8 February 2002.

O'Dowd, M (1974) The stages of economic growth and the future of South Africa, in A Leftwich (ed.) *South African economic growth and political change*. London: Allison & Busby.

O'Dowd, M (1978) The O'Dowd view: The stages of economic growth and the future of South Africa, in L Schlemmer and E Webster (eds.) *Change, reform and economic growth in South Africa*. Johannesburg: Ravan.

O'Meara, D (1977) The 1946 African mine-workers strike in the political economy of South Africa, in PL Bonner (ed.) *Working papers in Southern African studies*. Johannesburg: African Studies Institute, University of the Witwatersrand.

O'Meara, D (1983) *Volkskapitalisme: Class, capital and ideology in the development of Afrikaner nationalism 1934–1948*. Johannesburg: Ravan.

O'Meara, D (1996) *Forty lost years: The apartheid state and the politics of the National Party, 1948–1994.* Johannesburg: Ravan.

Padayachee, V (1998) Progressive academic economists and the challenge of development in South Africa's decade of liberation, *Review of African Political Economy* 25(77): 431–450.

Posel, D (2001a) Race and common sense: racial classification in twentieth century South Africa, *African Studies Review* 44(2): 87–114.

Posel, D (2001b) What's in a name? Racial categorisations under apartheid and their after-life, *Transformation* 47: 50–74.

SARS (South African Research Service) (1983) Introduction, in *South African Review 1: Same foundations, new facades.* Johannesburg: Ravan & SARS.

Saul, JS (1979) The state in postcolonial societies: Tanzania, in *The state and revolution in Eastern Africa: Essays by John S Saul.* New York and London: Monthly Review Press.

Shivji, IG (1976) *Class struggles in Tanzania.* London: Heinemann.

Sloth-Nielsen, J (2001) The child's right to social services, the right to social security, and primary prevention of child abuse: Some conclusions in the aftermath of Grootboom, *SA Journal of Human Rights* 17(2): 210–219.

Swilling, M & Phillips, M (1989) The emergency state: Its structure, power and limits, in G Moss & I Obery (eds.) *South African Review 5.* Johannesburg: Ravan.

Terreblanche, S (2003) *A history of inequality in South Africa 1652–2002.* Piermaritzburg: University of Natal Press.

Touraine, A (2000) *Can we live together? Equality and difference.* Cambridge: Polity Press.

Treatment Action Campaign and Others v. Minister of Health and Others (2002) Butterworth Constitutional Law Reports (BCLR) 4: 7.

The state of party politics: Struggles within the Tripartite Alliance and the decline of opposition

Roger Southall

> I think there are tendencies now of what some of us refer to as the zanufication of the ANC. You can see features of that, of a bureau-cratisation of the struggle: thanks very much. It was important that you were mobilised then, but now we are in power, in power on your behalf: Relax and we'll deliver ... It would be a renuncia-tion of the possibilities of the situation (the continuing existence of the Tripartite Alliance), to abandon the ANC to the neo-liberals ... For me what's most important about the breaking of the DA alliance ... it's the defeat of a particular project which was the most racial, subliminal mobilisation of minority communities in a pessimistic project about majority rule and democracy in our country. (Cronin 2002)

What was as fascinating as ANC MP and South African Communist Party (SACP) Deputy General Secretary Jeremy Cronin's interview with Irish aca-demic Helena Sheehan, was the ANC's reaction to the interview. Following a crude attack on him by Dumisani Makhaye (a fellow National Executive Committee (NEC) member) as both a Trotskyist and would-be 'white messiah' (*Sowetan* 29.07.02), Cronin was to be censured by the NEC and required to apologise, which he did. Yet ironically, what emerges from a reading of the Cronin interview is not only how he is defending the ANC against charges that it has sold out to capitalism and/or is sliding towards Stalinist bureaucratism, but also a consciousness of the enormous fluidity of the forces at play within the party and how its future remains underdetermined.

Much conventional analysis focuses on how the ANC, which took 63 per cent of the popular vote in South Africa's first democratic election in 1994, is becoming increasingly dominant at the expense of political opposition (Giliomee, Myburgh & Schlemmer 2001; Southall 1994). The ANC assumed office as the leading constituent of the government of national unity (GNU), which included representation of the former ruling NP (which had won 20 per cent of the vote) and the (largely Zulu-ethnic) Inkatha Freedom Party (IFP) (which had taken ten per cent). This left the task of opposition in the hands of the small Democratic Party (DP) (1,7 per cent) and three other minor parties.

However, the prospects for the viability of opposition had appeared to increase when, following promulgation of South Africa's final Constitution in 1996 (as provided for by the transitional agreement), the NP left the GNU. Subsequently, having seen its support (now seven per cent) wither away in favour of the more robustly critical DP (now ten per cent) in the second election in 1999, it had agreed to merge with the latter in the DA, designed to counter prospective ANC 'tyranny'. However, rapidly finding itself in danger of becoming subordinated to the DP, the by now New National Party (NNP) chose to negotiate re-entry into the government in junior partnership to the ANC. While the official rhetoric of renewed ANC-NNP cooperation pronounced a shift to racial co-operation in contrast to the DA's alleged national divisiveness, alternative opinion saw the NNP as undermining democracy in return for short-term gains of petty power and patronage. For some this merely confirmed the prognostication that democracy will only begin to flourish in South Africa when the Congress of South African Trade Unions (Cosatu) and the SACP, the ruling party's partners in the so-called 'Tripartite Alliance' (hereafter the Alliance), break away from the ANC to construct an opposition party of the left, whose socialist programme will enable it to attract a mass-based, popular following.

This paper will utilise the Cronin interview to explore the key aspects of this debate, which are indicated by the quotations above. By examining recent developments it will ask: Is the ANC becoming more bureaucratised and less internally democratic? Is the ANC becoming increasingly dominant over its partners in the Alliance? And is the ANC's extending dominance of the political arena leading to the decline of political opposition?

The bureaucratisation of the ANC?

In 2002 the ANC attracted widespread criticism for its endorsement of Robert Mugabe's Zanu, which stood accused of having rigged both parliamentary (2000) and presidential (2002) elections in a bid to retain power. However, what really seems to have irked the ANC about Cronin's interview, is his assertion that it is showing signs of 'zanufication', by which he meant tendencies to acute bureaucratisation at the expense of internal democracy.

Ottaway, writing before 1994, argued that the ANC's transition from a liberation movement to a political party would be difficult. Liberation movements inhabit environments which are uncongenial for democracy, while also stressing unity, rejecting partisan divisions and promoting the illusion that they stand for an entire nation. In contrast, political parties operating in a democratic environment do not pretend to represent an entire nation, but particular constituencies. 'Transition to democracy is not impossible, but neither is the much less attractive alternative of another form of authoritarianism' (Ottaway 1991: 82).

Cronin argues that many of the practices of today's ANC are inherited from exile, where the movement's social and geographical isolation encouraged an unquestioning intellectual certainty about the course of struggle that diverged from the realities on the ground. Priority was given to securing positions in a bureaucratic and military apparatus that would provide standing in the future, and factionalism and patronage prevailed. The exile tradition has translated into the ANC today exhibiting similar tendencies. The commitment to liberatory goals remains, yet the popular energies needed to realise them are subject to an institutionalisation and bureaucratism stemming from the movement's remoteness from its mass base. Hence, whereas the ANC swept into power on the basis of the highly progressive RDP, which put a premium on popular mobilisation, its replacement by the neoliberal Growth, Employment and Redistribution (Gear) strategy from around 1996 has seen a shift to the adoption of policies to be 'delivered' that may be 'people-centred' but are not 'people-driven'.

This transformation is not so much a product of betrayal by the ANC leadership as an outcome of the negotiated transition to democratisation having left large-scale capital in South Africa undefeated. In a post-Cold War world, the necessity of engaging with capital has led to the emergence of a new black capitalist class aligned to the ANC and not just bound to the state apparatus, as in Zimbabwe. This means that there are powerful forces within the ANC that have a financial independence, and that there are a multiplicity of centres of power within the broad movement. Cronin suggests that this imparts to the ANC a fluidity which, whilst making it prone to factionalism, also makes it open to influence from the left, not least because of the continued weight within the movement of a militant trade union movement. Even if a bourgeois, right wing of the party is dominant, it faces an internal challenge which indicates that the inevitability of bureaucratisation and the pursuit of untrammelled capitalism cannot be assumed.

Before exploring how recent developments within the ANC accord or otherwise with Cronin's analysis, it is instructive to note two major points. First, ANC-speak still attempts to justify the party's embrace of capitalism by reference to the two-stage theory of liberation (national independence first, socialism second), in which the present era is referred to as that of the national democratic revolution (NDR). This is a phrase which – as the late Joe Slovo observed – can be used so ambiguously that it can describe a whole range of situations whose only common feature is that successful assault on an existing social order has not yet matured into socialism. Slovo's position, writing in the mid-1970s, was therefore that, based on a revolutionary seizure of state power, the NDR would have to be characterised by the proletariat being politically dominant and playing the leading role in the post-revolutionary struggles to establish a new socialist order (Slovo 1976). Cronin, thinking aloud in the early 2000s, appears to have abandoned the historicist schema implied by the NDR, and is attempting to assess the balance of class forces within the liberation movement in the wake of the ANC's less-than-revolutionary acquisition of state power. Yet he also attacks Saul (2001), who views capitalism in South Africa as tragically triumphant, and McKinley (2001), who depicts ANC pro-capitalist policies as unambiguous evidence that the revolution has been betrayed, as both offering simplistic and demobilising analyses which foreclose a progressive future. The ANC may be subject to regressive tendencies, yet it is not beyond possible redemption.

The second observation is that Cronin is offering a far more nuanced analysis of the ANC than those who uncomplicatedly depict it as an overwhelmingly dominant party. Such a view is associated with those (Giliomee & Simkins 1999; Giliomee, Myburgh & Schlemmer 2001) who have proposed that since 1994 the ANC has misused its position as a democratically-elected government to extend its domination over state and society. The large African majority in society guarantees the ANC electoral dominance, and opposition is delegitimised as racist as, simultaneously, constitutional defences of minority rights are being weakened. Demographic representativity and affirmative action are being used to empower a black elite while a project of transformation is pursued to capture control of all major institutions in society. Meanwhile, a Leninist strategy of democratic centralism is employed to close down internal debate in its own ranks while the political opposition is increasingly inhibited by the manipulation of parliamentary and other rules in the ANC's favour. Opposition voters are being marginalised as the ANC marches South Africa along the road to African despotism.

Such a view would seem to overstate the capacity of the ANC to impose itself on a society that is hugely diverse, mobile and can, if necessary, call on deep traditions of popular protest to oppression. Yet what Cronin is also stressing is that, even if the party hierarchy aspires to dominance, the ANC itself is far from being a monolith. Instead, in his version of reality it emerges as an arena of marked contestation between different factions, classes and ideological tendencies, in which an emergent African bourgeoisie may at present be dominant, yet which is nonetheless constrained by democratic impulses that emanate from the trade unions and popular masses.

Cronin implies that rather than Ottaway's 'democratic' and 'authoritarian' styles of operation being alternatives for the ANC, they actually co-exist. This is scarcely surprising, for the ANC, in returning from exile, had to re-engage and absorb a popular-democratic political culture which not only resonated throughout its own earlier, pre-exile history, but also was made manifest by such internal organisations as the United Democratic Front (UDF) and Cosatu, which all claimed allegiance to the broader, historical Congress tradition. This simultaneity of political traditions almost inevitably results in mixed modes of behaviour by the party leadership. Nonetheless, Cronin seems to be largely in agreement with Friedman (*Business Day* 12.04.02) who suggests that the exile, authoritarian tendency is pre-eminent.

Centralising versus centrifugal tendencies

In so far as today's ANC is top-down, a major impulse derives from an effort to centralise power around the presidency. This has gained momentum particularly since 1999 under the presidency of Thabo Mbeki. Several examples of this tendency suggest themselves. One is structural: this has involved the creation of a Presidential Support Unit, whose particular role was announced to be the provision of advice to the President concerning international affairs, notably with regard to Africa (*Business Day* 22.02.02). This is a task that traditionally has fallen within the purview of the Department of Foreign Affairs. Instead, the new unit reports to the Minister of Intelligence, while simultaneously an internal restructuring of the presidency has been designed to enhance the latter's role to engage in 'critical strategic planning' (*Business Day* 18.02.02). While those around the presidency disclaim any aspirations to centralisation, Mbeki's hands-on style of governance would appear to be encouraging just that.

A common accompaniment of centralisation is the development of a politics of personalised supremacy, whereby dominant leaders impose policies, inhibit debate and suppress real or imagined challenges to their leadership. Under Mbeki this has most notoriously resulted in the AIDS debacle. Emanating from the presumed consequences of challenging the President's widely publicised doubts over whether the HIV virus leads to AIDS (as upheld by almost all leading scientists), government policy concerning treatment of the disease (notably distribution of prophylactic drugs) was to be hobbled by his Cabinet's acquiescence to his position. Yet it was also determined, on the one hand, by a sycophantic endorsement of his views by various party ideologists and, on the other, by the reluctance of leading ANC members to engage him in what was literally a matter of life and death for alarming numbers of the party's supporters. It was therefore left to civil society organisations, working closely with doctors, to break the logjam in policy by convincing the Constitutional Court that the government's inaction was unconstitutional. Ironically, they enjoyed the support of former President Nelson Mandela, who while professing his undying loyalty to the ANC, intervened publicly in favour of unhindered drugs provision to HIV-positive sufferers in order to increase pressure on the government to change its position (*The Sunday Independent* 10.03.02). It was precisely interventions such as these that led to alleged attempts by the party hierarchy to 'muzzle Madiba', to achieve the tricky business of preventing Mandela from embarrassing them politically (*Mail & Guardian* 01–07.03.02). Musings about the proper role of an ex-president, whether he should be constitutionally constrained from playing any active role in political affairs, appear to continue.

Widespread criticism of the government stance on HIV/AIDS, along with tensions arising out of its conservative economic policy, alleged lack of delivery of services to poor people at local level, and other discontents, were to fuel rumours that, for the first time in more than 50 years, the ANC might face an open contest for the party leadership at its five-yearly party congress in December 2002. Party culture had long upheld that such matters were best conducted well out of public view, but now it was being suggested that Mbeki might find himself facing a challenge. However, any such eventuality was averted by a revealing incident early in that year when (the late) Steve Tshwete, an Mbeki loyalist and then Minister for Safety and Security, launched a blistering attack on three major figures in the party (Matthews Phosa, Cyril Ramaphosa and Tokyo Sexwale) who were alleged to be planning to oust Mbeki, which he followed by setting up an official investigation. Although Tshwete later apologised to the trio (who had protested their innocence), the performance was designed to warn off anyone who might have the temerity to pretend to the throne (*Business Day* 28.03.02).

If the strangulation of debate about HIV/AIDS was one instance of the ANC's apparent continued preference for the political habits of exile rather than those of democracy, then its endorsement of the result of the presidential election in Zimbabwe was an even more blatant one. Mugabe secured re-election as president in February 2002 through a combination of outright thuggery, blatant intimidation of the opposition, manipulation of the voting process and a crude rigging of the vote-counting process (Bush & Szeftel 2002; Sachikonye 2002). Even so, the ANC – despite rejection of the result by international electoral monitors and (greatly to its credit) the SADC parliamentary monitoring team – joined fellow African governments and the then OAU in proclaiming the result as legitimate, in a display that was widely condemned as proclaiming that African leaderships would look after their own. To be sure, the Mbeki government wrapped the Zimbabwe issue in a package of 'quiet diplomacy', which was supposedly designed to find an 'African solution' (the essence of which was that the opposition Movement for Democratic Change, having been denied the election, should join Zanu as a junior partner in a government of national unity). Yet more revealing was the manner in which the ANC deployed its parliamentary majority to declare the election legitimate. As the *Mail & Guardian* (22–27.03.02) observed, the ANC – once the pride of democrats for the level of humanity and intelligence it brought to the struggle against apartheid – was betraying its own traditions. The writer, Rob Amato, added that by allowing the presidency to dominate the party on such a hugely symbolic issue, the ANC was undermining the independence of parliament and the separation of powers supposedly built into the Constitution (*The Sunday Independent* 24.03.02).

All this would appear to endorse Giliomee's thesis that democratic centralism is shutting down debate inside the ANC. Yet that interpretation is too simple, for the leadership is either permissive of, or unable, to wholly shut down independent internal activity. For example, Mbeki has consistently attempted to determine who becomes premiers of the seven (of the nine) provinces that are unambiguously controlled by the ANC, yet has not always succeeded.

Hawker (2000) has demonstrated how, initially, the ANC did not impose premiers on the new provinces, but sought to 'shepherd' them into office by adhering to the rule that every premier should first be elected by local party members as chair of the respective Provincial Executive Committee, before being ratified as premier. In practice, however, between 1994 and 1999 the central party intervened to replace three of the original premiers, and in two other cases, local party members defied the centre to elect their own preferred candidates to the provincial chairpersonship.

Similar tensions emerged in the run-up to the 2002 ANC National Congress. Popo Molefe, Premier of North West Province, who was seeking the appointment of Molefi Sefularo as his successor as provincial chair (and hence, by implication, also to his premiership following his intended retirement in 2004), decided to run for re-election himself to block the candidature of Thandi Modise, chair of the parliamentary portfolio committee on defence, who was being backed by the provincial ANCYL (*Business Day* 18.06.02). Winkie Direko, Premier of the Free State, and favoured by the central party, came off second best to Ace Magashule, who had previously been a key member of a group that had tried to oust Mosiuoa Lekota when he was that province's premier (*Sowetan* 29.07.02). Fish Mahlalela, previously sacked as a member of Mpumalanga's executive committee, defeated Premier Ndaweni Mahlangu, despite the central party's deployment of a team of heavyweights to support him (*Business Day* 25.03.02); and in Limpopo (formerly Northern Province), Premier Ngoako Ramatlhodi had to work hard to overcome vigorous challengers (*Sowetan* 28.10.02). Similarly, Makhenkesi Stofile, Premier of the Eastern Cape, faced down a campaign to replace him by Mluleke George, although in this case the national ANC overrode the election on the grounds of widespread electoral irregularities. Stofile's position was temporarily upheld, but only at the expense of his having to accede to national pressure to dismiss provincial ministers deemed to be responsible for provincial discontents (*Business Day* 25.11.02 & 02.12.02; *Sunday Times* 24.11.02).

There can be no denying the dominance of the central government (which provides over 90 per cent of the budget of the provinces), yet this has not always ensured its own way of imposing provincial leaders, especially in the context of provincial party elections where it has not wanted to stand accused of acting undemocratically. In any case, a centralisation of the party is by no means incompatible with the co-existence of factional power plays, which can pass as democracy. What is far more testing is where the party hierarchy is subjected to challenge over ideology and policy.

The right, the left and the Tripartite Alliance

Although the Alliance is formally a partnership, the ANC is the leading element. The communist wing (SACP) remains a separate political party, yet it has no autonomous public representation; those of its members who sit in parliament do so as ANC members of parliament (MPs). Meanwhile, a significant number of Cosatu federation and union officials have been elected to parliament under ANC auspices, at the cost of withdrawing from full-time trade union work. Hence, while the ANC claims that it provides for seamless representation of its tripartite partners in parliament, numerous commentators argue that they have been rendered subordinate (Habib & Taylor 2001, McKinley 2001), an impression which has gained ground by the easy manner in which leading ministers, who are SACP members, have attached themselves to the implementation of an economic strategy which leftist critics describe as unashamedly capitalist and neoliberal. In this context, strains have begun to appear within the Alliance, with mounting debate about its continuing viability and desirability. Most certainly there is developing debate, particularly within Cosatu, about the possibility of joining the SACP in leaving the Alliance and forming a labour-backed, mass party of opposition to an ANC which is becoming increasingly dominated by a bourgeois, right wing.

In his interview with Sheehan, Cronin attempts to locate the changes in relations between the Alliance partners in a historical context. His starting point is that by the late 1980s the SACP had become little more than 'a kind of network' inside the ANC, which was not asserting its own profile and vision of class politics strongly enough. During the growth inside South Africa of 'mass socialist organisation', centred around the new breed of trade unions that developed from the 1970s, the SACP had been sidelined. It was left to Slovo to re-think the relevance of the party, given its huge popularity within South Africa after its unbanning in 1990, even though by then the Soviet Union had collapsed.

Cronin identifies a post-exile widening of the divide between the right and left of the liberation movement as having taken place in 1990, when half the central committee of the SACP quietly resigned. Those who left 'constitute basically the core of the ANC leadership at present' (Cronin 2002). They argued that their open identification with the party would embarrass the ANC. Their departure was also a reflection of prior divisions between a grouping led by Mbeki (whose view was that the SACP would not be able to survive the struggle era) and another led by Chris Hani and Joe Slovo. So scepticism about the party came particularly, though not exclusively, from exile ranks. On the other hand, there were those such as Hani who had benefited enormously from Soviet solidarity yet were critical of the reality of actually existing socialism, and those like Harry Gwala, a hard-line Stalinist. The latter argued for the SACP to remain a tightly-disciplined vanguardist party; the former (with whom Cronin identified) favoured a more open approach to party membership and political debate. Whereas the Stalinist wing tended to view the negotiation process as a sell-out (arguing for insurrection to rescue the situation), the Hani grouping viewed mass mobilisation as necessary for negotiations to succeed. It was the latter, more pluralistic wing of the party, that became dominant after 1994.

The approach adopted by this wing of the party argued that although South Africa had been liberated politically, socialism had been rolled back and an emergent capitalist class within the ANC was rapidly linking up with 'an undefeated capital'. The task of the SACP consequently resolved into being a 'strategic force' within the ANC, which meant moving beyond being a handful of intellectuals to developing a mass organisation. Today there are about 80 000 signed-up members, yet the active cadreship is only around 18 000, many of whom are based in the union movement. Even so, argues Cronin, its influence within the Alliance 'is much greater than its membership', allowing it to engage an 'enormously complicated terrain' (Cronin 2002).

The ANC won the 1994 election on the basis of a highly progressive programme. The emphasis of the RDP was on coaxing and disciplining the dominant private sector into helping to overcome huge historical racial and social inequities, without which there could be no sustainable future for capitalism in South Africa. It was a multi-class project in which popular working-class forces were required to co-operate with capital, yet in which popular mobilisation was required to prevent the private sector from taking short-term profits. Nonetheless, argues Cronin, the ANC, or 'significant parts' of it, 'got seduced' by the neoliberal paradigm (Cronin 2002).

Cronin admits that the ANC right has probably won more rounds than the left. Gear was an attempt to establish capitalist hegemony yet, in order to succeed, it had to deliver. It aimed to succeed through privatisation, the attraction of massive flows of foreign, direct investment and, critically, the consolidation of a black bourgeoisie. In practice, however, macroeconomic constraints act as brakes on growth. Various inequality-widening accumulation trends may be hard to reverse. Yet there is nothing inevitable about Saul's 'tragedy', for not only is the neoliberal agenda losing direction globally, but within South Africa it has been strongly contested, and battles have been won by Cosatu about issues such as privatisation. For this reason, the SACP and Cosatu should stay inside the Alliance rather than launching their own party. The left project is not about running away from power, but using the state to realise whatever progressive potentialities exist.

Cronin recognises that such a strategy opens the SACP to allegations that it is betraying the revolution. Yet the ANC cannot be abandoned to the neo-liberals. To be sure, there has been massive fallout within the Alliance, with SACP and Cosatu opposition to privatisation leading to 'very nasty attempts' to expel the left from the ANC (Cronin 2002). Indeed, presidential anger was particularly aroused by Cosatu's anti-privatisation strike in August 2001, which was timed to embarrass the government during its hosting of the World Conference against Racism. Following the strike, there were moves to deal dictatorially with the left, yet the feedback which the ANC obtained was that there was overwhelming support for the Alliance and a sense that the SACP remained a guarantor of the movement's radical democratic credentials. So the objective must be to make the Alliance open to debate about policy and to correct the mistakes that are made.

Struggles within the Alliance: tensions between the ANC and SACP

Tensions between the ANC and its partners have been more open since the 1998 SACP Congress when then President Mandela and Deputy President Mbeki challenged the left to toe the line or leave the Alliance.

An Alliance summit in early April 2002 was designed to smooth strongly-held differences over Gear. It resulted in an announcement of a major shift in government policy away from reliance on foreign investment to domestic investment (with the pensions and life assurances industries being objects of particular attention). It also affirmed the working class as 'the leading social motivating force' in the NDR, and referred to the Alliance as playing an active role in promoting employment, wealth redistribution and local and community empowerment. It was hailed, therefore, as providing the Alliance with something of a new start in the wake of the anti-privatisation strike in August 2000. Yet differences remained, with Cosatu and the SACP tiptoeing around the issue of the ANC's treatment of HIV/AIDS, and the ANC urging its partners to assume a less hidebound approach to privatisation by viewing it as a 'restructuring of state assets' for growth and development (*Business Day* 05.04.02; *Mail & Guardian* 12–18.04.02). Mbeki's views of how the Alliance partners should conceive their role was to be underlined about a month later when he declared that South Africa needed a 'new worker' dedicated to the collective good of the nation, the continent and the world (*Business Day* 22.05.02).

The summit may have smoothed relations between the Alliance partners, yet by now questions relating to its continuation were commonplace. Hence a paper prepared for the SACP's 11th Congress in July 2002 and entitled 'A socialist approach to the consolidation of the National Democratic Revolution', faced up to the possibility of a future split: 'Is an eventual socialist transition likely to be led by the SACP in opposition to the ANC – or is it to be an SACP-inspired, but ANC-led, transition, the so-called Cuban option?' (*The Sunday Independent* 12.05.2000). Other documents called for the party to put up its own candidates in elections, stating that there was no contradiction between an independent SACP and the ANC continuing as the leading force in the NDR (*Sunday Times* 16.06.02). However, the run-up to the Congress was to be dominated by the row that erupted after Cronin's interview with Sheehan became public. Senior ANC figures, led by Smuts Ngonyama, the party's Head of Presidency, reacted furiously to Cronin's allegations about the ANC's 'zanufication' – claiming he was spreading deliberate lies and was totally out of order. Sam Shilowa, former Cosatu General Secretary, now Premier of Gauteng and still a member of the SACP's central committee, asserted that Cronin's views were not those held by the SACP (*Business Day* 16, 18, 19.07.02). However, Shilowa was the one out of tune, for the SACP leadership rapidly closed ranks, accusing Ngonyama of attempting to assassinate Cronin's character, and dismissing the ANC's utterances as unwarranted. Blade Nzimande, Secretary General of the SACP, attacked as racist accusations by some ANC members that the SACP was controlled by whites.

In the wake of all this excitement, the Congress was almost an anti-climax, foreshadowed by Nzimande's reassertion of the SACP's subordination to the ANC (*Mail & Guardian* 19–25.07.02). There were anti-socialists in the ANC, yet the message from the grassroots was that the Alliance organisations should resolve their differences. What Cronin had been saying with regard to the 'zanufication' of the ANC was that any liberation movement was in danger of becoming bureaucratised after getting into power. The role of the SACP, therefore, was to maintain the revolutionary morality of the liberation struggle. The SACP would not be putting up its own candidates for election in 2004, and it would not like to see the Alliance splitting up. 'What people don't realise is that breaking the Alliance means splitting all three organisations. You are talking of two million Cosatu workers, more than 80 per cent ANC members' (Cronin 2002). Alliance structures therefore needed to be re-examined for communist voices to be heard better.

At the Congress Mbeki pronounced that there were no problems in the relations between the ANC and SACP, and Nzimande declared that the Alliance remained central for advancing the gains made since 1994. Furthermore, although key Mbeki allies (notably Essop Pahad, Minister in the Presidency, and Jeff Radebe, Minister for Public Enterprises) were voted off the Central Committee, various prominent trade unionists withdrew their challenges to other ministers. The outcome was a central committee which the party stressed did not reflect anti-government sentiment. Even so, the party called for a comprehensive review of the government's plans for restructuring state enterprises (privatisation), and a more development-oriented economic strategy.

But beneath the surface of renewed goodwill, tensions remained. Cronin was re-elected Deputy Secretary General of the party with strong support, yet was soon to eat humble pie by issuing his public apology to the ANC for having spoken out of turn. Significantly too, in a report presented to the SACP central committee, a warning was given that the ANC was increasingly finding itself on the wrong side of mass campaigns against poverty, job losses and HIV/AIDS (*Sowetan* 21.07.02). Such warnings were issued following the announcement by Cosatu that a further planned anti-privatisation strike would go ahead in early October. This came as a surprise as Cosatu had earlier agreed with the government that it would suspend its anti-privatisation campaign until a growth and development summit that would be held under the auspices of Nedlac. However, Cosatu protested that the government had reneged on its promise to address its concerns before pressing ahead with privatisation (citing a recent announcement of the sale of 30 per cent of electricity generation and the concessioning of ports). Cosatu's move excited vocal support at the SACP Congress.

Such developments did not go down well with the ANC, which moved to quell dissent by declaring at a four-day policy conference at the end of September, that the resolutions it had adopted were all binding on its members. The SACP responded by repeating its warning that the ANC was increasingly on the wrong side of mass campaigns and that it was vacating political space that was being occupied by 'populist' organisations (*Business Day* 22.09.02).

Struggles within the Alliance: tensions between the ANC and Cosatu

On the eve of Cosatu's anti-privatisation strike, Mbeki launched a major attack on what he termed 'the ultra-left'. Without naming either the SACP or Cosatu, he criticised all those within the Alliance who treated the government and the ANC as their enemy, and accused 'the ultra-left' of abusing internal democracy by seeking to advance its agenda against policies adopted by the ANC's most senior decision-making structures. Paradoxically, he also attacked it as being in cahoots with 'right-wing' elements such as the DA, a party seeking to protect white minority privilege.

The attack on the 'ultra-left' reflected the ANC's increasing frustration at criticism to which it was especially vulnerable. Dismissing the DA as right-wing and racist was easy. Far less easy was the repudiation of criticisms from organisations that claimed to speak for the ANC's constituency. From this perspective, it was the duty of the SACP and Cosatu to educate the masses about the twists and turns of the struggle in a country where the bulk of capital remained in private hands. However, this was rendered particularly problematic by the fact that Cosatu admitted people who did not belong to the ANC and did not share its vision. It was they who provided the impetus for the formation of a workers' party to challenge the ANC. Such an ultra-left, explained Kgalema Motlanthe, ANC Secretary General, was an undisciplined international phenomenon that viewed the state as an employer, and hence an enemy of the working class (*Business Day* 03.10.02). Furthermore, a paper issuing out of the ANC's Policy Education Unit, written by NEC members Jabu Moleketi and Josiah Jele, argued that this left had consistently tried to mobilise other groups, domestically and globally, to join in a campaign against the government's neoliberalism. It claimed the ANC has become the instrument of the South African bourgeoisie, and has destroyed internal democracy and the independence of all organisations outside its orbit. Its hope is that it will trample over the ANC, and march on to a victorious socialist revolution, yet in so doing it is willing to work hand in hand with the forces of neoliberalism (*Business Day* 03.10.02).

Cronin responded, arguing that by lumping Cosatu and the SACP with fringe parties, Moleketi and Jele were guilty of McCarthyism (*Business Day* 06.10.02). Cosatu leaders also rejected the ultra-left labelling of the trade union movement as seeking to divert attention from real issues like economic policy, poverty, unemployment and disease.

However brave the face that they put on such matters, Cosatu (and by implication the SACP) were to be severely weakened by the extremely moderate response by workers to the privatisation strike. Cosatu claimed that 60 per cent of workers downed tools, but the South African Chamber of Business said the figure was only 15 per cent, while government claimed that only six per cent of public servants went on strike. Government ministers underscored the support for the strike given by organisations such as the Landless People's Movement and the Anti-Privatisation Forum and proclaimed the strike a failure, accused Cosatu of misleading workers and claimed a crisis in its leadership. Mbeki repeated the claim in his weekly column on the ANC's website, accusing Cosatu's leaders of using workers to 'destroy' the ANC by making them go on strike. Cosatu responded by accusing the ANC of attempting to drive a wedge between its leadership and its members, and complained that the government was seeking to undermine a number of its affiliates by infiltrating intelligence operatives into its membership (*Mail & Guardian* 04–10.10.02).

For the time being at least, the government had triumphed. It had ridden the strike with ease, and had forced Cosatu onto the defensive. Increasingly it looked as though the ground was being prepared for a major offensive against the left at the ANC's National Conference at the end of the year. In the event, however, the conference concluded in a truce: Cosatu failed in a bid to secure significantly increased representation on the NEC, yet it suffered no major attack. But a show of unity could not obscure the differences that remained, and the fact that Cosatu was regarded by ANC leadership as being as much a problem to be contained as an asset.

Perspectives on the Alliance

For the moment the Alliance remains in place, and there is every indication that it will do so for at least the forthcoming general election expected in 2004. Yet there can be no doubt equally that its foundations have been severely shaken by the bitter infighting. These internal travails would appear to have confirmed the political supremacy of the ANC, and a marked shift in the balance of forces against what the government and its representatives have labeled the 'ultra-left'. One interpretation of this transformation is that the SACP has had to learn the hard way that, after 1994, the communist tail is no longer in a position to wag the ANC dog. It has also had to learn that it does not represent the landless and the homeless any more than Cosatu can claim to represent the unemployed and the very poor. An alternative perspective is that the ANC is in peril of assuming a political arrogance that, like the apartheid government before it, may cause it to fall victim to popular resistance that began when those in power chose to decide what was good for the people. Yet another view is that the country has to be governed and that the ANC is determined to do so by dividing its opposition and occupying the centreground.

The decline of opposition

The decision by the NNP in November 2001 to leave the DA to again work in co-operation with the ANC was a massive setback for the opposition. The split in the DA was a result of the NNP's resentment at its alleged arrogant treatment by the 'old DP', difficulties in aligning its conservatism to the liberalism of the DP, doubts about the wisdom of the DA's robust oppositionist style, and not least, its discomfort at being totally removed from office. Whatever the reasons, the NNP's move signified to many the increasingly unassailable dominance of the ANC and the hollowness of South African democracy.

Cronin acknowledged that many on the left would characterise the ANC's new linkage with the NNP as getting into bed with the former oppressors. Yet for him the more important point was that the breaking of the DA signified the defeat of the latter's alleged project to mobilise minorities on racial grounds against the consequences of majority rule. At one level, the tie-up with the NNP was just short-term politics, yet at another it was far more profound: it was about developing a multi-party democracy. The NNP represented a mixture of neoliberalism and minority concerns, yet it was possible to enter a multi-party relationship with them. This was competitive 'but not just intransigence on every issue, which is where the Leon thing was going' (Cronin 2002).

Cronin's analysis touched a chord played by the DA's major critics, which was that party leader Tony Leon – who had presided over the increase in the DA's share of the vote between 1994 and 1999 – was mobilising support by fanning minority racial fears. For its part, the DA declared itself fully committed to non-racialism, and increasingly claimed that the ANC's strenuous pursuit of black empowerment was akin to a neo-apartheid racial nationalism. Not surprisingly, therefore, some commentators were to see in the NNP's withdrawal from the DA, a chance for a realignment of opposition politics. In a rather different spin from those hoping to see a new socialist opposition, this alternative vision looked to the formation of a new party which would fight the ANC on its own chosen turf, the political centre (*Business Day* 07.11.02).

Whatever the longer-term possibilities, the implosion of the DA appeared set to have far-reaching shorter-term consequences. First, it implied a rearrangement of coalitions at provincial and local government level in favour of the ANC and NNP; secondly, it undermined the DA's attempt to present itself as a party of principled competence; and thirdly, it threatened to extend the ANC's electoral hegemony.

The rearrangement of coalitions

In the 1999 elections the ANC swept to power (as it had done in 1994) in seven out of the nine provinces. The odd two out were KwaZulu-Natal and the Western Cape. In the former, the outcome was that the IFP – led by Mangosuthu Buthelezi – which mobilised around Zulu ethnic-nationalism, assumed the leadership (with 34 seats in the provincial legislature) in a coalition with the ANC (32 seats), with the DP and NNP taking seven and three seats respectively. In the latter, the ANC was the largest party, with 18 seats, but was scuttled into opposition by the formation of a coalition between the NNP (17 seats) and the DP (five seats). The NNP's withdrawal from the DA threatened both these coalitions. On the one hand, the ANC-IFP coalition at national level had been perpetually tense, with Buthelezi's authority as Minister of Home Affairs being constrained by ANC manoeuvrings, while provincially the IFP evinced concern that the ANC was determined to secure control. On the other hand, the ANC had felt cheated by its exclusion from power in the

Western Cape and seemed bent on revenge. Meanwhile, at the 2000 local government elections, which the DP and NNP fought in combination, the DA won control of a handful of municipal councils around the country, of which by far the most notable and wounding to the ANC's pride, was that of Cape Town. Again, the rift in the DA appeared likely to throw this to the ANC-NNP.

However, the fly in the ointment as far as the ANC and NNP were concerned was the provision in the Constitution that prevented floor-crossing. Hence, even after the NNP pulled out of the DA, it was left in a state of limbo. Although there was no constitutional barrier to NNP MPs and Members of Provincial Legislatures (MPLs) joining their party in new coalition agreements in the national and provincial legislatures, those who wanted to cross to the DA would lose their seats. At municipal level, where councillors elected on a DA ticket crossed to the NNP, they would similarly lose their seats.

The situation was further complicated by the NNP being split, with many representatives having to balance short-term calculations of political gain offered by coalition with the ANC against perhaps longer-term hopes of survival as members of the DA. The crisis in the NNP was dramatised by the revolt of Gerald Morkel, Premier of the Western Cape, against the NNP leader, Marthinus van Schalkwyk, moving his party into alliance with the ANC. After various legal challenges failed, Morkel was eventually ousted as premier and leader of the Western Cape NNP in November 2001, following which Peter Marais (previously DA Mayor of Cape Town) took his place as head of a new NNP-ANC provincial government.

Marais's move into the premiership was in line with a deal whereby the ANC would assume the mayoralty of Cape Town, while the NNP led the coalition at provincial level. Leadership of other municipalities that fell to the coalition would be decided according to which of the two parties had the larger number of councillors. There was also some indication that the NNP would also be rewarded at national level by positions in government. However, for all this to happen, the ANC-NNP had to overcome the constitutional barrier.

This was to be greatly facilitated by the dredging up of Section 13 of Annexure A of Schedule 6 of the final Constitution, which amended Section 23 of Schedule 2 of the Interim Constitution (1994). That clause allowed for a law enabling floor-crossing in national and regional legislatures to be passed without necessitating cumbersome constitutional amendments. The subsequent *Loss or Retention of Membership of National and Provincial Legislatures Bill* sought to provide for the legality of floor-crossing by representatives a year after their election, although it was to have been conditional on its being effected by the President after consultation with leaders of the political parties in the National Assembly and/or the premiers. Local councillors were to be accorded the same right through a similar amendment to the 1998 *Municipal Structures Act*. However, after public outcry claiming that these provisions would concentrate too much power in the hands of the President, who would be able to manipulate the process in favour of the majority party, a new measure was brought forward which would establish two pre-determined periods per annum in which representatives would be able to cross the floor without losing their seats. However, the proviso was that such a crossing would be allowed only if it involved at least ten per cent of the party's seats. This eventually passed through parliament in June 2002 (Habib & Nadvi 2002).

In the event, the legislation was challenged by the small United Democratic Movement (UDM) in a series of moves in the Cape High Court and the Constitutional Court, on the major grounds that it offended against the logic of proportional representation (whereby voters sent representatives to parliament in given proportions which should not be changed by floor-crossing). This put on hold an extensive game of musical chairs around the country before the Constitutional Court ruled in favour of the constitutionality of the floor-crossing legislation in October 2002. This opened the doors to floor-crossing at all levels, with the biggest impact taking place at local level where the DA lost control of half the councils it had won in 2000, these now falling to the ANC-NNP. During the 15-day period allowed, 555 local government councillors crossed the floor (417 from the DA – 340 back to the NNP, 51 to the ANC, the rest to other parties). Van Schalkwyk claimed it as a triumph, but as the DA was swift to point out, in the 2000 elections the NNP had taken 612 councillors into the DA (*Business Day*, 23, 25.10.02).

The one piece of the jigsaw that failed to fall into place was KwaZulu-Natal where five members of the legislature who had announced their decision to cross to the ANC – from the DA (2), IFP (2) and UDM (1) – found themselves expelled prematurely by their parties from the provincial legislature before the floor-crossing window was opened. This meant that leadership of the provincial government continued to lie with the IFP Premier, Lionel Mtshali, who proceeded to dismiss two ANC Members of the Executive Committee (MECs) and to replace them by DA appointees. When the ANC threatened retrospective legislation that would reinstate the five expelled MPLs and allow them to cross the floor, hence enabling it to take control of the provincial government, the IFP threatened to call a provincial election.

Relations between the ANC and IFP plunged into crisis as the former maintained that an early election would be unconstitutional in that, pending parliament's agreement on possible reform of the electoral system, there was no legislation in place concerning the running of an election. When the IFP held its ground, the ANC backed down (either because its constitutional case was weak and/or because it was reluctant to provoke renewed social conflict in KwaZulu-Natal), leaving the IFP in power. The incident highlighted mounting tensions between the ANC and IFP at national and provincial level, and increased speculation that the ANC's deal with the NNP foreshadows the end of its coalition with the IFP.

The erosion of the DA's reputation

The DA was always bound to be a difficult marriage of differing philosophies and practices. The DP had presented itself as a party of liberal principle and combative opposition; on the other hand, the NNP viewed itself as a party of conservatism, dedicated to the protection of minority rights, and inclined to political pragmatism. Yet the overwhelming membership of both parties swallowed their doubts when the DA was formed, not least because Tony Leon looked like a winner: he had hugely improved the DP vote in 1999, and he now evinced confidence in a future whereby the DA would work hard to cut the ANC's majority to less than 50 per cent of the popular vote in the next election, expected in 2004. *Sotto voce*, he seemed to be saying: the DA will clean up the combined white vote, take on board the majority of coloureds who would have been brought by the NNP, and aim to make significant inroads into African communities alienated by the failures of the ANC. Leon also projected his party as one of principled efficiency and determined to serve as a counterweight to ANC hegemony and excess. The problem was that he bit off more than he could chew.

The implosion of the DA was precipitated by an absurd saga that took place in Cape Town. After assuming office as Mayor of Cape Town in 1999, Peter Marais, one of the NNP's leading coloured politicians, went in search of quick credit by proposing to name two of the city's major streets after former Presidents Mandela and De Klerk. However, he became embroiled in a scandal when it emerged that a poll of residents to decide on the issue was being doctored. Marais was to be formally exonerated, but the DA was tarnished and Leon called for his resignation. When he refused, Leon threatened disciplinary action. The NNP fought back. Van Schalkwyk, deputy leader of the DA by virtue of his NNP leadership, attacked Leon, who responded with an ultimatum: accept Marais's expulsion or face disciplinary action. But there was a sub-plot to the action in that van Schalkwyk was also scheming to replace Morkel as premier. The upshot was that the NNP walked out of the DA and joined up with the ANC. Van Schalkwyk presented the NNP's shift as an act for the good of the country: the DP was committed to opposition for opposition's sake, and its background as the vehicle of well-off whites had transformed it into the new party of racial privilege. In contrast, the NNP saw opposition only as a means to an end, and were dedicated to racial co-operation. Such talk failed to go down well with many members of the ANC (Cosatu rejected the link with the NNP 'with contempt') (*Star* 08.11.01), or with the DA, which portrayed van Schalkwyk's move as about 'positions, privileges and perks' (*Mail & Guardian* 19–25.10.01). Nonetheless, it was the DA that suffered the most in the short term.

Leon's reputation for political acuity was severely damaged, and many now questioned the wisdom of his link with the NNP in the first place. Yet even more damaging were the allegations that emerged in the wake of the break-up that the DA had accepted donations from Jurgen Harksen, a hugely rich German who had ingratiated himself with the professional, social and political elite in the Cape and who apparently sought to use the influence he gained thereby to stall extradition proceedings against him instituted by Germany. The initial focus centred on the relationship between Harksen and Morkel, the Western Cape's DA leader. This was to be investigated by a commission established (with considerable glee) by the new NNP-led Western Cape government. Morkel and Harksen were hung out to dry, and in the process more and more evidence dribbled out that various DA leaders, including Leon, had been embroiled in dubious contacts with a fugitive from German justice. Although the DA insisted that it had not taken money from Harksen, although it would not have broken any law even if it had, and although there was strong suggestion that the ANC had also accepted money from him, the entire affair – which dragged on through early 2002 – undermined the party's self-alignment with the politics of principle and suggested that it would act as venally as any other one if and when it was placed in positions of power.

The extension of ANC hegemony

The status of the ANC as a dominant party has rested on its nearly two-thirds, largely African support amongst the South African population. Yet it was precisely the DP's hugely improved performance and the NNP's collapse in 1999 which gave the impetus to the formation of the DA. Subsequently, when the DA proceeded to take 22 per cent of the vote in the local government elections in 2000, Leon was buoyant about making inroads into the ANC's majority in the future.

Cronin's accusation that the DA was essentially engaged in a project of mobilising opposition around racial minority concerns was a theme loudly proclaimed by the ANC. Its seduction of the NNP, therefore, would be seen arguably to have had two objectives. First, to draw the NNP's remaining base among white and coloured voters into the ANC's camp, thereby rendering the DA more vulnerable to the charge that it was 'lily-white'. Second, to effectively suffocate the NNP, the party of apartheid, in a bear hug which offered short-term gains for highly dubious advantages in the future. While the DA continues to proclaim its determination to make inroads into black communities, its bid to construct a wider opposition has been halted in its tracks. To be sure, the closeness between the ANC and NNP has precipitated a warming of relations between the DA and the IFP, which could lead to a working relationship at the next election. Likewise, there is some talk about the DA working more closely with the UDM, formed by Bantu Holomisa, the former strongman of the Transkei military, following his expulsion from the ANC in 1997. Yet as the IFP is identified with Zulu ethnicity and the UDM has become principally a vehicle for promoting former Transkei discontents, linkages with either or both would be highly problematic. An opposition based on such an alliance would likely be a patchwork quilt of tensions, which could easily pull apart at the seams.

Finally, the implosion of the DA brings one more prospect into view – that of the ANC extending its direct control over all nine provinces. For the moment, attainment of that goal has been delayed, but the ANC is confident that what it regards as the final 'liberation' of the Western Cape and KwaZulu-Natal is just around the corner.

Towards 'low intensity' democracy?

South Africa's dominant party system seems embarked on the road to 'low-intensity' democracy. This implies that the formal requirements of democracy are met, yet under conditions of decreasing competition and declining popular participation. ANC domination of the political arena is being extended increasingly, challenges to its rule being steadily overwhelmed, and its own internal democracy eroded. As critics as disparate as Giliomee and McKinley suggest, this represents a substantial challenge to the quality and depth of democracy. Yet Cronin is correct to look beyond their essentially uniform views of the ANC/SACP as a monolith, for recent developments point to the correctness of his perspective of the Alliance as a site of struggle. This has to qualify his suggestion as to the extent of the ANC's bureaucratisation, a term which is far more appropriate than 'zanufication', which suggests not just Stalinist tendencies but also crooked militarism, corruption, basket economics, fraudulent elections and a dedication to lawlessness.

Two further points remain. First, the struggles within the Alliance are fought out according to certain ideological conventions and political constraints. Increasingly the leadership of the ANC makes no secret that socialism as a goal has been abandoned. Even so, internal battles continue to be fought out in the dreary phraseology of the NDR, a device which has lost all relevance in the post-Cold War era, and as Slovo pointed out so long ago, can be used to justify virtually anything. More to the point, the internal struggles have something of the quality of a phoney war in that all talk of the SACP and Cosatu hiving off from the ANC to form a left opposition is bounded by the recognition by its key protagonists of the huge risks involved. Hence Cronin's argument that it is wiser for the left to use whatever influence it has from within.

Second, it cannot be assumed from such developments that the ANC is becoming the unambiguous vehicle of an emergent Africa bourgeoisie and is moving uncomplicatedly to the right. To be sure, there is a significant element of this. The ANC's black empowerment strategy is deliberately intent on creating a black capitalist class that will challenge the hegemony of the white-run corporates, and the government's macroeconomic policy is fiscally conservative and designed to foster capitalist growth. Even so, such a strategy can only be legitimated in terms that are redistributionist, for although Cosatu remains on the periphery of policy-making, it possesses a potential veto-power, rooted in the capacity of the black working class to withdraw their political support and, at times, to strike. As Cronin implies, the continued existence of a relatively strong and militant trade union movement serves as a major constraint on ANC economic policy, and continues to force concessions.

However, what the recent campaign against the 'ultra-left' may indicate precisely is an attempt to undermine the trade union movement, thereby freeing the way for a shift towards a more flexible labour market that is more capital-friendly. It is here that classic questions abound about the relationship between the state and capital, about the former ruling on behalf of the latter and so on. Meanwhile, to make the matter even more complex, it would appear that by and large the party hierarchy is rooted more in government than anywhere else, and is constituting a political class which, although developing linkages to capital via the award of tenders and so on, remains distinctively a different stratum. Hence the exile faction, which is often identified with Mbeki, continues to fight its corner, at least against the left, with a tortured Marxian rhetoric that harks back to the days of Soviet solidarity. To confront the left it is deemed necessary to sound more correctly left than they, while simultaneously the party moves to capture the political centre from its various rivals.

If in nothing else, Cronin is correct to observe that the present era is one of enormous fluidity whose present meaning is difficult to identify.

References

Bush, R & Szeftel, M (2002) Sovereignty, democracy and Zimbabwe's tragedy, *Review of African Political Economy* 91 (29): 5–12.

Cronin, J (2002) An interview with Dr Helena Sheehan http:// www.comms.deu.ie/sheehanh/za/cronin02.htm.

Giliomee, H & Simkins, S (eds.) (1999) *The awkward embrace: One party domination and democracy*. Cape Town: Tafelberg.

Giliomee, H, Myburgh, J & Schlemmer, L (2001) Dominant party rule, opposition parties and minorities in South Africa, in R Southall (ed.) *Opposition and democracy in South Africa*. London: Frank Cass.

Habib, A & Taylor, R (2001) Political alliances and parliamentary opposition in post-apartheid South Africa, in R Southall (ed.) *Opposition and democracy in South Africa*. London: Frank Cass.

Habib, A & Nadvi, L (2002) Party disintegrations and re-alignments in post-apartheid South Africa, *Review of African Political Economy* 29 (92): 331–338.

Hawker, G (2000) Political leadership in the ANC: the South African provinces 1994–1999, *Journal of Modern African Studies* 38 (4): 631–658.

McKinley, D (2001) Democracy, power and patronage: Debate and opposition within the African National Congress and the Tripartite Alliance since 1994, in R Southall (ed.) *Opposition and democracy in South Africa*. London: Frank Cass.

Ottaway, M (1991) Liberation movements and transition to democracy: The case of the ANC, *Journal of Modern African Studies* 29 (1): 61–82.

Sachikonye, L (2002) Whither Zimbabwe: Crisis and democratisation, *Review of African Political Economy* 91 (29): 13–20.

Saul, J (2001) Cry for the beloved country: The post-apartheid denouement, *Monthly Review* 52 (8): 1–51.

Saul, J (2002) Starting from scratch? (A Reply to Jeremy Cronin), *Monthly Review* 54 (7): 43–50.

Slovo, J (1976) South Africa – No middle road, in B Davidson, J Slovo & A Wilkinson (eds.) *Southern Africa: The new politics of revolution*. London: Penguin.

Southall, R (1994) The South African elections of 1994: The remaking of a dominant-party state, *Journal of Modern African Studies* 32 (4): 629–655.

An imperfect past: The Truth and Reconciliation Commission in transition

Madeleine Fullard and Nicky Rousseau

On 30 October 1998, a five-volume report from the TRC was handed over to then President Nelson Mandela. The handover came two and a half years after the first public hearings held by the TRC in April 1996, years marked by a public and emotional process of testimony, disclosure, and investigation. This marked the end of the human rights violations work of the TRC, while the amnesty and reparations components were to continue for a further three years.

Yet the ceremonial report handover, instead of being the culmination of an internationally acclaimed process, saw TRC commissioners, reporters and victim representatives anxiously assembled awaiting the outcome of a court case. The ANC sought a last-minute interdict against the handover, claiming that the TRC had 'grossly misdirected itself in its findings on the role of the African National Congress' (ANC 1998). The ANC's legal effort was unsuccessful, and the handover ceremony took place, albeit in a rather grim and tense atmosphere.

The TRC, one of the flagship institutions created during the Mandela presidency to effect transition from an unjust past, thus ended its most public phase in a fractious and hostile relationship with the ruling party. That the ANC itself had been the initiator and most consistent proponent of the TRC made this response to the TRC's findings all the more ironic.

After the October 1998 handover, the TRC largely sank from public view. This article provides an overview of the TRC from its origins to its present inconclusive circumstances. In doing so, it suggests a range of possible reasons for the slide into virtual oblivion that seems to characterise the current state of the TRC project.

Genesis: national and international contexts

The genesis of the TRC in the early 1990s has been described by various commentators (Asmal, Asmal & Roberts 1997; Boraine 2001; De Lange 2000).

In 1993, the ANC appointed the Motsuenyane Commission to investigate allegations of abuse of ANC members in its exile camps, subsequently accepting its findings and collective responsibility for the abuses that the commission confirmed. At the same time, it reiterated an earlier call by NEC member, Professor Kader Asmal, for the establishment of a commission to investigate and report on human rights abuses committed by all parties during the apartheid era.

The call for a commission was consonant with broader international developments at the time as a number of countries, most notably in Latin America and Eastern Europe, searched for mechanisms to deal with the transition from authoritarian pasts to a democratic present. Truth commissions emerged as one possible route in dealing with the legacies of authoritarianism. Although the truth commissions in Argentina, Chile and El Salvador had received much international attention, a range of similar initiatives had also been undertaken in numerous other countries, including some in Africa (Hayner 1994, 2001). While these initiatives all had specific mandates, usually relating to disappearances and extra-judicial killings, they were also framed with broader concerns such as how to deal with contested and conflictual versions of the past with an ongoing purchase on the psyche of major protagonists, as well as how to confront issues of impunity and accountability. This move to truth commissions accompanied the growing strength of human rights discourses internationally. The ANC, with its well-developed international networks, also absorbed these impulses, although primarily at a leadership level. Following two conferences sponsored by Idasa (then called the Institute for a Democratic Alternative in South Africa) on truth commissions and issues of transitional justice in 1993 and 1994, these debates began to percolate into local human rights and NGO circles.

Neither the ANC nor the NGO community was able to model the truth commission on their own terms. As several analysts have pointed out, the TRC was part of the broader set of compromises wrought through the process of negotiation (Bundy 2000; Simpson 2002). The agreement to grant amnesty for politically-motivated acts was forged in the very last stages of negotiations, so late that the declaration containing this obligation was tacked on as a 'postamble' to the Interim Constitution. In some ways, this concession – largely made to satisfy the security forces and right wing – provided a second impetus for the establishment of the TRC. Rather than simply providing a framework for amnesty, the ANC took this concession and linked it to its own earlier call for a truth commission. As Simpson points out, not only was the linking of amnesty with the broader project of truth recovery and reparations unique in the history of truth commissions, but '[by] foregrounding the interests of victims, the TRC would attempt to restore the moral balance to an amnesty agreement born of political compromise' (Simpson 2002: 223).

The establishment of a truth commission continued to be hotly contested by those from the former apartheid regime who saw it as a thinly disguised witch-hunt, despite the provision for amnesty and the agreement to include all parties to the conflict, including liberation movements. The legislation finally adopted in 1995 was at the time the longest debated piece of legislation and underwent numerous adaptations. There was also considerable input from various NGOs and interest groups. It was primarily these interventions that ensured that the amnesty process would be held in public rather than behind closed doors.

The TRC's enabling legislation, the *Promotion of National Unity and Reconciliation Act* (No. 34 of 1995), was thus a hybrid document reflecting different concerns and concessions. On the one hand, largely to allay fears of a witch-hunt and consonant with the conciliatory nature of the Mandela presidency, the TRC was framed in terms of national unity and reconciliation. The reconciliatory impulse also reflected the highly charged and bloody four years preceding the 1994 elections, during which more people died than in the 30 years preceding 1990. In its final form then, it is unsurprising that issues of national unity and reconciliation loomed large.

On the other hand, another line of thought both from within the ANC and NGO sector was more concerned with the issue of accountability and of challenging impunity. Thus, the legislation specifically instructed the TRC to establish responsibility for gross human rights violations at both an individual and institutional level. These two points of emphasis were also reflected in the selection of commissioners. Some, particularly those drawn from the religious sector, tended to be drawn strongly to the discourse of reconciliation, while others, often from a legal background, were more concerned with determining responsibility and making perpetrator findings. The exercise of this latter aspect of the TRC's mandate led to significant discord with political parties (du Toit 1999).

An important strand of critical thinking around the TRC has pointed to the way in which truth commission-type mechanisms cannot simply be concerned with issues of justice, but are intricately involved in and reflective of broader processes of nation building. In this regard, they are seen as mechanisms to legitimise new governments. By effecting a notional break from the past, they enable the 're-visioning' of a new nation or order. As such, truth commissions and other transitional justice mechanisms do not exist impartially outside of power, but are deeply part of the broader lines of contestation within society.

In the eyes of some of its critics, the TRC's nation-building agenda was essentially a nationalist project, an 'imagining' of the 'rainbow nation', that echoed the reconciliatory nature of the Mandela presidency (Bundy 2000; Mamdani 1998). Mamdani thus refers to the TRC as creating the 'founding myth of the new South Africa' (cited in Hayner 2001: 74). Similarly, elsewhere in this volume Mangcu equates the TRC with the so-called 'sunset clauses'. The logic of this argument goes further in suggesting that the TRC was bound to produce a form of consensual and inclusive history. This view, to some extent, can be seen in Archbishop Tutu's 'Foreword' to the TRC report where he states 'we believe we have provided enough of the truth about our past for there to be a consensus about it. There is consensus that atrocious things were done on all sides' (TRC 1998 Vol. 1 Ch. 1: para. 70). However, this is in strong contrast to the rest of the report which establishes a strong hierarchy of responsibility for gross human rights violations.[1]

This type of one-dimensional and sometimes instrumentalist reading reduces the TRC to a rather narrow nationalism and ignores the more transformative impulse that characterised at least part of South Africa's transition. The TRC formed part of a fleet of institutions of redress and transformation rapidly established after the May 1994 elections, including separate Land, Human Rights, Youth and Gender Commissions and a Reconstruction and Development Programme. This battery of organs of change reflected the exuberant ethos of social justice and restitution that is as much enshrined in the Constitution as are individual property rights. Each was tasked with addressing particular sites of the legacy of apartheid. In addition, there were diverse voices and positions within the TRC, several with an uneasy and more critical relationship with the consensual and reconciliatory thrust, identifying the TRC within an activist agenda of social change.

Appraising the TRC

In terms of sheer publicity, impact and drama, the TRC was arguably the flagship of the fleet. Unlike the other bodies, which were to be permanent institutions, the TRC had a limited time frame of two years.[2] Yet its achievements were substantial. Internationally, the TRC was feted as a success story of massive proportions, acting as a precipitant to several other countries adopting truth commissions.

The TRC began its work in early 1996, commencing with statement-taking and 'victim' hearings that continued into 1997 in urban and rural locations across the country. This was accompanied by an array of both public and less visible activities relating to the different aspects of its mandate. These included the questioning of political parties and their officials regarding their policies and practices, sector hearings that examined the complicity of social institutions with apartheid, amnesty hearings, investigation and scrutiny of surviving state documentation, a range of specialised investigations, exhumations, and Section 29 in-camera investigative hearings. This was accompanied by an ongoing arduous process of investigation and corroboration of each individual victim statement. All these activities culminated in the five-volume report released in October 1998.

The TRC's public processes and modes of operation were among its more notable attributes. Its work was blazoned across the national media over a two-year period. In terms of sheer reach, there can be few South Africans who did not hear and grasp something of its import.

Although in fact only a limited number of cases were 'solved' by the TRC, mainly through amnesty applications, these revelations acted as symbolic reference points for the definitive confirmation of violent concealed practices. Often highly dramatic, involving shockingly gruesome and callous details – such as the description of perpetrators drinking and 'braaing' (barbecuing) while the victims were incinerated on a neighbouring fire – these perpetrator accounts extinguished the possibility of ongoing denials. The expressions of human pain in the faces, voices and images of victim testimony, the bleak accounts from perpetrators of torture and killings, the images of exhumed skeletons bearing bullet holes, marked a distinct rupture of the highly segregated forms of historical knowledge that characterised South African citizens. An important component of this rupture was the decimation of the moral underpinning of the NP and white right wing, the associated delegitimisation of the entire apartheid project and the destruction of the façade of legalism to which the apartheid state clung.

Amongst these various activities in the first two years, the TRC strove to achieve a strong orientation towards victims, not always with great success.

Probably the most lasting images and voices from this period remain those of the victims. Further, these were not on the whole the voices of political activists, who in some senses already constituted a 'voiced' segment through organisational channels, but of ordinary citizens who formed the overwhelming bulk of those who came to the TRC and who paid the price of political violence.

Alongside this centering of victims came official acknowledgement by the state (in the form of the TRC) and public acknowledgement of the wrong done. This official validation of experience was, before all else, the fundament of the TRC and the heart of its mission to wrest those physically and psychically bearing the scars of the past out of the peripheral and isolated spaces they occupied. Reparations were to be the most concrete expression of this official acknowledgement, in line with international human rights law.

Despite the initial centering of victims' voices, they were largely displaced in the amnesty process which pivoted around perpetrators. In addition, victims ended up at the end of the queue in terms of concrete material benefits. At the time of writing, no reparations have been forthcoming for victims, some six years after they made statements to the TRC. This is the central criticism directed at the TRC, although in truth it is misdirected – the TRC did not have the powers to allocate reparations, but only to make recommendations on reparations to government. For victims this distinction is confusing and immaterial, and the pain and sense of betrayal engendered by this debacle has at worst poisoned and at best soured their interaction with the TRC. Many who felt positive about their choice to participate in the work of the TRC now feel justifiably bitter and angry. For TRC staff and commissioners this post-TRC legacy is a painful nullification of the value and values of the TRC.

The TRC also tended to pander somewhat to political schisms and hostile political groupings, this propensity being reflected in its handling of the IFP, the South African Defence Force (SADF) and the NP. Internal dynamics within the TRC played some part in this, along with a failure of political will. In addition, the reconciliation mandate was articulated by some commissioners in a simplistic and naïve fashion, often loaded with Christian sentiment, that showed little complex reflection on the variousness of responses from and needs of victims.

Undoubtedly, the TRC failed to adequately situate the gross human rights violations that it addressed in the wider context of apartheid. One of the most searing criticisms of the TRC concerns its narrow focus on direct acts of political repression, to the exclusion of the far more widespread and numerous abuses of apartheid, including forced removals and the expropriation of land, the pass laws, racial classification and the whole host of legislative cruelties imposed upon millions of citizens in the name of apartheid. Some of these violations arguably constituted gross violations of human rights as internationally defined and thus fell within the TRC's mandate (see Asmal, Asmal & Roberts 2000). While the TRC would have been hard pressed in 18 months[3] to address these issues, and was of the view that they were being partly addressed by other institutional initiatives such as the Land Commission and the RDP, nonetheless it failed to deal with them even in a symbolic manner. The sector hearings were an inadequate and partial nod towards this important critique.

Similarly, the vast number of violations that occurred outside the borders of South Africa in the southern African region during the apartheid government's efforts to remain in power received only a modicum of investigative attention. Few statements were taken and no hearings were organised in any neighbouring countries, although the TRC's mandate included these 'external' violations. As the report points out, more people died as a result of apartheid outside South Africa's borders than inside, through the direct wars in South West Africa/Namibia and southern Angola, through state sponsorship of rebel groupings such as Renamo (Mozambique National Resistance) and Unita (National Union for the Total Independence of Angola), and through policies of destabilisation. Only one chapter in the report pays attention to these atrocities.[4]

The TRC's most explicit product, its 1998 five-volume report, was somewhat more controversial than its processes. The 1998 report elicited domestic protest and even legal action by several political groupings implicated in gross human rights violations.[5] While former President FW de Klerk, former Intelligence boss Niel Barnard and the IFP were amongst the organisations and individuals who protested the findings against them, it was the opprobrium of the ANC that had lasting consequences.

Although the TRC had accepted that apartheid was a crime against humanity and that the ANC had fought a just war against it, it also found that certain limited aspects of the ANC's armed struggle constituted gross human rights violations. These findings were based upon the principle that even when fighting a just war, just means must be employed. That the ANC had, in 1980, acceded to the Geneva Convention, indicated their willingness to adhere to such conventions and principles (TRC 1998, Vol. 1 Ch. 4: para. 64–81).

The ANC, however, took the view that the TRC's findings 'criminalised' the liberation movement and equated their actions with those of the state, an unacceptable form to it of 'moral equivalence'.[6] The ANC declared that it would:

> fight using all legitimate means, to defeat any effort which seeks to denounce the noble struggle the people waged, on the basis that it constituted a gross violation of human rights. (ANC 1998: para. 3.1)

This was despite the fact that the TRC found the primary perpetrator to have been the South African state, followed by the IFP. The findings against the ANC were modest and were not expected to elicit any controversy. As Archbishop Tutu commented:

> I must say that some of us were taken aback, since we had believed that the notice would be a mere formality with the ANC. The contemplated finding had been based on the ANC's own very substantial, full and frank submissions ... (Tutu 1999: 208)

Regretfully, the October 1998 report handover coincided with the departure from the TRC of most of its leadership figures. Indeed, even prior to the handover of the report, the TRC leadership was dispersing. This dispersal probably contributed to the breakdown of relations with the ANC over the findings issue.

With the handover of the report, the TRC went into suspension. Three commissioners were retained with responsibilities for the human rights violations (HRV), amnesty and reparations components, along with the Amnesty Committee. The others, notably its leadership of Chairperson Desmond Tutu and Deputy Chairperson Alex Boraine, departed to pursue other activities overseas, among them the promotion of the South African TRC model.

The consequence of this downscaling was a leadership vacuum and the TRC became almost entirely a bureaucratic agency for the next three years, administering amnesty applications, outstanding HRV and reparations matters. The Amnesty Committee placed great store on its independence from the rest of the TRC and confined its role exclusively to adjudicating applications. The collective institutional ability to argue and engage with the broader TRC project was no longer present and the public pronouncements of the TRC became almost exclusively bland announcements regarding the outcome of amnesty applications. At the crucial moment when the identity, value and mandate of the TRC was under critical scrutiny, the ship was rudderless.

The TRC was never able to repair its troubled relationship with the ANC and gradually became viewed with suspicion and some contempt by leading ANC officials. While there is evidence that this view was not universally shared by all in the ANC – many feeling that the accomplishments of the TRC were substantial and its findings appropriate – this antagonism became a powerful public expression. The parliamentary debate on the report in February 1999 built public perceptions that the TRC had misdirected itself. Few voices were heard to counter this. The TRC's remaining administrative shell could offer no input on the debate. Du Toit has commented:

> Within South African politics and public life, the TRC has not only effectively disappeared from the national agenda ... but the TRC process is widely assumed to have been less than successful, if not basically misconceived. (2002: 1)

After the parliamentary debate, the report and its recommendations sank like a stone into virtual oblivion in South Africa, although continuing to receive great acclaim and awards abroad. All of the above has resulted in a situation where a number of outstanding matters relating to the TRC, chief amongst them reparations, have fallen by the wayside.

Reparations

While the TRC had the power to grant amnesty, it had no similar power with respect to reparations. Instead, it was confined to placing recommendations before government (as it did in its 1998 report) and the payment of small 'urgent interim reparation' amounts to victims.

Although in the popular mind and ensuing controversies final reparations have become focused on individual monetary compensation, the TRC's recommendations were far wider.[7] The whole reparations package was devised in accordance with internationally-accepted approaches to reparations and rehabilitation and included different dimensions. In the first place, *individual reparation grants* were to be paid to victims or their surviving relatives/dependants. These grants would be paid by the President's Fund in six-monthly instalments for a period of six years. The amount would vary up to a maximum of R23 023 per annum.[8] *Symbolic reparations* were aimed at restoring the dignity of victims and survivors, and incorporated both legal/administrative measures as well as more commemorative aspects.[9] *Community rehabilitation* would give attention to those communities that were subjected to systemic abuse, most notably, although not exclusively, areas of KwaZulu-Natal.[10] In terms of the internationally recognised right to a guarantee of non-repetition of such violations, these measures were to be accompanied by *legal and institutional reform.*[11]

From the outset, government expressed caution regarding the individual monetary component. Some government figures rebuffed the notion of individual payments, stating that those who joined the struggle against apartheid did not do so for monetary gain. During the parliamentary debate, Dullah Omar, then Minister of Justice, reflected this unease with what was seen as 'financial reward':

> We will also bear in mind that our gallant sons and daughters did
> not participate in the struggle and did not sacrifice their lives for
> monetary compensation ... We must not reduce the victims of
> apartheid tyranny to beggars pleading for a hand-out of mercy.
> (Joint Sitting of the National Assembly and the NCOP, 1999:
> columns 64–65)

After the February 1999 debate, a long period of official silence ensued, broken only by intermittent verbal exchanges between government officials and increasingly anxious victim organisations, such as the Khulumani Victim Support Group.[12] While a committee was established consisting of director-generals of government ministries expected to contribute in some form to a reparations programme, no visible progress was reported. The TRC's official reparations policy gathered dust while its reparations' staff continued to be inundated by confused and desperate victims, who blamed the TRC for the silence.

Finance Minister Trevor Manuel's 2001 budget speech finally included some concrete financial indicators. He stated that allocations would bring the amount available for reparations in the President's Fund to about R800 million. These would be paid in once-off settlements and the process would be concluded within two years (Budget Speech 2001). The R800 million was not seen as a finite amount as government would seek additional funding from the business and civil society. This suggested that the reparations policy of a biannual pay-out over six years would not be adopted, but a smaller-scale single payment was preferred. If the full R800 million was used for individual payments alone, this would amount to approximately R40 000 per person.[13]

All subsequent references by Government to reparations indicated that only when the TRC's final volumes were handed over would it issue any further official announcements on its proposed reparations policy. This handover was first scheduled for late 2001, a date that continued to shift later and later, until being placed on hold in mid-2002 by the IFP's legal challenge to the findings made against it in the 1998 report. Following an out-of-court settlement in January 2003, the final report was set for handover on 21 March 2003, Human Rights Day.

The Khulumani Victim Support Group in the Western Cape attempted to force government to disclose its reparations proposals by using the *Access to Information Act*. The matter was still pending in court at time of writing. This did little to improve the poor relationship existing between the ANC or Government and victim-support groups. In one incident during a June 2000 visit by President Mbeki to Soweto township to commemorate June 16, members of Khulumani holding placards calling for the implementation of the TRC's reparations proposals, were manhandled and their placards destroyed by ANC supporters.

Although the Government pegged its prevarication on the delayed handover of the report, the TRC made it clear that the reparations proposals submitted in 1998 were its final recommendations. However, it was not only the reparations proposals that were ignored by Government.[14] None of the recommendations made in the October 1998 report have received official attention.

Some may argue that Government prefers to consider reparations as a broader social and economic development issue as opposed to individual compensation. Government has always articulated a preference for community and symbolic rather than individual reparations. This type of broader apartheid restitution framework was illustrated by a speech by Finance Minister Trevor Manuel at an NGO-hosted debate on reparations. His speech, which outlined the development challenges facing the country in the context of the legacy of apartheid, mentioned reparations but once, as follows:

> To promote sustainable but rapid development must be the most meaningful form of reparations for the vast havoc that apartheid wreaked on the lives of our people. (Manuel 2000)

While this is no doubt a paramount reparations approach for the country as a whole, the provision of electricity and water (which is in any event the function of a government) cannot be construed as reparations for a person paralysed by a police bullet – a person possibly mobilised into the streets by Minister Manuel himself in his earlier persona as UDF General Secretary! Furthermore, Government has not been consistent in this stance. Despite this apparent distaste for individual payments, Government has seen fit to compensate financially certain of its constituents via its veteran special pensions scheme, which provided for the payment of pensions to persons who, in the establishment of a democratic constitutional order, made sacrifices or served the public interest; and the dependants of those persons (*Special Pensions Act* [No. 69 of 1996]).[15]

Unlike the TRC reparations proposals that suggest biannual payments for a period of six years, no such time limit exists for those eligible for special pensions. The special pension annual amounts range from R24 000 to a maximum of R84 000, according to criteria of age and length of organisational service. The amount required for these pensions would clearly far exceed the annual amount required for the TRC reparation payments, where the maximum annual payment for a rural family with nine dependants is some R23 000. While the TRC reparations would involve some 22 000 victims,[16] just under 30 000 applications for special pensions had been received by December 2000. Furthermore, a recent proposed amendment to the special pensions legislation would allow for late applications to be received. According to the Chairperson of the Portfolio Committee, Barbara Hogan, 'we owe it to history to set up a record of everyone that was part of the struggle' (Finance Portfolio Committee and Select Committee Joint Meeting 21-08-02).

The special pensions process primarily privileges those who were members of organisations, as opposed to those who were engaged and even injured or killed in the political conflict in non-organisational ways. It is the latter group that came to the TRC. Whatever the specifics of the special pensions are (and the many problems associated with its implementation),[17] the principle of individual recompense by government for 'losses' suffered as a result of political involvement is clear. The difference in approach is stark. Perhaps this can be explained by the lack of political standing of the TRC victims, who are not on the whole a strong pressure or lobby group within the ANC. While former exiles, political prisoners, and Umkhonto we Sizwe (MK) combatants have also had a difficult journey to obtain and access what they saw as their just dues, they constitute groups with far greater access to the portals of power. As fairly organised groupings with pre-existing relationships with MPs, MPLs, Ministers and high-ranking officials, these ANC 'constituents' are able to lobby for their interests and mobilise a stronger sense of obligation in the ANC's conscience. By contrast, those who came to the TRC were not organised political activists in the main, but were mostly ordinary and often very poor township residents swept up in the conflicts of the mid-1980s and 1990s, with little more than a sense of identification with political movements.

Only a minority of TRC victims can be described as the organised membership of political parties. Even fewer high-profile activists and almost no parliamentarians made statements to the TRC. As Commissioner Hlengiwe Mkhize noted, TRC victims 'are mostly unemployed people with little education – not high profile or visible political people, but those who made sacrifices at a local level but are unknown and seen as insignificant' (*Cape Argus* 17.01.02).

Amnesty and prosecutions

The corollary of the amnesty process was the implicit assurance of prosecutions for those who did not apply, as well as those applicants refused amnesty for failing to meet the requirements.[18] To this end, shortly after the handover of the 1998 report, a unit was established in the National Directorate of Public Prosecutions. This was perhaps somewhat premature given that the amnesty process itself was far from complete and TRC records had yet to be handed over to the National Archives. It is thus unsurprising that the unit made little headway and not a single prosecution has been launched by it to date.

There are also difficult questions to be addressed surrounding prosecutions. As an unnamed source in the Justice Department noted:

> Government has a very serious dilemma. You do not want the next five years of South African politics to be dominated by sensationalist trials of high-profile figures. This country is hard enough to govern without opening up old fault lines. You do not want the politics of the future to be monopolised by the past. Yet you

cannot do nothing. If everybody denied amnesty walks free, the
Truth Commission turns into a mockery. The Commission was
acclaimed across the world. It cannot end in ignominy...
(*Business Day* 21.06.01)

Should prosecutions target the politicians, the generals or the footsoldiers?
While evidence may be more easily available for the prosecution of footsoldiers, charging only those who pulled the trigger is hardly a satisfactory
option.[19] David Unterhalter, director of the Nelson Mandela Institute at the
Wits University Law School, highlighted this dilemma:

> The crucial choice is whether to go for those who were politically
> responsible on one hand, or highly placed officials on the other.
> The morally sound choice is surely to go for those who were polit-
> ically accountable. It establishes principles germane to the present
> and the future – questions of moral responsibility for those who
> wield power. That's where Nuremberg was successful ... The
> Goebbelses, the Speers were brought to justice. Yet if the decision
> is a pragmatic rather than moral one, I guess government will go
> for officials instead of politicians. (*Business Day* 21.06.01)

The article suggested that one of the likely prosecution scenarios would be
'taking a few high-profile, symbolic cases to trial and letting the rest gather
dust' and asks who the 'sacrificial lambs' in such showcase trials are likely to
be. The same unnamed source in the Justice Department offered a response:

> A pretty cynical set of decisions will probably be made. Who is
> high profile enough for the trial to be a real showcase, but does
> not garner enough current support to provoke too many shock
> waves? Expect government to ask some pragmatic questions.
> (*Business Day* 21.06.01)

Justice Richard Goldstone, a Constitutional Court judge and an international
prosecutor, has also suggested that widespread prosecutions may not be
possible in transitional societies:

> All victims are entitled to full justice through trial and if proven
> guilty, then the punishment of perpetrators must follow. In
> transitional societies the problem is that there are too many
> victims and too many perpetrators for the latter to be tried.
> (*Cape Times* 04.10.01)

He further suggested that carefully-chosen prosecutions should follow according to three criteria:

○ The victim's desire to proceed.
○ The availability of sufficiently compelling evidence.
○ The heinousness of the crime.

The second dilemma confronting the prosecution authorities is the question of impartiality. Should prosecutions proceed against both state and liberation movements? Is it viable for prosecutions only to proceed only against those linked to the former state, and would this unleash a wave of protest? Rumblings from lawyers representing security-force interests, as well as victims of ANC bombs, suggest that should prosecutions proceed against former state operatives alone, a concerted effort will be made to counter this, including, for example, bringing civil claims against both ANC leadership and operatives.

At a more pragmatic level, the cost of such prosecutions is clearly an important factor in Government's considerations. In his budget speech in June 2001, Minister Maduna raised the question he claimed many South Africans would ask: whether to spend millions or even billions on prosecutions or whether to deploy scarce resources on pressing social needs such as housing and health? Responding to the issue of the costs of prosecutions, Venitia Govender, national director of the SAHRC, raises the danger of going the pragmatic route: 'How can we expect ordinary citizens to respect and uphold the law … if no real effort is made to deal with elements that snubbed the [TRC] process?' (*Mail & Guardian* 15.06.01).

Further, any post-TRC prosecution begins with a legacy of failure. Following the successful conviction in 1994 of Colonel Eugene de Kock, subsequent large-scale prosecutions of apartheid-era perpetrators have failed to secure convictions. In both instances, the failure of these prosecutions was blamed on an untransformed judiciary. In the case of former Defence Minister Magnus Malan and his co-accused, the prosecution's failure was widely blamed on prosecutor Tim McNally's alleged deliberate sabotage of the case. In the case of chemical biological warfare programme head, Brigadier Wouter Basson, the prosecutorial team (the same team which had been responsible for the conviction of de Kock) confronted a hostile apartheid-era holdover in Judge Willie Hartzenburg (Burger & Gould 2002).

While the failure of these prosecutions has been seen more as the result of unfortunate courtroom circumstances than the strength of the cases themselves, Judge Hartzenburg's refusal to grant key state witnesses immunity from prosecution is likely to have a more lasting negative impact. It is rumoured that several former security force operatives who had been co-operating with the Attorney General's office became reluctant to consider giving evidence in future trials as a result of this ruling. Two other local prosecutions, neither of which was initiated by the post-TRC prosecution unit, have also ended in acquittals.[20]

In the absence of effective prosecutions it may be said that a *de facto* general amnesty has been declared. Does this reflect a failure on the part of the national prosecutorial authority or does it reflect a broader lack of political will on the part of government itself?

Commentary by Government on the question of prosecutions has been some-what contradictory in recent years. The *TRC Act* was almost certainly promulgated with the intent of prosecutions following the amnesty process. Yet as time has passed, hints of other amnesty options have continually surfaced, primarily in the form of debate around a special amnesty for KwaZulu-Natal, where political violence continued after 1994, and ongoing amnesty calls by former SADF generals.

During the February 1999 parliamentary debate on the TRC report, both Mandela and Mbeki refuted the possibility of a general amnesty, but suggested that future prosecutions would be limited. Then-President Mandela stated:

> Accountability does need to be established, and where evidence exists of a serious crime, prosecution should be instituted … Yet a timeframe for this process is necessary, for we cannot afford, as a nation and government, to be saddled with unending judicial processes which can easily bog down our current efforts to resolve problems of the present. [The National Director of Prosecutions] will take into account not only the critical need to establish accountability and the rule of law, but also the need to advance reconciliation and the long-term interests of the country. (Joint sitting of the National Assembly and NCOP, 25.02.99: col. 55)

In the debate, then-Deputy President Mbeki concurred with much of this, adding that at the same time Government would need to address the situation in KwaZulu-Natal and the proposals put forward by former SADF generals. Another issue of concern alluded to by President Mandela was the trouble-some question of organisational liability that was not addressed by the amnesty provisions.[21]

These issues continued to surface with media suggestions that an elite pact might be underway to secure both the SADF and ANC leadership from prosecution.[22] Newspaper reports indicated that a working group consisting of Justice Minister Maduna and Deputy President Zuma, former generals of the SADF (including Generals Geldenhuys, Malan, Viljoen and Meiring), was established on Mbeki's initiative sometime in the period following the handover of the TRC report in 1998 (*Rapport* 10.06.01; *Business Day* 13.06.01). The group is said to have drafted a document in which they recommend the granting of amnesty to SADF generals and ANC leadership.[23] The proposal would not apply to persons who acted outside the normal recognised conventions of war and outside of a political framework. It also sought to secure SADC co-operation in preventing any prosecutions for incidents in neighbouring states.

The fragmented details of these meetings caused alarm when they came to public attention. Both the government and the former SADF generals hastened to reassure their subordinates that they too would be included in this amnesty proposal. For example, General Malan stated that this general amnesty would not be selective and it would include everyone involved before 8 May 1994 across the board. He argued that 'people desire the closing of the books' so that they can proceed without fear of prosecution, and he did not wish to see ANC leadership prosecuted (*Rapport* 17.06.01). In his budget speech in June 2001, Justice Minister Maduna stressed that these meetings were merely consultative and did not aim at securing a secret deal. He also gave an assurance that 'that there will be no blanket amnesty' (*SABC Pressclips* 19.05.02).

Despite the Minister's assurances, the presidential pardons granted in May 2002 to 33 prisoners in the Eastern Cape, including a significant number who had been denied amnesty by the TRC's Amnesty Committee,[24] fuelled speculation that these limited pardons were a precursor to a wider amnesty. Archbishop Tutu said if those pardoned included several people refused amnesty by the TRC, it would seem to be 'the thin end of a general amnesty wedge … It would make a mockery of the TRC and eviscerate the entire process' (*SABC Pressclips* 19.05.02). The pardons promptly elicited pardon applications from other serving political prisoners such as Eugene de Kock, Janusz Waluz and Clive Derby-Lewis, and a range of other right-wing prisoners, most of whom had been refused amnesty by the TRC. Newspaper reports suggested that the IFP and the Freedom Front had drafted lists of 'their' prisoners and were pressurising government with the hope of securing similar pardons. Indeed, it was reported at the time that the IFP had developed its own amnesty application form and that this form had been shown and approved by the Justice Department.

In the ensuing furore around these pardons, and in contrast to earlier statements, Cabinet confirmed that the possibility of a further amnesty for politically-related crimes was being considered, and that Government's view on the matter would be made known following the release of the TRC's final report. Indeed, it was rumoured at the time that following the submission of this report, Cabinet would announce its reparation programme and, at the same time, announce the parameters of such an amnesty.

A closer examination of the process leading up to the pardons suggests that they were possibly more of a local regional solution to a problem than an indicator of a future national amnesty. The pardons were the initiative of Eastern Cape Premier Makhenkesi Arnold Stofile who, more than a year before the pardons were announced, had criticised the TRC for leaving these amnesty applicants to 'rot in jail' and had publicly called for presidential pardons for all former Azanian Peoples' Liberation Army (APLA) and MK operatives.

At the time of writing, the final volumes of the TRC report are yet to be handed to Government. It is unlikely that Government will proceed with discussions around a further amnesty before their publication. At the same time, there have been renewed efforts by the National Prosecuting Authority to identify possible prosecutions. However, the unit responsible for this remains extremely modest and it is believed that even the most optimistic foresee only a handful of prosecutions materialising. Thus, even if a second form of amnesty does not come to pass, it is unlikely that prosecutions will occur on anything like the scale that human rights groups would deem desirable.

Yet without such prosecutions, those who snubbed the TRC will be vindicated. One such element was the SADF, and this is perhaps the most disturbing aspect of the discussions between Government and the SADF regarding further amnesty arrangements. If the efforts by the SADF and IFP to secure a further amnesty or pardons for their members are successful, it will in effect reward and endorse the contempt that both organisations displayed towards the TRC, and by extension to Parliament and the legal process that put the TRC in place.

Other unfinished business

While reparations and prosecutions are the two issues that loom largest on the post-TRC horizon, there are several others that should not be forgotten. The limited life span of the TRC inevitably constrained its ability to tackle and complete a host of investigations and activities that were terminated in October 1998 with the formal suspension of the Commission.

Most pertinent amongst these unfinished tasks has been the TRC's failure to provide any feedback concerning individual case investigations to the victims or their families. Of all requests made to the Commission, the most common was to find out what had happened, by whom, and so on? In many cases, families were not even aware of the publicly-available documentation that could have provided some information, such as police case dockets, post-mortem and inquest reports, as well as newspaper reports and NGO data. Neither these types of documents nor the final outcome of the TRC's investigation were made available to the victims.

Few victims have ever seen their own case file. All victims ever received from the TRC in the way of feedback was a *pro forma* letter with a ticked box indicating that they had/had not been declared a victim of a gross HRV, and that those declared to be victims could apply for reparations. In several cases involving amnesty hearings, the shortage of investigative capacity and the pressures of time meant that the relevant victims could not be traced and informed about the amnesty hearing. These victims have thus never heard the details of the perpetrator's account of the incident.

Two other areas of outstanding obligations relate to missing persons and the exhumations of human remains. Several hundred missing persons were reported to the TRC and most of these cases remain unsolved. The TRC conducted a limited exhumation programme of some 50 persons, primarily in the former Transvaal and Natal regions. All of these cases involved MK operatives killed in combat or ambush situations by the security forces. These exhumations were undermined by irregular procedures in certain cases, and potentially faulty identifications. Aside from the necessity of resolving these errors, there remain a significant number of anonymously buried combatants and civilians who have yet to be exhumed. There are, in addition, a large number of exiles who died on foreign soil in a variety of circumstances.

The return of human remains was one of the most emotive and tangible endeavors undertaken by the TRC. The heartfelt appeal by families for the bones of their loved ones remains a small but critical arena where real restitution and reparations can take place.

Conclusion

This article has positioned the TRC as one of the raft of institutions established post-1994 to redress past injustices and build a human rights culture. Whatever its shortcomings, the TRC is surely one of the most successful. While its impact on the public psyche was immense at the height of its operations, today its defendants are scattered and few, confined largely to sectors of the NGO community. Despite international acclaim, Government's response has been tardy and critical. This in turn has resulted in a widening sense of criticism and injustice from victims and the broader South African public, which has arguably squandered the potential energy of the TRC process to deepen the commitment to justice and end to impunity enshrined in the Constitution.

Various reasons have been suggested for Government's stance. First among these would be the tensions arising from the TRC's findings on the liberation movements. Beyond this, as the debate on prosecutions illustrates, Government is faced with competing agendas and limited resources, often drawing it towards other priorities. To what extent the lack of progress in expediting the TRC's unfinished business is a product of hostility to its findings, or a result of more urgent priorities, or even a more general muting of the more transformative impulses of the period, is unclear. Whatever the reasons may or may not have been, it undoubtedly remains a Government choice to keep the TRC on the backburner.

In his most recent 'State of the Nation' address to Parliament on 14 February 2003, President Mbeki referred to the prospect of future discussions on the way forward:

> It is in this spirit that we should engage in a national dialogue on how we take forward the report and recommendations of the TRC, which we hope will be presented to government in the next few months. This will afford us the opportunity to understand a critical part of our past and join hands in forging a people's contract for a better tomorrow.

It is as yet unclear as to whether this represents any significant commitment by Government to forefront the unfinished business of the TRC. Notably, the TRC was entirely absent from Minister Manuel's 2003 budget speech made two weeks later. Victim groups were dismayed to see no further financial provision made for reparations.

This article has perhaps unfairly focused on the shortfalls of Government. Yet others have pointed to the TRC's own abandonment of its project. Addressing a Chile/South Africa conference, Antjie Krog, an admirer of the TRC process, commented:

> As the process peters out and seems to leave hardly a ripple, I cannot help but question the commissioners' lack of foresight. If indeed, it rests with the ANC-led government to carry out reparations, sue perpetrators, implement prevention measures for foreign abuses and cultivate a human rights culture, then it is crucial to get it to understand what is at stake … The truth commission should have spoken to it, not once but a thousand times if necessary. Its failure to do so has done the process more harm than all the other criticisms and mistakes put together. (*Sunday Independent* 02.12.01)

Du Toit also argues that responsibility for the negative outcomes in the TRC aftermath, should not only be placed on the ANC government:

> These unfortunate results are as much the responsibility of the TRC itself. With its formal disbandment in 1998 the Commission has taken the view that its task had been completed and that the implementation of its recommendations now was a matter for the state. Technically this is correct … But, just as at the inception of the TRC process, civil society-based ways and means could have been found to ensure that the key issues remained on the national political agenda and were brought to the attention of the key political decision-makers. Instead it would seem that key figures in the TRC leadership have chosen to facilitate the export of the South African TRC model abroad in a range of international contexts while the local product has languished at home. (2002: 6)

Postscript

President Thabo Mbeki finally presented the Government's position on reparations and amnesty in Parliament on 15 April 2003, shortly after receiving the final two volumes of the TRC report. He announced a:

'once-off grant of R30 000 to those individuals or survivors designated by the TRC. Combined with community reparations, and
assistance through opportunities and services … [medical and
educational], we hope that these disbursements will help acknowledge the suffering that these individuals experienced, and offer
some relief'. (Mbeki 2003)

Even while announcing individual payments, President Mbeki continued to
express Government's misgivings: 'We do so with some apprehension, for no-
one can attach monetary value to life and suffering. Nor can an argument be
sustained that the efforts of millions of South Africans to liberate themselves
were for monetary gain' (Mbeki 2003). He also rejected the wealth tax
proposal made by the TRC.

While there was relief that Government had finally outlined its reparations
plan, there was widespread disappointment and anger amongst victims that
the individual reparations were only about one-quarter of what the TRC had
proposed. There may be further problems emerging from the proposed pay-
out. Only those who made statements to the TRC and were found to be victims are eligible for individual reparations. Yet, thousands of victims did not
come to the TRC for many reasons: inaccessibility, lack of information, the
brief life span of the TRC, or political objections. The 22 000 TRC victims by
no means constitute the entire victim pool. It remains to be seen whether
victims or groups representing their interests will challenge either of
these issues.

Mbeki and other Cabinet members also took the opportunity to lambast
efforts currently underway in courts in the United States to force certain
multinational companies to pay 'apartheid reparations.' Mbeki stated that 'we
consider it completely unacceptable that matters that are central to the future
of our country should be adjudicated in foreign courts' (Mbeki 2003). In
2002, two class-action lawsuits were filed in the USA against nearly 30 multinational corporations and international banks for their role in helping the
apartheid government 'do its dirty work' through the provision of finances, oil
and technology. The lawsuits, filed in the name of clusters of apartheid victims
and the Khulumani Support Group, sought individual compensation as well
as broader social development contributions. No doubt private initiatives
such as these and the prospect of investor unhappiness played some role in
urging Government to agree to some form of monetary compensation. At the

time of writing, initiatives brokered by Anglican Archbishop Ndungane are commencing to negotiate a settlement.

Government also put an end to further speculation around the issue of a general amnesty. President Mbeki stated unequivocally that:

> Any such approach, whether applied to specific categories of people or regions of the country, would fly in the face of the TRC process and subtract from the principle of accountability which is vital not only in dealing with the past, but also in the creation of a new ethos within our society. (Mbeki 2003)

The decision to pursue prosecutions would thus be left to the discretion of the National Directorate of Public Prosecutions (NDPP). At the same time, Mbeki continued, the NDPP would 'leave its doors open for those who are prepared to divulge information they have and to co-operate in unearthing the truth (Mbeki 2003),' thus opening the way to further disclosure by perpetrators in exchange for immunity from prosecution. At the same time, Government did not increase the resources of the NDPP unit working on TRC-related cases, thus signaling that it is unlikely that large numbers of perpetrators will be brought to book.

Somewhat surprisingly, neither President Mbeki nor the various ANC representatives who spoke during the ensuing parliamentary debate raised the issue that had previously caused so much ire and had bedeviled relations between government and the TRC, namely, the TRC's findings on the ANC. This was despite the fact that the TRC's final volumes confirmed its earlier findings on the ANC.

In the end, the final balance sheet will show that Government, while not wholeheartedly embracing the TRC's recommendations, stepped back from previously disputed terrain. Aside from symbolic reparations, identified TRC victims can expect to receive very modest monetary reparation, while a handful of perpetrators may find themselves facing criminal charges. With regards to the contested findings of the TRC, these have been left – arguably where they properly belong – to current and successive generations of South Africans and others to debate and research.

Notes

1   See for example the chapter on Findings and Conclusions, Vol. 5 Ch. 6.

2   After October 1998, the Amnesty Committee was enabled to continue its unfinished work, wrapping up its last amnesty hearings and decisions in 2001.

3   The life span of the TRC was originally set for 18 months, but this was extended to October 1998.

4   See TRC (1998), Vol. 2 Ch. 1.

5   The TRC found that three types of actions undertaken by the ANC constituted gross violations of human rights. These were the landmine campaign and the placing of certain bombs where civilians were killed or injured, attacks on suspected collabora-tors and state witnesses in trials, and the torture, severe ill-treatment and executions of ANC members in exile. There was also a finding that held the ANC accountable for the killing of political opponents in the 1990s period, primarily though its role in arming and training self-defence unit members without adequate structures of command and control, all of which contributed to the 'spiral of violence' engulfing areas of the country in that period. See TRC (1998), Vol. 5 Ch. 6, especially paras 130–138.

6   For a more detailed discussion of this issue see Cherry (2000), du Toit (1999) and Asmal, Asmal & Roberts (2000).

7   See TRC (1998), Vol. 5 Ch. 5.

8   The amount to be paid would be calculated according to three components: (1) an amount that acknowledged the suffering caused by the violation; (2) an amount that enabled access to requisite services and facilities; and (3) an amount to subsidise daily living costs according to socio-economic circumstances. Victims living in the rural areas would receive a slightly higher grant as the cost of living is higher there. The amount also varied according to the number of dependants.

9   The legal/administrative measures included, for example, the issuing of death certifi-cates, expunging of criminal records for politically related offences and other outstanding legal matters. Commemorative aspects included exhumations, tomb-stones, memorials or monuments and renaming of streets or public facilities.

10 These included programmes to demilitarise youth who had been been involved in or witnessed political violence over decades; programmes to resettle the many thousands displaced by political violence; mental health and trauma counselling; as well as programmes to rehabilitate and reintegrate into normal community life perpetrators of gross violations of human rights.

11 These included recommendations by the TRC as a whole relating to the judiciary, security forces and correctional services, as well as other sectors in society such as education, business and media.

12 While the Khulumani group was originally only active in the Gauteng area, a Cape Town group of victims also later affiliated to Khulumani. Other pockets of victim organisation also exist in other regions of the country, such as the Uitenhage Victims' Support Group in Uitenhage, Eastern Cape. Other NGOs such as the Healing of

Memories Institute, Khumbula and the Trauma Centres are also active in this area. An NGO Working Group on Reparations has also spearheaded pressure on reparations.

13 This was calculated in terms of some 17 000 victims. However the number of victims has grown substantially since then, which would lower the amount.

14 Even where Government has enacted measures in line with the TRC recommendations, such as the reform of public-order policing procedures, these have been done without reference to the TRC recommendations.

15 See the minutes of the relevant joint meetings between the Finance Portfolio Committee and Select Committee at the website of the Parliamentary Monitoring Group (PMG): http://www.pmg.org.za/.

16 The issues, problems and fairness concerning the TRC's 'closed list' of victims have not been canvassed in this article, yet will surely fall under the spotlight if and when actual payments become a reality. In short, the list of TRC victims who qualify for reparations is made up only of persons who were identified as victims either through HRV statements or through the amnesty process.

17 There are reportedly a host of problems associated with the implementation of the special pensions. In addition, according to Human Rights Media Watch, only some 9 500 of the 30 000-odd applicants have been accepted. Also see the minutes of the relevant parliamentary committees, available from the PMG at http://www.pmg.org.za/.

18 These requirements included: full disclosure, political objective, proportionality, and acting within the orders of a known political organisation.

19 The so-called 'German border guard cases' are intriguing examples of prosecution across hierarchies and functions. The Defence Minister and his deputy, members of the National Defence Council, as well as border guards themselves, were convicted and sentenced for fatal shootings of persons who attempted to flee from East to West Germany. See Arnold, Karsten & Kreicker (2002).

20 Two members of the Ciskei Defence Force who were involved in the Bisho Massacre and who had been refused amnesty were charged in respect of this event. The second trial involved a Western Cape policeman who was denied amnesty for killing a teenage protestor in Worcester in 1985.

21 For a discussion on the question of organisational and leadership liability and the problems of the South African amnesty process, see Klaaren & Varney (2000).

22 This was not the first time that rumours of secret negotiations regarding amnesty for the SADF have surfaced. Suggestions of such a deal brokered perhaps by Joe Modise or other leading MK personnel with the SADF have persisted. Modise is said to have assured SADF generals during bilateral discussions between the SADF and MK in 1993 that 'Nuremburg-style' trials were not on the cards and both sides are said to have been in agreement on the 'absolute necessity of a general amnesty'. (See Frankel 2002: 23–25.)

23 The SADF generals had refused to seek amnesty as they were of the view that they had fought a legitimate war, while a number of ANC leadership figures had been refused

amnesty as their applications were for general political accountability, rather than specified incidents or operations. The ANC amnesty decisions were the subject of a TRC-initiated court review. (See TRC 1998, Vol. 1 Ch. 7: 193–194.)

24   The 33 pardoned included various APLA operatives involved in attacks in the Eastern Cape in the early 1990s, a group of 12 UDF/ANC supporters from Mdantsane involved in 'community justice' killings and a UDF supporter refused amnesty for a farm killing in 1989. Also granted pardon was former Ciskei strongman and one-time South African security force agent, Kwane Sebe, jailed for attacks on two properties in 1989. The number of amnesty applicants is variously cited. Some had been granted amnesty for some offences or for certain aspects of the offence for which they applied.

References

Books and articles

African National Congress (1998) *Submission to the Truth and Reconciliation Commission in reply to Section 30[2] of Act No. 34 of 1996 on the TRC's Findings on the African National Congress.* Johannesburg.

Arnold, K, Karsten, N & Kreicker, H (2002) The German border guard cases before the European Court of Human Rights, *Criminal Law in Reaction to State Crime: Comparative Insights into Transitional Processes.* Freiburg: Max Planck Institute for Foreign and International Criminal Law.

Asmal, K, Asmal, L & Roberts, RS (1997) *Reconciliation through truth: A reckoning of apartheid's criminal governance.* Cape Town: David Philip.

Asmal, K, Asmal, L & Roberts, RS (2000) When the assassin cries foul: The modern just war doctrine, in C Villa Vicencio & W Verwoerd (eds.) *Looking back, reaching forward: Reflections on the Truth and Reconciliation Commission of South Africa.* Cape Town: UCT Press.

Boraine, A (2001) *A country unmasked.* Oxford: OUP.

Bundy, C (2000) The beast of the past: History and the TRC, in W James & L van de Vijver (eds.) *After the TRC: Reflections on truth and reconciliation in South Africa.* Cape Town: David Philip.

Burger, M & Gould, C (2002) *Secrets and lies: Wouter Basson and South Africa's chemical and biological warfare programme.* Cape Town: Zebra Press.

Cherry, J (2000) 'Just war' and 'just means': Was the TRC wrong about the ANC?, *Transformation* 42: 9–28.

De Lange, J (2000) The historical context, legal origins and philosophical foundations of the South African Truth and Reconciliation Commission, in C Villa Vicencio & W Verwoerd (eds.) *Looking back, reaching forward: Reflections on the Truth and Reconciliation Commission of South Africa.* Cape Town: UCT Press.

Du Toit, A (1999) Perpetrator findings as artificial even-handedness? The TRC's contested judgements of moral and political accountability for gross Human Rights Violations.

Paper presented at a conference, *The TRC: commissioning the past*, 11-14.06.99, University of the Witwatersrand, Johannesburg.

Du Toit, A (2002) The Truth and Reconciliation Commission: A critical appraisal. Unpublished paper, *Conference on reconciliation, restorative justice, remembrance*, Cape Town.

Frankel, P (2002) *Soldiers in a storm: The armed forces in South Africa's democratic tradition*. Boulder, Colorado: Westview Press.

Hayner, P (1994) Fifteen Truth Commissions – 1974 to 1994: A comparative study, *Human Rights Quarterly* 16: 597–655.

Hayner, P (2001) *Unspeakable truths: Confronting state terror and atrocity*. London: Routledge.

Klaaren, J & Varney, H (2000) A second bite at the amnesty cherry? Constitutional and policy issues around legislation for a second amnesty, *South African Law Journal* 117 (3): 572–593.

Mamdani, M (1998) A diminished truth, *Siyaya* 3: 38–40.

Mbeki, T (2001) *State of the Nation Address of the President of South Africa, Thabo Mbeki*. Parliament, Cape Town, 14 February.

Simpson, G (2002) 'Tell no lies, claim no easy victories': A brief evaluation of South Africa's Truth and Reconciliation Commission, in D Posel & G Simpson (eds.) *Commissioning the past: Understanding South Africa's Truth and Reconciliation Commission*. Johannesburg: Witwatersrand University Press.

Tutu, D (1999) *No future without forgiveness*. London: Rider Books.

Government and related sources

Budget Speech, Finance Minister Trevor Manuel, 21.02.01, Parliament. Available on http://www.gov.org.za/.

Finance Portfolio Committee and Select Committee Joint Meeting, 21.08.02: Special Pensions Board Progress Report. Available on http://www.pmg.org.za/.

'National Response to TRC Report', Joint Sitting of the National Assembly and the National Council of Provinces, 25.02.99.

Special Pensions Act (No. 69 of 1996) and *Special Pensions Amendment Act* (No 75. of 1998). Available on http://www.gov.org.za/.

Speech by Finance Minister Trevor Manuel, 14.09.00, Cape Town. Available on the website of the Institute for Justice and Reconciliation: http://www. ijr.org.za/.

TRC (Truth and Reconciliation Commission) (1998) *Truth and Reconciliation Commission of South Africa Report*. Cape Town: Government Printer.

The state of race relations in post-apartheid South Africa

Xolela Mangcu

Nelson Mandela and the discourse of reconciliation

South Africa's transition from apartheid to democracy has been hailed as one of the great stories of the twentieth century. Such was the exhilaration at the dawn of democracy in 1994 that the transition was described by Archbishop Tutu and others as 'a miracle'. Tutu also dubbed the new society 'the rainbow nation', a metaphor so powerful that it continues to inform the collective imagination and give psychological sustenance to an evolving democratic regime.

In the first years of the transition, both Archbishop Tutu and President Mandela came to embody the concept of racial reconciliation. Mandela's capacity for defusing tensions was displayed in the aftermath of the murder of Chris Hani by a Polish immigrant associated with the Afrikaner right wing. It was not so much that Mandela appealed for calm, but the manner in which he did so. He went on national television stating that 'a white man full of prejudice and hate came to our country and committed a deed so foul that our whole nation teeters on the brink of disaster. A white woman, of Afrikaner origin, risked her life so that we may know, and bring justice to this assassin' (Sampson 1999: 469). Again, Mandela's *leitmotif* was that of a black and white community united against evil.

In his public speeches at the time, Mandela kept on differentiating between the politics of the heart and the politics of reason. He suggested that his reconciliatory approach stemmed from a realisation that the ANC had not won the military struggle and that it had to find ways to neutralise white opposition. Speaking about Mandela's approach to the negotiations process, his long-time colleague, Ahmed Kathrada, stated that the aim of the armed struggle was never to overthrow militarily the South African government. It was a bargaining tactic to bring about a negotiated settlement and he complimented Mandela for preventing an eventual bloodbath:

With regard to overdoing reconciliation, Mandela always reminds us of the realities. He points to the few weeks preceding the 1994 election. There were preparations by the white right wing. The generals later took him into greater confidence, and gave him details of their plans to disrupt the 1994 elections. There would have been widespread bloodshed and violence. Being a realistic person, he had decided long ago that reconciliation was the course to take. Within the ANC and its national executive there was never a serious questioning of this approach. (*Business Day* 15.06.99)

It was for this reason of reassuring the white community that Mandela put his weight behind the controversial 'sunset clause' proposed by ANC and SACP veteran Joe Slovo. The idea was that the new government would guarantee security of job tenure for senior civil servants and security officials for five years into the new democracy. Like Mandela, Slovo reasoned that because the ANC had not won an overwhelming victory, white recalcitrants within the army and the civil service could still undermine the new government. It was therefore considered strategic to woo them onto the side of the new government by retaining them in their positions. This proposal caused a great deal of consternation in ANC ranks, with Pallo Jordan, for example, openly disagreeing with Slovo. With Mandela's backing, Slovo won the day. Ironically, Mandela would later complain about a lack of co-operation from white civil servants who were frustrating his government's development programmes.

As he cast his vote in the country's first fully democratic election, Mandela turned to the theme of racial reconciliation. He went back to the speech he gave at the Rivonia Trial before being sentenced to life imprisonment: 'I again repeat that I have throughout my life, as I pointed out in the Rivonia Trial, fought very firmly against white domination. I have fought very firmly against black domination.' He listed some of the major developmental challenges facing the new government and then said 'But we are also concerned about the minorities in the country – especially the white minority. We are concerned about giving confidence and security to those who are worried that by these changes they are now going to be in a disadvantaged position' (Mandela 1994).

The negotiations process produced a government of national unity with a place in it for the NP, and with its last leader, former State President FW de Klerk, serving as Mandela's second Deputy President. Early in his term President Mandela reached out to former opponents, visiting the racially-exclusive Orania to take tea with the widow of the architect of apartheid, Dr Hendrik

Verwoerd. He reached out to Percy Yutar, the prosecutor who led the case which resulted in his long-term imprisonment on Robben Island. He even appointed a former prison guard as part of his security brief. In perhaps his most public of reconciliation gestures, he donned a Springbok rugby jersey in support of the nearly all-white national rugby team in the final of the Rugby World Cup in 1995.

Tools of reconciliation: the 'sunset clause' and the TRC

In January 1996 President Mandela launched the TRC under the leadership of that other icon of racial reconciliation, Archbishop Demond Tutu. Its brief was, *inter alia*, to promote racial reconciliation. One of the key features of the TRC process was the possibility of amnesty for all those who came forward to tell the truth about human rights' violations they had committed, as long as those violations had occurred in pursuit of political objectives. The commission was also mandated to provide financial reparations for the victims of such violations. Some prominent political families, including those of Steve Biko and Griffiths and Victoria Mxenge, opposed the amnesty clause of the TRC's enabling legislation, the *Promotion of National Unity and Reconciliation Act*, arguing that it deprived them of their constitutional rights to justice through a court of law. They took the matter as far as the Constitutional Court but lost.

The first phase of the TRC process ended in October 1998 in some controversy with the release of the first five volumes of its final report. The ANC made its unhappiness with the TRC's findings clear, accusing the commission of drawing a moral equivalence between the liberation movement and the apartheid state. Earlier in August 1996, Thabo Mbeki (then ANC Deputy President) had argued that ANC members need not apply for amnesty on the grounds that its just war could not be equated with apartheid, leading TRC chair Archbishop Tutu to threaten to resign if the ANC did not participate in the amnesty process. While there can be no gainsaying the TRC's achievements in uncovering truths about the past, it cannot be said to have brought about reconciliation. That was perhaps too tall an order to have expected from a temporary institution.

In order for reconciliation to be achieved it also has to take on other more practical dimensions through real improvements in people's lives. As the distinguished African writer Chinua Achebe noted in a television interview on the SABC in 2002, the disappearance of an historical era like apartheid does not mean the disappearance of the problems that came with it. This reflected a feeling in black political circles that the white community had not reciprocated the gestures of goodwill extended to them by former President Mandela. Mandela himself, in the course of his term of office, began to shift towards a more critical posture, even questioning the wisdom of the 'sunset clauses'. In a speech to the ANC Congress in Mafikeng in 1997, he lambasted the lack of co-operation and reciprocity from his white counterparts. Some suggested the speech had the imprint of Deputy President Thabo Mbeki all over it. Whoever the author was, the speech burst the bubble of the racial honeymoon. Newspapers and commentators around the world reacted with shock at what they variously described as Mandela's 'attack', 'invective' or 'diatribe' against whites. Their choice of words was revealing, indicating how the white world at large had grown comfortable with the mood of reconciliation. Any criticism of their continued privilege was experienced as a form of assault. Both Mandela's legacy and the inevitability of a politics of reckoning was captured by Mandela's biographer, Anthony Sampson, thus:

> In his first months as president he enjoyed a brilliant honeymoon, particularly with white South Africans, to whom this tolerant old man came as a wondrous relief … at the end of the first hundred days in office the *Financial Times* could find no whites who had a bad word for him. It was a normality which carried its own dangers, as black militants saw the revolution betrayed, and younger ANC leaders, including Thabo Mbeki, knew they must make reforms which would offend the whites. (Sampson 1999: 504)

The Mbeki era: towards a new black radicalism

The assumption of the presidency by Thabo Mbeki signaled a more radical Africanist approach to national politics. This was heralded by his embrace of the concept of an African Renaissance, something which in the early days of his administration became a point of tension, with some black academics like Thobeka Mda questioning whether whites were indeed Africans. As noted above, Mbeki's attitude to the TRC was also very different to that of Mandela's. In contrast to the latter's unqualified acceptance of the TRC's final report, Mbeki, in his capacity as ANC chairman, resorted to the courts to try to prevent the TRC from releasing its report, which included some negative findings on the ANC. The court ruled against the organisation. But what this indicated was that Mbeki was moving towards a conception of reconciliation as transformation not absolution. As if to deliberately shake the comfortable assumptions of racial reconciliation of the Mandela era, Mbeki increasingly spoke of the continued threats posed by racism to South Africa's democracy. Asked on American television in July 1996 about the drop in the number of whites (from 70 per cent to about 34 per cent)who believed that race relations were good, Mbeki attributed that to the imperatives of change. He argued that one cannot just approach the process of transformation at the political level without addressing economic imbalances, and he continued: 'I would imagine that you would find whites who would be fearful of that kind of change' (http/www.pbs.org).

Speaking at the national conference held in preparation for the World Conference on Racism in 2001, Mbeki called on whites to become part of the movement against the continued existence of racism. He argued that 'despite our collective intentions, racism continues to be our bedfellow.' Mbeki has also made a practice of using his annual 'State of the Nation' address to Parliament to remind South Africans of the pernicious system of apartheid, and to use that as a benchmark for measuring social progress. In one of the most dramatic illustrations of the continued existence of racism, in his 2002 address Mbeki quoted an e-mail from an engineer who spoke about how the 'kaffirs had messed up the country.' The author spoke of black bastards and eerily complained that AIDS was not working fast enough to wipe out the black population. Mbeki concluded that:

> our successes in the struggle to move our country from apartheid
> to democracy have led many in our country to reach the prema-
> ture conclusion that racism in South Africa is dead. This is despite
> the obvious and naked fact that to this day and unavoidably, the
> racial divisions, inequalities and prejudices of the past continue to
> characterise our society.

Responding to the speech, opposition members criticised the President for generalising from one incident to draw inferences about the general prevalence of racism in the country.

Mbeki's 2001 'State of the Nation' address had been more conciliatory. He called for 'unity in action for change' in the struggle to combat racism. He specifically mentioned white South Africans like Carl Niehaus who had owned up to the past and the responsibilities which white privilege had brought with it. He specifically made mention of schools and white farmers who had volunteered their time to work in black communities. In more practical terms, Mbeki's government became a signatory to the United Nations Convention on the Crime of Apartheid, and Parliament passed legislation that made racial discrimination a crime. The legislation also actively promoted racial equality in the workplace.

The Mbeki presidency has thus been less concerned with appeasing whites than with redefining the terms of reconciliation towards the issues of transformation. If the earlier period of reconciliation was marked by what O'Meara described as 'a moment of absolution', the Mbeki approach has been characterised by calls for greater white responsibility.

The African nationalist/non-racialism debate

Mbeki's approach to race relations has occasioned an argument that he has been responsible for increasing racial hostility in the country. I differ with that assessment simply because whoever had taken power after the 'racial honeymoon' would, in the words of Sampson cited earlier, have had to 'burst that bubble' in confronting the vast disparities inherited from the apartheid era. But it is also important to locate the debate on Mbeki's approach to race within the context of the current race debate within the ANC. The role of whites has come up intermittently in the history of the ANC, and on occasions has led to splits within the organisation. One example was the breakaway of the PAC in 1959, another the expulsion of Tennyson Makiwane and the so-called 'gang of eight' from the ANC in 1975 for their opposition to the opening up of ANC membership to non-Africans (Ndebele 2002).

What these tensions, revolving around the shift away from an exclusive concept of nationalism to a more inclusive one, bore out was that, contrary to a widespread view (see Bernstein 1991; Frederikse 1990), non-racialism was a relatively late development in the history of the ANC, and it only came into full bloom in the late 1970s and 1980s (Ndebele 2002). This ascendancy of non-racialism brought to the fore a number of whites as equal and influential members of the ANC's leadership. For example, at the 1985 Kabwe conference of the ANC, Joe Slovo and Ronnie Kasrils were elected to the NEC. Likewise, inside South Africa throughout the 1980s and early 1990s non-racialism was the dominant philosophy of the ANC's internal allies, the UDF and the trade union movement. These structures provided the organisational base of Mandela's *leitmotif* of non-racialist politics.

However, by 2000 the old battles between black nationalists and white liberals had resurfaced within the ANC, and in society more broadly. Perhaps taking their cue from Mbeki's more radical variant of Africanism, the SAHRC, under the leadership of former black consciousness activist Barney Pityana, launched an inquiry into racism in the media – perhaps one of the most publicly-contested arguments about race in the post-Mandela era. This exercise exposed South Africa's racial fault lines. Black editors supported the SAHRC's enquiry, while white editors, with few exceptions, opposed it as a witch-hunt and a threat to freedom of speech. Months earlier, Barney Pityana had, on public television, accused a prominent jurist, Dennis Davis, of being a racist. At about the same time, at the liberal-inclined Witwatersrand University (Wits), Deputy Vice Chancellor William Makgoba was embroiled in a struggle for the position of Vice Chancellor. The stakes were high as Makgoba repeatedly spoke of an Africanist vision for Wits. This did not go down well with some of the senior staff at the institution. The Makgoba affair became one of the ugliest incidents of racial conflict with accusations going back and forth between Makgoba's largely black supporters and his largely white opponents, led by history professor Charles van Onselen. The latter alleged that Makgoba had embellished his curriculum vitae (CV). Blacks, on the other hand, pointed to Makgoba's academic reputation and argued that the issue of the CV was merely being used as a ruse to stop a black person from taking over the institution. In a symbolic gesture of support at the time, Mbeki wrote the foreword to Makgoba's autobiography.

The racism debate extended to other domains of public life, including the sports field, where South African rugby and cricket teams continued to be mostly white in composition, leading to the government calling for racial quotas in the selection of provincial and national rugby squads. The symbolism of Mandela walking onto the pitch donned in a Springbok rugby shirt in 1995 had been replaced in five short years with calls for the racial transformation of the national team. Blacks argued that Mandela had gone out on a limb for rugby, and yet there had been no reciprocity from the white rugby fraternity. In cricket, there was controversy when the president of the game's governing body overruled his selection panel and replaced a white player with a young coloured player, Justin Ontong, in the test team to take on world champions Australia. Months later the self-same board, however, announced an end to racial quotas in the selection of the national team, but backed down in the face of an attack by Sports Minister, Ngconde Balfour.

Such racial fault lines have also played themselves out in the schools and in the criminal justice system. In Vryburg in the mid-1990s, a black high school student, Andrew Babeile, was sentenced to a prison term for stabbing a white schoolmate whom he argued was being racist towards him. Yet, when white schoolboys at Bryanston High School attacked a black fellow pupil and damaged his eye, they were simply suspended and no charges were laid against them. These cases gave further credence to perceptions that the criminal justice system was still racially biased. Other incidents of racial violence include that of a white farmer who shot and killed a black baby on his mother's back because they were trespassing on his property; the white man who pulled a black man to death tied to the back of a van; and the group of white rugby players who beat Tsepo Matshoga to death. Most recently a group of Afrikaner right wingers belonging to an organisation known as the *Boeremag* were arrested for planting a series of bombs that rocked Soweto, killing one individual and disrupting public transportation in the township.

To be sure, there have also been racial incidents including black attacks on white farmers. Initially, these were politically motivated attacks associated with the military wing of the PAC. However, over time, these attacks seem to have become increasingly criminal in nature, with the PAC and farmers' groups sometimes forming joint patrols on farms.

Confronting denial

A high-water mark of the Mbeki presidency's anti-racism drive was the selection of South Africa as the site for a United Nations Conference Against Racism. This took place in 2001, but was preceded by a national conference on racism where leading black thinkers such as Barney Pityana, Patricia Williams and Pallo Jordan spoke. Jordan spoke directly to what he described as the problem of denial afflicting white society in the post-apartheid transition: 'Most white people say they are not responsible for apartheid. But they put the (whites only) Nationalist Party into government in 1948 and returned it to power again and again with a bigger majority until the late 1980s' (Racism Conference 31.09.2000). The issue of denial has increasingly become part of the discourse on race relations, with blacks seeking greater public acknowledgement of white complicity in apartheid. Some whites, organised under the auspices of the 'Home To All Campaign', signed a statement acknowledging the benefits they had derived from apartheid, even as they had battled with the Government in their own lives. These whites included struggle veterans such as Carl Niehaus, jailed for 15 years; Albie Sachs, who lost an arm and eye in an assassination attempt by a South African security police hit squad; and veteran anti-apartheid campaigner, Beyers Naude. The campaigners did not, however, collect a large number of signatures, an indication perhaps of lethargy or apathy in the political culture of whites. Or perhaps it reflected a refusal in the white community to accept any responsibility for South Africa's recent past. Many white politicians lamented the focus on the past with programmes such as affirmative action being presented as reverse racism.

Such responses stem from the formulaic, symmetric formulations of racism in South Africa. Peller (1995) has examined the genealogy of the concept of non-racial integration within the history of enlightenment universalism of the eighteenth century. In this history, racism is seen as an irrational prejudice which manifests itself through discrimination based on an arbitrary quality – such as skin colour. And because any individual is capable of irrationality, reverse racism is also possible. Black calls for affirmative action are in that sense then seen as being as irrational as, for example, Verwoerd's suggestion that blacks are inferior to whites. They are simply the other side of the same Verwoerdian coin. To be sure, a number of white people have sought to transcend the limits of liberalism by reaching out to black communities in a non-patronising manner. In a newspaper article entitled 'White racists raise your hands', Carl Niehaus, former ANC MP and then-Ambassador to the Netherlands, urged white people to show humility and admit that they come from a racist past in which they benefited on the backs of blacks:

> the underlying implications of the lack of preparedness to accept, and confront oneself with, the full evil of and depravity of apartheid has become a stumbling block for continued transformation in South Africa. As long as the deep and unmitigated racism that was the heart and essence of apartheid is denied by a substantial part of the white community, it will become impossible for them to become part of the new South Africa. (*City Press* 02.10.02)

Despite such appeals it is still not clear which way the tide of white political culture will ultimately go – towards a greater appreciation of playing a more active role in ameliorating the historic injustices of apartheid in their name, or towards more absolution for the past.

The race factor in white politics

One of the earliest cracks in the rainbow imagery of the new democratic dispensation was provided by the NP's decision to leave the GNU. This was not necessarily an intentional attempt to break the spirit of racial reconciliation. After all, the NP did what most coalition partners do when they are uncomfortable with the policies of the majority party. However, the break had the effect of signaling a further racialisation of South African politics. For one thing, the withdrawal led to a sharp fall in share values on the Johannesburg Stock Exchange, as well as a drop in the currency value of the Rand. This reflected the racial biases of the global financial community. Much the same thing had happened when Trevor Manuel became the first black Finance Minister in South African history.

In opposition, the NP seized on the issue of crime as the major public policy challenge facing the country. In everyday discourse blacks saw in this an attempt to depict black people as criminals and whites as the sudden victims of a lack of protection under the new black government. The message of crime reverberated around the world in newspaper headlines and television footage. Black people complained that they had been terrorised by criminals for ages without anyone as much as raising a voice about that, and that in the new era they still constituted the majority victims of crime. And yet the issue was represented as an onslaught on white South Africa.

No sooner had the NP entered the opposition space than it received a challenge for that space from the predominantly English-speaking liberal DP. The DP has its origins in the Progressive Party, which was formed in 1959 as a breakaway from the then official opposition party, the United Party. It later became the Progressive Federal Party. It established its credentials as a parliamentary opposition to the NP, first through the sole representation of Helen Suzman, and later under the charismatic leadership of Frederik van Zyl Slabbert.

The post-apartheid DP was under the leadership of Tony Leon. His ambition was for the DP to emerge as the official opposition after the second national elections in 1999. Leon argued that the DP had not sullied itself by going into the GNU. It had remained an independent and fierce critic of the government, and that was exactly the kind of opposition the ANC needed to confront. This hard-edged, confrontational style provided the essence of the DP's so-called 'fight back' campaign against the ANC. Leon's strident and uncompromising politics worked. It attracted white voters disillusioned with the NP's dalliance with the ANC. They, as well as other liberals and conservative Afrikaners, joined the DP and turned it into South Africa's official opposition. Leon was unapologetic about the right-wing inflow into the DP. In an interview in July 1998 with the conservative *Focus* magazine, mouthpiece of the Helen Suzman Foundation, Leon described whites as a minority that was now being excluded under the new democracy. His party's strategy was to exploit the *gatvol* factor among these 'excluded' minorities, and then reach out to black voters.

The strategy worked. In the 1999 elections, the NNP suffered a tremendous setback, with its share of the vote dropping from 20 per cent in 1994 to seven per cent, while the DP's jumped from 1,7 per cent in 1994 to ten per cent. These gains notwithstanding, the ruling ANC still obtained a massive 66 per cent of the vote. With numbers so lopsided in favour of the ANC, it quickly became clear to the opposition that the best strategy was to come together, especially around municipal elections. To this end, the DP and NNP coalesced into the DA. The strategy worked to a degree and in the 2000 municipal elections the DA gathered about 25 per cent of the total vote. The ANC described the new alliance as a racist ploy to fight a black government at all costs, even labelling the DA's black chairman, Joe Seremane, as yet another bantustan leader (ANC statement 26.06.2000).

This accusation against Seremane was a reflection of what by 2001 was becoming a worrying trend within the governing party and within the debate on race. Increasingly, white critics of the government were being labelled as racists, and black critics as reactionaries and counter-revolutionaries. This name-calling happened particularly around the questioning of government's policies on HIV/AIDS and Zimbabwe. Even Jeremy Cronin, a longstanding member of the liberation movement who expressed some critical comments in an interview with an Irish journalist, was accused by ANC leaders of presenting himself as a white knight out to save the blacks in the ANC. He was eventually forced into an humiliating apology. Likewise, the respected black academic and immunologist Professor William Makgoba, whom Mbeki had backed in the leadership fight at Wits, was rebuked and harassed for his questioning of the HIV/AIDS dissidents who were advising government on its AIDS policy. Delivering The ZK Matthews Lecture at the University of Fort Hare on 12 October 2001, President Mbeki, in what was seen as an allusion to his HIV/AIDS stance, criticised those who sought to depict black people as germ carriers:

> And thus does it happen that others who consider themselves to
> be our leaders take to the streets carrying their placards, to
> demand that because we are germ carriers, and human beings of a
> lower order that cannot subject its passions to reason, we must
> perforce adopt strange opinions, to save a depraved and diseased
> people from perishing from self-inflicted disease.

What had started as a legitimate questioning of the racial assumptions of the
reconciliation process had, by 2001, seemingly degenerated into a game of
racial name-calling.

Conclusion: the limits of the reconciliation discourse

The post-apartheid discourse of racial reconciliation was perhaps necessary
for the stable transition to democracy. Mandela's overtures and assurances to
the white community worked insofar as they averted a white backlash,
whether in the form of right-wing military revolt or just sheer lack of co-operation with the new regime. In that respect, South Africa has avoided the fate
of some other settler-type colonies where the white colonists went so far as to
rip out telephones and remove light bulbs before leaving for their mother
countries. Even though a significant number of skilled white and Indian
South Africans have emigrated since 1994, the great majority of non-African
South Africans have stayed. The theme of reconciliation has also helped draw
the favourable attention of the international community in a period when
other societies in transition, such as some of those of the former Soviet Union
and Eastern European bloc, were in chaos and engulfed in bloody conflict.

This politics of reconciliation is deeply lodged within the dominant motif of
the ANC's politics, a motif that centres on the inclusion and accommodation
of peoples of all races. It is of no small significance that the opening line of the
ANC's most important policy document, the Freedom Charter, reads 'South
Africa belongs to all who live in it black and white.' However, the ANC has
never articulated the detailed terms of this political inclusiveness. O'Meara's
description of Mandela's inaugural speech as 'a moment of absolution and
unity the likes of which the country had not known since the first white settlement at the Cape 342 years ago' (1996: 414) is in that sense very apt. Even
though Mandela himself became exasperated by the lack of co-operation and
reciprocity from the white community, he remained true to his conception of
reconciliation as reaching out to the white population.

Mbeki's departure from that model has had its pros and cons. He has tried to define or redefine the terms of reconciliation. The effect, however, has been that many whites regard this as a form of reverse racism. But, as Sampson noted in his biography of Nelson Mandela, this was an inevitable step in holding whites to account for the country's past history. However, Mbeki's otherwise legitimate transformative approach to reconciliation has been marred by the use of race as a shield against criticism. The challenge going forward is to come back to the very necessary issue of racial transformation without resorting to racial name-calling of opponents, black or white. Whether the NNP is the partner for putting the issues of race on the agenda or whether this is yet another case of 'a marriage made in hell' is still unclear. It will become clearer with time. As for the DA, it is interesting to note that it has shifted its rhetoric from the 'fight back' mode and now presents itself as a party for all the people. What its future role in race relations will be is uncertain.

The issue of racial reconciliation is still an open and vexed one, made more so by the struggle for power at various levels of government and the shifting nature of coalition politics. In some ways it could be argued that these struggles for political power with their cross-racial alliances are resulting in a lessening of racial tensions as individuals and political parties form coalitions around common issues. But race is also being used at times to buttress those in power and to mobilise sectarian interests. It remains an open question as to which way the absolutely necessary discourse on race and racism in South Africa will go in the years ahead.

References

Bernstein, H (1991) The breakable thread, *The Southern African Review of Books*, 3.

Frederikse, J (1990) *The unbreakable thread: Non-racialism in South Africa*. London: Zed.

Mandela, N (1994) *Nelson Mandela's statement after voting in South Africa's first democratic election*. Available on http://www.anc.org.za/ancdocs/history/mandela/1994/sp940427.html.

Ndebele, N (2002) The African National Congress and the policy of non-racialism: A study of the membership issue, *Politikon* 29 (2): 133–146.

O'Meara, D (1996) *Forty lost years: The apartheid state and the politics of the National Party 1948–1994*. Johannesburg: Ravan.

Peller, G (1995) Race consciousness, in D Danielsen & K Engle (eds.) *After identity: A reader in law and culture*. New York: Routledge.

Sampson, A (1999) *Mandela: The authorized biography*. Johannesburg: Jonathan Ball.

The state of local government: Third-generation issues

Doreen Atkinson

The South African local government sphere has seen vast changes since 1990. During this tumultuous period, a phase of community-based resistance was followed by a complete redesign of local government. The heady period of constitutional negotiations (1992–1996) has been followed by a more businesslike concern with municipal delivery, especially to address questions of poverty, infrastructure backlogs, the need for economic development, and the consequences of HIV/AIDS. This paper will argue that the creation of developmental local government, as envisaged in the *White Paper on Local Government*, has created unforeseen challenges and difficulties.[1] The requirements of local development are only gradually becoming understood and it is likely that the entire intergovernmental order will have to make developmental municipal government a key priority.

The apartheid legacy

Towards the end of the 1980s the municipal order was in a profound state of disarray. It had become one of the most visible and controversial aspects of the apartheid order. Municipalities were constituted on a racial basis, as white local authorities, black local authorities and coloured or Indian management committees. This design was seriously out of gear with the spatial, financial and political circumstances. Spatially, the central business districts' (CBD) tax bases were invariably located within white local authorities, which meant that black, coloured and Indian local governments were systematically starved of funding. The payment culture was virtually non-existent because of poverty. But these problems paled into insignificance in the face of political resistance. A wide array of civic associations, linked to other oppositional movements, kept resurfacing, despite the most draconian measures. A long-term beneficial consequence of these harrowing experiences is that a class of local political leaders emerged who were committed to community and municipal development. These leaders were the natural inheritors of the local government system after the first municipal elections in 1995.

The anti-apartheid period laid the foundation of post-apartheid local government in many ways. First, the many years of government-imposed fragmentation created a strong interest in the concept of integration (i.e. spatial integration and functional or sectoral integration). This laid the groundwork for the Integrated Development Planning (IDP) philosophy that emerged many years later. Second, and more negatively, it created a heritage of non-payment and popular suspicion about financial extractions at local level. This is only now being combated, to some degree successfully. Third, and perhaps most importantly, it drew attention to the importance of local government in contrast to many other centralising trends within the country. This laid the groundwork for the concept of a sphere of local government, which is one of the foundation stones of the current constitutional system of intergovernmental relations.

Three distinct phases or generations of change have taken place. First-generation issues (1995–1998) concerned primarily political questions such as the amalgamation of racially-defined municipalities, in the light of the *Local Government Transition Act* of 1993. This phase was explicitly transitional, and there was no overarching paradigm for steering municipal capacity-building, with the result that local governments around the country developed very different styles of functioning. At the time analysts lacked a normative paradigm to evaluate or guide the process of amalgamation, and studies tended to focus on the minutiae of particular municipalities.

Second-generation issues began to be raised as part of the 1998 Local Government White Paper process. The compiling of the preliminary discussion document, and subsequently the *Green Paper* and *White Paper on Local Government* (Department of Constitutional Development 1998) were highly consultative processes. These debates attempted to flesh out the meaning of the constitutional provisions on local government. During this phase, overarching normative questions were addressed, culminating in the key concept of developmental local government. This period provided a valuable window for the design of long-term local government policy in terms of the *White Paper on Local Government* (1998), which remains a feat of far-reaching thought and consensus-seeking. This phase culminated in the drafting of the *Municipal Structures Act* (1998) and the *Municipal Systems Act* (2000). It was taken forward in the redemarcation of local government and the election of new municipalities in December 2000. Unlike the first-generation phase, the second-generation phase emphasised the overall normative vision and rationale of local government.

Third-generation issues have prevailed since January 2001 (see for example, DBSA 2000; DPLG Ministerial Advisory Committee 2001). These concern questions of practical development management, within the normative framework of the *White Paper* and key legislation. Third-generation issues concern the desirable outputs of municipal activity (i.e. municipal developmental policies and programmes), as well as which activities should be conducted (for example, by means of integrated planning, public participation and alternative service delivery).

It was only in December 2000 – a full six years after the enactment of the Interim Constitution of 1994 – that fully-fledged democratic local and district councils were elected. This gave most municipalities a period to figure out some of the new third-generation ground rules of the developmental game. The December 2000 elections were a watershed because full-blown democracy was achieved for the first time at local level. In the majority of municipalities this meant that the ANC achieved complete supremacy and, in a few other municipalities, politics remain furiously contested between the ANC and smaller opposition parties. In 2002, the political order at local government level has not yet settled down fully, and many councillors are still grappling with their new roles and political responsibilities.

Post-apartheid reconstruction: the development challenge

The term 'developmental local government' was coined in the *Local Government White Paper* (1998): 'Developmental local government is local government committed to working with citizens and groups within the community to find sustainable ways to meet their social, economic and material needs, and improve the quality of their lives' (1998: 17). Furthermore, the *White Paper* continues, 'developmental local government' has four interrelated characteristics: (1) maximising social development and economic growth; (2) integrating and co-ordinating development activities of a variety of actors; (3) democratising development by empowering communities to participate meaningfully in development; and (4) providing leadership, promoting the building of 'social capital', and creating opportunities for learning and information-sharing (1998: 18–22).

The two key pieces of municipal legislation (the *Municipal Structures Act* and the *Municipal Systems Act*) have given substance to these characteristics by innovations such as ward committees, cross-border municipalities, a code of conduct for councillors, integrated development planning, performance management, development partnerships, and alternative service delivery.

A new culture of municipal governance is envisaged by recent municipal legislation. New service-delivery models include strategies that should be customer oriented; have a strong emphasis on performance; measure performance within the organisation, as well as against other municipalities and private-sector organisations; work in partnerships in service delivery with the broad community, including the private sector; provide for continuous evaluation of results through performance audits; and use results as a basis for continuous quality improvement.

These are formidable strategic guidelines for new municipalities in a developing country. Furthermore, a range of new institutional innovations have added to the difficulties of democratic and administrative consolidation. The Department of Provincial and Local Government (DPLG) has not drafted adequate policies and programmes to provide administrative support to municipalities and, in general, there has been a substantial policy void.[2] One of the challenges has been the redemarcation of municipalities' jurisdictions.

The travails of demarcation

After the demarcation of December 2000, municipalities faced the huge task of administrative amalgamation. Typically, each municipality now consists of several towns, as well as their rural hinterlands. Various national grants were made available to build municipalities' administrative capacity. These are, first, the Local Government Support Grant, aimed at assisting medium and small municipalities experiencing severe financial problems to restructure their financial positions and organisations over the medium term; second, the Financial Management Grant made available by National Treasury to promote reforms to municipal financial management practices, including the modernisation of budgeting, financial management, accounting, monitoring systems, and implementation of the *Municipal Finance Management Bill*, which is to be passed soon; and third, the Restructuring Grant made available by the National Treasury, which is aimed at modernising large municipalities.

These grants have been far from sufficient. The impression is gained that the sheer scale of the administrative integration process caused by the new demarcation, has been radically underestimated by decision-makers. The integration of administrative, financial and information technology systems of several previously autonomous municipal administrations has proven to be time-consuming, complex and difficult. Some of these problems are due to the sheer logistics of very different municipal administrative systems. For example, staff with very different task descriptions, and who received different levels of remuneration, have had to be integrated into a common organogram. The new municipalities have had to integrate different tariff structures for municipal services, as well as different levels of municipal rates. Different credit control policies and indigent policies had to be aligned. Asset registers and insurance policies had to be consolidated – often in municipalities with poor systems of data management. Rural municipalities, with few skilled staff, have been particularly hard hit by these organisational changes.

The fact that many of the old municipalities (Transitional Local Councils [TLCs]) were bankrupt did not help matters since that created a double whammy – institutional amalgamation and financial reorientation needed to be undertaken simultaneously. In fact, in many municipalities, the TLCs with positive bank balances have found their financial reserves used to pay the outstanding debts of other TLCs within the new municipalities.

There is a great need for research on what the DPLG's support grants were actually spent on, and whether it was adequate to meet the needs of municipalities. Part of the difficulty is that the actual impact of consultants on municipal processes may vary widely, in terms of the uptake of consultants' advice by municipal officials and councillors. But it is also due to DPLG's evident lack of understanding of the real dynamics taking place in municipalities, and therefore the support mechanisms do not always address the real political or administrative problems.

Financial consultants have been appointed in several municipalities, under the Municipal Support Programme (MSP). In several interviews in the Northern Cape and Free State, many municipal officials did not speak highly of the support provided by MSP consultants. MSP consultants tend to be financial experts, and some of them do not have sufficient grounding in municipal administration and development management to be able to make useful restructuring proposals. Some debate needs to be undertaken on the selection of MSP consultants, possibly with a view to teaming them up with development specialists. A much greater focus on capacity-building needs to be created – but the effective and flexible programmes still need to be designed.

What should municipalities do?

Curiously, more than two years after the December 2000 municipal elections, there is still little clarity on the allocation of powers and functions to South Africa's two tiers of local government – local and district municipalities. Before 1996, district municipalities had very limited functions, viz. allocation of capital grants (derived from their levy revenue) to municipalities, and management of a few district-level 'bulk' functions (eg. large-scale water supply).

There are now clear signs of a rethink of this allocation of powers and functions. Two schools of thought have emerged:

○   District municipalities should serve as the primary developmental tier: This approach argues that most developmental functions should be concentrated at district municipality level. This has three key advantages. First, it is more cost-efficient to build up developmental capacity at the 47 district municipalities, rather than at the 231 local municipalities. Second, it enables a degree of redistribution from the wealthier towns within a district municipality's jurisdiction, to poorer areas. Third, some development functions are best addressed at district-wide level. Some functions involve several local municipalities (eg. district-based tourism), whereas other functions can be done at scale if done within several municipalities simultaneously (eg. rapid roll-out of sanitation projects).

○   Local municipalities as the primary developmental tier: A contrasting point of view is that most developmental functions are deeply labour-intensive, requiring a great deal of personal contact between programme managers and communities. This would require a primary role for local municipalities (and, possibly, for branch offices of local municipalities). An additional argument is that the main virtue of local municipalities is precisely that they are 'local', and thus better attuned to the specific needs of localities. Local diversity may require different local developmental policies and programmes and, ultimately, local municipalities should be politically answerable to their communities for the developmental choices they make. This argument puts the developmental ball squarely within the local municipalities' court.

The argument for the primacy of local municipalities is much more attuned to the policy position as spelt out in the *Local Government White Paper*, as well as subsequent government policy documents.[3] A key argument was made then that delivery of municipal services should be located as close as possible to the communities the services are meant to serve. In the same vein, it should be noted that district municipalities do not have wards or ward councillors, with the result that the interests of specific geographic areas cannot be carried forward easily to district municipalities.

Currently, the approach by institutions such as the DPLG and the Demarcation Board is that functions should be allocated to institutions where 'capacity' (a term that seldom seems to be defined) exists. This is not a particularly helpful approach since inherited capacity may not be located at the most appropriate level. An alternative approach would be to consider the nature of a function, and the type of developmental activities associated with it. For example, it may be argued that hard (infrastructural) services may well be more effectively delivered at a district level (i.e. to achieve economies of scale), whereas soft (human) services may be more appropriately placed at local level. A different example is the case of local economic development (LED): attracting investment capital may be more effectively done at district level (i.e. marketing the district as a whole as an investment destination), whereas poverty-alleviation projects may be better placed at local level (i.e. promoting close interaction with indigent individuals or groups of poor people).

The argument made here is that administrative effectiveness has to be decided on a service-by-service basis. If each service – as well as all the subcomponents of each service – is examined, it may become fairly evident which services should be provided at which level. Take environmental management as an example: it can be argued that, whereas littering and environmental awareness may be best dealt with at local level, a district-based air pollution strategy may be better located at district municipal level because air pollution may well straddle local boundaries. There is an urgent need for a function-by-function assessment of appropriate allocation of responsibilities.

There is an urgent need for debates and negotiations with various national and provincial line departments on the issue of powers and functions. Unfortunately, the debate has prematurely hardened and has now assumed a distinctively ideological tinge, with different institutions adopting implacable views on the matter. The Department of Water Affairs and Forestry and the

Demarcation Board, for example, have become strong proponents of district municipalities as the key locus of development, whereas many municipalities have opted for defending the powers and functions of local municipalities. The DPLG remains steadfastly ambiguous on the entire matter.

Form should follow function? Creating viable organisational structures

How should a developmental municipality be structured? In many South African municipalities, basic organisational and developmental questions have not been addressed at all – for example, the relationship between municipal head offices and outlying offices; the creation of co-operative mechanisms among municipal departments; and improving municipalities' public relations within their communities.

According to the old adage, 'form should follow function'. This means that the restructuring of municipalities should be based on their developmental goals. In this context the emphasis has been placed primarily on the drafting of IDPs, on the grounds that IDPs should be the foundation for municipal structure.

The argument that form should follow function is, generally, a good one. Presumably, organisational design should depend on the organisational functions that are identified. However, in the case of municipalities during 2001–2002, it is possible to argue that the redemarcation of local government should have been dealt with first, and that the basic amalgamation of TLCs and Transitional Rural Councils into new municipalities should have preceded any discussion of either form or function. With the benefit of hindsight it is possible to argue that, during the first two to three years after amalgamation, the new municipalities' first and primary task was to continue with the provision of the services for which the erstwhile TLCs and Transitional Rural Councils were responsible. The inordinate focus on drafting IDPs has drawn attention away from this basic requirement of administrative competence.

According to the *Municipal Systems Act* (sections 51 and 153), a municipality must 'establish and organise its administration in a manner that would enable the municipality to … be performance-oriented and focused on … its developmental duties as required by section 153 of the Constitution.' But there is still no clarity on what a developmental municipality should look like.

A few observations can be made regarding smaller and more rural municipalities. Traditionally, smaller municipalities in South Africa consist of three departments: administration or corporate services, finance, and technical. The technical department is often the most important delivery department at present since it carries responsibility for the ongoing operations and maintenance of municipal infrastructure, roads, pavements and open space.

By default, technical departments usually become responsible for development – which is not surprising owing to the heavy bias towards infrastructural projects (such as projects funded by the Consolidated Municipal Infrastructure Programme or the Department of Water Affairs and Forestry). These departments are given the nominal responsibility of overseeing (they would prefer to call it 'project management') the building of things that are usually undertaken by external service providers. The real oversight (project management) responsibility often lies with the consultants (engineers, architects or other professionals who designed the project). Thus the technical department is responsible for managing and ensuring compliance with massive contracts (in terms of volume and complexity), but they lack contract management skills.

This type of structure leaves little scope for real community development to take place on a significant scale. The current system of municipal organisation overloads the senior staff in the finance, administration and technical department. Department heads often become swamped in a variety of projects, usually in addition to their normal line staff functions. Many of these staff members lack project and contract management skills and, in particular, skills of interacting with developing communities. Due to the existing levels of overwork in municipalities – often due to staff cuts, in turn caused by rising wage bills, in turn caused by trade union pressure – many municipalities simply outsource development projects to consultants. While consultants may have specialised knowledge, they cannot offer prolonged support to communities during and after implementation of projects. In rural areas, consultants typically pay fleeting visits to project sites. They are also very expensive.

There are other management pathologies. One of the paradoxes of local government is that municipalities spend too much money on the wages and salaries bill (more than 40 per cent of their budgeted operating expenditure, due to increased salaries at all levels) because they have bloated administrations but, at the same time, a lot of work (most of it of a routine nature) does not get done. They have too many people with inappropriate skills. A second part of the problem is the lack of proper supervision. Many municipalities have top management and frontline workers with almost no middle-level management and supervisors.

Also, managers do not manage, for numerous reasons: because they do not know how to manage, or because councillors manage their departments on their behalf, or because the trade unions have become the *de facto* manager, or because they do not care, or because they are spending all their time assisting underskilled subordinates. A further reason is that they do not face the consequences of poor or non-existent management – nothing bad will happen whether they do or they don't. This is because many senior officials, municipal managers and councils do not know how to evaluate staff performance.

In this context, senior officials find themselves dealing with all aspects of project and contract management – liaising with consultants, dealing with beneficiaries, managing public participation, trouble-shooting community conflicts, interacting with donors and writing project reports – often without significant experience in project or programme management.

An alternative scenario is for municipalities to be primarily output-based. Such municipalities would focus on developmental outputs such as infra-structural projects, poverty alleviation, community projects or investment promotion. In smaller municipalities this may involve the creation of a single, strong developmental department as the primary centrepiece of the municipal organisation.

In such an output-oriented municipality, the administrative, financial and technical departments would be primarily aimed at supporting the developmental department. Their allocation of resources would be substantially project-oriented. The development department would be able to call on the supporting departments for resources, in different combinations, on different programmes or projects.

It should be noted that the developmental department should not be a modest sideline affair, begging the other line departments for resources to do its job. On the contrary, it should be the flagship department, probably with the largest number of senior and middle-level staff (although the technical department is likely to retain the largest number of staff, to undertake infrastructure maintenance).

The main point is that developmental municipalities need developmental staff. Such staff should have some qualifications and experience in development management, programme management or project management. In a typical smaller or more rural municipality it is possible to envisage a head of development department, assisted by at least three project managers. In the context of amalgamated municipalities, such project managers should be spatially distributed, i.e. located within each town or rural settlement so that they can offer hands-on project guidance and support. It goes without saying that the appointment of development staff should avoid the pitfalls of political patronage, and focus strongly on their experience within development organisations and programmes.

Linking centres and satellites: the spatial structure of new municipalities

The new municipalities are geographically much larger than before. In the Northern Cape most local municipalities consist of three to four towns, and have a diameter of up to 150 km. In the Free State, huge local municipalities were created – the most radical case is that of Kopanong, which combines nine erstwhile municipalities and has a diameter of 150 km.

The challenge of administrative amalgamation in such contexts is huge. The challenge of effective development administration is even more daunting. All lessons in development management (see, for example, Lowndes 1996) point to the fact that only a limited number of development functions can be performed from far away. Development, especially in very underdeveloped contexts, is highly labour-intensive. Mentors and guides and managers have to be available regularly, often at unscheduled times, to promote local leadership skills, build institutions, deal with practical problems, and give advice to beneficiaries.

Despite such obvious developmental pressures for spatial devolution of functions within municipalities, this issue has rarely been put on the agenda. Most municipalities are still too engrossed in amalgamating the administrations of the erstwhile TLCs to think through the far-reaching implications – in particular, the developmental tasks and staff – required for the implementation of their IDPs. At a more fundamental level, however, there is a lack of political clarity about the merits of devolution of functions. Many councillors are more concerned about consolidating unified municipalities than contemplating the spatial devolution of functions. In some municipalities, councillors believe that spatial devolution will amount to some kind of fragmentation or balkanisation of communities within a single municipality. Clearly, some investigation and debate are required about the merits and problems associated with the spatial distribution of municipal capacity and functions.

Integration of municipal departments: a challenge for municipal managers

Whether or not a development department is created, the need for municipal departments to co-operate in the implementation of development projects remains. In small municipal establishments this need not be a severe problem since most of the senior and middle-level officials will probably be able to co-ordinate their activities informally.

However, as soon as IDPs are implemented in earnest and a development implementation begins to be performed at scale, it is likely that the development department will grow. This department will need constant inputs from the support departments (administration, finance and technical). This creates a classical problem of cross-departmental co-ordination and co-operation. For example, an LED or poverty alleviation or land reform project may require financial inputs (capital or operating expenditure), administrative inputs (eg. staff, training, buildings or facilities), and technical inputs (eg. equipment and vehicles).

Elements of 'matrix organisation' will be needed to resolve this situation. This means that specific programme or project managers will be given the responsibility for liaising directly with senior and middle-level officials within the support departments. Clearly, there is scope for clashes and confusion as support officials become subject to the demands of their line department heads and the programme managers simultaneously. However, given the multi-sectoral and multi-disciplinary nature of most development projects, there is simply no other way to do this. A way has to be found of giving programme managers sufficient authority to lever resources from the support departments.

Each municipality will probably resolve this problem in its own way. Various suggestions can be made for possible solutions. First, all programmes and projects need to become cost centres with their own budgets. Second, the resources of municipal support departments need to be costed (eg. rate per hour of staff time, and vehicles). Third, municipal support departments need to specify, in their annual budgets, the amount of resources they can provide to each development programme or project. Fourth, programme or project managers will need to do their own cost accounting. Finally, a uniform, easy to implement and understandable financial management system should be introduced to assist head office staff and branch managers to manage revenue and expenditure.

Co-ordination and mutual adjustment of priorities will be the order of the day. This will require a high degree of leadership from the municipal manager, who will need to be sufficiently and constantly informed of project require-ments and dynamics. Turf jealousies and rivalries about resources will need to be sorted out amicably.

Clearly, this approach will require a high degree of management skill on the part of the municipal manager (or his or her nominee). Municipal managers must exert a strong integrative force to secure consensus and co-operation between the spatially-based development officers and the head office staff of the municipal line departments. Such municipal managers need to have suffi-cient developmental knowledge and experience, as well as personal qualities, to integrate the spatial and vertical lines of authority within a municipality.

Section 55 of the *Municipal Systems Act* makes rigorous demands on munic-ipal managers. Managers are tasked with (and held accountable for) 'the formation and development of an economical, effective, efficient and accountable administration', which is equipped to carry out a municipality's IDP, which is also operating according to the municipality's performance management system and which is responsive to the needs of the local commu-nity. Clearly, the Act envisages the appointment of managers who have substantial abilities regarding strategic development management.

In this context, the low level of development skills and expertise of many municipal managers is a cause for concern. In the light of the debate on third-generation issues in municipal government, an important issue will be an examination of the types of skills and experiences which should be obligatory for municipal managers.

Frontline staff – municipalities' best-kept secret

Much of the emphasis regarding municipal restructuring has been placed on the higher echelons of municipal establishments. The role of the frontline staff is sel-dom discussed. Nevertheless, this is where the municipality meets the citizen/

resident/consumer, or put differently – 'where the rubber hits the road'. The question of a positive client interface is a critical and deeply neglected matter.

A recent study of a Northern Cape municipality (Bekker & van Zyl 2002) makes several useful recommendations: a community education and development programme should be undertaken as a matter of urgency; training and development programmes for councillors and staff should be undertaken to change the mindset of the municipality towards client service; where development projects have been undertaken, after-care programmes should be provided. This should include monitoring and evaluation of client opinions. Furthermore, councillors should meet with ward committees on a regular basis. Such meetings should be synchronised with council meetings. Agendas and minutes of council meetings should form the basis of discussions at meetings of ward committees. Training for ward committee members should be provided. Venues for council meetings should be rotated between the various towns of the municipality, and this should include roadshows in each town (including meetings with ward committees, with interest groups, council meetings, and community feedback meetings).

Consultative strategic planning process should be undertaken in conjunction with key social and economic interests in the municipality (eg. agriculture, business, HIV/AIDS groups, SAPS). Innovative communication methods should be designed, eg. newsletters, road shows, and informed communication by frontline staff. A public relations officer should be appointed, who should issue a regular municipal newsletter, co-ordinate press releases, act as secretary for ward committees, and organise community meetings. One-stop service desks should be provided at head office and all the satellite offices. Officials will need multi-skilled training for these tasks. Community members should be provided with guidance in identifying development projects. Communication with all national and provincial line departments should be promoted.

This formidable list illustrates the extent of cultural changes that many municipalities will need to experience before they become truly responsive to community needs for services, information and empowerment.

Information management, monitoring and evaluation: the costs of ignorance

Information management will become an increasingly important aspect of municipal functioning for at least two reasons: (1) the requirements of effective planning in the IDPs, and (2) adhering to the requirements of performance management. For example, section 46 of the *Municipal Systems Act* requires that a municipality must prepare an annual report for each financial year, showing its performance in comparison with targets. Such reporting will inevitably require sufficient information regarding baseline conditions (i.e. socio-economic and infrastructural conditions before development projects are undertaken), as well as information on the implementation and impacts of development programmes.

Many municipalities encountered their first information-related difficulties when the IDPs were drawn up. IDPs must include an analysis of the current level of development in a municipal area. One of the many benefits of the IDP process is that it has exposed how little information municipalities have. For example, many councillors – and even senior officials – have only the vaguest idea of how many residents live within their jurisdictions. Senior staff who are concerned about information gaps acknowledge that they simply do not have the information, and deplore the outdated and unreliable nature of the information that is available. Consequently, planning is mostly based on opinion and not fact. The urban bias of many IDPs compounds this problem. Owing to the accidental exclusion of rural communities from some IDP processes, the level of development or, in many cases the lack of development, in rural areas remains very poorly understood.

In the case of water and sanitation infrastructure, for example, three key types of information are necessary:

○ Demographics: how many people live in the municipality? Where (rural or urban)? What is their level of income? This is needed to determine both levels of service as well as appropriate levels of subsidies to the poor.

○ Financial management information: are water bills sent to all households? Are all indigent households listed? Are all erven listed, and does the municipality have an address for each household? (What about informal settlements, i.e. before township establishment?) Do all households actually receive their bills? Are all meters read? (Households that do not receive bills, and therefore do not pay for services, are a massive drain on the finances of the municipality). Is there proper budgeting (effective cash flow) for operation and maintenance of water services infrastructure?

○ Physical information: where are the pipes underground? Are there infrastructure maps?[4] Are there bulk and reticulation meters? How much water flows into the system and is used by households? How much sewerage water is transported to oxidation dams? How much water loss takes place in the reticulation network? How many spares and supplies are kept in the store?

Several practical issues need to be considered when setting up a monitoring and evaluation system. What theoretical methodologies will be employed? Is data quantitative or qualitative? How will be information be processed, and how will the reporting system function? Will data be verified for quality? What staffing and financial resources will be made available? What level and quality of data analysis will take place? How, and to whom, will information be distributed? How will information actually be utilised in municipal decision-making? How will feedback be ensured?

There is an urgent need for possible information systems to be designed and tested, possibly in a few pilot municipalities, and then transferred to all municipalities. This must include not only computers and software, but funding for information management staff.

Local governments as political systems

Service delivery is only one side of the coin. The other is effective political representation. Municipalities are polities in their own right. They are not only bureaucratic edifices; they are also elected directly by the citizenry, and party politics plays an important role in municipal governance.

Several consequences flow from this basic fact of municipalities as polities. The first is that the calibre of performance by councillors has to be improved in many municipalities. The second is that relationships between councillors and officials need to be clarified and institutionalised. The third is that the role of other representatives – in particular, ward committees – have to be clarified and institutionalised. And finally, public participation needs to be enhanced and made more effective.

It should be noted that the December 2000 elections were a radically new experience, not only as a result of the new demarcations, but also because they were based on a new political landscape – notably, the protected white, Indian and coloured franchise fell away, and strong majority-party tendencies have emerged.

Many councillors are serving as councillors for the first time. The turnover rate of councillors has been high, with few bringing experience from pre-December 2000. Even where erstwhile councillors have been re-elected, the political dynamics have changed massively, and much of their experience has not been used. In many cases, dominant political parties have selected candidates for councils on criteria other than merit or developmental potential, with the result that councils have become arenas for patronage, turf wars and factionalism.

In the wake of the December 2000 election, new staff appointments have been the order of the day. These have exerted enormous, and often chaotic, influence on the appointment of municipal staff, with the result that the existing fragile skills base of municipalities has been even further eroded. Many of the new appointments have been justified in terms of affirmative action, although the impression is gained that many appointments are also based on political patronage by dominant political parties.

Research in the Northern Cape has shown the serious consequences of poor council-staff relations. In the Karoo district, four of the eight local municipalities have experienced significant periods of virtual breakdown in municipal organisation. In these cases councils have suspended municipal managers, leading to a situation of limbo until the cases are resolved. In two cases, councils want certain senior staff members to leave but do not have the funds to pay them retrenchment packages, and therefore an uneasy and quite unproductive stalemate prevails, with a significant decline in staff morale. In such conditions it is almost impossible to continue with normal municipal activities, let alone initiate any development programmes.

Many councillors are also overwhelmed by the magnitude of their job descriptions, particularly in the light of the prescriptions of the *Municipal Systems Act*. Two provisions have had a dramatic impact on the role of councillors: (1) the relationship between executive councillors (often full-time) and ordinary councillors (typically part-time), and (2) the introduction of ward committees as representative bodies.

As regards the relationship between executive and ordinary councillors, several critical issues are noted by the Ministerial Advisory Committee, which was appointed by the Minister for Provincial and Local Government in 2001 to investigate the problems of local government. The committee's findings make depressing reading. The investigators found that ordinary councillors receive information almost only through caucus structures; ordinary councillors find themselves serving on committees and structures without much purpose, real mandates, or meaningful links to the rest of council or any real powers; and the discrepancy in remuneration between executive councillors and ordinary councillors leads to feelings of exclusivity and complicates deployment to meaningful and demanding roles.

In addition, committee meetings (in the form of portfolio or *ad hoc* committees) are seen as a waste of time because all decision-making powers are effectively centralised at executive level. The discipline, momentum and transparency that previously characterised the standing committee system in large local authorities has not been replaced by any meaningful mechanism, thus resulting in ordinary councillors and officials feeling disempowered and disconnected from meaningful debate and opportunity to influence decision-making. Centralised decision-making at the executive mayoral committee or executive committee level, coupled with a reluctance or inability to agree on sound political and administrative delegations has resulted in decision bottlenecks at the executive mayoral committee or 'exco' level. These decision bottlenecks may have dire consequences for operational efficiency. Council meetings have now become caucus-driven rubber stamps for decisions taken by 'mayco' or 'exco' without any real accountability. Finally, media coverage of council affairs has become restricted to the attendance of open sections of 'exco' meetings, and the interaction between the media and communications officers acting on behalf of the executive.

Ward committees are another emerging political arena, providing a fertile opportunity for communities' interests to be represented. But the practical problems facing ward committees should not be underestimated. Most ward councillors are part-time (in contrast to many councillors elected by proportional representation) and do not have constituency offices or administrative staff. Some wards, particularly in the rural areas, are spread over large distances.

Many municipalities do not have the funding to give administrative support to ward committees. The fact that members of the committees will not be paid for their participation does not help and so it is important to sustain their enthusiasm in other ways.

The legislation provides no more than a general framework for ward committees. Municipalities are meant to provide the specifics – but most have yet to do so. National and provincial regulations and guidelines were meant to help – but these have been slow in coming. Some councillors, understandably, may feel threatened by ward committees who attempt to pressure their councillors into becoming 'delegates' (i.e. bound by narrow ward mandates) instead of 'representatives' (allowed to engage in council debates with an open mind, and allowed to use their discretion). Should councillors be 'delegates' or 'representatives'? The jury is still out on this question.

Ward committees can also become sites of narrow, sectarian, political turf battles, not least within the same political organisation. It cannot be ruled out either that ward committees can become estranged from the residents, and become elitist and self-serving. Ward committees, clearly, have to be managed sensitively.

Impressionistic evidence indicates several problems in the system of ward committees. First, ward committees become *de facto* frontline officials, assisting understaffed municipalities with indigent policies and credit control. This creates an uneasy blurring of representative and official boundaries. Second, some ward committees totally exclude key economic, spatial and racial communities. Third, some ward committees are used by councillors as a source of political patronage. Finally, in some municipalities, ward committees have resulted in the balkanisation of the municipality, and in some cases a ward committee in one geographic area does not have the right to voice opinions with regard to issues in other geographic areas.

Ideally, ward committees should be used to mobilise the broadest range of progressive interests in a ward community and ensure their active representation in the municipality. Attempts should be made to ensure representation from civic, development, business, trade union, taxi, women, youth, religious, cultural, professional, sport and other organisations in the committee. Organisations can be clustered and asked to forward representatives for election to the ward committee. Women and rural residents have to be appropriately represented in the committee. While committee members may not be paid salaries, municipalities can consider allocating them modest allowances, where it can be afforded. Effective ward committees will certainly serve to strengthen community participation – and community participation will serve to strengthen ward committees. Managed appropriately, ward committees and political parties can also benefit from each other. Again, if they work properly, ward committees can lessen the burden on ward councillors. A key test of the success of community participation will be the way the ward committees function.

Some serious thinking needs to be devoted to exactly what ward committees should be, and what should be expected of them. They are curious representative devices, with a great deal of potential for both good and harm.

Conclusion

Municipal government in the post-1999 era is in a state of flux. This is nothing new – it has been evolving and transforming relentlessly since 1992. In fact, the remarkable phenomenon is probably the fact that service delivery has – in most communities – continued to take place. This suggests that the inherited municipal system had a great deal of vibrancy, in spite of its apartheid origins; and that the local government order continues to attract people who are determined to make a contribution to their communities.

Nevertheless, it is clear that many municipalities need a helping hand. Changes are taking place simply too fast for many municipalities to assimilate effectively. The challenge to build developmental municipalities is much greater than previously envisaged. The dilemma is that numerous government programmes are already looking to municipalities to be the primary implementation agent of development programmes, and therefore their programmes will falter until strong municipalities are in place. By placing additional expectations on fragile municipalities, those departments are contributing to the strain experienced by municipalities.

In the meantime popular expectations of service delivery are high. There are increasing signs of public dissatisfaction with municipalities and many are steadily losing the political credibility they gained in the December 2000 election. Only a concerted, interdepartmental approach to building municipal capacity will unblock the obstacles to developmental local government.

Notes

1   The paper focuses primarily on non-metropolitan areas.

2   One exception to this negative picture is DPLG's support of the IDP-writing process.

3   For example, the DPLG's *Policy Framework for the Division of Powers and Functions* (July 2000); and the Financial and Fiscal Commission's *Division of Municipal Powers and Functions between District and Local Municipalities*, July 2001.

4   Tales abound of municipalities that have no infrastructure maps. They do not know where the pipes and valves are. Many engineering consultants keep these maps, or

local authorities have lost them. The result is that municipalities have to shut down the whole water system when they do maintenance and repairs.

References

Bekker, K & Van Zyl, N (2002) *Promoting a development-oriented client interface.* Local Government Learning and Support Network/Department for International Development Programme, Northern Cape.

DCD (Department of Constitutional Development) (1998) *Green Paper on Local Government.* Pretoria: DCD.

DCD (1998) *White Paper on Local Government.* Pretoria: DCD.

DPLG (Department of Provincial and Local Government) Ministerial Advisory Committee (2001) *Interim report on the challenges facing local government.* Pretoria: DPLG.

DBSA (Development Bank of South Africa) (2000) *Development report: Building developmental local government.* Midrand: DBSA.

Lowndes, V (1996) Locality and community: choices for local governments, in S Leach, H Davis et al. *Enabling or disabling local government.* Milton Keynes: Open University Press.

Part II: The economy

The state of the economy: A crisis of employment

Nicoli Nattrass

Introduction

In his 'State of the Nation' address in February, President Mbeki (2002) argued that macroeconomic stability had been achieved, the structure of the economy had changed for the better, and that the basis for sustainable growth and poverty alleviation had been laid. In several important respects, the State President is correct. After increasing sharply in the mid-1990s, the budget deficit and total national government debt has fallen as a percentage of gross domestic product (GDP) since 1996,[1] South Africa's export performance and balance of payments situation has improved, and inflation has dropped sharply.[2] These trends are in what Finance Minister Trevor Manuel frequently refers to as South Africa's 'sound economic fundamentals'. Echoing Manuel, Mbeki concluded that 'barring the exchange rate' (which at the time had depreciated in real terms by about one-third since 1994), 'all critical economic indicators have improved' (2002: 11).

What is surprising, however, about this 'State of the Nation' address is that it paid no attention to trends in one very critical economic indicator indeed: employment. In this respect, South Africa's performance has been nothing short of dire. Total formal non-agricultural employment fell by 1,6 per cent in 2001, and has fallen almost every year since 1989. As can be seen in Figure 6.1, overleaf, employment in the mining sector almost halved between 1990 and 2001. Manufacturing employment increased marginally in the mid-1990s, but nosedived thereafter. Public sector employment helped boost overall employment until the mid-1990s. Since 1996, however, public employment has contracted, alongside private sector non-agricultural employment.

The net result of these trends is that between 1990 and 2001, non-agricultural formal employment declined by over 20 per cent. South African non-agricultural employment is now lower than it was 20 years ago. In other words, as far as employment is concerned, things have certainly not improved.

The steady haemorrhaging of jobs in South Africa spells only hardship and suffering for those unable to find work.

Figure 6.1 *Trends in non-agricultural formal employment in the 1990s*

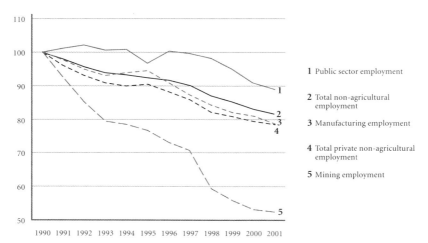

1 Public sector employment

2 Total non-agricultural employment

3 Manufacturing employment

4 Total private non-agricultural employment

5 Mining employment

Source: South African Reserve Bank

South Africa's welfare system provides support for the elderly and the disabled – but nothing for the bulk of the unemployed.[3] The life chances and living standards of entire households are thus compromised when working-age adults cannot find employment.[4] According to the government household and labour force surveys conducted from the mid-1990s onwards, over one-third of those who stated that they wanted jobs reported that they were out of work.[5] This is a socio-economic crisis of major proportions. The failure of the South African economy to expand the number of formal jobs, (let alone provide enough employment growth to absorb new entrants into the labour market), is clearly worthy of being classed as a fundamental and structural problem. Without job creation, South Africa's already high levels of inequality[6] will continue to worsen.[7]

Given the importance of the jobs crisis, this review of the South African economy focuses specifically on trends in unemployment, employment earnings and job creation. It describes the historical roots of unemployment and then turns to a discussion of trends in employment and earnings over the past decade. The chapter concludes with some discussion of policy options.

The rise of unemployment

Until the mid-1970s the South African economy was plagued by chronic labour shortages. In this regard, South Africa experienced the typical sub-Saharan problem of labour-constrained development: either a labour supply had to be created through extra-economic coercive mechanisms, or relatively high wages had to be offered in the capitalist sector (Karshenas 2001). The uniquely South African solution to this problem comprised a set of coercive policies which undermined independent peasant production and channelled relatively cheap African labour to mines, commercial farms and industry via influx control and the labour bureaux system.[8]

Not only was the process of de-agrarianisation and proletarianisation more extensive in South Africa than elsewhere in sub-Saharan Africa, but the pace of industrial development far outstripped the rest of the continent. Development, fuelled in part by gold revenues and foreign capital, sucked labour out of traditional agriculture and facilitated rapid urbanisation. But this engine of growth slowed down sharply in the mid-1970s. Apart from the brief (gold-financed) boom in the early 1980s, the South African economy has performed poorly ever since. This has had serious consequences for average living standards. As can be seen in Figure 6.2, gross national product per capita is lower in real terms in 2001 than it was in 1973.

By the end of the 1970s, open unemployment had become a major problem. Unemployed men crowded the rural labour bureaux in unprecedented numbers, queued outside urban factories, and sat without work in the denuded and overcrowded rural areas. The situation worsened as the economy limped through the late 1980s and early 1990s. At the dawn of democracy in 1994, over one-third of the African labour force was unable to find work (Nattrass 2000). Unemployment is now a (if not the) defining feature of the South African political economy.

A range of economic factors appear to have contributed to this abrupt turn-around in the fortunes of the South African labour market. The most important of these was the slowdown in economic growth from 5,6 per cent per annum in the 1960s, to three per cent in the 1970s, and then to about 1,5 per cent in the 1980s. To some extent, South Africa's slowdown mirrored the end of the long post-war boom in advanced capitalist countries (Armstrong, Glyn & Harrison 1991), although increases in the gold price provided some initial cushioning. But the situation was further complicated in South Africa by developments relating to the general growth strategy.

Figure 6.2 *Real gross national product per capita (1995 prices)*

Source: South African Reserve Bank

From the mid-1920s South Africa had followed a Latin-American style inward-industrialisation strategy. This strategy initially supported strong employment growth in labour-intensive consumer goods industries, but by the 1960s had lost momentum. At that point, rather than opting for more outward-oriented export strategies (as in the East Asian economies), the South African government extended protection upstream into evermore capital-intensive industries. This, together with large-scale strategic investments by the state (eg. Sasol) and negative real interest rates and accelerated depreciation allowances, contributed to rising average capital-intensity in the 1970s,[9] especially in manufacturing (Kaplinsky 1995) and agriculture (Simbi & Aliber 2000).

During the 1970s and early 1980s, the coincidence of rising wages and negative real interest rates meant that the cost of capital relative to labour fell to about half the level it had been in the 1960s (Meintjes 1998). Tax breaks for capital investment further encouraged firms throughout the economy to adopt more labour-saving techniques. The change to positive real interest policies and the depreciation of the Rand in the mid-1980s reversed the downward trend in the user cost of capital, but failed to boost employment growth significantly. Rising levels of industrial conflict may have contributed to this.[10] The net result was that the South African industrial sector became steadily more capital-intensive over time. This can be seen in Figure 6.3, which plots the rise in the manufacturing capital:labour ratio between 1960 and 2001.

Figure 6.3 *Key trends in South African manufacturing, 1960–2001*

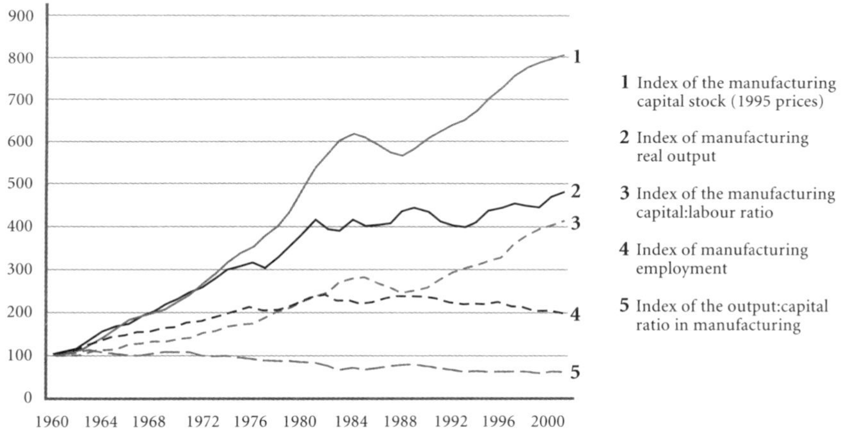

1 Index of the manufacturing capital stock (1995 prices)

2 Index of manufacturing real output

3 Index of the manufacturing capital:labour ratio

4 Index of manufacturing employment

5 Index of the output:capital ratio in manufacturing

Source: South African Reserve Bank

Figure 6.3 shows that it was the dramatic increase in the capital stock which was the primary driving force behind the rise in capital intensity. Manufacturing employment doubled during the 1960s and 1970s – but the real manufacturing capital stock increased almost five-fold over the same period, thus increasing the capital:labour ratio sharply. Most of the increase occurred in the 1970s when conditions were most conducive to capital investment. During the 1980s, there was a sharp drop in the capital stock as political and social unrest dampened investor confidence. This, together with a slight growth in manufacturing employment in the mid- to late-1980s, resulted in the only period in South African economic history when manufacturing actually became more labour-intensive. This trend was, however, short-lived.

The capital stock resumed its rapid growth during most of the 1990s. As this was a time of falling employment, capital-intensive manufacturing increased at its fastest pace ever.

Rapid capital accumulation is, under most circumstances, a positive development. The larger the capital stock, the greater the capacity for production and the larger the surplus available for distribution between capital and labour. Unfortunately, the growth in South Africa's manufacturing capital stock was not that efficient in generating new output. Figure 6.3 shows that the rise in the capital stock exceeded that of real output, with the result that the output:capital ratio (a measure of capital productivity) actually declined. The manufacturing sector was producing 40 per cent less output per unit of capital in 2001 than it was in 1960. This strongly suggests that South Africa's rate of capital accumulation was over-rapid in manufacturing and that resources were wasted in the process. For a middle-income developing country like South Africa where capital is relatively scarce and labour relatively abundant, great care should be taken to use capital as efficiently as possible. Rather than capital productivity increasing alongside employment, the exact opposite took place over the past two decades – with the trend worsening significantly in the 1990s.

One of the contributing factors to this trend was developments in the labour market. Under apartheid, independent African trade unions were denied access to industrial councils (where wage bargaining took place at industry level). In 1979, the Wiehahn Commission recommended full trade union rights for Africans. This was implemented shortly thereafter, and by the mid-1980s, African trade unions were participating in industrial councils (now called 'bargaining councils').[11] African trade unions were able to use their new-found institutional muscle to push up wages – especially for relatively low-paid workers (Hofmeyr 1994). To the extent that such wage pressures encouraged firms to adopt labour-saving techniques, these trends would have contributed to the increase in capital-intensity.[12]

Another factor behind the rise in unemployment was structural change in the South African economy – and in particular the decline in the gold mining industry. The major site of job losses was in the manufacturing and (especially) mining sectors. Employment grew in the other private sector activities (most notably in commerce, finance, real estate and business services) and in the public sector (until the early 1990s). However, this growth was not enough to prevent an overall decline in formal non-agricultural employment.

Wages, employment and profitability: 1990–2001

Those who lost employment (or failed to find it) were the big losers in the 1990s. By contrast, most of the employed and owners of capital did relatively well. Figure 6.4 shows that real average remuneration rose as employment fell during the 1990s. Given that average labour productivity rose over the same period, one can assume that it was the relatively skilled workers who retained their jobs and experienced increasing real wages.

How have these trends affected capitalists? On the one hand, firms have had to contend with sharp increases in labour costs. On the other hand, they have been able to secure an increase in labour productivity. By restructuring and down-sizing their workforces, they have ensured that each remaining worker contributes more to output than had been the case when employment was higher. This has been good for profitability.

Figure 6.4 *Index of labour productivity, employment, average wages and the profit share*

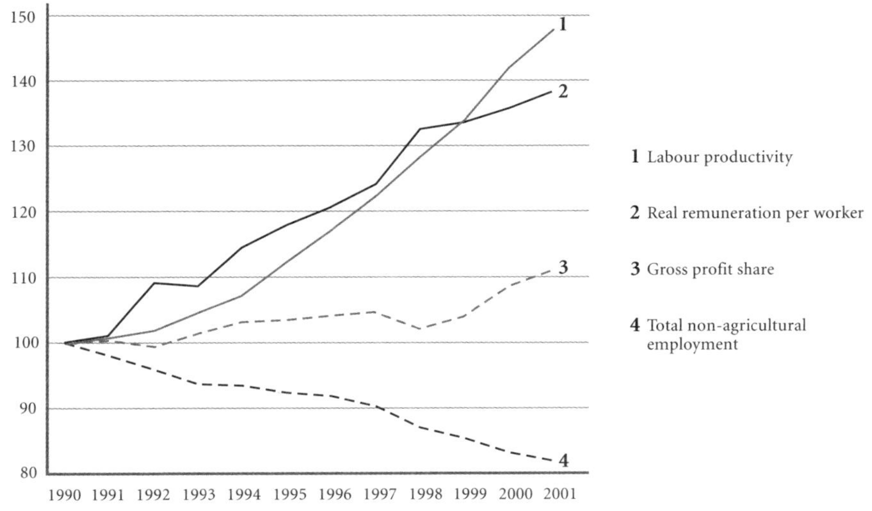

1 Labour productivity

2 Real remuneration per worker

3 Gross profit share

4 Total non-agricultural employment

Source: South African Reserve Bank

One rough indication of profitability is the gross profit share (i.e. the share of gross output going to the owners of capital). Broadly speaking, if the growth in labour productivity is greater than the growth in real wages, then workers are contributing more to output growth than they are getting back in wages, and hence the share of output going to capitalists (the profit share) will rise and the wage share will fall. As can be seen in Figure 6.4, the average rate of growth of productivity exceeded that of real wages for most of the 1990s. As a result, the aggregate profit share was about ten per cent higher in 2001 than it was in 1990.

The general rise in labour productivity in the 1990s, and in the proportion of skilled workers in total employment, is consistent with government policy to drive the economy 'up the value chain' – that is, to cajole and force the economic structure to shift towards a more skill-intensive growth path. This 'high productivity now' strategy entails a mixture of incentives to encourage training and the development of high value-added forms of economic activity – and continued support for those aspects of labour market policy that hinder low-wage, labour-intensive job creation (Nattrass 2001). As argued above, the strategy appears to have benefited those workers who managed to keep their jobs because real wages grew significantly. But it has done little yet to improve the economy's capacity to create jobs.

Capitalists have also benefited in the sense that a greater proportion of income now accrues to owners of capital (because the profit share has risen). They have also benefited from rising rates of profit (i.e. the rate of return on capital) in most sectors. This can be seen in Figure 6.5 which tracks net profit rates for key economic sectors. The only sector to have experienced an overall decline in the rate of profit during the 1990s was manufacturing. As this was primarily the result of a faster rate of growth of the capital stock than in value-added,[13] this trend is not necessarily a bad sign for future profitability. It indicates that capitalists have been renewing the capital stock they neglected in the 1980s when economic times were turbulent. Overall, the net profit rate for the private economy (that is, all economic sectors excluding community social and personal services[14]) was two-thirds higher in 2001 than in 1990.

As shown in Figure 6.5, the profit rates fell in almost all economic sectors from 1960 until the mid-1980s. The exception was the mining industry, which experienced a huge boost to profitability during the early and late 1970s. For most of the 1990s, the mining sector acted as a major drag on overall profitability – although mining fortunes appear to have shifted in 2000 and 2001. The major source of support to overall profitability in the 1990s came from commerce (wholesale and retail trade, catering and accommodation) and finance, real estate and business services. The process of structural change in favour of these sectors is thus likely to continue (because investment will be tempted into those areas offering the highest rate of return on capital).

Figure 6.5 *Trends in the profit rate, 1960–2001*

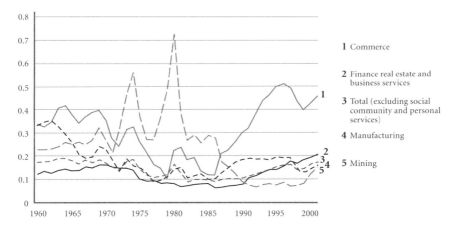

Source: The South African Reserve Bank

Economic policy: recent performance and future prospects

South Africa's growth strategy may well deliver benefits in terms of income growth in the longer term. Its success, however, is dependent on skills development and sustained investment. The orthodox fiscal policy stance (dubbed Gear) adopted in 1996 was premised on investment becoming the driving force for growth. The hope was that investors would respond well to falling inflation and the budget deficit. Unfortunately, investment has not responded as quickly or as extensively as hoped for by the Gear macro-modellers. Private investment grew at about one-tenth the rate hoped for by the Gear modellers between 1996 and 1999 (Nattrass & Seekings 2001a).

Investment is a volatile but crucial component of growth. As can be seen from Figure 6.6, investment was buoyant through the 1960s until the late 1970s. It grew strongly in the early 1980s (with the gold boom) and then again in the mid-1990s – but then turned negative in the late 1990s.

Some of the reasons for this lacklustre performance were beyond the control of the government. The Asian crisis and over-zealous monetary policies by the

Reserve Bank both acted as unexpected economic brakes. It is, however, a moot point whether the government should have continued with its restrictive fiscal policies given the recessionary conditions of the time (Weeks 1999). There is mounting evidence that pursuing anti-inflationary policies undermined growth in the developing world (Stiglitz 1998) and South Africa is unlikely to have been an exception to the rule. Furthermore, by continuing with trade liberalisation in the absence of labour market reforms, the government probably contributed to employment losses (Nattrass 1998). Import-competing industries (particularly the ultra-labour intensive industries) have been particularly hard-hit, and South Africa's export industries are becoming increasingly capital-intensive (Bell & Cattaneo 1997; ILO 1999).[15]

Figure 6.6 *Trends in investment and economic growth, 1960–2001*

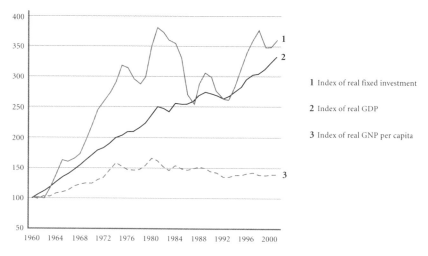

1 Index of real fixed investment

2 Index of real GDP

3 Index of real GNP per capita

Source: The South African Reserve Bank

As noted earlier, rapid capital accumulation – and even rising capital-intensity – is desirable if it is accompanied by significant growth in employment. The policy gamble taken by the South African government is that the shift to greater capital- and skill-intensity will provide a new engine for sustainable growth in the medium- to longer-term. Unfortunately, skill shortages (which are currently driving up the price of skilled labour relative to unskilled labour) will continue to act as a constraint on growth – and the brain drain of young white professionals will exacerbate the situation for some time. The AIDS pandemic – which has affected predominantly unskilled (especially migrant) labour – is already exercising a dampening impact on growth (Arndt & Lewis 2000). As it takes more of a hold on skilled labour, the burden on South Africa's growth path will increase exponentially.

But even if the growth path is eventually successful in generating a sustainable increase in employment and income, what is to be done for the unemployed in the short- to medium-term? One option is to embark on massive public works programmes. Job creation initiatives such as the 'Working for Water' scheme, which pays unemployed people to remove alien vegetation, is an example of the kinds of intervention which could make material difference to poor people's lives. Recent government statements in favour of providing people with the 'dignity of work' suggests that an expansion of public works programmes is possibly on the agenda. But whether sufficient unemployed people can be reached in this way, remains to be seen. It would require a massive redeployment of government resources.

Another option is to provide a basic income grant (BIG) for all South Africans. There appears to be widespread support for the introduction of a BIG – ranging from the opposition DA to the socialist left (Matisonn & Seekings 2002). But while there is agreement about the need for a BIG, there is less agreement about how to finance it. The recent Taylor Committee report (2002) on comprehensive welfare reform endorsed the notion of a BIG, but was curiously silent about how it should be financed.[16]

Samson *et al.* argue that there is room for increased taxation to finance a BIG because South Africa's average tax rate is below that of other countries at similar levels of development (2000: 17). The People's Budget 2002 (supported by Cosatu, the South African Council of Churches and the South African NGO Coalition) proposes that part of the needed revenue could be raised through a solidarity levy in the form of a 17,5 per cent surcharge on income tax for the top two quintiles – and the rest in the form of increased taxation of 'the high income group'. This is broadly in line with Cosatu's 7th National Congress' resolution that the cost of the BIG must 'fall on the rich'. By contrast, Le Roux (2002) proposes that the BIG be financed out of taxes on consumption with certain items (such as cigarettes and alcohol) being taxed especially heavily. The advantage of his proposal is that it is broad-based and redistributive (those with high expenditures contribute most). Those who spend more than

R1 000 a month end up paying more in consumption taxes than they benefit from the R100 universal grant.

Given that income-earners (particularly the skilled) benefit from the current growth path relative to the unskilled and unemployed, an appropriate social-democratic response may well be higher taxation in order to finance a BIG. That the beneficiaries of economic growth (capital and employed workers) should provide a minimum level of support to those not fortunate enough to benefit from it, was the implicit social contract behind the Scandinavian social-democratic model (Nattrass 1999). At present, the burden of supporting the unemployed in South Africa falls on the employed who face social and personal pressures to remit a portion of their earnings to unemployed family members. This is probably why Cosatu is in favour of a BIG – even if it means that some of their members may have to pay higher taxes as a result (Matisonn & Seekings 2002).

Despite the fact that the ruling ANC relies on a large constituency of poor people to keep it in power, the government has so far rejected the idea of a BIG. Perhaps this is because a BIG has never before been introduced in a middle-income developing country and our government is too conservative to be the first to try it? Or perhaps it is because the government is worried about its capacity to deliver a BIG to all South Africans (witness the problems with delivering old-age pensions in the Eastern Cape). As neither of these obstacles is insuperable, it is more likely that the government opposes a BIG primarily on ideological grounds.

As noted earlier, the government's Gear strategy is premised on attracting private investment through its commitment to fiscal discipline (most notably through lower government debt, expenditure and taxation). The government's economic policy discourse is, accordingly, one of entrepreneurial capitalism rather than social democracy. The Ministry of Finance is thus probably doubly opposed to a BIG: first because of the additional tax implications; and second, because of the adverse signal that consideration of a BIG may send to investors.

If this is the case, then the government may be seriously misjudging the situation. Investment is notoriously difficult to model and predict, and there is very little evidence to suggest that investors respond well to fiscal discipline *per se*. Instead, it appears that investment typically responds positively to demand (Nattrass 2001). In other words, when the economy is growing well investors are more upbeat about expected profitability, and investment rises. It may well be that introducing a BIG boosts demand (and hence investment) by putting income into the hands of poor people. Samson *et al.* (2000) model precisely this result.

But even if the macroeconomic benefits are not great, a BIG could impact on investor confidence through its social implications. South Africa is a highly unequal society with a reputation for high levels of violent and property-related crime. To the extent that a BIG helps reduce the socio-economic pressures that encourage crime, it will impact favourably on the investment climate via this route. Under the circumstances, there is a strong case for adopting a bolder and more experimental approach to welfare reform. There is a strong social case for a BIG, and there are no compelling economic reasons against it.

The greatest socio-economic challenge facing South Africa is to address the unemployment problem. Ideally the government should be proceeding on several fronts. Industrial and labour market policy should support labour-intensive production, public works programmes should be expanded, and the welfare system should be reformed to help alleviate the plight of the unemployed. Opinion polls regularly show that unemployment is regarded as the biggest problem facing South Africa (Nattrass & Seekings 2001b). Adopting a more energetic and creative policy stance on the matter would make good economic and political sense.

Notes

1 The budget deficit dropped from 5,1 per cent of GDP in 1996 to two per cent in 2001, and total national government debt as a percentage of GDP decreased from 49,6 to 45,8 over the same period. This turnaround is dramatic given that national debt as a percentage of GDP had risen from 39 per cent in 1990 to 55 per cent in 1995.

2 Between 1995 and 2001 exports as a percentage of GDP rose from 18,9 per cent to 27,9 per cent, the current account deficit on the balance of payments fell from –1,5 per cent of GDP to –0,2 per cent, and consumer inflation dropped from 8,7 per cent to 5,7 per cent. There was a sharp increase in basic food prices in mid 2002, but the subsequent strengthening of the Rand appears to be dampening subsequent increases.

3 The Unemployment Insurance Fund (UIF) provides 36 weeks of income support to those who have previously contributed to the fund. As only about five per cent of the unemployed have access to the UIF, this is a very low level of coverage.

4 Households with working members are predominantly in the top half of the income distribution – whereas those without any members in employment are amongst the

poorest, and can be regarded as comprising a marginalised 'underclass' (Seekings 2000).

5   This is the broad measure of unemployment – i.e. it includes those who report that they want work and does not require that they also be searching actively for it. See trend unemployment data for the 1990s in Nattrass 2000: 74.

6   South Africa is infamous for having one of the most unequal income distributions in the world (Leibbrandt et al. 2000: 32). Despite the decline in racial inequality between 1975 to 1996, overall inequality remained persistently high. This is because inequality within race groups grew as inequality between race groups declined (Whiteford & van Seventer 2000). Inequality within the African population increased as skilled workers experienced real wage growth and upward mobility, whilst unemployment increased amongst the ranks of the less skilled. It is this growing gulf between the employed and the unemployed which is now a major driver of inequality in South Africa (Leibbrandt et al. 2000; Nattrass & Seekings 2001a).

7   There are strong indications that inequality worsened during the 1990s. According to census data, the Gini coefficient (a measure of inequality ranging from 0 to 1) increased by 1 point between 1991 and 1996 (Whiteford & van Seventer 2000). Household survey data from KwaZulu-Natal reported an increase in the Gini coefficient of 4 points between 1993 and 1998, as did data from the Income and Expenditure surveys of 1995 and 2000. According to the KwaZulu-Natal survey (which collected information on the same households in 1993 and 1998), the proportion of poor households rose from 35 per cent to 42 per cent over the five-year period.

8   This aspect of the South African political economy was highlighted by radical historians in the 1970s. See Wolpe (1972) and Johnstone (1976) for classic renditions of this argument. While such analyses were correct to stress the importance of coercive nature of South Africa's labour supply policies, they typically underestimated the negative effect of other apartheid policies (eg. the job colour bar) on overall profitability. As can be seen in Figure 6.6, profit rates fell in most economic sectors over the apartheid period.

9   Between 1970 and 1980, the average capital:labour ratio (in constant 1995 rands) in South Africa shot up from R59 334 to R91 197, i.e. grew by an average annual compound growth rate of 4,5 per cent.

10 The number of worker-days lost through strike action increased substantially during the 1970s and 1980s. Such disruption raises the costs of production and places further upward pressure on wages. A 1991 survey of manufacturing employers found that 'labour problems' were cited as the most common cause of the continuing drift towards capital intensity (Welcher cited in Meintjies 1998: 11).

11 Not all workers, however, were covered by industrial council agreements. The impact of deracialising the industrial council system was thus to 'recycle' the old apartheid wedge between white and black workers into a wedge between 'insiders', i.e. workers covered by industrial councils, and 'outsiders' i.e. those in poorly-paying uncovered sectors such as agriculture and services, and the unemployed (Moll 1996).

12   Most calculations of employment elasticity in South Africa indicate that the labour demand curve is relatively elastic. Estimates range from –0,66 to –0,85, which suggests that a ten per cent increase in wages will result in a drop in employment of between 6,6 per cent and 8,5 per cent (reported in the Eager Report No.10, Spring 1999: 7).

13   The profit rate, i.e. profits/capital stock (P/K) is equal to the profit share, i.e. profits/value-added (P/Y) multiplied by the output:capital ratio (Y/K). The growth in the profit rate is thus equal to the growth in the profit share plus the growth in the output:capital ratio. In the 1990s, the rate of capital accumulation in manufacturing exceeded the increase in output, and hence the output:capital ratio fell. This fall more than offset the small increase in the profit share, thus resulting in a decrease in the profit rate.

14   Community social and personal services comprise mostly government services and is hence best left out of aggregate profit rate calculations.

15   This is not to say that the net impact of trade liberalisation has been to reduce jobs. Indeed, there is evidence that the overall impact has been marginally positive as export industries have helped boost labour-intensive downstream industries like transport and services (Edwards 2000). The point is simply that a more flexible labour market would probably have reduced the negative impact of trade liberalisation.

16   Pieter Le Roux and Charles Meth provided detailed work on financing a BIG to the Taylor Committee. It seems that pressure was put on the Taylor Committee not to include any discussion of financing in the report.

References

Armstrong, P, Glyn, A & Harrison, J (1991) *Capitalism since 1945*. Oxford: Basil Blackwell.

Arndt, C & Lewis, J (2000) The macro implications of HIV/AIDS in South Africa: A preliminary assessment, *South African Journal of Economics* 68(5): 856–887.

Bell, T & Cattaneo, N (1997) *Foreign trade and employment in South African manufacturing industry*. Occasional Report No. 4, Geneva: Employment and Training Department, International Labour Office.

Edwards, L (2000) *Globalisation and the skill bias of occupational employment in South Africa*. Unpublished paper, School of Economics, UCT.

Hofmeyr, J (1994) *An analysis of African wage movements in South Africa*. Research Monograph No. 9, Economic Research Unit, University of Natal, Durban.

ILO (1999) (drafted by Hayter, S, Reinecke, G & Torres, R) *South Africa: Studies on the social dimensions of globalisation*. Final draft, February 1999, Task Force on Country Studies on Globalisation, International Labour Office, Geneva.

Johnstone, F (1970) White prosperity and white supremacy in South Africa today, *African Affairs* 69: 124–140.

Kaplinsky, R (1995) Capital intensity in South African manufacturing and unemployment, 1972–90, *World Development* 23 (2): 179–92.

Karshenas, M (2001) Agriculture and economic development in sub-Saharan Africa and Asia, *Cambridge Journal of Economics* 25: 315–42.

Leibbrandt, M, Bhorat, H & Woolard, I (2000) Understanding contemporary household inequality in South Africa, *Journal of Studies in Economics and Econometrics* 24 (3): 31–52.

Le Roux, P (2002) *A targeted and affordable South African universal income grant.* Paper delivered to the 9th International Conference of the Basic Income European Network, Geneva, 12–14 September.

Matisonn, H & Seekings, J (2002) *Welfare in wonderland? The politics of the Basic Income Grant in South Africa, 1996–2002.* Paper presented to the Development Policy Research Unit/Friedrich Ebert Stichting Conference on Labour Markets and Poverty in South Africa, Johannesburg 22–24.10.02.

Mbeki, T (2002) *State of the Nation Address*, Parliament, Cape Town.

Meintjes, C (1998) *Impediments on the labour absorption capacity of the South African economy.* Discussion Paper No. 2, Halfway House: Development Bank of Southern Africa.

Nattrass, N (1999) Globalisation and social accords: A comparative analysis of Sweden, Australia and South Africa, *Labour, Capital and Society* 32 (2): 158–190.

Nattrass, N (2000) The debate about unemployment in the 1990s, *Studies in Economics and Econometrics* 24 (3): 73–90.

Nattrass, N (2001) High productivity now: A critical review of South Africa's growth strategy, *Transformation* 45: 1–24.

Nattrass, N & Seekings, J (2001a) Two nations: Race and economic inequality in South Africa today, *Daedalus*, Winter 45–70.

Nattrass, N & Seekings, J (2001b) Democracy and distribution in highly unequal economies: The case of South Africa, *Journal of Modern African Studies* 39 (3): 470–498.

Samson, M, Babson, O, MacQuene, K, van Niekerk, I & van Niekerk, R (2000) *The macroeconomic implications of poverty-reducing income transfers.* Paper presented to the conference: Towards a Sustainable and Comprehensive Social Security System, hosted by the Institute for Social Development, UWC.

Seekings, J (2000) Visions of society: Peasants, workers and the unemployed in a changing South Africa, *Journal of Studies in Economics and Econometrics* 24 (3): 53–72.

Simbi, T & Aliber, M (2000) *The agricultural employment crisis in South Africa.* Paper presented at the Trade and Industry Policy Secretariat Policy Forum, Muldersdrift, September.

Stiglitz, J (1998) *More instruments and broader goals: Moving towards the post-Washington consensus.* Annual Lectures 2, United Nations University, Helsinki.

Taylor Committee (2002) *Transforming the present: Protecting the future.* Report of the Committee of Inquiry into a Comprehensive System of Social Security for South Africa, RP/53/2002, Pretoria: Government Printer.

Weeks, J (1999) Stuck in low Gear? Macroeconomic policy in South Africa, 1996–98, *Cambridge Journal of Economics* 23 (4): 795–811.

Whiteford, A & van Seventer, D (2000) South Africa's changing income distribution in the 1990s, *Studies in Economics and Econometrics* 24 (3): 7–30.

Wolpe, H (1972) Capitalism and cheap labour power in South Africa: From segregation to apartheid, *Economy and Society* 1 (4). Reprinted in W Beinart & S Dubow (eds.) (1995) *Segregation and apartheid in twentieth century South Africa.* London and New York: Routledge.

The state of employment and unemployment in South Africa

Miriam Altman

Introduction

The unemployment problem in South Africa is not a recent phenomenon (Altman 2001a, 2001b; Bhorat & Hodge 1999; Edwards 2000; Kaplinsky 1995; Klasen & Woolard 2000; Meth 2001; DoL 1998). Net employment has been stagnant or falling since the early 1980s. The structural characteristics of falling employment have been caused by a number of factors related to the apartheid government's policies aimed at promoting 'separate development'. For example, the supply of labour suitable to a middle-income economy was constrained by a complementary set of adverse education, population control and labour market measures, whilst at the same time having the effect of diminishing household incomes and therefore a nation's greatest resource: its people. At the same time, markets were constrained by a closed economy and legal constraints to black entrepreneurship amongst others. The direction of development has further limited labour absorption by putting the economy on a firmly capital-using path, as will be argued in this paper.

So a large stock of unemployed people has built up over many years, and each year the economy has trouble absorbing not only this stock, but new entrants as well. The overall picture is quite complex: many formal jobs were lost, but since the mid-1990s, total formal employment has simply stagnated (Altman 2002a; Edwards 2000; Meth 2001). Most of the job loss was found in resource-based industries, construction and the public sector, generally due to a range of technological and policy-induced decisions. Inside the picture of no net growth was considerable private sector restructuring, where any job creation that did occur absorbed higher-skill labour, sometimes in new sectors: those retrenched have either shifted to outsourced businesses or are unemployed. The main source of employment growth for lower-skill labour was found in the informal sector until 2000 – primarily in street trade and domestic work – but even this sector seems to be stagnant or declining since then. Alongside stagnant formal employment, is a context of high population growth and large net inflows into the labour market. The labour market expands on average by about 600 000 net new entrants each year. By 2001, the strict and broad unemployment rates had risen to 30 per cent and 41 per cent respectively. Even by the strict definition, unemployment continues to rise by about two to three per cent each year.

From a policy perspective, employment depends on both economic growth and the labour-absorption capacity of the economy. Policy must target both of these. Higher growth rates can be achieved through productivity improvements (technology, industry restructuring, improved know-how, and so on) and/or growth in domestic or foreign market demand. Higher growth rates are difficult to achieve, and do not in themselves guarantee labour absorption as we have seen in recent years. This is partly because South African growth has been more reliant on *intensive*, rather than *extensive* growth. Moreover, in a distorted market, particularly in the context of the apartheid legacy, extracting more employment per unit of investment and output requires forceful stimulation and market reforms.

This chapter outlines the experience of employment, under employment and unemployment, and then moves on to explain possible causes and policy implications.

Unemployment in South Africa

Measuring unemployment is a tricky affair. Properly calculating employment and unemployment across the full population is really a new activity: there have been many changes in the measurement instruments over the 1990s as Stats SA has sought to make improvements. The Labour Force Survey (LFS) is currently by far the most reliable source of information. It is thus preferable to draw broad trends rather than focus on precise point estimates.

Unemployment can be measured in a number of ways. The accepted international norm focuses on 'strict' (or 'official' or 'narrow') measures that include only workers still actively looking for work. The 'broad' (or 'expanded') definition includes those parts of the labour force that say they would like to work, but have become discouraged. In South Africa, the review of both measures is important due to racial and gender biases: by far, the majority of discouraged workers are African rural women. Of the 7,7 million workers who were unemployed in 2001, 3,2 million were discouraged. The *chronic nature* of unemployment is demonstrated by the fact that only 41 per cent and 32 per cent of *urban* men and women respectively that were defined as strictly unemployed, had previously had a job. One-third to one-half of the 'strictly-defined' unemployed had been out of work for more than three years. Although some (eg. Schlemmer) argue that many of these people may well be working in small piece jobs or in the informal sector, the LFS is covering any and all economic activity, including unpaid labour, so should be capturing this possibility. Labour force participation rates are quite high and more people are looking for work: this may mean that people are more hopeful or alternatively, more desperate, as the picture is still quite bleak.

Even by the strict definition, unemployment is expanding each year. While unemployment is rising for all race groups, the racial incidence is enormous, mostly falling on African workers. The main contributors to *growing* unemployment include: expanding labour force due to population growth, increased participation rates (with the end of apartheid – freedom of movement to urban areas, increased hopefulness; increased female participation) and no net increase in the number of job opportunities.

Table 7.1 *Unemployment trends (percentages)*

	1994	1995	1996	1997	1998	1999	2000	2001
Strict definition	20.0	16.9	19.3	21.0	25.2	23.3	25.8	29.5
Broad definition	28.6	26.5	34.9	38.9	37.5	36.2	35.9	41.5

Sources: October Household Survey (OHS) 1994–99, Labour Force Survey (LFS) Sept 2000, 2001

Table 7.1 presents unemployment trends between 1994–2001. As noted, care should be taken in reviewing these figures, and year-on-year trends deserve less attention than overall direction over the period. The official unemployment rate rose by ten per cent between 1994–2001, reaching almost 30 per cent of the labour force. The broader definition of unemployment that includes discouraged workers, increased from 28,6 per cent to 41,5 per cent over the same period. The recorded unemployment rate would have grown much faster if not for the massive growth in the informal sector. There is some debate as to whether the pace of informal sector growth is real, or whether Stats SA has improved its data capture: for simplicity sake, this submission will work on the assumption that the growth is real.

Unemployment by race

As Figure 7.1 clearly shows, unemployment rates for African workers are much higher than for other groups. However, it also reveals that unemployment rates have been growing substantially for every other group, aside from whites, particularly from the mid-1990s. Even so, 35,5 per cent or 3,9 million African workers were unemployed in 2001; compare this to 21,8 per cent of coloured and 18,2 per cent of Asian workers, numbering only 0,5 million.

Figure 7.1 *Unemployment by race, 1994–2001 (strict definition)*

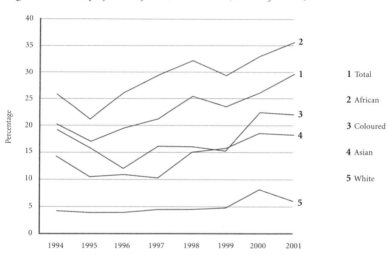

Sources: OHS (1994 – 1999) and LFS (Sept 2000, 2001)

Unemployment by gender and location

The experience of unemployment by gender and location is well known. Figure 7.2 shows strict and broad rates of unemployment by gender, also presenting variations by rural and urban location. The most significant point is the substantially higher rate of discouragement amongst rural African women than for any other group, reaching 58 per cent by the broad definition. The large dip in unemployment numbers between 1999–2001 may well be explained by a corresponding recorded rise and fall in subsistence agriculture, which appears to be more statistical than real.

Figure 7.2 *Percentage of unemployment by gender and location, 1994–2001 (strict [A] and broad [B] definition compared)*

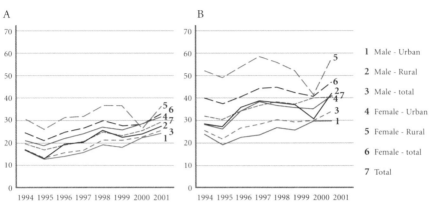

Sources: OHS (1994–1999) and LFS (Sept 2000–2001)

Unemployment by age

The importance of focusing on flows, and particularly on the inability of the economy to absorb new labour-market entrants, must be underlined. Figure 7.3 presents unemployment rates by age group, comparing 1994 to 2001. Generally, one expects higher rates of unemployment amongst younger people as they find their way in the labour market. However, Figure 7.3 shows that the number of young unemployed is growing much faster than any other group, thereby boosting the economy-wide unemployment rate each year. We see that young people are 'queuing' for work, only finding work after age 30. To put this into context, almost 72 per cent of the unemployed are under age 35 (LFS Feb 2002). Of the unemployed under 30 years of age, 73 per cent had never worked before. The involuntary nature of this situation is highlighted by the difficulty in finding a job: 30 per cent of unemployed aged less than 30 had been searching for more than three years, while another 30 per cent had been searching for 1–3 years.

These are people who should be economically active, supporting older relatives and children; instead, many young people are joining the stock of long-term unemployed. This has serious implications for economic policy seeking to reduce long-term unemployment. Is this a problem of skills and experiential mismatches and poor labour market information, or is it deficient demand? The identification of appropriate policy interventions will depend on the extent to which it is one or the other.

Figure 7.3 *Number of unemployed by age, 1994 and 2001*

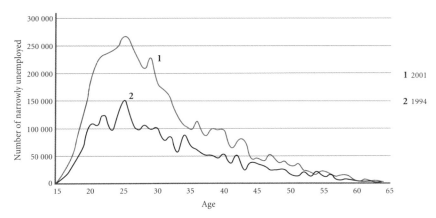

Sources: OHS 1994 and LFS 4 (2001)

Employment and underemployment

Broad employment trends

Employment is a fuzzy concept in developing countries, and many prefer to map out livelihoods. The contribution of employment to household income is particularly important since there tends to be more reliance on families than on individuals. The 'employment rate' masks much lying underneath, with substantial implications for households, and for policy. Trends in different types of employment and their welfare implications are discussed below.

Figure 7.4 and Figure 7.5 show trends in formal and informal employment. In the non-agricultural formal sector, employment has been stagnant, ranging between 6,4 million and 7,1 million workers. Commercial agriculture lost 750 000 jobs between 1994 and 1996, and is now stagnant, with employment in the region of about 660 000. It is estimated that about 1,2 million people work in the public sector.

Figure 7.4 *Formal sector employment, 1994–2001 (millions)*

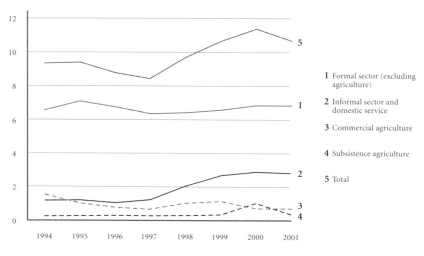

1 Formal sector (excluding agriculture)

2 Informal sector and domestic service

3 Commercial agriculture

4 Subsistence agriculture

5 Total

Sources: OHS (1994 – 1999) and LFS (Sept 2000, 2001)

Stagnant employment does not mean that there has not been change: it is now well known that there have been considerable shifts in labour demand, away from lower-skill labour toward the absorption of higher-skill labour. This is found in every sector, except for community services. This may partly be explained by a regrouping of activity to improve productivity in an increasingly competitive environment. In addition, employment-output ratios (or the number of people employed relative to output) have fallen in every sector except community services.

Overall, the main employment growth has been found outside the formal sector. The main variations in employment figures rotate around the informal sector. Reports on job-creating growth or the recent 'job destruction' are probably more related to teething problems in statistical collection, than to real change. Stats SA has been actively working to improve its estimates of the informal sector. In this context, drawing a trend is not advisable. Rather, it is more prudent to focus on the most recent measurements at a point in time.

Demarcating informal employment is a little confusing and the categories require explanation. Essentially, it is worthwhile following definitions used by the *October Household Survey* (OHS) and the *Labour Force Survey* (LFS).

These surveys distinguish between the informal sector, domestic work, and subsistence agriculture.

Figure 7.5 *Informal sector employment, 1994–2001 ('000s)*

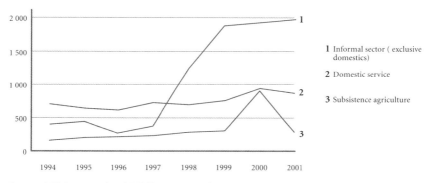

1 Informal sector (exclusive domestics)

2 Domestic service

3 Subsistence agriculture

Sources: OHS (1994–1999) and LFS (Sept 2000, 2001)

In this vein, the 1999 OHS and September LFSs for both 2000 and 2001 all found that the informal sector comprised about 1,9 million participants. This represented a dramatic increase from previous levels of around 450 000 until 1997. It appears that about 200 000 more domestic workers were employed, ultimately reaching about 0,9 million workers in 2001. The other variations in employment measurements arise from subsistence agriculture, first measured in the LFS 2000. About 960 000 workers were found in 2000, falling to 360 000 in the following year! In the absence of any economic or environmental shocks, the peak was probably more related to measurement than any underlying occurrence. So it is estimated that informal employment had a total of about 3,2 to 3,7 million participants by 2001. Surprisingly, only 30 to 40 per cent are classified as 'elementary workers' and so the informal economy should not necessarily be seen as unskilled. The other three-quarters are mostly semi-skilled.

The quality of work

The quality of work can be measured in a number of ways, such as the prevalence of underemployed people wishing they could work more hours, contract flexibility, benefits and remuneration.

We looked at trends in hours worked and found that by far the majority of those employed in the formal sector worked more than 35 hours per week.

The variations in work quality were more related to contract flexibility and earnings. Although the legislation is often seen as onerous, there is actually substantial contract flexibility in the formal sector. This was found by the International Labour Organisation review looking back on the early 1990s (Standing, Sender & Weeks 1996). Counter-intuitively, the figures below show that there is more, not less, flexibility (or at the very least stability, depending on the reliability of the shift from the OHS to the LFS).

Figure 7.6 shows that just over half of formal sector workers have written contracts or pension plans. Just less than two-thirds are allowed paid leave. In fact, this overstates the contractual obligations in the formal *private* sector. The public service skews the average contractual obligations in the formal sector upwards.

Figure 7.7 shows that by far the majority of public sector workers (comprising about one-fifth of the formal sector) have contracts, pensions and paid leave. This may indicate that either there has long been substantial flexibility, or else that firms are locating strategies to introduce flexibility. Either way, employment should not be constrained by contract inflexibility, except possibly on the margins.

Figure 7.6 *Formal sector work conditions, 1999 and 2001*

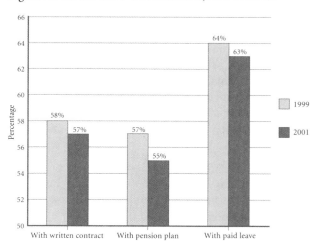

Sources: OHS 1999, LFS Sept 2001.

Figure 7.7 *Comparison of work conditions in the public and private sector, 2001*

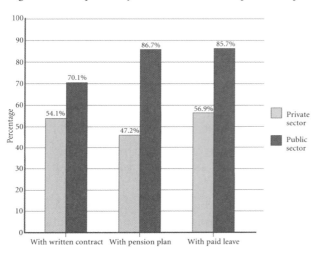

Source: LFS Sept 2001

Average manufacturing wages are often the minimum living level. Mean monthly incomes in 1999 are presented in Table 7.2. Formal wages for African workers ranged from R599 to R2 204 per month. It is estimated that more than four million formal sector workers earn less than R23 000 per year. As many households depend on only one wage earner, the sector worked makes a very large difference to poverty levels. As shown below, informal sector workers earn between one fifth to almost a half of their counterparts in the formal sector.

Table 7.2 *Mean monthly incomes (Rand, 1999)*

	Rand		As a percentage of formal African male earnings	
	Men	Women	Men	Women
White workers				
Formal (urban)	7 514	4 774		
African workers				
Formal (urban)	2 204	2 068	100	94
Informal (urban)	1 012	845	46	38

Informal (non-urban)	705	524	32	24
Domestic (urban)	903	537	41	24
Domestic (non-urban)	347	397	16	18
Agricultural (formal)	1 011	599	46	27
Agricultural (informal)	386	306	18	14

Source: Meth (2001)

Variations in experience of employment by race, gender and location

The persistence of gender and racial segmentation (and discrimination) in the labour market is apparent. While found at all levels, it becomes more stark further down the skills ladder.

Even at the highest levels, the returns to education for black graduates is lower than for white graduates. This is partly explained by choice of institution, but also due to mistaken choice in course of study and weak job-search capabilities. It does appear that insider-outsider phenomena are important even at this level (Moleke & Fourie 2003).

At lower levels, the persistence of gender discrimination is also stark. The returns to education for African women is much lower than that for African men. Although educational attainment is the same or better for women, at least half of African women are crowded into few low-level occupations such as domestic work or 'elementary' work categories such as tea ladies, cleaners and the like. Male workers with the same education find jobs in a much wider variety of occupations such as trades, and across manufacturing sectors. This partly explains the variations in earnings between men and women. Then earnings by location also clearly differ substantially, with lower earnings in rural areas.

This has implications on households and on firms:
- It results in persistence in cycles of poverty for *female*-headed households in particular. This may have implications for the focus of policy on the particular needs of female-headed households and the reduction of cost of living, for example, through child-care services and so on, and in the longer term, more forceful policies to enable career pathing of women out of dead-end jobs, and improved focus of education and work placements for girls.

○ It reduces the potential skills pool as firms choose from only a portion of the workforce on the basis of gender and race, rather than capability.
○ It raises policy questions insofar as rural livelihoods are concerned, where the required balance between social grants and earnings from economic activity may differ from urban areas.
○ It is probable that the weak contract coverage and benefits provision apply mostly to African workers: this raises questions in respect of the role of the state in connecting benefits to work, or at least in enabling some kind of 'forced' savings (in addition to just the state pensions).

Implications of employment trends

Alongside renewed GDP growth in the 1990s was an expectation that jobs would be created. Instead unemployment has risen. There has been some debate as to whether South Africa has experienced jobless or job-creating growth. That is, have we turned the corner where the economy is finally on a path to job-creating growth? Is the main problem that employment growth is being outstripped by labour force expansion?

Over the 1990s, more output was squeezed out of fewer people, so there was stagnant formal employment in the context of GDP growth. Some job losses are blamed on productivity improvements and technological change. The idea that we might be 'turning the corner' refers to the possibility that the substantial restructuring and productivity improvements made in the 1990s will slow down, and further increases in output will rely on more horizontal expansion.

The idea of job-creating growth arises from the fact that, at the very least, there has been some net growth in employment. So the economy 'turned the corner' in 1998, after almost a million jobs were lost between 1994 and 1997 alone. This was an important turning point. However, the only net gains arose in the informal sector, where measurement is difficult (and so trends difficult to ascertain).

So, is this really job-creating growth? Or is it 'jobless growth'?

One way to assess whether employment is growing in accordance with economic growth, and 'turning a corner', is to assess whether there is some trend or reversal over a number of years. A comparison of growth in GDP and employment is offered in Figure 7.8. It does appear that total employment grew substantially in four of the past seven years, averaging 2,6 per cent compound growth between 1994–2001. The same cannot be said about employment in the formal sector and commercial agriculture, which grew in only three of seven years. While there was substantial change (or both entry and exit) in net terms, there was no net growth in formal-sector employment over this period. According to these statistics, 2001 was a disastrous year.

Overall, the correlation to growth is difficult to ascertain, partly because of the restructuring over the 1990s. Informal employment is the only discernible source of job growth, and even that is now slowing and even falling. So in absolute terms it does seem that some jobs were created. Does it matter that they were informal?

From a policy perspective, the critical question is whether the growth trajectory can generate sufficient employment to meet some minimum expectation, thereby underpinning an upward growth cycle, in turn generating further employment, and so on.

Figure 7.8 *Employment and growth*

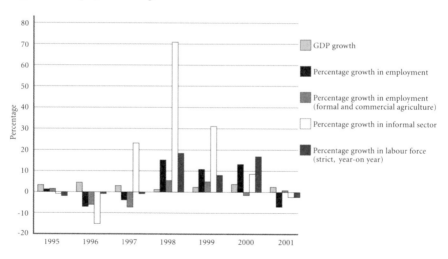

Sources: OHS (1995–1999) and LFS (Sept 2000, 2001)

Employment is important from a number of perspectives, including:
○   Improved income distribution and household welfare *per se.*

- ○ Sustainable growth path:
  - • a growing productive sector to support less productive parts of the economy (via intra-household transfers, fiscal transfers and consumption linkages);
  - • longer upswings in the business cycle (with household demand being the single most important contributor (see Laubscher 2002).
- ○ Non-economic considerations that arise from participation, well-being, social interaction, social cohesion, self respect, good health, and a feeling of making a contribution to family and community.

If government is tracking figures as one measure of improvement in these considerations, then aggregate employment figures can be very misleading. If the broadest brushstrokes are applied, the picture drawn in Figure 7.8 is one of stagnant formal employment and growing informal employment, within the context of a fast-growing labour force. At the same time, productivity is improving, so GDP growth is still higher than it was and more is squeezed out of fewer people. Some argue that this nevertheless means overall employment has increased in accordance with GDP growth. There are a number of concerns with this view. First, there is little reflection of the proportions required to uphold sustainable development – in other words, a certain minimum productive sector is required to support less productive parts of the economy. Unless Government plans to offer very substantial transfers as found in welfare economies, it is essential that economic growth be partly derived from broader economic participation. Instead, more people were unemployed than were working in the formal sector in 2001. Of a broad labour force of 18,5 million, 7,5 million were employed in the formal sector and commercial agriculture, 3,2 million were working in the informal sector, subsistence agriculture and domestic work, and 7,7 million workers were unemployed (of which 3,2 million were discouraged). At least one-fifth of formal sector workers were employed in 'elementary' occupations.

Dramatic expansions in the labour force from 1997 are the most noticeable trend. The distinction between formal, under- and un-employed is a loose one based on broad Stats SA definitions. Formal employment refers to those categorised as falling within formal sector employment including commercial agriculture. Underemployed refers to those in the informal sector, domestic service and subsistence agriculture. Unemployed refers to the official or narrow definition of unemployment. If further analysis were done, the 'under-employed' category would expand at the expense of formally employed, as there are many other categories of worker (for example, cleaners, tea ladies, underemployed care givers).

Figure 7.9 offers a clearer set of implications. Two pie charts are provided, comparing the proportion of productive, underemployed and officially unemployed in 1994 and 2001. As noted, ideally the aim of national policy is to raise incomes through employment opportunities, thereby promoting spread effects through the economy. These spread effects arise from a range of linkages, whether in the household, through increased expenditure, and via state revenues. Instead, the proportion of formal sector workers fell from 69 to 49 per cent. At the same time, those underemployed rose from 14 to 21 per cent, and unemployed from 17 to 30 per cent. In summary, the economy had previously been supported by more than two-thirds of the labour force, whereas it is now supported by only a half. This is unsustainable and poses a certain brake on long-term growth and human development. An economy needs a minimum proportion of its labour force sufficiently active to support less productive groups, with the exception of oil-exporting economies that have so much income that they support large welfare states.

Figure 7.9 *Proportion of productive and unproductive labour, 1994 and 2001 (percentages)*

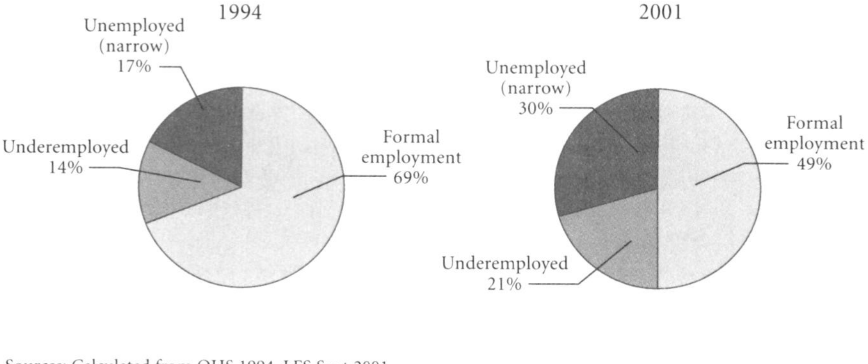

Sources: Calculated from OHS 1994, LFS Sept 2001.

In a context of rising household dependence on fewer wage earners, the proportion of workers in the formal vs. informal sector matters a great deal. Figure 7.10 shows returns to education in the formal and informal sector. Note the massive difference in earnings: workers in the informal sector with primary or secondary education earn average monthly wages of between R535 and R1 392. Their counterparts in the formal sector earn about twice as much. Those with tertiary education earn 2,5 times as much in the formal sector.

Figure 7.10 *Earnings in the formal and informal sector by level of education, 2001*

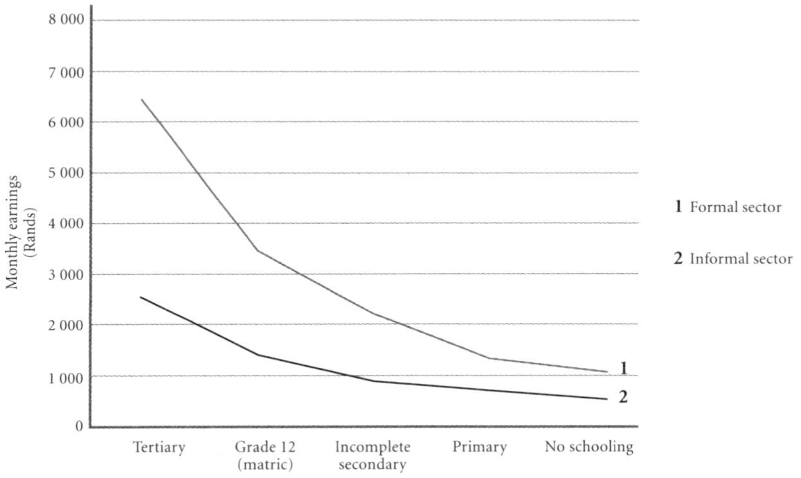

Source: LFS 4, 2001

There are two main implications that can be drawn. First, the shift to informal sector employment has serious welfare implications at all levels of educational attainment. Second, there is much societal waste, where the large portion of net new opportunities available offers far lower returns to education.

This would not be a problem if employment were growing overall, with both formal and informal sectors expanding. However, there is a very serious problem if the shift is from productive to less productive labour, with the labour force contributing less and less to household incomes and to the economy in general.

It does appear that the South African economy has experienced 'jobless growth'. In other words, there does not seem to be a strong correlation between GDP and employment growth. Generally, the shift has been from formal to informal, with fewer returns to education, low wages, and fewer contractual obligations or benefits. If both the formal and informal sectors were growing and drawing in the unemployed, that could be a positive scenario. Instead, the experience is the opposite. From the perspective of households, this would indicate that there is a vicious downward cycle, not an upward virtuous development cycle: this is not a sustainable growth path in a middle-income economy.

What explains persistent unemployment?

Rising unemployment is a serious concern, particularly in the context of improved growth, and expanded exports. Will this problem correct itself once the economy adjusts through all the regulatory and political changes, or is more dramatic intervention required?

The build-up of unemployment in South Africa over the past decades can most accurately be attributed to the demise of jobs in traditional resource-based industries in agriculture and mining, without a concomitant employment take-up in more advanced industrial sectors, as would be expected in a process of structural change and development.

Employment in major primary resource-based industries fell, primarily due to commodity price trends, technical conditions (in mining), domestic market deregulation and fear of potential land tenure claims and labour rights (in agriculture). The slow pace of land reform and the protectionist stance of the United States and the European Union further limit the expansion of new agricultural activity.

The dramatic fall in primary resource-based employment in the 1990s was not compensated for in other industries. Gross fixed capital formation fell by an average 1,5 per cent per year between 1990–1994, and subsequently grew by an average of only 4,7 per cent per year between 1995–1999. This latter growth was primarily driven by investment in public sector corporations. Growth rates of private capital formation fell over the 1990s, particularly with the demise in construction and mining sectors: gross fixed capital formation as a percentage of GDP has been below 17 per cent through the 1990s, as compared to rates of around 27 per cent in 1983 (SARB 2000). To offer perspective, in 1998 gross domestic investment as a percentage of GDP in South Africa was about half that in Malaysia or Thailand. Most economies that have sustained real growth rates of three per cent or more have had investment and savings levels in excess of 20 per cent of GDP. Ultimately, South Africa needs growth rates that are even higher.

The main investments prior to 1984 were largely directed to capital-intensive resource-based projects in basic chemicals and metals. Minerals revenues enabled the spending on defence and on capital-intensive projects that marked the inward focus of the former regime. For example, basic chemicals and basic metals accounted for 66,7 per cent of investment made between 1972 and 1990: by 1990, basic chemicals and metals sectors accounted for over half South Africa's capital stock. The politically-driven synthetic fuels projects, Mossgas and Sasol, alone accounted for more than half the growth in manufacturing investment over this period. The ANC's Macro-Economic Research Group recognised this and attributed growing unemployment to the crowding out by the capital intensive minerals-energy-complex (MERG 1993).

Employment growth depends on human and physical capital formation, the latter ideally applied to labour-absorbing investments. While labour-intensive industries such as clothing have been promoted in South Africa since the 1920s, this was done within a context that severely limited its growth: a closed economy with constrained domestic demand due to apartheid. So between 1972–1990, the capital stock in the clothing sector *fell* by 19 per cent. Similarly, there was only marginal investment in the four most labour-intensive industries over this 18-year period (Kaplinsky 1995). Between 1984–1990, the manufacturing capital stock actually diminished.

In the 1990s, the substantial restructuring that took place in manufacturing in response to globalisation leaned towards an ever more capital-using base. Manufactured exports rose from five to 20 per cent of total exports between 1988–1996. Yet the majority of manufactured exports are still material-intensive products such as beneficiated iron and steel, processed chemicals, processed foods, paper and paper products, and non-ferrous metals, which by 1996, constituted 62 per cent of manufactured exports.[1]

Since the mid-1990s, substantial growth in exports of mechanical machinery, motor vehicles, electrical machinery, transport equipment and wine has taken place, although increasing from a small base and primarily destined for African markets (Black & Kahn 1998).[2] The restructuring and export expansion has not resulted in net employment gains.

To explain stagnant or falling employment it is necessary to look to the causes of weak human and physical capital formation. The historically slow growth in secondary and tertiary sectors can be attributed to the apartheid minerals economy that restricted international interaction, small business entry, effective demand and labour market functions such as skilling, spatial and occupational mobility, affordable cost of job search, and circulation of market information. These conditions were created by the approach to import-substitution industrialisation, international sanctions, legal restrictions on ownership of assets and businesses by the black population, and controls over the labour market and access to education. One legacy is the severe gap in skills attainment: for example, less than a third of African men and women that work in the urban formal sector have completed high school. Generally less than ten per cent of informal and non-urban African workers have finished high school (Meth 2001; OHS 1999). The 'human development indices' such as life expectancy, infant mortality and calorie intake more closely resemble the quality of living in low-income economies.

The separate development strategy entailed that the black population would be kept out of the central urban areas, and that production became increasingly capital intensive to reduce dependence on black workers. The black population would be moved to outlying (and generally uneconomic) areas, where labour-intensive industries were encouraged to move. So, most legislation was aimed at saving economic opportunity for the white population. Examples of these controls included job reservation, the bantu education system, severe limits by race on access to occupation, certification and education, the *Group Areas Act* and influx control, and racial applications of labour law. Since the black population could own neither a business nor property, large parts of the population now lack assets to put forward as collateral.

So, in the South African context, severe distortions are related to the distribution of asset ownership, spatial dislocation, skills gaps, and the attraction of investment into more profitable, spatially determinist, capital-intensive resource-based projects. Explaining high unemployment as the result of factor price distortions, particularly emphasising wages and low savings rates, is quite simplistic (Fallon & Pereira da Silva 1994; Fallon & Lucas 1998; Fedderke, Henderson & Kayemba 1999). Falling wages and rising savings rates would not in themselves solve such a severe experience of high and growing levels of unemployment.

Most of the elements that underpin growth and the efficient co-ordination of factor and product markets were purposefully undermined by the apartheid government. The minerals base made this possible on a sustained basis, with the misallocation of mineral rents, particularly in the context of dramatic increases in the gold price in the early 1970s.

The *misallocation* of resource rents has left South Africa as a highly distorted middle-income economy, with a cost structure and domestic market-oriented production sectors that reflect this middle-income status, but a human development index, skills level and export profile that is more reflective of a less developed country (Black & Kahn 1998; Klasen & Woolard 2000).

Some implications for future policy directions

There are two complementary variables that will impact on future employment trends – economic growth and the capacity of the economy to absorb labour.

Growth and employment

With rapid technological and productivity improvements, diminishing links between employment and output are not uncommon in many countries. However, this link seems to be even weaker in minerals economies. Within this context, what is the relationship between growth and employment? What if government were to set a minimum expectation or policy target at stabilising unemployment rates at current levels? What rate and type of growth would be required?

As at 2001, the economy would need to generate about 450 000 net new jobs each year, compared with an average 240 000 net new jobs created annually since 1994, almost all in the informal sector. To achieve the higher rate of job creation, employment would need to grow by 3,9 to 4,4 per cent annually. What rate of GDP growth would be needed in the current environment to achieve this minimum target? It is difficult to pinpoint a precise relationship between employment and growth in South Africa, particularly in the context of such dramatic structural change. However, it is possible to look at the experience of other countries, and of sectors that have transformed less dramatically.

In the high-performing Asian economies, employment growth rates of 2,5 to four per cent would normally be associated with GNP growth rates around five to eight per cent or more (Mazumdar & Basu 1997). In these south-east Asian countries, employment and growth depended on the rapid expansion of low-cost manufactured exports, made possible by a low cost structure.

Developed economies that have overcome high unemployment have relied substantially on the expansion of high-value market services (such as business and professional services) and low-value social and personal services, such as health, education and child care. Ireland is one example, where in this way employment growth rates averaged 2,6 per cent between 1991–1997, but GDP grew by more than eight per cent per annum (O'Connell 1999).

It seems quite unlikely that more than four per cent employment growth could be achieved within the current policy framework, particularly at projected GDP growth rates of around 2,5–3,5 per cent. South Africa has a capital-intensive structure of production, with many supply constraints limiting employment and investment multiplier effects. This is reinforced by globalisation, where it is the high-skill, capital-intensive export industries that are mostly benefiting. At the same time, services industries are expanding and entry is easier for small- and medium-sized formal and informal firms. The comparison to Ireland above is offered to show what ratio of employment to GDP growth might be expected in a context of high rates of labour absorption per rand invested. What could we expect where the economy has a low capacity to absorb labour? The South African economy is likely to generate less than one per cent annual growth in 'market-based' employment in the short-to-medium term (Altman 2001b; Lewis 2001).

Increasing the capacity of the economy to absorb labour

There is much value in building such labour-intensive market-based sectors, promoting industrial diversification and deepening domestic linkages, but the impact on employment will be at best moderate for some time to come. A mix of approaches aimed at raising employment-output ratios without undermining competitiveness and long-run formal sector growth, must be pursued. It is clear that the pursuit of higher GDP growth rates is essential, but equally important is the question of how to squeeze more employment out at each rate of growth, investment and output.

Ultimately, the drivers from the demand side by which the South African economy can become more labour-absorbing depend on a number of interconnected legs, involving:

- The expansion of low productivity non-traded goods and services, such as construction, and social and personal services.
- The stimulation of investment linkages arising from key investments and export opportunities. This entails the promotion of small business with more strategic use of procurement by government and business.

- ○ Active labour-market policy – some of the central functions of any market would include: signalling, response, mobility and reproduction. It could be argued that labour markets in South Africa are not well developed from a perspective of information provision, skills response, occupational and geographic mobility, nor even in supporting the reproduction of labour. For example, learning institutions may be getting a signal that certain skills are increasingly in demand, but they may not respond due to inappropriate institutional incentives. Poorly developed labour markets with weak information flows, substantial exclusion, rigidities in spatial and occupational mobility, and weak skills development are a legacy of the apartheid regime.
- ○ Household expenditure is the single most important contributor to upswings in the business cycle (Laubscher 2002). In South Africa, weak household consumption expenditure has therefore resulted in shorter upswings and longer downswings. Are there ways that government could more forcefully stimulate or even emulate household expenditure, whether directly or indirectly? Examples include financial transfers, food vouchers, and food grants. Alternatively, employment expansion (eg. in construction and personal services) and reduced forms of inefficient household indebtedness (eg. multiple insurance policies, high interest costs, defaults) could contribute to household consumption.
- ○ The inflation-unemployment relationship is not well understood, but nevertheless has a substantial impact on policy decisions. Given current knowhow, government is limited in its capability to stimulate the economy for fear of inducing self-defeating inflationary pressures. It may be that low-level inflation under current circumstances requires strict unemployment rates of around 30 per cent. This is explained by path dependence in the economy, where the institutions underpin a continued link between inflation and unemployment. Some examples include: wage-setting institutions, administered prices and the extent to which markets are competitive. How can the inflation-unemployment relationship be unbound? The concept of 'hysteresis' or path dependence requires investigation. One would look at underlying market and institutional structures to see where institutional reform could help to unlock the relationship between unemployment and inflation. The line of inquiry is this: if government seeks to stimulate demand for say food, with the aim of eradicating child malnutrition, would it be inflationary and could these pressures be avoided through market restructuring or voluntary price restraints?

Conclusions

In employment terms, the economy has shifted to a smaller productive base that supports a larger under- and un-productive base. Fewer people at higher-skill levels are producing more output. Larger parts of the labour force are in very low or zero productivity activities. This is unsustainable since although output has grown, lower rates of employment (and income derived from employment) means higher household dependency ratios, weaker 'spread effects' and distribution of income, thereby undermining any sustainable growth trajectory.

The most critical problem lies in the very slow uptake of young entrants. It is one thing to have a 'lost generation' as a result of apartheid. It is quite another to generate a *new* generation of people who have little link into the economic and social participation offered by the world of work.

The policy solutions are varied and complex, but there are two complementary interventions: the one entails active stimulation of low-productivity labour-absorbing non-traded goods and services to increase the number of opportunities in the market. This is one measure, in combination with active labour market policy, that raises employment created at any rate of national growth.

Notes

1   For example, in 2000 merchandise exports increased by ten per cent (and imports increased by nine per cent), but most of this growth can be explained by the R2 billion in capital exports by SA contractors during the construction of the Mozal smelter in Mozambique (Budget Review 2001).

2   Opening up to the rest of Africa has been important in this regard, where two-thirds of manufactured exports are destined. The share of exports excluding gold destined for Western Europe has fallen from 50 to 41 per cent, while Africa's share has grown from nine to 18 per cent between 1998–1996.

References

Abedian, I (2001) *The impact of the structural change of the South African economy on labour*. Editor's brief. Economics Sector Briefing Notes, Economics Division, Standard Bank, Johannesburg, September.

Altman, M (1998) *Memo to the Department of Labour: Special employment programmes.* Memo No. 18.

Altman, M (2001a) Employment promotion in a minerals economy, *Journal of International Development* 13: 1–19.

Altman, M (2001b) Paths to employment expansion in a minerals economy, *Urban Forum* 12 (3–4), Special Issue: WORK 2001, First International Conference on Employment Creation in Development.

Altman, M (2002a) Employment policy in a 'minerals economy', in E Carlson & W Mitchell (eds.) *The urgency of full employment.* Sydney: CAER-University of New South Wales Press.

Altman, M (2002b) *Progress in addressing employment and unemployment.* Paper prepared for the Policy Co-ordination and Advisory Services, Office of the Presidency, Pretoria.

Bell, T & Cattaneo, N (1997) *Foreign trade and employment in South African manufacturing industry.* Occasional Report, No. 4, Employment and Training Department. Geneva: ILO.

Bhorat, H & Hodge, J (1999) Decomposing shifts in labour demand in South Africa, *South African Journal of Economics* 67 (3): 348–380.

Black, A & Kahn, B (1998) *Growing without gold? South Africa's non-traditional exports since 1980.* Mimeo, Department of Economics, University of Cape Town.

Cassim, R (2000) Some notes on foreign direct investment in South Africa, *Trade Monitor* 15: 12–15.

Collier, P & Gunning, JW (1999) Why has Africa grown so slowly? *Journal of Economic Perspectives* 13 (3): 3–22.

Cosatu (1996) *Social equity and job creation – The key to a stable future. Proposals by the South African labour movement.* Cosatu. Johannesburg.

Department of Labour, RSA (1998) *Creating jobs, fighting poverty: An employment strategy framework.*

Edwards, L (2000) Globalisation and the skill bias of occupational employment in SA, *South African Journal of Economics* 69 (1): 40–71.

Fallon, P & Lucas, R (1998) *South African labour markets: adjustments and inequalities.* Informal Discussion Papers on Aspects of the South African Economy, World Bank.

Fallon, P & Pereira de Silva, L (1994) *South Africa: economic performance and policies.* World Bank Discussion Paper, No. 7, Southern Africa Department, World Bank.

Fedderke, JW, Henderson, S & Kayemba, J (1999) *Changing factor market conditions in South Africa: The capital market – a sectoral description of the period 1970–1997.* Report prepared for the TIPS, ERSA Paper No. 5, University of the Witwatersrand.

Galbraith, JK, Conceição, P & Ferreira, P (2000) Inequality and unemployment in Europe: The American cure, *New Left Review* 237: 28–51.

Heese, K (1999) *Foreign direct investment in South Africa (1994–1999) – confronting globalisation.* Prepared by BusinessMap for the TIPS Annual Forum, Muldersdrift.

HSRC (1999) *SA labour market: Trends and future workforce needs: 1999–2003.* Pretoria: Human Sciences Research Council.

Kaplinsky, R (1995) Capital intensity in South African manufacturing and unemployment, 1972–90, *World Development* 23 (2): 179–192.

Kitson, M, Michie, J & Sutherland, H (1997) The fiscal and distributional implications of job generation, *Cambridge Journal of Economics* 21: 103–120.

Klasen, S & Woolard, I (2000) *Surviving unemployment without state support: Unemployment and household formation in South Africa.* Paper presented at Annual Meeting of European Society for Population Economics, Bonn 15–17.06.00.

Laubscher, P (2002) *The South African business cycle over the 1990s: What can we learn?* Paper presented at the TIPS Annual Forum, Glenburn Lodge, Muldersdrift.

Lewis, J (2001) *Policies to promote growth and employment in South Africa.* Informal Discussion Papers on Aspects of the Economy of South Africa, No. 16, World Bank.

LFS (various) *Labour Force Surveys.* Pretoria: Statistics South Africa.

Mazumdar, D & Basu, P (1997) Macroeconomic policies, growth and employment: The East and South-East Asian Experience, in AR Kahn & M Muqtada (eds.) *Employment expansion and macroeconomic stability under increasing globalisation.* London: ILO Studies Series, MacMillan.

MERG (1993) *Making democracy work: A framework for macroeconomic policy in South Africa.* Cape Town: OUP.

Meth, C (2001) *Unemployment in South Africa – what the latest figures tell us.* Unpublished paper, University of Natal.

Ministry of Finance, RSA (1996) *Growth, employment and redistribution: A macroeconomic strategy* (Gear).

Moleke, P & Fourie, K (2003) *The employment experience of graduates.* Pretoria: HSRC, (forthcoming report).

Moore, D (1999) The Aids threat and the private sector, *Aids Analysis Africa* 9 (6): 1–2.

National Treasury (2001) *Budget Review.* Pretoria.

O'Connell, PJ (1999) *Astonishing success: Economic growth and the labour market in Ireland.* Employment and Training Papers, No. 44, Employment and Training Department, ILO, Geneva.

OHS (various) *October Household Surveys.* Pretoria: Statistics South Africa.

SARB (2000) *Annual Economic Report.* South African Reserve Bank.

South African Foundation (1996) *Growth for all.* Discussion document. Johannesburg.

Standing, G, Sender, J & Weeks, J (1996) *Restructuring the labour market: The South African challenge.* An ILO Country Review, International Labour Office.

Syrquin, M & Chenery, HB (1989) *Patterns of development, 1950 to 1983.* World Bank Discussion Papers, No. 41, World Bank, Washington, DC.

Weeks, J (1999) Stuck in low Gear? Macroeconomic policy in South Africa, 1996–98, *Cambridge Journal of Economics* 23 (6): 795–811.

The state of trade unionism in post-apartheid South Africa

Sakhela Buhlungu

Introduction: Trade unions and the double transition

The trade union movement has played a pivotal role in South Africa's history, and never more so than from the 1980s. This chapter focuses primarily on how the political and economic changes of the post-1990 transition era in South African politics have impacted on the trade union movement, changes which some have characterised as a 'double transition' (Webster & Adler 1999).

For the greater part of the twentieth century the South African trade union movement was divided into insiders and outsiders, a cleavage that coincided with race, occupation and access (or lack thereof) to legal recognition and protection. As insiders, white workers had industrial and political citizenship and their unions enjoyed legal recognition, rights and protection. On the other hand, black workers[1] and their unions were outsiders and were denied the rights of industrial and political citizenship that their white counterparts enjoyed. This duality ended in 1979 when the apartheid state accepted that worker militancy could no longer be contained through repression alone, and adopted the Wiehahn Commission's recommendations to unify the labour relations dispensation under one law, the *Labour Relations Act* (LRA).

Today the majority of organised workers belong to unions affiliated to one of three major federations, namely, Cosatu, the Federation of Unions of South Africa (Fedusa) and the National Council of Trade Unions (Nactu). Although it was formally founded in 1985, Cosatu's history goes back to the early 1970s with the emergence of unions for black workers inspired by the strikes of 1973. In 1986 those black unions which for largely ideological reasons had opted not to join the Charterist-aligned Cosatu, formed the more racially-exclusive Nactu. With an initial paid-up membership of 200 000, Nactu had a predominantly black blue-collar membership.

Fedusa is a relatively new federation, but its affiliated unions are not. Originating mostly as craft unions and staff associations, these unions represent a predominantly white white-collar membership. Their decision to regroup under the federation was motivated by fears of marginalisation in the post-apartheid era.

Cosatu today overshadows the other federations in terms of membership size, campaigns and activities, the public profile of its leadership, and the influence it has in relation to employers and the state. It is the largest trade union federation in the history of South Africa, with a paid-up membership of 1,8 million members organised into 20 affiliates. By contrast, Nactu claims a total membership of about 397 106 in 19 affiliates[2] and Fedusa approximately 530,000 in 26 affiliates.[3] In addition to the three federations, there are other smaller federations and a number of independent or unaffiliated unions, most of which are very small.

Cosatu has an overtly political orientation with its alliance with the ANC and the SACP. Although Nactu is a political federation it has not aligned itself to any political party. It draws its membership from two different traditions in the liberation movement, namely Pan-Africanism and Black Consciousness and insists on black leadership of the union movement, a view that contrasts with what it regards as the colour-blind non-racialism of Cosatu. Fedusa pursues a policy of apolitical non-alignment and is particularly critical of Cosatu's alliance with the ANC and the SACP.

Fedusa unions have weak grassroots structures and power tends to be concentrated in national structures run by powerful full-time officials. By contrast, the other two federations, particularly Cosatu, were until recently characterised by a greater degree of decentralisation of power and vibrant grassroots structures such as shop stewards' committees and local councils and branch and regional structures.

The development of black trade unionism in the late apartheid era occurred in the context of opposition to racist and authoritarian workplace regimes. Its power derived from its ability to organise and to render first the workplace and then the country 'ungovernable'. In short, the militant unionism of this period, its ability to unite black workers and the influence it exercised in the rest of society, was a product of racial despotism in general, compounded by employer intransigence and state repression. And one of its legacies was an entrenched tradition of opposition to management and managerial plans and decisions.

Until the mid-1990s the black trade union movement retained their strength and occupied a powerful position *vis-à-vis* the state and capital, impacting significantly on the process of political and economic restructuring then underway. This influence translated into concrete gains including legislative provisions such as those embodied in the new *Labour Relations Act* of 1995 and participation in labour market and macroeconomic policy formulation through such institutions as the tripartite Nedlac.

However, the movement has not been able to sustain this level of influence or to take full advantage of some of its gains. The advent of democracy and the acceleration of processes of globalisation are producing today a realignment of political and class forces, largely to the detriment of the union movement. Today, the labour movement confronts a dramatically altered political economy. It has had, consequently, to revise notions of 'the enemy' and 'the oppressor' and to modify its attitude to both the state and employers. Many unionists now find themselves working in some kind of partnership with employers and or the government, and have had to jettison the 1980s notion of 'smashing' capitalism in favour of a discourse of reconstruction and social partnership.

Union organisation in transition

In the 30 years since 1973, two major changes have had a profound effect on the character of South African labour unions. The first was the granting of official recognition to black unions in 1979. This paved the way for spectacular union growth in the 1970s and 1980s. For example, overall union density figures in the non-agricultural sectors of the economy grew from 14,8 per cent in 1973 to 57,5 per cent in 1996. This was largely due to a growing unionisation of African workers. From 1981–1988 African union membership grew by almost 700 000, while the membership of other racial groups declined (Macun 2002).

As significantly, union recognition by the state and employers made possible the institutionalisation of trade unionism for black workers. For example, recognition accorded unions the right to stop-order facilities for membership subscriptions, the right to negotiate on behalf of workers and sign binding agreements with employers, the right for union officials to gain access to the employer's premises and the right to elect shop stewards.

The stop-order facility resolved what had been a perennial problem for black unions in South Africa, namely their lack of a sustainable resource base. Unions could now employ full-time officials and guarantee them a monthly salary and, in some cases, a few basic benefits. The right of unions to negotiate on behalf of their members served to entrench the position of these full-time officials. Even during the heyday of 'the worker-control tradition' (or democratic unionism), the full-time official was expected to be present at all important negotiations and to be the chief signatory to agreements concluded. Importantly, these reforms of the late 1970s failed to produce the bureaucratic tendencies many sociological studies of trade unionism had warned about. Industrial citizenship in the workplace did nothing to diminish the black worker's aspiration for full political citizenship; indeed, it served as a catalyst to the struggle for political liberation.

By contrast, the second of the significant changes of the post-1973 era – political democratisation – ironically has impacted negatively on the union movement in a number of different ways. First, it opened up new opportunities[4] for upward mobility for black people in general, and union activists in particular. Since 1994, hundreds of union officials have left worker ranks for political office, while many others have been the beneficiaries of the affirmative action and black economic empowerment policies of the new dispensation (Buhlungu 1994b). Furthermore, with the unbanning of political movements, unions lost their monopoly of legitimacy as 'struggle employers' as new 'struggle job opportunities' appeared within the ANC, the SACP and other organisations. Likewise, with their new legitimacy acquired after the ANC came to power in 1994, state institutions like the civil service attracted union workers into their ranks where they enjoyed much higher salaries and superior benefits. At the same time, managerial jobs, which were previously regarded with suspicion by unionists, now attracted a growing number of unionists. A new discourse of 'going into management' to 'influence a culture change from within' encouraged many union officials and shop stewards to take up positions at management level.

Accompanying this process has been another significant development, namely an erosion of those notions of altruism and collective solidarity which had characterised the struggle era, and the concomitant emergence of a new value system based on individualism. Comradely relations among activists have, to a not insignificant degree, been replaced by competition for positions and power. Within unions themselves, top positions such as those of regional secretary, general secretary and president into which officials were previously elected unopposed, have now become arenas for fierce competition. By contrast, at the other end of the membership scale there has been a demobilisation on the part of the rank-and-file membership, something which has manifested itself in diminishing levels of participation in such union activities as mass meetings and rallies.

Ironically, the introduction of a labour-friendly labour relations dispensation[5] with legitimate centralised institutions for negotiation and consultation between labour, the state and employers (such as Nedlac and Industry Bargaining Councils) has intensified this depoliticisation process as it has entrenched a corporatist trend within the union movement. This corporatist tendency has engendered an often secretive, unaccountable and elitist bargaining style wholly at variance with the painstaking processes of mandating and reporting back that was established practice in the apartheid era. This trend has also left lower-level union structures, such as shop stewards' committees and local shop stewards' councils, in a state of some powerlessness.

Finally, the advent of democracy has introduced new pressures on unions to abandon their social-movement character and to operate like conventional social institutions. New practices or operational styles have emerged ranging from abandoning township church venues for meetings in favour of upmarket hotels and international convention centres, to the introduction of grades and differential remuneration based on market trends and the professionalisation of union activities in general. There have also been changes to the dress code, to the cars which officials drive, and in general, the social circles in which they move.

In short, the political democratisation of South Africa marked the deepening of the process of institutionalisation of the union movement that began with the granting of recognition at the end of the 1970s. Today trade-union education courses on organisational development are standard menu for labour-supporting organisations and in internal union education programmes. They borrow concepts and principles contained in standard business management textbooks. In addition, mainstream economics and industrial relations theories find their way into the unions via union officials and shop stewards who enrol for custom-made courses at local universities and technikons, many of which run courses jointly with foreign, principally British and Australian, universities.

Meanwhile, academic disciplines such as sociology and economic history that were intimately associated with the birth and development of the post-1973 unions, are increasingly finding themselves without a role in the new union movement. During the formative years of the new unions, the Marxist orientation of these disciplines, as well as their focus on collective action, provided a generation of activists with intellectual skills to support the labour movement. It also created the space for intellectuals and activists to engage critically with the goals and practices of this movement. However, in recent years both the theoretical framework and the substantive issues have shifted away from social movements towards human-resource management. Importantly too, other academic institutions and disciplines have been more adept than these traditional disciplines in repositioning and marketing themselves to the unions. For example, some technikons and management faculties at universities have been developing courses and services that respond to the instrumental notions of knowledge in a movement that is under pressure to find quick solutions to complex problems.

For many years some observers and union activists assumed that the militancy of the workers and the democratic union traditions that were developed in the 1970s and 1980s would endure into the future. However, today these practices and traditions have been eroded in ways that mirror established movements elsewhere in the world. The erosion of the tradition of grassroots unionism or worker control has resulted in a shift of power from workers and constitutional structures to full-time officials and national leadership (Buhlungu 2002a).

A related theme is that of leadership issues in the unions. Leadership is now less accountable to the rank-and-file and its vision and goals are murkier. In recent years, countless reports of undemocratic behaviour and even corrupt practices by union leaders have been reported in the media. Although some of the media reports tend to contain some exaggerations and distortion of facts, the picture that is emerging is of a union movement whose democratic character is being contested by new forces driven by individualism. Larger unions which are under threat of being destabilised by these changes include the National Union of Metalworkers of South Africa (Numsa), the National Union of Mineworkers (NUM), the National Education, Health and Allied Workers' Union (Nehawu) and the South African Commercial, Catering and Allied Workers' Union (Saccawu), all Cosatu affiliates.

There have also been reports of late that all three union federations and several of their affiliates are facing serious financial problems (Grawitzky 2002; Hlangani 2002). Although many of these problems are related to a diminishing membership base as a result of job loss and the inability of unions to organise atypical workers, there have also been cases of fraud and corruption (Grawitzky 2002). It should be pointed out, however, that both unions and the federations have been attempting to adapt union strategies to changing circumstances with a view to maintaining their strength. In the mid-1990s, Fedusa's predecessor, the now defunct Federation of South African Labour (Fedsal), took a conscious decision to reposition itself by, among other things, launching an aggressive drive to recruit African members and by seeking to revive its shopfloor structures. It has also worked hard to improve its public profile, particularly through use of advertising. According to an observer at the Federation's 2002 national congress, some of this is beginning to pay off:

> Fedusa is increasingly beginning to represent a broader category of workers. The federation has a strange mix of unions: from traditionally white unions to those more multi-racial and almost exclusively black unions. This diversity was far more evident at the congress than in previous years. [O]ne could see that the federation is hard at work seeking a higher degree of legitimacy both from within government and from amongst its fellow trade unionists in other federations such as Cosatu. (South African Labour Bulletin 2002: 63)

Nonetheless, the general features of the crisis facing trade unions are still present in Fedusa. Decision-making in the federation remains highly centralised and there is little participation by members in the affairs of their respective affiliates.

Of the three federations Nactu has kept the lowest profile since 1994, but it is common knowledge that its structures are weak and that the organisation is hierarchical and run in a top-down manner (Macun 2000). It remains, as it has always been, the smallest of the three federations.

Since 1994, Cosatu has continued to occupy centre-stage as the largest and most active labour centre in the country. Furthermore, it has on several occasions engaged in introspective exercises to assess its strength, and has produced some of the most interesting and innovative initiatives to revitalise its structures and affiliates. In developing these strategies, Cosatu has often tried harder than its sister federations to engage constituencies and activists outside the union movement itself. In this way it has managed to place itself and its issues firmly in the public domain. This has been achieved by using such innovative methods as placing its discussion documents and resolutions on the internet, effective media use, establishing a mouthpiece in *The Shopsteward*, and making use of the services of researchers and other intellectuals based outside the movement.

Soon after the 1994 elections, Cosatu acknowledged that its structures had taken a heavy toll from the federation's campaign in support of the ANC, and from the departure of scores of union leaders. It undertook to 'go back to the basics' to ensure organisational renewal (Buhlungu 1994a). Although little came of the 'back-to-basics' campaign, the acknowledgement of weaknesses was significant in itself, particularly because it later gave birth to several initiatives to revitalise the federation and its affiliates. For example, in 1994 Cosatu established a research centre, the National Labour and Economic Development Institute (NALEDI), to provide research back-up to the federation and its affiliates. At the end of 1996, Cosatu and Fedusa jointly launched the Development Institute for Training, Support and Education for Labour (DITSELA) which provides education and training to union leadership, with a strong emphasis on skills development.

However, the most ambitious initiative in recent years was Cosatu's Commission into the Future of Unions tasked with investigating and recommending strategies for the future of the federation and its affiliates. It comprised a 12-member team of current and former unionists chaired by Cosatu's then second Vice President, Connie September. Its final report was published in August 1997 and represents a detailed assessment of the problems facing the unions in the post-1994 dispensation.

The commission recommended several strategies for organisational renewal. Most important of these was that the federation should embrace what it termed 'social unionism', that is, a model of unionism combining a strong commitment to grassroots unionism and a strong shopfloor base with an engagement with the social and political concerns of its members and the broader working class beyond the workplace. This implied a commitment to building alliances to further the interests of its members (September Commission 1997).

Notwithstanding these and other initiatives undertaken by unions and federations, the state of union organisation has not improved much. This is partly
due to the fact that unionists have continued to leave the movement en masse
to take up jobs in other spheres, principally in politics, management and business. This point is explored later in this chapter.

Trade union activity

In the run-up to the first democratic election in 1994, many observers of the
union movement predicted that the post-election period would see increased
efforts by the movement to achieve unity. This prediction has not materialised
as the union movement still remains fragmented both at industry and federation levels. Between 1990–96 the number of unions increased from 198 to
248 but many of these were small and unaffiliated to any federation (Macun
2000). In 2001 the number of unions registered with the DoL stood at 485,
down from an all-time high of 499 in 1999 (DoL 2002). Apart from the emergence of many small unions, the post-1994 period also saw divisions within
some of the largest unions that often resulted in the formation of splinter
unions – as in the cases of the NUM, the Food and Allied Workers' Union
(Fawu), the Transport and General Workers' Union (TGWU), Numsa and the
Chemical Workers' Industrial Union (CWIU).

In line with the recommendations of the September Commission, Cosatu
decided in the late 1990s to establish super-unions, which brought together
groupings from different industries or sectors. The rationale was to pool
resources to achieve economies of scale in an environment where some sectors of the economy were in decline. Since then at least three super-unions
have been established in the mining/construction, paper/printing/chemical
and the transport/security sectors services. It is too early to assess the success
or otherwise of this strategy.

On the positive side, though, considerable progress has been achieved by many
unions in terms of attracting new constituencies, particularly members from
occupational and racial groups that were formerly not part of those unions'
traditional constituencies (Baskin 1996; September Commission 1997). This is
particularly the case with unions affiliated to Cosatu and Fedusa.

At the level of unity of the federations, success has continued to elude the
union movement. Indeed, the subject of unity of the three federations has not

been broached since the mid-1990s. Even Cosatu's September Commission avoided the issue, and today it would appear that the vision of 'one country, one federation' has fallen off the agenda of the union movement. The chief obstacles to trade union unity seem to be the different histories and political and organisational traditions of the three major federations (outlined earlier in this chapter). In addition, in an environment where union leaders have become part of the new polity's power elite, unions are now important power bases that those aspiring to leadership will not abandon easily.

Unions and the economy

Concurrent with its political transition, South Africa has shed its economic isolation and its inward-looking industrialisation strategy and actively sought to reintegrate itself into a globalising economy. This has confronted the union movement with an additional set of challenges. First, it has tilted the capital-labour balance of power in favour of the former. In the late 1980s, the unions had the initiative and were able to dictate the pace and direction of change through the use of various forms of mass action. However, the globalisation process of the 1990s has enabled capital to seize the initiative and put unions on the defensive. Although unions are still able to mobilise and take industrial action, such tactics are now essentially back-to-the-wall defensive strategies in a context where workers are faced with unemployment and retrenchment.

Second, globalisation has facilitated capital mobility from one country to another and from one region of the world to another. Locally, this has been evident in the relocation of both South African and foreign companies to other African countries where labour markets are perceived to be more flexible. The relocation of a number of Taiwanese firms from the Ciskei to Swaziland after 1994 is a case in point. This mobility has drastically limited the options of unions in dealing with capital.

Third, globalisation has accelerated the restructuring of work and work modes and seen the introduction of more flexible forms of work (such as sub-contracting and home-based work). This has undermined the capacity of unions to organise and build membership. In South Africa, the sectors most affected by these developments have been retail (especially the shop assistant level) and manufacturing, especially clothing and textiles.

The above trends have all affected membership levels in the trade union movement. Membership trends in Cosatu provide a good illustration of this point (this is partly because only Cosatu and its affiliates have been consistent in making their membership records publicly available). Table 8.1 below shows membership changes between 2000 and 2001, and compares the 2001 figure with the union's all-time high membership figure.

Table 8.1 *Cosatu membership 2001, 2002 and all-time high membership figures* [6]

Affiliate	Membership 2000	Membership 2001	Change from 2000 – 2001	All-time high (year)
CEPPWAWU	73 720	65 000	– 8 720	98 900 (1996) *
CWU	35 008	35 008	0	40 398 (1999)
FAWU	119 302	119 302	0	139 810 (1995)
NEHAWU	234 607	234 607	0	234 607 (2001)
NUM	290 070	279 099	– 10 971	339 430 (1996) **
NUMSA	200 000	200 000	0	220 000 (1991)
PAWE	2 571	2 571	0	2 571 (2001)
POPCRU	70 618	66 681	– 3 937	70 618 (2000)
RAPWU	18 317	18 317	0	18 317 (2001)
SAAPAWU	22 163	22 163	0	33 000 (1993)
SACCAWU	102 234	102 234	0	118 417 (1999)
SACTWU	119 930	119 792	– 138	185 740 (1991)
SADNU	8 128	8 128	0	8 128 (2001)
SADTU	218 747	214 547	– 4 200	218 747 (2000)
SAFPU	400	22	– 378	400 (2000)
SAMWU	119 792	119 792	0	120 109 (1997)
SASAWU	18 000	18 003	+ 3	18 003 (2001)
SASBO	63 046	60 824	– 2 222	74 145 (1995)
SATAWU	103 218	103 218	0	103 218 (2001)
Total	1 819 871	1 789 308	– 30 563	N/A

Sources: Naidoo 1999 and Cosatu 2001

* CEPPWAWU did not exist in 1996. This figure was obtained by adding up the membership of its predecessors, CWIU and PPWAWU, in that year.

** In 1999 the construction union, Cawu, was absorbed into NUM in terms of the federation's policy of building 'super unions'. This figure was obtained by adding up the membership of NUM and Cawu in 1996.

Fourth, globalisation is also emerging as a threat to labour rights. After 1994, the new democratic government promulgated a new set of labour laws which granted workers new rights and protections. From that day, organised capital in South Africa has mounted a frontal attack on these new protections. The South African Foundation (SAF), a lobby group representing powerful business interests, has led the charge against the creation of what they consider to be an extremely inflexible labour market. What the Foundation proposes instead is a two-tier labour market, with one enjoying labour rights, while a second free-entry tier is exempted from labour rights and minimum standards. There are indications that notions of economic liberalisation such as these enjoy significant support within the ANC, but the party has thus far resisted pressures to dismantle the post-1994 labour-friendly dispensation. Even so, the new government has been shifting to the right since it assumed office in 1994 and this shift is characterised by a largely uncritical acceptance at Cabinet level of the logic of neoliberal globalisation. The clearest indication of this shift was the adoption of a neoliberal macroeconomic policy known as Gear and a downgrading, or rather dismantling, of the RDP. Neither the SACP nor Cosatu were party to or informed about any of these radically important changes in political direction.

The union movement's response to Gear took the form of a discussion document issued by the labour caucus at Nedlac. The document sought to steer the government in an interventionist direction so that union concerns about social equity and job creation could be prioritised (Cosatu, Nactu & Fedsal 1996). However, after the document had been issued the three federations failed to build a common front and Cosatu tended to go it alone, while the other two kept a low profile. Since then, Cosatu has led several struggles against Gear and policies associated with it such as privatisation. Since 2000 the federation has mounted three general strikes (2000, 2001 and 2002). These have been to little avail, although they have certainly slowed the pace of planned privatisations. Eroding Cosatu's stance has been the fact that neither of the other two federations supported the second and third of the general strikes, while in the wider political arena only the SACP has steadfastly backed all of Cosatu's mass actions. Despite these shifts in the ANC government's economic policies and the tensions they have generated between the federation and the ruling party, Cosatu has, however, remained part of the Tripartite Alliance and has continued to throw its electoral weight behind the ANC. The significance of this is discussed in the next section of this chapter.

Despite the labour movement's opposition to the government's embrace of the market economy, it has itself entered the marketplace through the formation of investment companies which have acquired equity in some of the major corporations in the name of 'black economic empowerment'. Likewise, even though unions have adopted strident anti-privatisation and anti-outsourcing positions, some union investment companies have been amongst the bidders when state corporations have gone up for sale or when their activities have been outsourced. This strategy will be examined and its failures or successes assessed. The long-term implications of this seeming contradiction in union policies and actions are not clear at this stage. But what is clear is that the contradiction opens the union movement to accusations of hypocrisy.

Unions and politics

As indicated above, the Tripartite Alliance has in recent times come under stress, but an inevitable fracture should not be assumed. There are compelling reasons for Cosatu to remain inside the tent. One is the access the Alliance gives it to the patronage which the ANC is able to bestow on those loyal to it; another is the avenue it opens up for upward social mobility (Buhlungu 2002b). But perhaps the most compelling reason of all is the fear that a break-up of the Alliance would leave the federation in the political wilderness. In other words it would be the big loser.

In recent years the ANC has changed from treating Cosatu as a special ally to treating it as just one among many forces in society. It now finds itself having to compete along with big business, black business, international financial institutions, foreign governments, traditional leaders and even other union federations for the ANC's attention. At the same time, the ANC has attacked what it calls an 'ultra-left element' within Cosatu which it believes wish to take control of the party and turn it into a socialist organisation (Mbeki 2002; Moleketi & Jele 2002).

With regard to civil society, most unions and union federations have since 1994 tended to stand apart from other civil society bodies and adopt a go-it-alone approach. While this is not so surprising in regard to Nactu and Fedusa in that they have never had strong ties to civil society, it is a new development for Cosatu. Instead, Cosatu has invested its coalition-building efforts in trying to maintain their alliance with the ANC and the SACP. But this is not the sole reason. Ever since its formation in the 1980s, Cosatu has adopted a

vanguardist-type approach in its relationship with other movements. Its attitude is that it is the historic leader of civil society and that other movements
need it more that it needs them. As a result, in the post-1994 period, the federation has invested little time and resources in trying to build coalitions
outside of the Tripartite Alliance. This approach has left the union movement
increasingly isolated and few organisations have come either to its assistance
or defence when it has been under attack. This was well illustrated during the
October 2002 general strike organised by Cosatu where the federation along
with a weak SACP, fought a near lone battle. Even the South African National
Civic Organisation (Sanco), Cosatu's traditional ally from the struggle days,
distanced itself from the strike.

The other area in which the union movement has lost tremendous support is
amongst intellectuals. Historically, most black unions which emerged in the
early 1970s (and today are mostly in Nactu or Cosatu) had strong bonds with
progressive intellectuals, many of whom were in universities and labour-supporting organisations. Most of these intellectuals shared the radical political
orientation of these unions and, in many cases, the unions looked up to these
intellectuals. Today, most of this support is no longer there, with some intellectuals having shifted their energies to other social movements and causes.
However, as significantly, many others from this intellectual corps have themselves changed their spots and embraced a different politics that emphasises
market regulation of social life.

Many activists and observers now look back nostalgically to the era of social
movement unionism of the 1980s and early 1990s, and imagine that this form
of unionism can be revived. However, as von Holdt (2002) has argued, the
concept of social-movement unionism is an ambiguous one and the movement it describes derived its vitality not only from class identities but also
from pre-modern and non-class identities. Thus, any strategy that is intended
to revitalise the union movement should locate itself within what von Holdt
(2002) calls the 'era of democratic post-colonial reconstruction'. Not only does
this imply new approaches by unions to alliance-building, it also means that
unions have to develop new approaches of engaging the democratic state on
the basis of the present and the future rather than sentiment and history.

Unions and the democratic state

Today the democratic South African state enjoys legitimacy in the eyes of the
union movement. This has occasioned a shift in relations with the state from

an exclusive one of adversarialism and confrontation to one which has a degree of co-operation. Even in those cases where unions have since 1994 taken mass action against state institutions, the legitimacy of the state has never been questioned. In addition, the democratic dispensation has created new avenues for all unions and federations to influence policies in ways that were not imaginable before 1994. Today, at least two of the union federations (Cosatu and Fedusa) have permanent parliamentary offices staffed by experienced unionists whose job it is to lobby parliamentarians and members of the Cabinet and to make submissions to portfolio committees.

In addition, all three federations are active participants in Nedlac where they have an opportunity to influence government policies before they are taken to parliament. Union influence has also been exercised through other means and platforms, such as the Presidential Job Summit of 1998 and the Millennium Labour Council. In most of these platforms employers are also involved, which ensures that capital and labour have equal access to the state.

However, this recognition of the union movement as an important social force under the democratic dispensation has had its downside too. Union leaders now spend an inordinate amount of time in meetings and consultations with state and business representatives with the result that internal democratic processes in the unions have been neglected. National engagement of this kind has also engendered a different style for union leaders with the emphasis now being on deal-making and complicated agreements which, in turn, has generated a reliance on so-called 'experts' rather than rank-and-file activists.

This element of co-operative relations with the state should not be over-emphasised, however. There is still a high degree of conflict occasioned particularly by the government's adoption of Gear and the related policy of privatisation. Disagreement at the collective bargaining table has been the other source of conflict between public sector workers and state institutions at local government and national levels. In the last nine years, the most traumatic clashes have been those involving nurses, teachers and municipal workers.

Confrontation is set to deepen in future, particularly when the government intensifies its drive to privatise parastatals and reduce the size of the public sector. This will bring the state into confrontation with various public sector unions, whose membership overall in 1999 stood at 656 748, with two (Nehawu and Sadtu) having over 200 000 members each. There has been some drop in membership since then, but these two remain formidable bodies and they and other unions will resist any assault on the size of the public sector.

International relations

The South African union movement has a long history of solidarity and links with unions in Africa and the rest of the world. Prior to 1994, these links mostly took the form of international unions providing moral, political and material support to local unions. Since 1994, there has been a change to these relations. Instead of always being on the receiving end of outside help, the South African union movement has become a proactive player internationally. Today Cosatu is an active member of the Southern African Trade Union Co-ordinating Council (SATUCC), the Organisation of African Trade Union Unity (OATUU) and the International Confederation of Free Trade Unions (ICFTU). In 1998, it hosted the World Congress of this confederation in Durban. For the last 11 years Cosatu has played an active role in forging union linkages in the south, particularly through the Southern Initiative on Globalisation and Trade Union Rights (SIGTUR), which brings together union federations from 14 developing countries. Finally, Cosatu (and to some extent Nactu) affiliates have regional and international links with sister unions in various parts of the world, mostly through industry-based trade union secretariats.

Conclusion

Overall, the democratic era in South Africa has been paradoxical for the union movement. It has brought some important victories (the 1996 LRA in particular) and a significant degree of influence. I have tried to provide an overview here of these achievements while also seeking to highlight the immense challenges and problems now confronting the movement. Most of these, as I have shown, flow from the changed political circumstances in the country as well as from the insertion of South Africa into the modern global economy. Of these problems, I have highlighted the loss of organisational vibrancy, the threat of a fragmentation with the potential to paralyse the movement, and the consequences flowing from the restructuring of the workplace and the broader economy.

The history of the South African labour movement offers few lessons for how this paradox of victory and setbacks can be confronted. Indeed, there is an extent to which an aspect of that history has become a burden and hinders the search for creative strategies to confront the situation. One such burden is the ongoing Tripartite Alliance, which makes it difficult for Cosatu to think creatively about coalition formation in a democratic environment. As a result, the federation has thus far excluded one of trade unionism's historic weapons, namely, the use of the unionised workers' vote either to win ruling-party support or to withhold it where the party adopts anti-labour positions. This failure has forced Cosatu to rely exclusively on the strike as its most potent weapon at an inopportune time when the economy is shedding jobs.

The state of the union movement as presented in this chapter has several implications for the state of the nation in South Africa. First, a union movement that is weakening politically and organisationally poses negative consequences for the consolidation of democracy. This concern becomes more serious when we consider the general weakness of opposition political parties and the dismal state of other civil-society organisations in the country. A successful consolidation of democracy requires both strong opposition parties and independent extra-parliamentary movements, which collectively can act as a counterweight to a dominant ruling party. In the context of South Africa, it is important that such a countervailing party or movement should have 'struggle credibility' and that it should draw the bulk of its membership from the black population. The role of such independent forces is not simply to oppose government when it adopts and implements misguided policies, but also to articulate and represent the interests of their constituencies in ways that the ruling party is unable to do. In this context, the labour movement has a vital role to play.

Second, there is a risk of the current crop of unions becoming discredited in the eyes of many South Africans, including some workers. I have argued earlier that trade unions are generally isolated from the rest of civil society in that they tend to adopt a go-it-alone approach to engaging with political issues. In addition, some unions have responded in contradictory ways to some of the recent changes in the country, causing some to accuse unions of acting in a hypocritical manner. The danger is that the more unions become discredited, the more they will want to prove their relevance by embarking on militant actions, which may not be the most appropriate way of achieving best results.

Third, in the short term the corporatist relationship that has existed between unions, employers and the state, as well as the alliance between Cosatu and the ANC, have been beneficial in terms of political stability. Terminating these relationships could therefore be politically destabilising for the country. However, a continuation of these arrangements does not carry any long-term benefits for the unions. As shown above, the ANC has demonstrated before that Nedlac and the Tripartite Alliance can be bypassed. In the meantime, union internal democratic practices have become eroded while many union leaders have found themselves trapped in patronage relationships with the ruling party. The challenges posed by the democratic transition and neoliberal globalisation necessitate that unions should jealously guard their political and organisational independence. This further implies that unions should explore new kinds of coalitions and ways of exercising influence that are different to those that worked well in the past in social democratic countries, namely, corporatism and alliances with ruling parties.

Finally, none of the above should be construed to suggest that South Africa's unions are facing imminent collapse. Instead, what is suggested is that trade unionism in post-apartheid South Africa is changing. The unionism of yesteryear that was based on mobilisation, collective action and grassroots participation is gradually giving way to one based on deal-making by a few national leaders. Under these changed circumstances, unions are judged by the ruling party less on their ability to articulate and represent the interests of their members and more on their ability to act in what is perceived or articulated as the national interest. Whether such a form of unionism is positive in regard to democratic consolidation is open to debate, but what is certain is that the era of militant unionism in which millions of South and southern African workers played a leading role in bringing democracy to South Africa is for now dead and buried. The times have changed and the unions are changing with it.

Notes

1   However, it must be pointed out that some black workers, namely Indian and coloured workers, enjoyed full trade union rights from the start. Thus, strictly speaking, only African workers were outsiders.

2   See http://www.nactu.org.za/index2.html.

3   See http://www.fedusa.org.za/affiliates.index.htm.

4   The September Commission (1997) also identified similar changes which had occurred since the end of apartheid. These were: a weakening vision and shared ideology within the unions; engagement with many complex issues; a shift from mass militancy to national negotiations; loss of experienced staff and worker leaders; massive growth of unions; growth of a black middle class and a culture of self-enrichment which undermines the culture of solidarity in unions; and negative organisational trends such as lack of service to members, lack of skills, lack of discipline and lack of commitment (168).

5   The centrepiece of this labour-friendly dispensation is the LRA of 1995. Other pieces of legislation include the *Basic Conditions of Employment Act* of 1997, the *Employment Equity Act* of 1998 and the *Skills Development Act* of 1998.

6   The 2001 Secretariat Report to the 1st Central Committee of Cosatu noted that despite 'massive job losses' in manufacturing and mining, most affiliates had not revised membership figures from those submitted for the federation's congress in 2000. The report also noted that SACCAWU had 'not modified its membership since 1994!' (Cosatu 2001). Thus figures should be treated with extreme caution as affiliate figures submitted to federations for credentials tend to be inflated above their actual levels. This is because bigger numbers mean larger delegations to the central committee and the national congress.

References

Baskin, J (1996) Unions at the crossroads: can they make the transition, *South African Labour Bulletin* 20 (1): 8–16.

Buhlungu, S (1994a) Cosatu and the elections, *South African Labour Bulletin* 18 (2): 7–17.

Buhlungu, S (1994b) The big brain drain: union officials in the 1990s, *South African Labour Bulletin* 18 (3): 25–32.

Buhlungu, S (2002a) *Comrades, entrepreneurs and career unionists: organisational modernisation and new cleavages among COSATU union officials.* Occasional Paper No. 17, Friedrich Ebert Stiftung, Johannesburg.

Buhlungu, S (2002b) From 'Madiba magic' to 'Mbeki logic': Mbeki and the ANC's union allies in S Jacobs & R Calland (eds.) *Thabo Mbeki's world: myth, ideology and the politics of Thabo Mbeki.* Pietermaritzburg: University of Natal Press.

COSATU (2001) *Secretariat report to the 1st Central Committee*, 19-21.11.01, Esselen Park, Kempton Park (http://www.cosatu.org.za/cc2001/orgarep.htm – accessed on 10 March 2003).

COSATU, NACTU & FEDSAL (1996) *Social equity and job creation: the key to a stable future.* Johannesburg: NEDLAC Labour Caucus.

DoL (Department of Labour) (2002). *Preliminary Annual Report, 2001/2002.*

Grawitzky, R (2002) Financial crisis hits unions, *South African Labour Bulletin* 26 (3): 61–62.

Hlangani, M (2002) Labour federation NACTU is under pressure, *The Star*, 03.09.02.

Macun, I (2000) Growth, structure and power in the South African trade union movement, in G Adler & E Webster (eds.) *Trade unions and democratisation in South Africa 1985–1997*. London: Macmillan.

Macun, I (2002) *The dynamics of trade union growth in South Africa, 1970-1996*, Labour Studies Report No.10, Sociology of Work Unit, University of the Witwatersrand, Johannesburg.

Mbeki, T (2002) *Statement of the President of the African National Congress, Thabo Mbeki*, ANC Policy Conference, Kempton Park, 27.09.02.

Moleketi, J & Jele, J (2002) *Two strategies of the national liberation movement in the struggle for the victory of the National Democratic Revolution*. Discussion document, October 2002.

Naidoo, R (1999) *Unions in transition: COSATU into the new millennium.* Johanesburg: NALEDI.

September Commission (1997) *Report of the September Commission.* Johannesburg: COSATU.

South African Foundation (1996) *Growth for all: an economic strategy for South Africa.* Johannesburg: SAF.

South African Labour Bulletin (2002) Fedusa: a congress with a difference, *South African Labour Bulletin* 26 (3): 63–64.

Von Holdt, K (2002) Social movement unionism: The case of South Africa, *Work, Employment and Society* 16 (2): 283–304.

Webster, E & Adler, G (1999) Towards a class compromise in SouthAfrica's double transition: Bargained liberalisation and the consolidation of democracy, *Politics and Society* 27 (2): 347–385.

The state of the labour market in contemporary South Africa

Percy Moleke

Introduction

The state of the labour market in South Africa today is a reflection of the crippling legacies of the apartheid years and, as such, is a major challenge confronting the government. Wherever one looks in the workplace that sector's HRD is characterised by racial inequalities. There are pockets of progress, but this progress has been minuscule in relation to the magnitude of the inequities inherited from the apartheid era.

Historical overview

The inherited state of HRD can be characterised by the following:

○ Race and gender inequalities in the occupational structures.
○ Education and training structures and systems perpetuating and reinforcing the occupational inequities.
○ Huge income inequalities.
○ A shortage of skills in critical areas and an abundance of unproductive skills.
○ Huge unemployment and underemployment rates among Africans.

While there are several reasons for this, the most relevant in the South African context is discrimination in both the pre-labour market and the labour market. Major sectors of the economy, including the public sector, developed rigid forms of division of labour along racial lines. Race was the determining factor in the allocation of people to jobs, particularly in occupations that were largely outside the apprentice system, and those that required a professional qualification: i.e. accountants, engineers, doctors, and so on. However, even in these occupations job opportunities were largely reserved for whites, especially white males. As a result, Africans and women were concentrated in low-skill work and unskilled labour.

The division was established and reinforced by legislation and other barriers to access. Skilled and supervisory job categories were reserved for white workers, while black workers were restricted to unskilled, low-paid job categories. White workers used the trade unions and their institutional and political power to influence the shape of labour laws to their advantage. A system of job reservation was instituted for whites in key occupational categories and sectors. Efforts to employ Africans in higher-level positions reserved for whites were thwarted by closed-shop agreements and other prescriptions, such as higher wages for certain occupations (Webster 1985).

Excluding Africans and women from key occupations in industry and government meant that there was a restricted pool of skilled workers. This undermined the development of essential technical and managerial skills within the economy. Thus the country experienced qualitative and quantitative skill constraints.

Job reservation automatically implied that training, when it took place, was limited and concentrated in the types of skilled jobs reserved for whites. The apprenticeship system, for example, was the main form of industrial training and took place in racially-separate colleges administered by racially-defined education departments. When Africans received apprenticeship training it was concentrated in the relatively low-skill trades, such as welding, boiler-making, fitting and sheet-metal working (Lundall & Kimmie 1992). Even then, those who did receive apprenticeship training found it hard to find placements within industry.

Qualitatively the training had a number of shortcomings. This was underlined by the 1995 World Competitive Report, which ranked South Africa last out of 32 countries in terms of total quality management. The report noted that South African managers were appointed without much training and had low awareness of productivity issues. The National Training Board confirmed the lack of formal management training in South Africa (Standing, Sender & Weeks 1996), which could be attributed to the poor quality of training.

Working practices within firms strengthened and perpetuated the inequities. Hiring policies were such that white males were placed in jobs with training provision and opportunities to enjoy upward mobility within the internal labour market; other groups were placed in jobs requiring least in the way of formal skills, with little scope for occupational advancement. In other words, white males enjoyed an absolute advantage in terms of access to internal promotion paths.

The inequalities in the labour market were aggravated by the shortcomings of the education system. Lack of access to education meant that a large section of the population was functionally illiterate. The 1996 census estimated that about 36 per cent of the population aged 20 years and above were illiterate (SAIRR 2000).

Where Africans did have access to education, the quality and standard was not adequate to ensure a satisfactory supply of potentially productive members of the labour force. The disparities in education were evident in expenditure and resource commitment. A lack of resources created pressure on teachers who had to deal with overcrowded classes, and the low quality of education was reflected in the educational output of Africans. In the mid-1980s it was estimated that the drop-out rate for Africans was about 50 per cent for those between the first year of primary education and first year of secondary education, while that of white pupils was below one per cent. African matriculants also had high failure rates, although a small proportion did matriculate with good maths and science grades.

The result was that few Africans obtained matric results of a standard that enabled them to proceed into higher education. And those who did enter higher education could not meet the requirements for registration in fields that would prepare them for a profession. For example, in 1993 fewer than 20 per cent of black matriculants studied mathematics or physical science, and of those who did, fewer than 20 per cent passed those subjects on the higher grade. In contrast, 61 per cent of white matriculants studied mathematics, a third at the higher grade, and 44 per cent did physical science, half at the higher grade (FRD 1996). As a result, the output of Africans from institutions of higher learning was skewed towards the non-professional degrees, except for teaching.

Historical trends in training

One of the main drawbacks in analysing the state of HRD is the lack of comprehensive research in the area. Some micro-studies do exist, but these are not sufficiently comprehensive. For this reason the Department of Labour (DoL) commissioned a study to 'capture the extent of training prior to the implementation of the new training dispensation' (Kraak, Patterson, Visser & Tustin 2000: Executive Summary). This study provides the baseline information with which to compare subsequent data on training.

The DoL study revealed trends that were common in the apartheid era. It was found that overall, on average, firms spent about 4,4 per cent of their budget on training. This varied by sector, however. For example, forest industries, manufacturing and engineering, food and beverages, and services spent 0,2 per cent, 0,7 per cent, 0,7 per cent and 0,3 per cent respectively of their total remuneration on training (Kraak et al. 2000). The low level of spending was confirmed by a study of manufacturing firms in the greater Johannesburg area, which found that 16 per cent of respondents spent nothing on in-house training and 27 per cent spent nothing on external training (Bhorat & Lundall 2002).

The baseline study also revealed common trends in terms of differentiated spending by size of firm. Small- and medium-sized firms were spending less on training, especially externally-accredited training. Overall, firms recorded a higher rate of on-the-job training. The report showed that whites dominated training in the managerial, professional and technical occupational categories. Africans, on the other hand, were the main participants of training in operative and clerical occupation categories. For example, in the operative occupational category, 83 per cent of those trained were African compared to 4,9 per cent of whites. In the managerial and professional category, whites constituted 71 per cent of those trained compared to 16 per cent of Africans.

Table 9.1 *Training recipients within occupational groups by race*

Occupational group	African	Asian	Coloured	White
Professional	16.4%	7.4%	4.9%	71.3%
Technicians	27.8%	8.6%	8.6%	55.1%
Clerical	30.9%	15.3%	15.8%	37.9%
Services	44.3%	16.2%	17.3%	22.2%
Craft	49.0%	2.6%	8.8%	39.6%
Operators	83.6%	2.3%	9.3%	4.9%
Unskilled	89.4%	0.6%	9.6%	0.4%

Source: Kraak et al. 2000

Women were not only under-represented in certain occupations, especially those requiring high levels of skill, but they also had limited access to training opportunities within these occupations. As the data shows, it was only in the clerical/administration category where, relatively, they enjoyed more training opportunities, (57,9 per cent of those being trained). Women constituted only 28 per cent of trainees in the management/professional category (Kraak et al. 2000).

Table 9.2 *Training recipients within occupational groups by gender*

Occupational group	Percentage male	Percentage female
Professional	71.9	28.1
Technicians	82.9	17.1
Clerical	42.1	57.9
Services	67.0	33.0
Craft	93.5	6.5
Operators	77.9	22.1
Unskilled	79.1	20.9

Source: Kraak et al. 2000

Legislation

Two major pieces of legislation have been enacted since 1994 to address issues of equity and skills shortages in the South African labour market – the *Employment Equity Act* (EEA) and the *Skills Development Act* (SDA). The EEA was passed in 1998, the first piece of legislation dealing specifically with equity that recognised racial and gender disparities affecting labour market opportunities. The EEA aims to eliminate discrimination and establish specific measures to accelerate the advancement of designated groups – i.e. women, blacks and people with disabilities – by using affirmative action. Affirmative action measures are aimed at ensuring that suitably qualified people from designated groups have equal employment opportunities and are equitably represented at all levels in all occupational categories. The Act prohibits discrimination by a 'designated employer' (direct or indirect) on the basis of race, gender, age and sexual orientation, among others. A 'designated employer' excludes an employer of 50 or fewer employees and whose annual turnover is less than that stipulated for a small business in Schedule 4 of the Act. The EEA was complemented in the public sector by the *Public Service Laws Amendment Act* of 1997. This Act focused on the drive to achieve equality in public sector appointments, and the constitutional goals of a public service broadly representative of the South African population with regard to race, gender and disability.

Supporting both these acts are the SDA and *Skills Levies Act* passed by Parliament in 1998 and 1999 respectively. The main focus of the SDA was the development of workforce skills, with particular emphasis on the previously disadvantaged. Overall, the SDA aims not only to develop the skills of the workforce, but also to increase levels of investment in education and training in the labour market, encourage employers to use the workplace as an environment for active learning, improve employment prospects of the previously disadvantaged through education and training, assist work-seekers to find work, whether first-time job seekers or those re-entering the labour market. Through the SDA the traditional apprenticeships would be replaced by learnerships that would lead to registered qualifications and be linked to the NQF. The *Skills Development Levy Act* requires companies with a remuneration bill of more than R250 000 to pay one per cent of the total remuneration bill to fund skills training.

The two acts provide the legal underpinnings that support the National Skills Development Strategy (NSDS). 'A key aim of the NSDS is to help achieve equity in the labour market and in the acquisition of skills by the population of this country' (DoL 2001b: 20). The NSDS has five main objectives:

- Developing a culture of high-quality lifelong learning.
- Fostering skills development in the formal economy for productivity and employment growth.
- Stimulating and supporting skills development in small businesses.
- Promoting skills development for employability and sustainable livelihoods through social development initiatives.
- Assisting new entrants into employment.

The strategy is comprehensive and aims to bring a much broader view to skills development, guided by the ultimate outcomes that it aims to achieve, namely an economy with skills which will '… enable it to compete more successfully in the global economy, attract investment, enable individuals and communities to grow to eradicate poverty and to build a more inclusive and equal society' (DoL 2001b: 20).

The SDA set out institutions for skills development that are not far removed from the pre-1994 institutional framework, although refined and improved. The SDA provided for the establishment of the National Skills Authority (NSA), the Sectoral Education and Training Authorities (SETAs) and institutions within the DoL. The NSA, which is primarily an advisory body to the

Minister of Labour, resembles the National Training Board. The SETAs, whose responsibilities involve facilitating education and training in their sectors, disbursing grants and promoting quality assurance, resemble the Industry Training Boards (ITBs). A key change is that the current set-up is stakeholder-driven, while the old dispensation was more employer-driven. The skills levies have a precursor in the training levies introduced and administered by the ITBs. The other key development is the role given to the DoL, which is expected to play a proactive role in steering skills development and in ensuring delivery of training.

Current state of occupational distributions

While few people would quarrel with the basic proposition that conditions for Africans and women are better than they were say 20 years ago, the argument now is about the speed and spread of these gains, and the reasons for them. Admittedly it is still too early to assess the full effect of transformation policies in regard to HRD, but there have been some tangible results.

However, when it comes to high-level occupational categories, especially at management level, white males remain dominant in spite of initial gains by Africans. The table below compares management composition for 1992 and 1994, with the projections for 2000 made in the light of trends emerging from affirmative action policies, and the actual figures for 2000. These show, for example, that it was expected that by 2000 at least 32,8 per cent of managers would be African, whereas the actual figure achieved was 9,5 per cent. The enthusiasm with which policies of affirmative action were begun appear to have diminished over time, and this was the case for all race groups.

Table 9.3 *Management composition by race group: October 1992, September 1994 and projected for September 2000*

Race	October 1992	September 1994	Projected: September 2000	Actual
African	2.3%	3.8%	32.8%	9.5%
Asian	1.6%	2.2%	6.9%	5.5%
Coloured	2.5%	3.0%	6.9%	5.3%
White	93.4%	90.9%	53.5%	79.6%

Sources: *South Africa Survey* 1995–1996 and *Breakwater Monitor* 2000–2001

The table below reflects the continued domination of white males in high-level occupation categories, especially at management levels. This was the case across almost all sectors. What is of particular interest is the extent to which whites dominated management positions across the sectors despite being a smaller proportion of the total workforce, except in the accounting and other financial services sector.

Table 9.4 *Sectoral staff profile by skills level, race and gender*

Sector	Level	Race (percentage)			Gender (percentage)		
		African	Coloured	Indian	White	Male	Female
Accounting and other financial services	Management	7	2	6	85	68	32
	Skilled	20	6	10	64	28	72
	Total staff	26	5	8	61	35	65
Banking	Management	6	4	6	84	68	32
	Skilled	12	15	14	59	28	72
	Total staff	20	16	11	53	35	65
Chemical and allied industries	Management	16	5	8	71	84	16
	Skilled	27	9	9	55	77	23
	Total staff	49	8	5	38	82	18
Construction	Management	5	7	8	80	89	11
	Skilled	25	15	11	49	83	17
	Total staff	67	11	4	18	90	10
Education, training and development	Management	5	2	1	92	72	28
	Skilled	16	10	4	70	49	51
	Total staff	25	15	2	58	59	41
FMCG (food and consumer goods)	Management	10	5	6	79	83	17
	Skilled	23	18	8	51	77	23
	Total staff	51	21	6	22	76	24
Forestry, pulp and paper, board, furniture, wood	Management	6	1	7	86	90	10
	Skilled	22	5	22	51	89	11
	Total staff	66	5	10	19	82	18
IT, electronics and telecoms	Management	22	6	7	65	87	13
	Skilled	18	9	7	66	79	21
	Total staff	36	13	6	45	74	26
Insurance	Management	7	4	2	87	80	20
	Skilled	30	13	5	52	52	48
	Total staff	32	16	4	48	48	52

Table 9.4 (continued)

Sector	Level	Race (percentage)			Gender (percentage)		
		African	Coloured	Indian	White	Male	Female
Local government, water and related services	Management	6	15	2	77	82	18
	Skilled	21	40	1	38	72	28
	Total staff	30	48	0	22	82	18
Media, publishing, printing and packaging	Management	13	7	7	73	80	20
	Skilled	18	20	16	46	75	25
	Total staff	41	22	15	22	80	20
Metal engineering, plastics, motor retail, auto manufacturing, new tyres and rubber	Management	5	3	3	89	90	10
	Skilled	21	10	10	59	86	14
	Total staff	54	10	5	31	86	14
Mining and minerals	Management	5	2	1	92	95	5
	Skilled	24	6	1	68	92	8
	Total staff	84	2	0	14	97	3
Primary agriculture	Management	9	3	12	76	91	9
	Skilled	24	6	32	38	83	17
	Total staff	59	4	19	18	90	10
Services	Management	8	6	8	78	90	10
	Skilled	36	38	6	20	92	8
	Total staff	49	38	5	8	88	12
Tourism and hospitality	Management	11	3	4	82	78	22
	Skilled	32	11	12	45	51	49
	Total staff	68	10	6	16	61	39
Transport	Management	8	4	5	83	87	13
	Skilled	20	13	7	60	62	38
	Total staff	35	12	6	47	68	32
Wholesale and retail	Management	9	12	7	72	57	43
	Skilled	23	25	9	43	34	66
	Total staff	41	27	7	25	36	64

Source: *Breakwater Monitor*, 2000–2001

The data also show the continued under-representation of women in management, constituting about 21 per cent of employees at this level. According to the Employment Equity Report, white females were doing better than their counterparts in other race groups (15 per cent of the legislators, senior officials and managers occupational category), compared to Africans at three per cent, coloureds at two per cent and Asians at one per cent. There were more white females than black males even within this occupational category (see table below).

The racial and gender composition of the professional category is interesting. It shows that there are almost equal proportions of white males and African females, and African males and white females. The high proportion of African females could be explained by their concentration in the nursing and teaching professions.

Table 9.5 *Occupational distribution by race and gender*

Occupational category	African		Asian		Coloured		White	
	M	F	M	F	M	F	M	F
Legislators, senior officials and managers	11	3	4	1	5	2	59	15
Professionals	16	26	3	3	3	4	28	17
Technicians and associate professionals	17	12	4	2	7	6	33	19
Clerks	19	15	4	5	6	11	8	32
Service and sales	38	14	3	2	7	8	17	11
Craft and related	41	4	4	0	11	1	37	2
Plant and machine operators	63	9	3	1	10	7	6	1
Elementary occupations	63	13	1	0	8	6	8	1

Source: DoL 2001a

The above portrays the national picture. Micro-level studies are also used to reinforce the national data and to provide a better understanding of the distribution within professions and sectors/industries.

Distribution of employment across a sector

Information from two sector studies – the financial, accounting, management consulting and other financial services (FASSET), and the mining and minerals sectors – are used here to provide a snapshot of human resource distribution. They were selected because they are based on comprehensive research undertaken and available recently.

The financial sector

By its nature this sector is comprised of high-skill personnel with only a few in low and semi-skilled positions. Whites constitute 66 per cent of employees within the sector, with Africans, coloureds and Asians at 17, 8 and 10 per cent respectively. White managers and owners of business constituted about 81 per cent, professionals were 70 per cent, while Africans constituted about 83 per cent of those in elementary and labourer occupations, and 77 per cent of plant and machine operators.

Table 9.6 *Racial distribution of workers according to occupational categories*

Occupational category	Percentage African	Percentage coloured	Percentage Asian	Percentage white
Legislators, senior officials, managers and owner managers	7	4	8	81
Professionals	14	7	10	70
Technicians and associate professionals	14	5	23	59
Clerks and administrative workers	18	10	10	62
Service and sales workers	21	12	5	62
Plant and machine operators	77	16	1	5
Labourers and elementary occupations	83	10	0	6
Trainees	14	4	22	61
Other	20	8	9	63
Total	17	8	10	66

Source: HSRC 2003

The financial sector consists largely of professionals and as a result is regulated by professional bodies. The professional bodies clearly reflect the inequities still extant in this sector. The major professional bodies within the sector are those of the accountants – South African Institute of Chartered Accountants (SAICA) – and of the auditors – Public Accountants' and Auditors' Board (PAAB). In 2002, 91 per cent of SAICA members were white, while Africans, coloureds and Asians constituted 1,9 per cent, 1,2 per cent and 5,5 per cent respectively of its membership across all the categories. PAAB members were 92 per cent white, while Africans, coloureds and Asians constituted 1,4 per cent, 0,3 per cent, and 5,4 per cent respectively of its membership.

Gender distribution within the sector shows slightly more women (56 per cent) than men (44 per cent). However, a detailed look at the figures reveals the inequalities: women constituted 32 per cent of managers, 83 per cent of clerical and administrative workers, and 67 per cent of labourers and elementary occupations. Unfortunately the gender figures do not show the breakdown across racial groups. However, a look at the figures of the professional bodies indicate that it is largely white females who are making significant progress compared with their counterparts in other race groups. For example, African females represented only 0,5 per cent of SAICA membership, while white females were 16 per cent, coloureds 0,4 per cent and Asians 1,1 per cent. PAAB's white female membership was 11 per cent, while African, coloured and Asians constituted 0,2, 0,1 and 0,3 per cent respectively.

Table 9.7 *Gender distribution of workers according to occupational categories*

Occupational category	Percentage male	Percentage female	Total percentage
Legislators, senior officials, managers and owner managers	68	32	100
Professionals	52	48	100
Technicians and associate professionals	50	50	100
Clerks and administrative workers	17	83	100
Service and sales workers	50	50	100
Plant and machine operators	97	3	100
Labourers and elementary occupations	33	67	100
Trainees	47	53	100
Other	50	50	100
Total	44	56	100

Source: HSRC 2003

The mining and minerals sector

In contrast to the financial sector, mining and minerals largely employs workers with low- and medium-level skills, i.e. 40 per cent of the workforce are labourer-related, 37,9 per cent are plant and machine operators and assemblers, 9,9 per cent are craft-related, 1,5 per cent are professionals, 0,8 per cent managers, 4,5 per cent are technicians and associated professionals, 3,25 per cent are clerks and 3,2 per cent are service workers, shop and market sales workers. Africans constituted 83,7 per cent of workers, while whites, Asians and coloured constituted 12,4, 0,2 and 3,7 per cent respectively.

The sector is largely male dominated and so reflects the inequities in the labour market generally. African males were 82,6 per cent of the total workforce, but only 3,8 per cent of management, 10,8 per cent of professionals and 21,8 per cent of technicians and associated professionals. In contrast they constituted 94,3 per cent of plant and machine operators and 95,9 per cent of labourers.

Women constitute only three per cent of the workforce in this sector, most of whom are white females. They constitute about five per cent of management (mostly white females). While there were more males (African) within the clerical occupations, there were more white females as well (23,6 per cent). It is the only occupational category where there was a higher proportion of females.

Table 9.8 *Racial distribution of workers according to occupational categories*

Occupational category	African		Asian		Coloured		White	
	M	F	M	F	M	F	M	F
Senior officials and managers	3.8	0.8	2.5		4.6	0.1	83.9	4.3
Professionals	10.8	2.2	3.9	2.3	1.7	0.2	71.8	7.2
Technicians and associated professionals	21.8	0.7	2.8	0.3	0.5	0.03	67.8	6.1
Clerks	52.3	6.6	3.9	5.9	0.3	0.8	6.6	23.6
Service workers, shop and market sales workers	66.7	6.7	3.9	3.1	0.1	0.01	15.8	3.6
Craft and related workers	43.2	0.6	7.0	1.0	0.6	0.003	46.7	0.9

Plant and machine operators and assemblers	94.3	0.5	2.9	0.3	0.03	0.001	1.6	0.4
Labourers and related occupations	95.9	1.1	2.0	0.5	0.01		0.5	0.1
Total	82.6	1.1	3.0	0.7	0.2	0.03	10.8	1.5

Source: HSRC 2000

The financial and mining sectors represent extremes of the labour spectrum, but it is reasonable to assume that they offer a picture that is common to all sectors of the economy. The data above on the sectoral breakdown of the distribution of occupational levels confirms the continued domination of whites in high-level occupations, especially management.

Measures to improve on HRD and redress

On-the-job training, recruitment and promotion practices have all played and continue to play a major role in shaping the labour market outcomes described above. The extent of a firm's HRD and its willingness to redress past inequities is reflected in its commitment to training and the way it organises promotion and recruitment practices. In the post-apartheid labour market it is expected that the previously disadvantaged should benefit the most from training. This, in turn, should lead to an increased level of recruitment of the previously disadvantaged, matched by an increase in the number of promotions, compared to the rest. However, other studies reveal that the pattern in training, promotions and recruitment continues to reflect the skewed trends observed in the occupational studies referred to in this paper.

Training

Training – whether on-the-job or off – is significant to the acquisition of skills and formal qualifications for those who have left the education system, because of its role in improving the skills level of the country. Training is also imperative for firms as a means to improving the productivity of workers and, hence, performance and competitiveness. It is surprising, therefore, that South African firms have a reputation for being averse to training.

On-the-job training is hard to measure, and encompasses formal and informal learning to acquire skills. Formal training can be measured to some extent, although it can also take many forms. There is external accredited training, for example apprenticeship training, and in-service training that is not accredited externally, but may lead to the acquisition of skills and increased productivity, eg. learning to operate a bulldozer. Informal training, i.e. learning by 'sitting next to Nellie', occurs almost daily on the job. However, it is of little help if it fails to improve promotion prospects or the potential to enter a job outside the firm. Therefore, the type of training individuals receive is important. Unfortunately, there are no studies to date that have evaluated training at that level of detail.

Information from the DoL's NSDS Synthesis Report for April to June 2002 shows that between April 2001 and the first quarter of 2003, a total of 1 345 213 workers participated in structured learning programmes. Black males constituted 41,7 per cent, black females were 22,2 per cent, while white males and females constituted 21 per cent and 14,7 per cent respectively. Unfortunately, the information does not distinguish training participants by occupational category.

However, that information has been separated out by the SETAs and an assumption of participation by occupational categories can be made based on that work. This is shown below and is based on the information of the two SETAS, taken from the NSDS report, which appeared to be the most comprehensive.

Table 9.9 *Training participants in the Services SETA*

Quarter	Number of workers participating in NQF Level 1 training including NQF level 1				Number of workers participating in structured learning programmes			
	Black		White		Black		White	
	Male	Female	Male	Female	Male	Female	Male	Female
02/1								
02/2	24 703	20 988	1 995	2 504	43 072	34 350	11 526	14 755
02/3								
02/4	21 006	19 890	1 333	1 667	33 758	29 971	8 826	10 630
03/1	228	127	0	1	562	342	195	322

Source: NSDS Synthesis Report, DoL 2002

Table 9.9 is extracted from the DoL report and shows the numbers participating in training within the Services SETA. It compares training participants on NQF level 1 and the total number of those participating in training. It shows that there were more blacks participating in training within this SETA. It also emerges that while there is a higher proportion of workers participating in training, within this SETA the higher proportion was participating in training on NQF level 1. This was especially the case for black workers.

Table 9.10 *Bank SETA training participants*

Quarter	Workers participating in structured learning			
	Black		White	
	Male	Female	Male	Female
02/1	7 960	10 817	9 536	13 629
02/2	8 041	10 948	9 556	13 642
02/3	8 987	11 725	10 571	11 836
02/4	10 670	16 333	9 505	13 914
03/1	5 975	7 198	11 292	13 7441

Source: NSDS Synthesis Report, DoL 2002

The Bank SETA information extracted from the DoL report indicates that while there are higher numbers participating in structured learning programmes, the participation is still skewed. More whites participate than blacks, and more females than males, which might be a reflection of the concentration of females in the bank sector. Overall, the information from the two SETAS confirms that blacks and women continue to be represented in training at lower occupational categories.

The trend is underlined when learnership agreements are examined. Based on submissions to the DoL, there were only 5 839 learners in learnership agreement 18(1) registered during the same period, that is, April 2001 and first quarter of 2003. Across all SETAs represented, there were more whites (2 505) in learnership agreements than blacks (1 594). White males had the highest proportion. FASSET SETA had the highest number of registered learners in learnerships, which reflects the racial occupational distribution within that sector. An overwhelming majority of the learners were still white. There were

1 279 white males and 1 119 white females, compared to 498 and 406 for black males and females respectively.

Training for the unemployed appeared to have taken place at an even slower pace. There were only 1 055 learners who completed learnership agreement 18(2), of whom 688 were black and 367 white.

Promotions and recruitment

The DoL Employment Equity report (2001) shows that 47 per cent of total promotions went to Africans, 32,7 per cent to whites, while for Asians and coloureds it was 6,3 and 14 per cent respectively. Within management, 35 per cent of promotions went to blacks. In top management, nine per cent of promotions went to blacks. Confirming these figures, the Breakwater Monitor Report (2000) indicated that while black promotions were about ten per cent higher than those for whites, white promotions were significantly higher at management (71 per cent) and skilled levels (52 per cent) than for blacks. The DoL reports more promotions for men (65 per cent) than for women (35 per cent). While the Breakwater Monitor shows that women's promotions were two per cent higher than those for men, it also shows that at management level more men were promoted (69 per cent) than women, while at skilled job levels more women were promoted (54 per cent) than men. The difference in the two reports could be attributed to the fact that the DoL report does not make an occupational breakdown.

Recruitment trends indicate that, overall, four per cent more Africans were recruited. However, whites accounted for most of the recruitment at management levels (66 per cent), compared to 20, six and eight per cent for Africans, coloureds and Asians respectively. A higher proportion of whites (43 per cent) also accounted for most of the recruitment at skilled levels compared to Africans, coloureds, and Asians where the figures were 35, 12 and nine per cent respectively (Breakwater Monitor 2000).

Trends in higher education

Overall, participation in higher education has increased. However, the increased participation is, as Cooper and Subotzky (2001) stated, 'a skewed revolution'. The proportion of those obtaining three-year qualifications is still higher than those obtaining four-year qualifications. The latter are largely profession-oriented, while three-year qualifications are largely general, without any form of specialisation.

Table 9.11 *University qualifications*

Type of qualification	1991	1998
Bachelor degree (3 years)	45.4%	43.3%
Bachelor degree (4 years)	16.5%	18.5%
Postgraduate diploma	8.0%	7.8%
Honours degree	21.4%	21.3%
Masters degree	7.3%	7.9%
Doctorate	1.4%	1.2%

Source: SA Survey 2001/2

Historically, Africans and women were denied access to education but this has changed over time and their participation has increased. In 1991 Africans constituted 24 per cent of total awards in tertiary institutions; in 1998 the figure had increased to 49 per cent. However, they are still over-represented in three-year qualifications, which carry less weight in the labour market. Most Africans are graduating in fields that do not prepare them for a profession, i.e. engineering, architecture, medicine, and so on, and these trends correspond to some extent with occupational distributions. For example, the fact that FASSET has a lower proportion of Africans employed could be attributed to the lack of Africans graduating in fields related to the sector.

Conclusion

A number of observations can be made, therefore, about the state of HRD in relation to the labour market, in particular.

1. Whites still dominate high-level occupations; white males predominate in management; Africans and women are still concentrated in secondary sectors and occupations with the characteristics of the secondary sectors.
2. While there is progress in terms of redress, it has been relatively slow. There is little change in the racial and gender composition within occupations, with whites dominating high-level occupations. What is interesting is that white females are progressing faster than their counterparts, and even faster than African males at management level.
3. On-the-job training, promotions and recruitment reflects limited commitment towards redress. These are still skewed towards whites and are concentrated on higher levels.

4. Beneficiaries of training reflect the demographic profile of sectors and occupations, i.e. it is still mostly whites who receive training at higher occupational levels because they form the majority of those within those groups.
5. Education and training is still supply-led. There is little if any labour market information on demand for skills. As a result, in higher education for example, people pursue qualifications for which the labour market outcome is unknown, while in the labour market, skills analysis studies are not undertaken. The question then is: on what basis is the recorded training taking place?
6. Lack of basic education is a major challenge in HRD. Numeracy and literacy affects access to good jobs and hence training.

Emphasis on training – and hence improving the human resources of the country – is heavily concentrated within enterprises. While it is in firms' best interests to invest in training, there are shortcomings to this approach when it comes to redressing the inequities of the past. The structure of the labour market as it developed historically poses a major challenge when seeking redress. Access to jobs – and therefore to work-related training – is limited and unequally distributed across different groups. Those in short-term employment, part-time work and who work in small- or medium-sized firms, have poor literacy and numeracy, are less likely to receive work-related training. Their jobs require relatively low skills and offer little advancement within the internal labour market. Technological advancement and its diffusion biases training towards the highly-skilled, pressuring firms to prioritise retraining of the highly-skilled over that of the low-skilled. As a consequence, past inequities are perpetuated because most of those in high-skill occupations are white.

The problems are such that they need to be tackled both within and outside the labour market. High unemployment rates and marginalisation of Africans and women needs to be tackled through active labour market policies, i.e. basic literacy and numeracy training, job-search assistance, vocational guidance and counselling. Active labour market policies would improve the employability of the unemployed, increase the efficiency of job searching, secure job outcomes and improve equity. These cannot be provided by private enterprise so become a responsibility of Government.

This is not meant to underplay the importance of equity legislation and the role it can play in redress. The continued domination of whites in highly-skilled occupations cannot only be accounted for by the poor basic education of Africans. It reflects the deep entrenchment within internal labour-market systems of patterns of occupational segregation and the difficulties associated with overcoming them. Thus, they affect the major sources of redress, i.e. training and promotion opportunities. Hence, even after the abolition of racist legislation, apartheid patterns in employment continue to reproduce themselves. There is thus a need to strengthen affirmative action policies.

The HIV/AIDS epidemic poses another major challenge, especially with regard to training provision. High levels of infection in the working population may result in a need for the replacement of formerly productive workers. However, the epidemic could also become a disincentive to training provision, resulting in inefficiencies in this regard.

In conclusion, owing to a lack of detailed research on training in the South African labour market, it is hard to provide answers to pertinent questions about the impact of training on both the individual and the firm. As a result, it is not possible to distinguish between training that simply enables an individual to perform the job better, and that which not only enables them to do the job better, but also provides opportunities to move up the job ladder. While each individual worker needs training that will enable them to do both, the emphasis is different for workers at differing occupational levels and categories. A manager might emphasise training that enables the job to be done better, while a semi-skilled or unskilled worker might emphasise training that enables them to move up the job ladder (better performance is embedded in this type of training). As a result we cannot say what the end result of training is – do people move up a higher level as a result of the training they receive and, if so, how does it differ by race, gender and occupational category, and what is the impact on firms and the economy?

References

Bhorat, H & Lundall, P (2002) *Employment, wages and skills development: Firm-specific effects, evidence from two firm surveys in South Africa.* Pretoria: Development Policy Research Unit, UCT, in association with Skills Development Policy Unit (DoL).

Breakwater Monitor Report (2000) *Monitoring employment equity in South Africa.* Cape Town: Graduate School of Business, UCT.

Cooper, D & Subotzky, G (2001) *The skewed revolution: Trends in South Africa higher education, 1988–1998.* Cape Town: Education Policy Unit, UCT.

DoL (Department of Labour) (2001a) *Report on Employment Equity Registry.* Pretoria: Department of Labour.

DoL (2001b) *National Skills Development Strategy: Skills for Productive Citizenship for All.* Pretoria: Department of Labour.

DoL (2002) *National Skills Development Strategy: Synthesis Report.* Pretoria: Department of Labour.

Foundation for Research and Development (FDR) (1996) *Survey on factors affecting the quality of research.* Pretoria: FDR.

HSRC (2000) *Skills analysis in the mining and minerals sector, report for the mining qualification authority.* Pretoria: HSRC.

HSRC (2003) *Skills development in the financial, accounting, management consulting and other financial services sector.* Draft report to FASSET. Pretoria: HSRC.

Kraak, A, Patterson, A, Visser, M & Tustin, D (2000) *Baseline survey of industrial training in South Africa.* Pretoria: HSRC & Bureau of Market Research (UNISA).

Lundall, P & Kimmie, Z (1992) Apprenticeship training and artisan employment: Changing numbers – but maintaining job reservations, *South African Labour Bulletin* 16 (6): 42–45.

SAIRR (South African Institute of Race Relations) (1996) *The South African survey 1995–1996.* Johannesburg: SAIRR.

SAIRR (2000) *The South African survey 1999–2000.* Johannesburg: SAIRR.

SAIRR (2001) *The South African survey 2001–2002.* Johannesburg: SAIRR.

Standing, G, Sender, J & Weeks, J (1996) *Restructuring the labour market: The South African challenge.* Geneva: ILO.

Webster, E (1985) *Cast in a racial mould: Labour process and trade unionism in the foundries.* Johannesburg: Ravan Press.

Part III: Society

State-civil society relations in post-apartheid South Africa

Adam Habib

> The basic twin expectations of government are that NGOs will firstly continue to act as monitors of the public good and safeguard the interests of the disadvantaged sections of society. This performance of this social watch role requires both transparency and accountability on the part of NGOs. The government's second expectation is that NGOs will assist in expanding access to social and economic services that create jobs and eradicate poverty among the poorest of the poor. This requires cost-effective and sustainable service delivery.(Zola Skweyiya in Barnard & Terreblanche 2001: 17)

> For many of the activists … working in different spaces and having different strategies and tactics, there was a binding thread. There was unmitigated opposition to the economic policies adopted by the ANC … Activists spoke of how the right-wing economic policies lead to widespread and escalating unemployment, with concomitant water and electricity cut-offs, and evictions even from the 'toilets in the veld' provided by the government in the place of houses. More importantly, there was general agreement that this was not just a question of short-term pain for long-term gain. The ANC had become a party of neoliberalism. The strategy to win the ANC to a left project was a dead end. The ANC had to be challenged and a movement built to render its policies unworkable. It seems increasingly unlikely that open confrontation with the repressive power of the post-apartheid state can be avoided. (Desai 2002: 147)

Two quotations and two very different visions of post-apartheid state-civil society relations. The articulators of these visions have as their goal the empowerment of, and service delivery to, the poor. Both individuals are located in different institutional settings. The first is a cabinet minister responsible for the Department of Social Development. The second is a civil society activist, one among many leaders in the new and emerging civic struggles that are challenging local governments in their imposition of a cost-recovery paradigm to the provision of social services. Which vision is appropriate for the conditions of post-apartheid South Africa?

Both quotations reflect at least one element of our post-apartheid reality. But the absolute and categoric character of their visions make them inappropriate models for a contemporary state-civil society relationship. Implicitly these visions imagine a homogenous civil society. They project a single set of relations for the whole of civil society. Is civil society, however, not plural by its very nature? And should not this plurality infuse our understandings of state-civil society relations in contemporary South Africa?

This chapter takes as its departing point a definition of civil society that celebrates its plurality. It recognises that the set of institutions within this entity will reflect diverse and even contradictory political and social agendas. As a result, state-civil society relations will reflect this plurality. Some relationships between civil society actors and state institutions will be adversarial and conflictual, while others will be more collaborative and collegiate. This state of affairs should not be bemoaned. Instead it should be celebrated for it represents the political maturing of our society. Under apartheid, the adversarial-collaborative divide largely took a racial form with the bulk of white civil society establishing collegiate relations with the state, and the majority of black civil society adopting a conflictual mode of engagement. This racial divide began to blur in the transition period as significant sections of white civil society began to distance themselves from the apartheid regime. In the contemporary era, the racial divide has all but disappeared, with adversarial and collegiate relations extending across the entire ambit of civil society.

Elsewhere I have defined civil society as 'the organised expression of various interests and values operating in the triangular space between the family, state, and the market' (Habib & Kotze 2002: 3). This definition conceptualises civil society as an entity distinct from both the market and the state. Of course traditional Hegelian definitions of the term include the market. I am, however, persuaded by Cohen and Arato's comprehensive and defining work on the subject, which makes a coherent case for why the market should be excluded from the definition of civil society. For Cohen and Arato, the actors of what they call 'political' and 'economic' society control and manage state power and economic production and this imparts to them a different strategic purpose and function from civil-society actors. In their words, political and economic actors cannot 'subordinate (their) strategic and instrumental criteria to the patterns of normative integration and open-ended communication characteristic of civil society' (Cohen & Arato 1992: ix). This then makes it essential for civil society to be analytically distinguished from:

> both a political society of parties, political organisations, and political publics (in particular, parliaments) and an economic society composed of organisations of production and distribution, usually firms, cooperatives, (and) partnerships … (Cohen & Arato 1992: ix)

This chapter is divided into three separate sections. The first, which serves as a backdrop to the analysis, describes the set of relations between the state and civil society agencies in the apartheid era. This is followed by a description of the initiatives undertaken by the state, sometimes independently and at other times at the instance of other actors, to redefine the post-apartheid civil society arena. The chapter then analyses how different civil-society actors have responded to these initiatives and to the challenges of the post-apartheid moment, and how this has informed their relations with the state. Finally, the conclusion reflects on current assessments of, and advances my own view on contemporary state-civil society relations in South Africa.

Historical context

There are two distinct phases in the evolution of contemporary civil society in South Africa. Before identifying these, however, it may be useful to note that contemporary civil society is distinguished by the fact that it not only reflects the demographic realities of South African society, but also transcends the racialised form of the adversarial-collaborative dichotomy that typified civil society relations with the state in earlier epochs. In any case, the diverse racial profile of contemporary civil society has its roots in the early 1980s when there was a phenomenal growth in associational life in this country. Indeed, the distinctive feature of this period is not only the longitudinal growth of the sector, but the formal emergence, or at least the surfacing in the political sphere, of a significant part of it, namely black civil-society actors who had hitherto been either banned or prevented from operating in the public arena. The second phase dates back to 1994 when the character and operations of a significant part of the civil society, once again anti-apartheid black civic actors, fundamentally changed as a result of new opportunities and challenges. Both phases of course neatly coincide with key moments in the evolution of the political system: the first with the liberalisation phase, and the second with the democratisation phase of the transition.[1] Civil society has thus influenced and been moulded by the political transition in South Africa.

Prior to the liberalisation in the early 1980s, the dominant element in civil society were organisations and institutions that were either pro-apartheid and/or pro-business. Agencies critical of the state and the socio-economic system were either actively suppressed or marginalised from the formal political process. The major political contest within civil society seemed to be between pro-apartheid institutions like the Broederbond and Nederduitse Gereformeerde Kerk (NGK) and liberal-oriented organisations like the Institute of Race Relations and the National Union of South African Students (NUSAS).[2] As the 1970s approached, anti-apartheid NGOs like the unions and the array of organisations associated with the Black Consciousnesss Movement (BCM) began to make their presence felt (Marx 1992). But constant harassment from the state and miniscule resources ensured that they really served as a sideshow to the more formal contest and engagement within civil society and between it and the state.

This all changed in the 1980s. The anti-apartheid elements within civil society resurfaced and within a few years became the dominant element within the sector. Two developments underpinned this growth in anti-apartheid civil society organizations. The first was the liberalisation of the political system unleashed by the PW Botha regime in the early 1980s. This involved reform of the more cruder aspects of Grand Apartheid, the attempted political cooption of some sections of the disenfranchised communities, and allowing the emergence of some civic activity within, and representation of, the black population. It is indeed ironical that credit for facilitating the re-emergence of civil society, the agencies responsible for the destruction of apartheid, should go to one of South Africa's most authoritarian political leaders. But such are the quirks of history.

In any case, the reform of the political system in the early 1980s did indeed enable the re-emergence of anti-apartheid civil society. The Soweto revolt in 1976, and the more general upsurge in protest including union activity throughout the 1970s, created a struggle between reformers and conservatives within the heart of the state. The former wanted to reform apartheid, make it compatible with the modernising imperatives of the economy, and co-opt some elements of the black population by giving them a stake in the system. The latter wanted a recommitment to the traditional project of Grand Apartheid. The success of PW Botha and his reformist coalition in the leadership succession dispute of the NP in the late 1970s created the opportunity for the promulgation of the reformist project (Sparks 1990). A series of institutional reforms followed, a significant component of which included the recognition and legalisation of independent black unions and the establishment of a political space that permitted the re-emergence of anti-apartheid civil society. Moreover, the state provided the rationale for mobilising this sector by proposing a reform that attempted to co-opt some and marginalise other elements of the black community. Anti-apartheid civil society was thus enabled by and provided the rationale for mobilisation by the state's liberalisation initiative.

Not all of this scenario was positive. In fact, very soon into the reform programme the state began actively to repress elements within the anti-apartheid camp. But despite this repression (which became quite severe under the states of emergency of the 1980s), anti-apartheid civil society retained its popular legitimacy. This enabled it to re-emerge very quickly when De Klerk took over the leadership reins in a palace coup that replaced Botha as President, and reintroduced and even extended, the state's liberalisation initiative. The ultimate result was that by the 1990s the anti-apartheid camp had become the dominant element in the civil society sphere.

The second development facilitating the re-emergence of anti-apartheid civil society was the increasing availability of resources to non-profit actors in South Africa. Two types of resources are crucial in this regard. The first – human resources – increasingly became available in the early 1980s as university students and graduates politicised by the activities of the 1970s, and political prisoners, many of whom were released in the early 1980s, came together in myriad of ways to not only organise community and political activities, but to also establish non-profit institutions to support these mass struggles. The second – fiscal resources – initially emerged from private foundations and foreign governments who were moved to act largely due to the fact that the 1976 June 16 revolt and its consequences made its way to the televisions screens in the advanced industrialised world. The increasing tempo of struggle within the country, however, also gradually compelled local actors, particularly corporates and churches, to begin to underwrite anti-apartheid non-profit activity in South Africa (Stacey & Aksartova 2001). This increasing availability of resources from both foreign and domestic sources established the second plank that enabled the re-emergence and growth of anti-apartheid civil society in South Africa.

Two points need to be underscored in this very brief and cursory history of the emergence of contemporary civil society. First, the historical overview provides support for two theories of social movements: political opportunity structure, and resource mobilisation. The political-opportunity structure theory emphasises the opening of political opportunities in explanations of the rise of social movements and social struggle (Tarrow 1994). Resource-mobilisation theories, on the other hand, explain the rise of social formations through a focus on resources and their availability to different social groups (McCarthy & Zald 1987; Tilly 1978). The explanatory variables emphasised by both theories, then, are crucial for understanding the emergence of contemporary civil society.

The second point that needs to be stressed is that, despite the fact that anti-apartheid civil society was born within the womb of the state's reform programme, state-civil society relations tended to take an adversarial form throughout the 1980s. This is because the liberalisation initiative was not democratic and enabling. Indeed, like all liberalisation initiatives in transitional societies, it needs to be conceptualised in relative terms. Thus, anti-apartheid civil society maintained its distance from, and was treated with suspicion by, what was still an apartheid state. The legal environment, including the tax regime, while allowing anti-apartheid NGOs and community-based organisations (CBOs) to emerge, was nevertheless still hostile to their operations. Similarly, the political and security environment remained repressive and became even more so after states of emergency were declared in 1985 and 1986. This hostile environment ensured that state-civil society relations took an adversarial form in the first decade of the anti-apartheid civil society organisations (CSOs). This was to change only in the middle of the second decade when South Africa entered the democratisation phase of its political transition.

Civil society in the democratic era

Regime change can have significant impacts on society. This is all the more so if it occurs in an era of globalisation. Nowhere is this more evident than in

South Africa where the transition to democracy and globalisation have fundamentally transformed the society. In the process, civil society has itself been remoulded in significant ways, the effects of which are only now becoming evident. Nine years after the transition, the most obvious outcome of the remoulding process is the evolution of civil society into three distinct blocs, each of which is a product, to different degrees, of separate transitional processes.

Establishing an enabling environment

The first bloc, which comprises formal NGOs, has largely been influenced by the political restructuring which the democratic state undertook in order to create an enabling environment for civil society. Three initiatives were undertaken in this regard. First, the security environment was reorganised in significant ways. Repressive legislation was repealed and a political climate permitting public scrutiny and protest activity was established. This was in no way unqualified. Indeed, in the last nine years there have been occasions when security officials and even some politicians reacted to legitimate scrutiny and protest in ways reminiscent of their predecessors. But any overall assessment would have to conclude that the security environment is far more enabling now than it has ever been in this country.

Second, the post-apartheid regime moved quickly to pass legislation and adopt practices to reorganise the political environment. Thus, a *Non-Profit Act* was passed that officially recognised civil society, created a system of voluntary registration for its constituents and provided benefits and allowances in exchange for NGOs and CBOs undertaking proper accounting and providing audited statements to government. A Directorate for Non-Profit Organisations was established in the Department of Social Welfare to co-ordinate the above processes. In addition, Nedlac, the country's premier corporatist institution, was established with four chambers, the last of which was to cater for representation from civil society. Most important in creating a new political environment, however, was the state's willingness to partner with NGOs in the policy development and service delivery arenas. This opened up a whole new avenue of operations for NGOs and fundamentally transformed their relations with the state.

Third, an enabling fiscal environment was created to enable the financial sustainability of this sector. This was in part forced onto the state very early on in the transition as NGOs confronted a financial crunch when foreign donors redirected their funding away from CSOs to the state. Again legislation was passed and institutions were established to facilitate a flow of resources to the sector. The *Fundraising Act* of 1978, which limited NGOs' capacity to raise funds, was repealed. Institutions like the National Development Agency (NDA) and the Lottery Commission were established with a mandate to fund legitimate non-profit activity, and, a reform of the tax regulations was promulgated in 2000/2001 to grant registered CSOs tax-exemption status, and to encourage a philanthropic culture in the country.

The net effect of these legislative changes and restructuring has been the establishment of a fiscal, legal and political environment that has facilitated the development of a collaborative relationship between the state and formal NGOs. The latter have increasingly been contracted by the state to assist it in policy development, implementation and service delivery. This has been encouraged by donors who sometimes fund such partnerships, and who regularly advocate for the professionalisation and commercialisation of NGOs. The positive result of this is that it has facilitated the financial sustainability of a number of these organisations. But it has come at a cost. Commercialisation and professionalisation have blurred the non-profit/profit divide, and have led to questions around the lines of accountability of these organisations. As Habib and Taylor argue:

> The existing literature of the non-profit sector is replete with suggestions that NGOs are institutions that service the interests of the poor and marginalised. But can one really argue this when NGOs have become so commercially-oriented and dependent on the resources of donors and the government? … Can one really assert that (they are) community-driven or answerable to marginalised sectors of South African society? (1999: 79)

Reaping the costs of neoliberalism

The second and third constituent blocs of contemporary civil society are largely products of processes associated with globalisation and its particular manifestation in South Africa. South Africa's democratic transition, like so many in the so-called 'third wave of democracies' (Huntington 1991), has been characterised by two distinct transitional processes, political democratisation and economic liberalisation. The goal of the former is representative government. The latter has as its aim the integration of South Africa into the global economy, and is informed by a particular configuration of power in the global and national arenas, defined largely by the fact that the leverage of multinational corporations and the domestic business community has increased dramatically vis-à-vis other social actors as a result of the techno-logical transformations of the last decade or two.[3]

This increasing leverage of multinational corporations and the domestic busi-ness community has translated in South Africa into the ANC government's adoption of neoliberal economic policies (Habib & Padayachee 2000). Other than the odd commentator or two who dispute this, or who every now and then on the basis of one or other development read a change of heart on the part of South African political elites (Padayachee & Valodia 2001), most ana-lysts across the ideological spectrum recognise the neoliberal character of the post-apartheid government's economic trajectory. The effects of this neo-liberalism − read as the liberalisation of the financial and trade markets, the deregulation of the economy, and the privatisation of state assets − have been negative in many respects. Even by its own terms, the government's macro-economic policies have not performed to expectations. Foreign investment, the enticing of which is a primary rationale of these policies, has not flowed into the country in the volumes predicted or hoped for. Moreover, the prospects for increased flows are slim given the current problems of crime, HIV/AIDS and regional instability as a result of the rise of authoritarianism in Zimbabwe.

The problem is aggravated by the relaxation of exchange controls, which have enabled South African companies and individuals to export capital, resulting in substantial outflows from the country. As a result, the currency markets have been volatile. Initially, the Rand devalued, pressurising inflation and forcing the Reserve Bank to increase interest rates by four percentage points in 2002. Subsequently, it strengthened by approximately 40 per cent, but it could well devalue again as the US dollar stabilises. Finally, the state's privati-sation programme has registered little success in terms of capital generation for the state.[4] It has, however, had the effect of ideologically polarising the country and alienating the ruling party from its alliance partners.

The net achievement of this programme has been the realisation of the state's deficit targets, but at the cost of employment, poverty and inequality. Massive job losses have occurred in almost all sectors of the economy. Tighter fiscal

constraints have compromised the state's poverty alleviation and development programmes. State officials often claim credit for having met the targets
of the RDP, especially in the areas of water, sanitation, telephony and electricity. But the most comprehensive independent study in this regard estimates
that there have been approximately ten million cut-offs in water and electricity services because people have not paid their bills, and a further two million
people have been victims of rates and rent evictions (McDonald & Pape
2002). Moreover, a number of other studies have shown that poverty and
inequality has increased in real and measurable ways. For example, Carter and
May (2001), in a study of approximately 1 200 black households in KwaZulu-
Natal, demonstrated that poverty rates increased from 27 to 43 per cent
between 1993 and 1998. Economic liberalisation has benefited the upper
classes of all racial groups, and in particular, the black political, economic and
professional elites who are the primary beneficiaries of affirmative action
policies and black economic empowerment deals.[5] But Gear has had a devastating effect on the lives of millions of poor and low-income families. As
Habib and Padayachee have argued:

> the ANC's implementation of neoliberal economic policies has
> meant disaster for the vast majority of South Africa's poor.
> Increasing unemployment and economic inequalities associated
> with neoliberal policies have also pushed even more of South
> Africa's population into the poverty trap. (2000: 24)

In order to respond to this challenge civil society has been reconstituted in
two very distinct ways. The first involves the proliferation of informal, survivalist community-based organisations, networks and associations, which
enable poor and marginalised communities to simply survive against the daily
ravages of neoliberalism. According to the recently published study of the
Johns Hopkins survey on the shape and size of civil society in South Africa,
these associations comprise 53 per cent of 98 920 non-profit organisations
and thereby constitute the largest category of institutional formations within
the sector (Swilling & Russel 2002). Care must be taken not to fall into the trap
of much of the writings on the informal economy, and to celebrate these associations as representing the energies and vibrancy of South African society.
Indeed they should be recognised for what they are, which is survivalist
responses of poor and marginalised people who have had no alternative in the
face of a retreating state that refuses to meet its socio-economic obligations to

its citizenry. As I have argued elsewhere, anecdotal evidence suggests that these 'informal, community-based networks are on the rise, particularly in the struggle to deal with the ever-increasing repercussions of the government's failure to address the HIV/AIDS and unemployment crises' (Habib 2002: viii).

The second bloc that has emerged within civil society in response to the effects of neoliberalism is a category of organisations that have been described by some studies as social movements (Desai 2002). This category is made up of a diverse set of organisations, not all of whom actually meet the criteria of social movements. Some of them, like the TAC, are more nationally-based associations, and, in this case, focus on challenging the state's AIDS policy and enabling the provision of anti-retroviral drugs to AIDS sufferers. Others, like the Soweto Electricity Crisis Committee and the Concerned Citizens Group, are located at the local level, and organise against electricity cut-offs in Soweto and rates evictions and water terminations in Chatsworth and surrounding townships in Durban respectively. Nevertheless, when compared to the above category of associations, both of these types of organisations are more formal community-based structures, which have a distinct leadership and member-ship, often supported by a middle-class activist base. Moreover, their mode of operations is fundamentally different. They are not survivalist agencies, but are more political animals. Indeed, they have been largely established with the explicit political aim of organising and mobilising the poor and marginalised, and contesting and/or engaging the state and other social actors around the implementation of neoliberal social policies. As a result, they implicitly launch a fundamental challenge to the hegemonic political and socio-economic dis-course that defines the prevailing status quo.

These two very different blocs within civil society, which have emerged in response to globalisation's neoliberal manifestation in South Africa, have very different relations with the state. The informal organisations and associations have no relationship with the state. They receive neither resources, nor do they covet recognition, from the state. They are preoccupied with the task of sim-ply surviving the effects of the state's policies. Indeed, it is doubtful whether the majority of these associations even recognise that the plight of the com-munities in which they are located is largely a result of the policy choices of political elites. The second bloc of more formal organisations whose activists covet the status of social movements have an explicit relationship with the state. This relationship, depending on the organisation and the issue area, hovers somewhere between adversarialism and engagement, and sometimes involves both (Bond 2001; Desai 2002). But even when engaging the state this is of a qualitatively different kind to that of the formal NGOs. The latter has a relationship with the state that is largely defined by its sub-contractual role, whereas the former is on a relatively more even footing, engaging the state in an attempt to persuade it through lobbying, court action, and even outright resistance. The reconstitution of civil society in response to globalisation and neoliberalism, then, has led to the evolution of a plurality of relationships between civil society and the post-apartheid state.

A plurality of relations: Marginalisation, engagement, and adversarialism

In summary, the post-apartheid era has witnessed the normalisation of South African society in a neoliberal global environment. Poverty, inequality and the attendant problems of marginalisation and governance that the 'Washington Consensus' and 'Third-Wave' model of globalisation and democracy respectively have wreaked on other parts of the world, are now the hallmarks of South African society. The legacy bequeathed by apartheid has not only not been addressed, but in fact, has in many ways been reinforced and even aggravated. How to respond and address this is the primary challenge confronting South African civil society?

The response by civil society in South Africa to these developments has been similar to that of the so-called 'third sector' in other parts of the world. In response to the effects and challenges of democratisation and globalisation it has reconstituted itself into three distinct blocs, each of which is defined by a different set of relationships with the state. On the one end of the spectrum, there are a set of informal community-based organisations mainly in marginalised communities, which have no relationship with the state. These organisations are preoccupied with assisting people to survive the ravages of neoliberalism. On the other end of the spectrum, there are a range of more formal social movements and/or CBOs, which are actively challenging and opposing the implementation of neoliberalism. Although these organisations also engage the state, their relations with the latter tend often to take on an adversarial tone. Finally, the third and perhaps the most powerful bloc is a set of more formal service-related NGOs, which, as a result of the more enabling environment created by the democratic regime, have entered partnerships with and/or sub-contracted to the state. These organisations have more engaging and collegiate relations with the state.

Of course these distinctions within civil society are not as stark nor rigid as depicted here. In the real world, there are many organisations that straddle the divide and blur the boundaries between one or more of these blocs. Some, like the TAC, display adversarial relations with the state on one issue and more collegiate relations on another. Others, like the Homeless Peoples Federation, challenge and oppose some state institutions but have established partnerships with others. What is important to remember of the contemporary era is that democratisation and globalisation have facilitated the reassertion of the plural character of civil society and undermined the homogenous effects that the anti-apartheid struggle had on this sector.

This plurality of civil society is recognised by most activists, politicians, and government officials, at least at the rhetorical level. But in most cases its meaning has not been internalised for, had it been, we would not have the kinds of demands from these actors evident in the quotations at the start of this chapter, for a single homogenous set of relations between civil society and the state. A recognition of the heterogeneity of civil society must as a corollary recognise the inevitable plurality in state-civil society relations. This, it should be noted, is beneficial for democracy and governance in the country. The informal CBOs enhance democracy at the simplest level because they enable ordinary people to survive. The establishment of more formal relations between them and the state would subvert their character and thus compromise this role. The more formal NGOs' collaborative relationship with the state is largely a product of the services they render for the state. And, in a society confronted with massive backlogs and limited institutional capacity, this role can only be to the benefit of democracy since it facilitates and enables service delivery to ordinary citizens and residents. Finally, the adversarial and conflictual role of new social movements and more formal CBOs enhances democracy for it creates a fluidity of support at the base of society. This can only be beneficial for it permits the reconfiguration of power within society, forcing the state not to take its citizens for granted, and effecting a systemic shift to the left which may create the possibility for a more people-centred, Keynesian-oriented developmental agenda.

These diverse roles and functions undertaken by different elements of civil society, then, collectively create the adversarial and collaborative relationships, the push and pull effects, which sometimes assist and other times compel the state to meet its obligations and responsibilities to its citizenry. The plurality of civil society and the diverse sets of relations that it engenders with the state is thus the best guarantee for the consolidation of democracy in South Africa.

Notes

1 Following O'Donnell and Schmitter's four-volume study on the subject, it has now become common in the literature to distinguish democratic transitions into these two distinct phases. Liberalisation refers to the moment when authoritarian leaders open up the political system, whereas democratisation is the period in which representative political systems become institutionalised (O'Donnell & Schmitter 1986).

2 Some of the leaders of NUSAS were fairly radical and anti-business from the early to mid-1950s. However, the bulk of the rank-and-file student membership tended to remain largely liberal in orientation until at least the late 1970s and early 1980s.

3 It is this power configuration that underpins the existing model of globalisation defined, and now increasingly questioned, as the 'Washington Consensus'.

4 The privatisation programme is expected to pick up pace in 2003, and the year did start off with the listing of Telkom in Johannesburg and New York.

5 This point has been made by a number of studies of, and commentators on, the South African political scene. For one of the earlier studies in this regard, see Adam, Slabbert & Moodley 1997. In recent months, however, a number of government officials, black entrepreneurs and intellectuals have responded to the charge by accusing critics of racism.

References

Adam, H, Slabbert, F & Moodley, K (1997) *Comrades in business.* Cape Town: Tafelberg.

Barnard, D & Terreblanche, Y (2001) *PRODDER: The South African Development Directory.* Pretoria: HSRC.

Bond, P (2001) *Against global apartheid.* Cape Town: UCT Press.

Carter, MR & May, J (2001) One kind of freedom: Poverty dynamics in post apartheid South Africa, *World Development* 29(12): 1987–2006.

Cohen, J & Arrato, A (1992) *Civil society and political theory.* Boston: MIT Press.

Desai, A (2002) *We are the poors: Community struggles in post-apartheid South Africa.* New York: Monthly Review Press

Habib, A (2002) Editor's introduction, in *The size and scope of the non-profit sector in South Africa.* Johannesburg and Durban: University of the Witwatersrand School of Public and Development Management and The Centre for Civil Society.

Habib, A & Kotze (2002) *Civil society, governance and development in an era of globalisation.* Unpublished manuscript.

Habib, A & Padayachee, V (2000) Economic policy and power relations in South Africa's transition to democracy, *World Development* 28(2): 245–263.

Habib, A & Taylor, R (1999) South Africa: Anti-apartheid NGOs in transition, *Voluntas* 10(1): 73–82.

Huntington, S (1991) *The Third Wave: Democratization in the late twentieth century.* Oklahoma: University of Oklahoma Press.

Marx, A (1992) *Lessons of struggle: South African internal opposition 1960–1990.* New York: OUP.

McCarthy, J & Zald, M (1987) The trend of social movements in America: Professionalization and resource mobilization, in M Zald and J McCarthy (eds.) *Social movements in an organizational society.* New Brunswick: Transaction Books.

McDonald, D & Pape, J (2002) *Cost recovery and the crisis of service delivery in South Africa.* Pretoria: HSRC.

O'Donnell, G & Schmitter, P (1986) *Transitions from authoritarian rule: Tentative conclusions about uncertain democracies* Vol. 4. Baltimore: Johns Hopkins Press.

Padayachee, V & Valodia, I (2001) Changing Gear? The 2001 Budget and economic policy in South Africa, *Transformation* 46: 71–83.

Sparks, A (1990) *The mind of South Africa.* New York: Ballantine Books.

Stacey, S & Aksartova, S (2001) The foundations of democracy: US foundations support for civil society in South Africa, 1988–1996, *Voluntas* 12 (4): 373–397.

Swilling, M & Russel, B (2002) *The size and scope of the non-profit sector in South Africa.* Johannesburg: School of Public and Development Management; Durban: Centre for Civil Society.

Tarrow, S (1994) *Power in movement.* Cambridge: CUP.

Tilly, C (1978) *From mobilisation to revolution.* Reading, Mass: Addison-Wesley.

The state of families in South Africa

Acheampong Yaw Amoateng and Linda Richter

Introduction

While scholars may debate its merits and demerits, there is general agreement that one of the most significant influences in the nineteenth century was the emergence of the industrial-capitalist revolution in Europe. Even though there were several facets to the revolution, for the purposes of the present chapter two related outcomes are worthy of note. First, as Schumpeter (1976) rightly observed, capitalism changed the material conditions of people both qualitatively and quantitatively. Second, the industrial-capitalist revolution marked a paradigm shift in family theorising, as in other fields, from the domination of traditional beliefs and philosophical speculations to the use of the scientific method, with its aspirations to freedom from the influence of values and its rigorous methodology (Doherty, Boss, LaRossa, Schumm & Steinmetz 1993).

The increased rationalisation of society led to the systematisation and for-malisation of family theory because the small social group, termed variously the family, household or domestic unit, continued to be regarded as one of the basic constituent institutions of the capitalist economy. For this reason family concepts were increasingly used to investigate the operations of capitalism on a world scale (Martin & Beittel 1984). One of the products of this process of systematisation and formalisation was the emergence of two prominent, seemingly competing, theoretical traditions that continue to be used to analyse family structure and process, namely structural-functionalism and Marxist-conflict theory. Even though scholars are quick to note the differences between the two theoretical traditions, they both make similar assumptions about the institution of the family and society (see Duke 1976).

For one thing, both theories are evolutionary in nature and emphasise the interface between the family institution and other institutions in society. Moreover, both theoretical traditions regard industrial-capitalism as a promi-nent co-ordinate of change in society, and thus underscore the importance of rational economic factors as an engine of change in social structures such as the family.[1] As a result of industrial-capitalism and its modernising influences such as urbanisation, several writers over the years have commented on the implications of such changes for the institution of the family using one or other of the two theoretical perspectives. For example, the evolutionary model of family life has sought to relate family structure to the level of modernisation or development of society (Goode 1963; Parsons 1951).

Writing in the 1950s under the influence of the 'family-as-an-endangered species' view, the American sociologist Parsons (1951) popularised the notion that the nuclear family was a logical product of the industrial-capitalist order, the survival of which depended on a gendered division of labour in the household. According to this view, the husband-father performs the more public or instrumental/breadwinning role, while the wife-mother performs the private expressive roles. Following Parsons, Goode (1963) focused on the homogenising effects of industrial capitalism with regard to family patterns. Specifically, Goode's position was that the penetration of capitalist ethos around the world led to the nucleation of the family in Western and non-Western societies alike.

Like their functionalist counterparts, family scholars who write from within the Marxist conflict tradition have also drawn attention to the interface between the family and broader society, although they see conflict and competition in family life, where functionalists see consensus and co-operation. For example, writing at the height of the industrial revolution of the nineteenth century, Engels observed that the kind of work women did varied a great deal from one society to another, and that the form of ownership in the society was a crucial determinant of the benefits women reaped from their work. Specifically, Engels observed that the subjugation of women was caused by an economic change, the institution of private property.

In recent times, Giddens (2000) has noted that globalising forces are impacting on the family in a number of ways, as seen in the separation of sexuality from reproduction, the emergence of more egalitarian relationships between men and women, the increasing participation of women in work outside of the home and in public life, and the growing tendency for family relations to be based on the sentiments of love rather than economic or social concerns, with the intimate couple being the primary family unit. However, notes Giddens, this depiction does not apply equally in all parts of the world. This is especially true in poor developing countries where gross inequalities between men and women persist, where extended families are maintained for reasons of cultural preference as well as survival in the face of poverty, and where immigration, employment opportunities and regional turbulence and war, have 'dispersed families across national borders and stretched kinship networks across vast geographic space' (Turner 2002).

Why a focus on the family?

Why take stock of the state of families in a volume that seeks to assess the state of the nation since the inception of democracy in South Africa? The essence of the state of the nation project is to act as a guidepost for the government's social and economic transformation agenda through the provision of empirical databases for policy formulation and implementation. In other words, the conventional expectation is that the end product of a project of this nature will be to enhance the development of policies in areas such as education, trade, tourism, politics, race relations, the environment, and so on.

It is something of an irony that, with respect to an institution that is generally regarded as the basic unit of society, family policy has not achieved a status commensurate with that of, say, economic, education, or even environmental policy. As has been shown by the brief overview of the two theoretical traditions that have conventionally been used to examine both family structure and process, the fortunes of the family have been bound up with those of all other institutions that have been the target of sustained state intervention in the pre- and post-apartheid eras. Both historically and contemporaneously, families perform a number of vital social functions. These include: the socialisation of children and the inculcation of moral and social values; the provision of material and emotional sustenance to family members and care of dependent family members, including children, older persons, and sick and disabled individuals; the control of social and sexual behaviour, including the restraint of aggression, antisocial behaviour and the infringement of taboos; the maintenance of family morale and identity, which creates mutual obligations and responsibilities and the motivation to perform pro-social roles inside and outside the family; and the launch of young people into roles and functions in the wider society.[2]

Thus, families are regarded as the building blocks of communities and the source of individual development and identity among young and old members, men and women, providers and dependants. Values and behaviours assumed to be present in adult members, which are key to the functionality of a society – for example, honesty, perseverance, care for vulnerable groups and so on – are acquired during development, and maintained and reinforced through experiences in a family group. The importance of the family is evidenced by the fact that issues such as stress and ill-health, the care and support of children and aged persons, school retention, labour force stability, substance use, and crime cannot be considered without attention to family life.

The balance of family resources to provide for and support family members, and the costs in doing so, is critical to the functionality of families (Mattessich & Hill 1987). Families with fewer resources (for example, insufficient income and individuals capable of performing needed activities) and high costs (a large number of dependent or needy individuals) may cease to perform traditional family functions because they are not able to provide for the material or social needs of members. For these reasons, poverty and unemployment, as well as high rates of social dependency (such as disability or substance use), place severe strains on the resources of families.

It is in the interest of communities and the state to ensure that families have sufficient resources to provide for the basic needs of their members. When families are able to perform traditional care-giving functions it reduces the burden on the state in terms of the long-run costs of addressing social problems that might arise from the failure of families to perform their normative roles. Such family functions also positively determine higher levels of individual functionality than is usually achieved without family support and assistance. This is more the case in the current macroeconomic policy environment. With minimal state intervention, government social safety nets tend to shrink, and families and communities assume a larger role in providing for their members, socially and economically.

This overview of families in South African society is provided against this background of the importance of family life for national development. The aim is to give a perspective that includes the past as well as anticipates some future trends as far as the institution of the family is concerned. Specifically, we take stock by looking at four aspects of family life in the society, namely residential, marriage, childbearing and divorce patterns. We expect that the examination of household structure and the three central family formation and dissolution events will provide some insight into the state of the family in the society for the purposes of policy intervention. Since the 1996 population census was the first all-race census undertaken, we examine the state of the family in South Africa through empirical evidence provided by this data source, although we draw on other sources whenever appropriate. To accomplish our aim, we put the discussion into an historical context by briefly reviewing the evolution of family scholarship in the society.

Major developments affecting families and family scholarship

Writing about the African social experience, Mazrui (1986) has used the phrase 'the triple heritage' to refer to the cultural syncretism that resulted from the continent's historical contact with both Arabs and Europeans. It has become conventional to use the establishment of these *alien* institutions as the point of departure for any analysis of change in an African society. European culture was introduced as part of the colonial project, and colonisation resulted in a profound transformation of many social institutions in most traditional African societies.

For instance, as far as the family institution is concerned, the adoption of Christian and Islamic beliefs and practices through the mechanisms of, for example, formal education, affected family patterns that served important functions in pre-modern African societies, such as polygamy and preference for large families. Moreover, the family's primary role in the organisation of political, economic, and social life was undermined by the introduction of the nation-state with its reliance on modern institutions of governance, production and distribution. For example, commenting on the extent of penetration of European culture in South Africa, Schapera argued:

> Native culture in South Africa is everywhere in contact with ever widening channels of European civilisation, which are gradually but effectively modifying its traditional manifestations. The customs of the Natives are being altered by the action of the European economic system, through the teachings of missionaries and educators and through contact with whites in innumerable other ways … Bantu culture will change and develop, drawing most of its impetus from the elements of our own civilisation, no matter what we (Europeans) can do or how we attempt to control it. The best we (Europeans) can hope to achieve is to regulate our active participation in the process of change so as to avoid conflict and disaster. (1967: xi)

In South Africa, colonisation through such processes as land expropriation and industrial development resulted in large numbers of people migrating to earn cash income to meet imposed taxes, to supplement declining agricultural resources, and to ward off poverty. The resulting urbanisation, and subsequent politically imposed residential and work restrictions, affected black families particularly, and reinforced dual urban-rural homesteads and circular migration as organisational mechanisms of economic and social adaptation (Okoth-Ogendo 1989). It was against this backdrop of colonial domination and racial oppression in the society that structural-functionalist family theory, with its evolutionary flavour, held sway.

With its ideology of political quietism, structural-functionalism provided a justification for the colonialists' mission to bring modern civilising values and norms to otherwise primitive peoples. Second, this theoretical perspective served as an analytical tool for scholars in organising the masses of data they had accumulated on the transformations occurring in traditional institutions as a result of their coming into contact with a supposedly superior culture. Thus, the predominant theoretical approach to understanding the family institution posited a functional relationship between families and society whereby families were seen as performing tasks such as the socialisation of children, sexual and reproductive control, economic co-operation, social support, and so on, in ways that co-ordinate with and serve broader social and political goals (Parsons 1951).

The family in South Africa was understood in the context of this intellectual tradition for close on a century until well into the late 1980s. Based on the assumption that the western, independent and isolated nuclear family had evolved from a supposedly complex, multi-generational type, the nucleated family type was held up as the ideal form to which every modern person or group aspired.[3] Within this theoretical tradition, family theory and research sought to define as a family a social unit that comprised a husband, his wife, and their dependent children living in the same dwelling. By this view, any domestic unit other than the idealised nuclear family was seen primarily as a deviation from an essentialist or universalistic notion of the family (see Chambers 2003; Pauw 1963; Steyn 1993a, 1993b; Steyn, Strijdom, Viljoen & Bosman 1987). This politically-biased paradigm of family life began to shift as the apartheid edifice began to crumble in the face of mounting social crises generated from the political left.

The demise of apartheid and the emergence of critical family scholarship

The evolutionary-functionalist model of the family was incorporated into the apartheid status quo through its commitment to Western values of family life, but began to shift as the challenge to the state gathered momentum from the late 1970s onwards. Several writers contested what is called the rhetoric of African family breakdown (Barrow 2001) and the portrayal of the African family as an illegitimate white family (Chambers 2003; Nobles 1979). African families were portrayed as a disintegrating institution, with strong moral overtones, because they deviated from the nuclear family in terms of two defining features – marriage and co-residence of members. As a result, research on African families tended to focus on 'dysfunctional' family patterns such as polygamy, extra-marital sexual relations, illegitimacy, delayed marriage, teenage pregnancy, and female-headed households (see eg. Chambers 2003; Pauw 1963; Steyn et al. 1987; Steyn 1993a, 1993b). In addition, in some respects research on the African family became a by-product of another ideological and political concern – the control of fertility and population growth.

Branding the evolutionist model of family change as paternalistic, and therefore conservative, critique centred on both substantive-theoretical and methodological considerations (see eg. Murray 1987; Russell 1994; Ziehl 1994). Citing the same data sources as those used by adherents of the convergence thesis, critical scholars argue that African families are not evolving with urbanisation into the assumed universal nuclear form in a linear and unproblematic way (Siqwana-Ndulo 1998). Rather, Africans, in adhering to their cultural beliefs about family life and kin relationships, have continued to live in extended families, even in the face of countervailing forces in the urban-industrial milieu (see eg. Russell 1994; Ziehl 1994, 2001).

Household structure, marriage, childbearing and divorce

In this section, four selected aspects of family life are considered: the residential dimension of the family or household structures, as well as patterns of marriage, childbearing and divorce, which are examined within the context of the conflict orientation to illustrate the shortcomings of apartheid-era family research.

The structure of households

A household has been defined as a 'person or a group of people that usually live and eat together regardless of whether they are related or unrelated' (Institute for Resource Development 1987). While a household is not the same as a family, it is nevertheless the unit through which demographers understand the family. The household is a basic social, consumption and pro- duction unit, and the arena where most people spend a major portion of their lives (de Vos 1995). With increasing separation of family and household as a result of migrant labour, as well as new forms of household headship by women and even children, households are being problematised in South Africa (Budlender 1997).

However, given the importance of the household as far as the family is concerned, it is hardly surprising that a considerable amount of time was spent by family scholars in studying household structures. In fact, the view that the family patterns of blacks were converging towards those of their white counterparts was based on data on urban household structures (see eg. Steyn 1991). The question we pose is: what is the state of households in the popu- lation? Part of the answer to this question can be found in Table 11.1 which shows the distribution of households in the population.

Table 11.1 *Distribution of household types by race and urban-rural location (percentages)*

Urban/rural	Race	Extended	Non-family	Nuclear	Other
Urban	African/Black	32.5	20.7	44.1	2.7
Urban	Coloured	32.3	7.9	52.2	7.6
Urban	Indian/Asian	27.6	5.4	62.1	4.9
Urban	White	8.9	21.4	61.9	7.8
Rural	African/Black	43.3	13.4	40.9	2.5
Rural	Coloured	25.4	14.4	54.6	5.7
Rural	Indian/Asian	25.3	8.0	63.0	3.7
Rural	White	9.1	15.2	71.2	4.6

Source: Stats SA (1996) Population Census Data

Several issues regarding household structure are illustrated above. First, the importance and salience of the family is evidenced by the fact that most households consist of family groups, regardless of urban-rural residence. Second, there are almost equal proportions of nuclear and extended family households in rural and urban areas (45 per cent and 40 per cent respectively). Third, extended family households predominate in rural areas, while nuclear family households predominate in urban areas. Finally, while extended family households prevail among coloureds and Africans, nuclear family households are identifiable with whites and Indians/Asians.

On the face of it, Table 11.1 appears to lend credence to the thesis of convergence espoused by functionalist family scholars, especially the finding on rural-urban differentials. Given the absence of time-series data, analyses of change have been done conventionally by rural-urban comparisons on the assumption that urban status is progressive over time. However, a critical analysis of the data reveals that, to a very large extent, there has been continuity in household – and hence family – patterns in the society. For instance, much has been claimed about the similarities in family patterns of coloureds and Africans because of their shared historical circumstances under apartheid. More detailed analyses of the data show that African and coloured households are more likely to include children, grandchildren, siblings and other relatives of the head of the household.

Moreover, in similar parallels, Indians and whites are said to have similar socio-economic characteristics, again because of historical circumstances. This assertion is also confirmed as far as their family patterns are concerned, although they exhibit some important differences. For instance, even though the most common household type for the two cultural groups is the nuclear family, Asians simultaneously have a relatively high prevalence of extended family households. A proportion of South African Indian families exhibit crucial elements of the joint family system, which is a family household with three contiguous generations, conventionally associated with eastern Asian cultures (de Vos 1995).[4]

The cultural heritage of white South Africans is invariably European and, to all intents and purposes, this heritage has been kept intact as far as family patterns are concerned. Up until the publication of the work of Laslett and the Cambridge school of historical demography (Laslett 1983), the conventional wisdom was that the nuclear family normally associated with whites is a creation of modern industrial society. Analysing historical documents such as parish records from seventeenth- and eighteenth-century England, the Laslett group found that the nuclear family has always been the characteristic family pattern of Europeans.[5] The continuity in white family patterns is evidenced by the fact that white households are the least likely to include extended family members, such as grandparents, parents, siblings, grandchildren and other relatives, even their own children. Households headed by whites are heavily weighted in favour of the marital dyad or the conjugal unit, and are the most likely to include non-relatives.

The functionalist lenses its adherents wore prevented family scholars from engaging in a critical interpretation of the data at their disposal,[6] and hence became open to attack by Marxist-oriented family scholarship. For instance, the functionalist commitment to a universal family form led them to ignore the ethnic nuances that challenge notions of a universal family. The functionalist-evolutionist model of family change was accused of being paternalistic and therefore conservative; that the view of convergence only sought to justify the superiority of the family patterns of the ruling class that happened to be white (see Murray 1987; Russell 1994; Ziehl 1994). The new generation of critical family scholars argued that African families are not evolving with urbanisation into the assumed universal nuclear form in a linear way (Siqwana-Ndulo 1998). Rather, Africans, in adhering to their cultural beliefs about family life and kin relationships, have continued to live in extended families, even in the face of countervailing forces in the urban-industrial milieu (see Russell 1994; Ziehl 1994, 2001). This position is consonant with family scholars in Western societies who concede that it is not easy to arrive at definitions of families that accommodate the wide variety of family forms evident around the world (Walker 2002). Goode (1964, 1982), for instance, noted that families existed in a variety of forms, according to a life cycle involving different stages of growth, size and composition.

A related issue to that of family diversity, and which challenged traditional approaches to family and household research, was the treatment of the family and homestead as coterminous, a conception which is at variance with empirical evidence. Though subject to different drivers and manifestations, in both resource-rich and resource-poor environments, the links between family and residence, or household, are loosening. Co-residence is not a defining feature of family. In fact, the acceptance of the family dimension of social relatedness within, and even across, households allows one to better understand household livelihood strategies as emanating from complex social processes involving competing historical, contemporary and envisaged future individual and group interests. It also helps one to reach beyond a pathology or deficit model of families as disorganised and disintegrating, towards an understanding of family adaptation and coping (Siqwana-Ndulo 1998). In addition, by focusing on families as well as households, one is able to take account of the fact that women, men and children do not operate as purely autonomous and isolated individuals or rational collectives of individuals of equal standing and claim in a shared material space (Mbiti 1969; Walker 2002).

Rather than a universal progression from extended to nuclear family types with modernisation, broad consensus has developed that families are extremely diverse. In fact, families can be no more closely defined than as social groups related by kinship, residence or close emotional attachments, which share a number of systemic features. These include, but are not restricted to, intimate interdependence, boundary maintenance, the preservation of identity and adaptation of identity to change over time, and the performance of family tasks (Mattessich & Hill 1987).

Marriage

Marriage has been pivotal in demographic change. It marks the start of one form of family activity and identifies a critical transition in a person's history from which intervals to subsequent family events can be assessed. The importance of the institution of marriage for both family and society in Africa is demonstrated by the fact that almost all women marry (Adegboyega 1994). In South Africa, as elsewhere on the continent, the centrality of marriage in pre-colonial times is underscored by the fact that marriage alliances between lineages provided the basis for the power of patriarchal lineage heads, while the payment of the bride wealth by junior men was the means of acquiring wealth by their seniors (Lekhele & Ntsime 1984). Bozzoli (1991) has noted that the phenomenon of marriage and the related activity of building a household was central to the migration of Batswana women. Judging from accounts of historical demographers in European societies, we now know that the conjugal unit is central to the nuclear family system with which white South Africans are identified, a fact that reflects the importance of marriage in the family life of whites as well.

The absence of racially-motivated laws prohibiting inter-group marriages also contributed to raising the marriage rate. Several commentators have noted that hundreds of Afrikaner white families intermarried with non-whites in the early history of South Africa. These relationships were often a result of white bachelors living on frontier farms who sought the company of non-white women. Although such interracial sexual encounters and mixed marriages were confined to a minority of people, these practices were by no means uncommon in early South Africa (Attwell 1986; Thompson 1990).[7]

As the foregoing review shows, marriage has always been an important family event in South Africa regardless of race and/or ethnicity, as indicated by the fact that the bulk of childbearing in the society occurs within the context of marriage (52 per cent). However, as already noted, the historical contact with alien cultures through colonisation, and the subsequent development of industrial capitalism, brought about significant alterations in most social institutions. Given its central role in the organisation of production and consumption, fundamental changes also occurred in the family. The emergence of the cash economy and the expropriation of land for commercialised farming by the colonialists led to the migration of large numbers of able-bodied African males to the emerging towns and cities to search for work.

In view of the fact that both the timing and incidence of marriage depend largely on the sex ratio in the marriageable ages, several scholars have commented on the deleterious effects of this economic transformation on marriage rates among Africans (see Simkins & Dlamini 1992). The absence of males in the marriageable age range in the African community, coupled with persistent poverty in the face of increasing commercialisation of the *lobolo* (bride wealth), meant either the postponement of marriage or its absence altogether. Conversely, the relative privilege and affluence of groups such as whites and Indians, and to some extent coloureds, ensured that marriage was maintained among them.

What then is the state of marriage in South African society? While this question requires empirical knowledge about past and present marriage patterns, the paucity of reliable and valid historical data compels an answer based on recent empirical data. Again, recourse is made to the 1996 census data in which respondents were asked to indicate their current marital status (see Table 11.2, overleaf).

Table 11.2 shows the distribution of marital status in the population. Two issues are noteworthy in the table. First, in general, the marriage rate is low compared to the nearly universal marriage pattern that has been observed in most sub-Saharan African societies (Adegboyega 1994). Specifically, just over one-quarter of the population is married (26 per cent), while almost two-thirds of the population are single and have never been married (66 per cent). The second issue is the very large race differentials in the marriage rates. For instance, while the crude marriage rate for Africans is 212 marriages for every 1 000 persons, for coloureds, Asians and whites it is 282, 430 and 509 respectively.

Table 11.2 *Distribution of marital status by race (percentages)*

Marital Status	African/Black	Coloured	Indian/Asian	White	Total
Never married	70.45	61.87	49.37	39.94	65.79
Married	21.24	28.24	43.20	50.98	25.63
Living together	3.52	3.76	0.72	2.13	3.31
Widow/widower	2.90	3.42	4.39	3.03	3.00
Divorced/separated	1.19	2.27	1.91	3.53	1.56

Source: Stats SA (1996) Population Census Data

Cross-sectional data makes it difficult to address the issue of change with regard to marriage and other family events in the population. Yet knowledge about past levels of marriage as a family event is required to assess the state of the institution. To glean information about the past, a cohort analysis was carried out to portray changes in marriage patterns over time.[8] Tables 11.3 and 11.4 show the results of the analyses.

Table 11.3 *Distribution of marital status by birth cohort (percentages)*

Marital Status	1878–1901	1902–1921	1922–1941	1942–1961	1962–1981
Never married	17.95	8.35	9.30	18.94	71.08
Married	37.61	50.96	65.31	65.05	20.96
Living together	1.52	1.32	2.65	6.41	5.25
Widow/widower	39.98	37.14	19.03	4.10	0.33
Divorced/separated	1.23	1.48	3.21	4.91	1.01

Source: Stats SA (1996) Population Census Data

Table 11.4 *Distribution of marital status by birth cohort and race (percentages)*

	African					Coloured				
	1878–1901	1902–1921	1922–1941	1942–1961	1962–1981	1878–1901	1902–1921	1922–1941	1942–1961	1962–1981
Never married	18.18	9.37	11.21	23.44	75.26	20.75	10.65	10.46	17.12	65.11
Married	39.57	50.94	61.46	59.63	16.85	15.09	31.38	57.96	65.38	26.40
Living together	1.50	1.49	3.16	7.66	5.51	0.00	1.54	3.21	6.58	5.71
Widow/widower	38.18	35.98	20.64	4.49	0.32	64.15	54.05	23.72	4.29	0.35
Divorced/separated	1.18	1.46	3.00	4.18	0.69	0.00	1.85	4.36	6.28	1.59

	Indian/Asian					White				
	1878–1901	1902–1921	1922–1941	1942–1961	1962–1981	1878–1901	1902–1921	1922–1941	1942–1961	1962–1981
Never married	6.67	6.88	4.84	6.51	53.25	14.63	3.54	2.64	4.20	49.21
Married	46.67	35.81	67.26	82.56	42.57	24.39	60.04	82.60	83.85	42.91
Living together	0.00	0.22	0.48	1.03	1.11	4.88	0.66	0.94	2.43	4.06
Widow/widower	40.00	56.34	25.17	5.40	0.55	53.66	33.88	10.00	2.05	0.28
Divorced/separated	6.67	0.32	1.98	4.20	1.76	0.00	1.61	3.57	7.21	2.80

Source: Stats SA (1996) Population Census Data

Table 11.3 shows that the marriage rate increased from about 38 per cent among the 1878–1901 birth cohort to 65 per cent among the 1942–1961 birth cohort. Thereafter, it declined dramatically to slightly over one-fifth among the 1962–1981 birth cohort. As expected, there has been a dramatic increase in the proportion of single people, from less than one-fifth (18 per cent) among the 1878–1901 cohort to almost three-quarters (71 per cent) among the 1962–1981 birth cohort. While marriage has declined, there has been a steady increase in the rate of non-marital cohabitation over the years among all race groups, suggesting that, increasingly, younger generations of South

Africans are choosing this type of living arrangement. As far as race and marriage is concerned, the period effects persist even after adjusting for race effects: that is, there has been a decline in the prevalence of marriage in the society among all race groups, as shown in Table 11.4. The greatest decline in marriage rates occurred among Africans, with a 23 percentage point decline between the 1878–1901 and the 1962–1981 birth cohorts. Coloureds started with a relatively lower marriage rate among the 1878–1901 birth cohorts and increased steadily until it began to decline again among the 1962–1981 birth cohorts.

What might explain the decline in marriage and the increase in cohabitation in the society? Again, the absence of time-series data makes it difficult to answer this question with any degree of certainty. In a separate analysis in which we examined the levels of education over time, we found that the older generation are less educated than the younger generation. For example, only two per cent of the 1878–1901 birth cohort had matriculated while 23 per cent of the 1962–1981 cohort had matriculated. The majority (62 per cent) of the 1962–1981 cohort who had matriculated had never been married, compared to only 26 per cent of the 1878–1901 cohort. Increasing education is thus associated with the decline in marriage. One consequence of the decline in marriages among the younger generation is the increase in non-marital fertility, especially among Africans, as shown in Table 11.5. Almost one-third of births among Africans occur outside marriage, compared to only two per cent of non-marital births among whites and three per cent among Indians; coloureds have 24 per cent non-marital births.

Table 11.5 *Distribution of married parents by race (percentages)*

Race	Marital status	
	Single/never married	Ever married
African/black	32.43	66.98
Coloured	24.49	75.18
Indian/Asian	2.74	96.99
White	2.32	97.43

Source: Stats SA (1996) Population Census Data

Divorce

Marriages dissolve through either divorce or death. It is generally believed that African marriages tend to be stable. The stability is attributed to the role of lineage or extended family in marital arrangements and, in some cases, practices such as endogamy. In contrast, individualism and the ethos of romantic love that prevail in Western societies make marriages in such societies relatively unstable. Commenting on the relative stability of traditional Tswana marriages, Lekhele and Ntsime observe:

> In traditional Tswana society, marriage between a Motswana damsel (girl) born in a particular *kgoro* (ward) to a complete stranger was a taboo. Acceptable matrimonial unions were those in which the bride and her spouse had common family or clan ties, so that not only the spouses, but their parents as well belonged to the same or allied clans. If one's daughter were to get married to a blood relation or to a clansman the couple naturally share the heritage of common customs and traditions. This had the added advantage of impartiality for those family members/ clansmen involved in settling any dispute or misunderstanding within the marriage. (1984: 1)

Divorce is a relatively rare occurrence in South Africa, although race groups exhibit different patterns of divorce. For the country as a whole, the crude divorce rate is 15 per 1 000. In fact, as Table 11.2 shows, marriages in South Africa are more likely to dissolve through death than through divorce.

Whites have the highest divorce rate at 35 per 1 000, compared to Africans among whom only 11 marriages in 1 000 dissolve through divorces; coloureds and Indians have 22 and 19 divorces out of every 1 000 marriages respectively. The cohort analysis in Table 11.3 shows that while the divorce rate for the country as a whole is relatively low, it increased steadily over the years before starting a dramatic decline. For example, the crude divorce rate increased almost 37 per cent – from 12 divorces per 1 000 marriages among the 1878–1901 cohort to 49 divorces per 1 000 marriages among the 1942–1961 cohort. Thereafter it declined by almost 40 per cent to ten divorces per 1 000 marriages among the 1962–1981 cohort. This suggests that the younger generation of South Africans is choosing to stay in marriages longer than their older compatriots.

As far as racial patterns of divorce are concerned, Table 11.6 shows that, with the exception of Indians who had an extremely high divorce rate around the turn of the twentieth century, all the other race groups show the same general pattern of a steady increase in divorces, reaching a peak among the 1942–1961 cohort, and then a gradual decline among the 1961–1981 cohort.

Table 11.6 *Changes in crude divorce rate (per 1 000) by race and birth cohort*

Race	1878–1901	1902–1921	1922–1941	1942–1961	1962–1981
African	11	14	30	41	6
Coloured	0	18	43	62	15
Indian	66	3	19	42	17
White	0	16	35	72	28

Source: Stats SA (1996) Population Census Data

Childbearing

Like marriage, childbearing or fertility is an important event in the course of family life. The importance of fertility behaviour lies in the role it plays, not only in demographic change, but also in the social and economic development of a society. The importance of childbearing is further illustrated by the observation that, in traditional African societies, a mother and her children formed the nucleus of the elementary family to which the father was attached (Colson 1970). In fact, the practice of polygamy has been linked to the premium that African societies place on childbearing, as was noted by a colonial official among the Batswana:

> I know the ordinary native. If he has a wife who has no child, then he will take a second wife simply with the idea of having children. If he is a Christian – well, he does not worry about that – he takes a second wife whether it is right or wrong. He does not care … So you can see, it is not voluntary that they have small families. There is something wrong, and I cannot find out what the reason is.
> (Native Economic Commission Report 1932: 977)

Even though there are several aspects of fertility, here we restrict ourselves to completed fertility, measured by children ever born in the 1996 population census. Changes in fertility also help us to assess the state of the family in the society.

Table 11.7 shows the distribution of children ever born by age. The importance of childbearing is demonstrated by the fact that only 29 per cent of the women interviewed are childless compared to almost three-quarters (72 per cent) who have at least one child. The incidence of childlessness also declines as women get older, suggesting that the younger generation of women is increasingly choosing to delay childbearing or to remain childless. For example, while 62 per cent of women aged 15 to 24 have borne no child, only six per cent aged 55 to 64 are childless. In a study of the timing of parenthood, it was found that the estimated proportion of childless women in South Africa is 6,3 per cent (Amoateng, Kalule-Sabiti & Ditlopo 2003).[9]

Table 11.7 *Children ever born by age*

Age	0	1	2	3	4	5	6	7	8	9	10	11	12
0–14	98.85	0.50	0.18	0.11	0.11	0.08	0.07	0.04	0.02	0.03	0.01	0.00	0.00
15–24	62.04	26.73	8.33	1.95	0.51	0.17	0.11	0.06	0.04	0.03	0.02	0.01	0.00
25–34	15.53	23.43	27.42	17.24	8.88	4.16	1.91	0.79	0.36	0.17	0.07	0.03	0.01
35–44	6.93	9.92	20.32	20.02	15.27	10.52	7.16	4.53	2.69	1.41	0.77	0.32	0.15
45–54	5.83	7.36	15.68	16.61	14.53	11.32	9.20	7.05	5.20	3.42	2.16	1.03	0.62
55–64	5.95	6.21	11.10	13.33	12.97	11.34	10.12	8.65	7.43	5.28	3.98	2.16	1.48
>65	10.58	7.11	10.53	11.29	11.02	9.91	9.25	8.25	7.38	5.56	4.63	2.51	1.97
Total	28.81	15.55	15.54	11.95	8.54	5.93	4.40	3.21	2.40	1.59	1.12	0.57	0.39

Source: Stats SA (1996) Population Census Data

As with all aspects of family life in South Africa, childbearing behaviour is changing. As far as Africans are concerned, changes in childbearing was noted as far back as the 1930s. For instance, commenting on the change in this aspect of family life among the Batswana of the Northwest, the Native Economic Commission Report noted: 'The birth figures are becoming less and less. There are many households without children, and there are many households with only two or three children' (1932: 987).

While there are problems associated with coverage, especially among blacks, in past censuses and surveys, nonetheless they give us a picture of trends in fertility levels (Makiwane 1994). To analyse changes in the childbearing behaviour of women, we present the findings of a cohort analysis in Tables 11.8 and 11.9, which show the mean number of children born in general and for each race group respectively. What the tables show is that fertility levels have been falling steadily over the years for all race groups in the country, with the largest decline being observed among whites and Asians. For example, among Africans, the mean number of children born declined from 5,29 among the 1878–1901 cohort to 1,37 among the 1962–1981 cohort. Among whites it fell from a mean of 2,57 (1878–1901) to 0,90 (1962–1981).

Table 11.8 *Children ever born by birth cohort*

Birth cohort	Children ever born	
	Mean	Standard deviation
1878–1901	5.29	3.42
1902–1921	5.07	3.21
1922–1941	4.96	2.99
1942–1961	3.75	2.39
1962–1981	1.30	1.50

Source: Stats SA (1996) Population Census Data

Table 11.9 *Children ever born by birth cohort and race*

Race	Birth cohort	Mean	Standard deviation
African/black	1878–1901	5.44	3.38
	1902–1921	5.49	3.20
	1922–1941	5.44	3.02
	1942–1961	4.17	3.53
	1962–1981	1.37	1.56
Coloured	1878–1901	4.90	4.23
	1902–1921	5.19	3.56
	1922–1941	5.08	3.18
	1942–1961	3.38	2.05
	1962–1981	1.23	1.30

Indian/Asian	1878–1901	3.00	3.00
	1902–1921	5.16	3.30
	1922–1941	4.15	2.57
	1942–1961	2.78	1.52
	1962–1981	1.06	1.20
White	1878–1901	2.57	2.16
	1902–1921	2.95	2.08
	1922–1941	2.96	1.73
	1942–1961	2.34	1.25
	1962–1981	0.90	1.10

Source: Stats SA (1996) Population Census Data

Summary and conclusion

Our aim in this chapter was to assess the state of the family in South Africa, a task motivated by the watershed democratic transition in 1994. Given the complexity and the multi-dimensional nature of families, four crucial aspects of family life were selected for examination based on secondary analyses of the 1996 population census data and other anecdotal sources. The features of family life examined were the residential dimension of the family or household structure, and patterns of marriage, childbearing and divorce. To accomplish our aims, the study was put into an historical context by critically examining the nature of family scholarship in the country, especially during the apartheid and post-apartheid eras, to give a sense of how the perceived state of the family has been affected by the very nature of this scholarship.

Several issues have emerged from our analyses that have implications for the state of the family as a social institution and its possible future trajectory. As far as the residential dimension of family life is concerned, we found that the search for the South African family, a fundamental goal of functionalist-oriented family scholars, is not warranted. Consistent with its multi-cultural and adaptable nature, there is no one family form that can clearly be identified with South Africa. There is a multiplicity of family forms in the society, of which two family patterns predominate, namely the nuclear and extended family forms. Culturally, the nuclear family is clearly identifiable with whites, while the extended family pattern is identifiable with Africans. Coloureds and Indians exhibit a mixture of the two family patterns.

A profile of a household at a specific point in time, as is inevitable in an analysis of once-off national census and survey data, obscures the movement of family members in and out of different households over their life courses. Individuals go through a series of life transitions that impinge not only on their own lives, but also on the structure of their families and households (Hareven 1982). While analyses of the rural-urban variations in household types suggests that non-family households are likely to increase among all population groups as a result of both macro- and micro-social forces, most South African households are still family-oriented. Interesting changes in family patterns are beginning to emerge with respect to urban-rural residence; for example, white South Africans are beginning to show a decline in nuclear-family types in urban as compared to rural areas, a change that is also evident in post-industrial Europe.

Conventionally, marriage marks the beginning of the family-building process, which makes it an important family event. However, unlike most sub-Saharan African societies where marriage tends to be universal, the marriage rate in South Africa is relatively low, especially among Africans and coloureds. Moreover, we found evidence of the decreasing prevalence of marriage in society, especially among the younger generations, although the importance of marriage is underscored by the fact that the bulk of childbearing still occurs within the context of marriage. In place of legal marriage, non-marital co-habitation appears to be increasing, especially among the younger groups. The decrease in marriage-coupled childbearing has resulted in a progressive increase in non-marital fertility over the years.

People may be reluctant to marry in South Africa but once they do so, they tend to remain attached, judging by the relatively low rate of divorce. The cohort analysis suggests that divorce rates are continuing to fall. In fact, marriages in South Africa have a higher probability of being dissolved through the death of a spouse than through divorce. Even though Africans have the lowest marriage rate, their divorce rate is the lowest of all the race groups, while white marriages tend to be the most unstable.

Childbearing continues to be normative, judging by the fact that nearly three-quarters of women become parents at some stage in their life course. In fact, the increasing tendency to bear children outside of marriage may attest to the importance of parenthood in the society. However, the birth rates are relatively low compared to the rest of the continent, and continue to fall among all race groups. White people have the lowest birth rate, followed by Indians, while Africans have the highest fertility rate, followed by coloureds.

The family, in all its diversity, appears to be alive and well in South Africa. While forces of modernisation such as industrialisation and urbanisation have brought about certain obvious changes, the resilience of family forms as a key social unit is demonstrated by the persistence and continuity of certain elements of family life.

Worldwide, governments are increasingly developing policies to strengthen family life in recognition of the fact that family groups play irreplaceable roles in the socialisation of children, in the promotion of pro-social behaviour, and in the care and support of vulnerable members of the population. There is now good evidence of the relationships between school achievement, mental health, behaviour control, and retention and productivity effects in the workplace, and the quality of family life. Although the view is frequently expressed that healthy families are the building blocks of a stable and productive society, South Africa is only now beginning to formulate an explicit family policy.[10] In 1982 the Cabinet appointed a task group to investigate family life in South Africa with a view to formulating a national family programme. In 1987, the South African Welfare Council was tasked with the implementation of what was called the National Family Programme.[11]

The HSRC was responsible for the execution, co-ordination and administration of a research programme on family life, and several influential documents were produced as part of the research programme (Harvey 1992). However, no substantial effect was given to the National Family Programme. In addition, it was structured within the political framework of apartheid and narrowly focused on marriage, child care and social security. For most of the last century, political and economic policies in South Africa were determined without their implications for family life being taken into account. Examples include influx control, migrant labour, the freezing of family housing, and transport and labour regulations. The new family policy currently being formulated has to take account not only the changing nature of a democratic South Africa, but also the mechanisms required to redress the negative impact of apartheid policies on families.

Notes

1   This view is contrary to conventional wisdom, which branded structural-functional-ism as static and therefore conservative in its basic assumptions of the nature of man and society.

2   In fact, an impetus for the tendency towards putting families on the political agenda is the recent call by the political leaders of the country for a moral regeneration, where one of the emphases is on strengthening and supporting families to perform their traditional functions of moral education.

3   See Laslett (1983) for a critique of this notion of the nuclear family.

4   In the ideal joint family system, family members continue to reside with other family members from birth until death; daughters leave the natal home to join the household of their husbands' parents, while a son stays in the parental household and brings his wife to live in this household upon marriage.

5   Adegboyega (1994) has argued that rather than modernisation or industrialisation being the cause of nuclear families, nucleation appears to be associated with any economic activity with an inherent geographical mobility. For example, the family structure of pastoralists tends to be nuclear in nature, while that of agriculturalists tends to be extended.

6   It is significant to note that Russell's (1994) critique of the convergence thesis was based on analysis and re-interpretation of tables from Steyn's (1991) work.

7   Following the passage of the *Prohibition of Mixed Marriages* and *Immorality Acts* of 1949 and 1950 respectively, the incidence of inter-racial marriages gradually became less common in the late nineteenth century and in mid-twentieth century. Jacobson, Amoateng & Heaton (2003) found that all race groups in South Africa have homogamy rates in the high 90s.

8   A cohort is a group of people who experience an event together. The census data had information on respondents' age. This enabled us to create a 20-year interval birth cohort variable by subtracting age from 1996, the year of the census. Cohort analysis has become a popular technique among demographers because it provides insight into the effects of human ageing and the nature of social, cultural, and political change (see Glenn 1977).

9   A comparable figure for women aged between 15 and 44 in the United States was found to be 44 per cent (Hird & Abshoff 2000).

10   Linda Richter and Yaw Amoateng have a contract from the Department of Social Development to provide research information to support the development of a family policy.

11   Co-operative Research Programme on Marriage and Family Life.

References

Adegboyega, O (1994) *The situation of families in East and Southern Africa*. Unpublished manuscript.

Amoateng, AY, Kalule-Sabiti, I & Ditlopo, P (2003) Analysing cross-sectional data with time-dependent covariates: The case of age at first birth in South Africa, *Journal of Biosocial Science* 35.

Attwell, M (1986) *South Africa: Background of the crisis*. London: Sidgwick & Jackson.

Barrow, C (2001) Contesting the rhetoric of 'black family breakdown' from Barbados, *Journal of Comparative Family Studies* 32: 419–441.

Bozzoli, B (1991) *Women of Phokeng: Consciousness, life strategy, and migrancy in South Africa, 1900–1983*. Portsmouth, New Hampshire: Heinemann.

Budlender, D (1997) *The debate about household headship*. Pretoria: Central Statistical Services.

Chambers, D (2003) 'Civilising the natives': Customary marriage in post-apartheid South Africa, in R Shweder, M Minow & H Markus (eds.) *Engaging cultural differences* (in press).

Colson, E (1970) Family change in contemporary Africa, in J Middleton (ed.) *Black Africa: Its peoples and their cultures today*. London: Collier-Macmillan.

De Vos, SM (1995) *Household composition in Latin America*. New York: Plenum Press.

Doherty, WJ et al. (1993) Family theories and methods: A contextual approach, in WJ Doherty, PG Boss, R LaRossa, WR Schumm & SK Steinmetz (eds.) *Sourcebook of family theories and methods: A contextual approach*. New York: Plenum Press.

Duke, JT (1976) *Conflict and power in social life*. Provo, Utah: Brigham Young University Press.

Giddens, A (2000) *Runaway world: How globalisation is shaping our lives*. New York: Routledge.

Glenn, ND (1977) *Cohort analysis*. Beverly Hills: Sage Publications.

Goode, WJ (1963) *World revolution and family patterns*. New York: The Free Press.

Goode, WJ (1964) *The family*. Upper Saddle River, New Jersey: Prentice Hall.

Goode, WJ (1982) *Explorations in social theory*. New York: OUP.

Hareven, T (1982) *Family time and industrial time*. Cambridge: CUP.

Harvey, E (1992) *Social change and family policy in South Africa, 1930 to 1986*. Pretoria: Co-operative Research Programme on Marriage and Family Life, HSRC.

Hird, MJ & Abshoff, K (2000) Women without children: A contradiction in terms? *Journal of Comparative Family Studies* 31: 347–366.

Institute for Resource Development, Inc. (1987) *DHS Interviewer's manual*. Basic Documentation No. 6. Columbia, Maryland: Institute for Resource Development/ Macro Systems.

Jacobson, CK, Amoateng, AY & Heaton, TB (2003) *Interracial marriages in South Africa*. Unpublished manuscript.

Laslett, P (1983) Family and household as work group and kin group: Areas of traditional Europe compared, in R Wall, J Robin & P Laslett (eds.) *Family forms in historic Europe*. New York: Cambridge University Press.

Lekhele, SM & Ntsime, JM (1984) *Setswana marriage*. Unpublished manuscript. Mmabatho: Institute of African studies, University of North West.

Makiwane, BM (1994) *Fertility in South Africa*. Unpublished PhD dissertation, Department of Sociology, University of Witwatersrand.

Martin, W & Beittel, M (1984) The hidden abode of reproduction: Conceptualising households in Southern Africa, in JI Guyer & PE Peters (eds.) *Conceptualizing the household: Issues of theory, method and application*. Cambridge, Mass: Harvard University Press.

Mattessich, P & Hill, R (1987) Life cycle and family development, in M Sussman & S Steinmetz (eds.) *Handbook of marriage and the family*. New York: Plenum Press.

Mazrui, A (1986) *The Africans: A triple heritage*. London: BBC Publications.

Mbiti, J (1969) *African religions and philosophy*. Suffolk: The Chaucer Press.

Murray, C (1987) Class, gender and the household: the developmental cycle in Southern Africa, *Development and Change* 24: 755–785.

Native Economic Commission Report (1932) *The Native Economic Commission Report*. Union of South Africa Parliamentary Paper, U.G. No. 22, Pretoria.

Nobles, W (1979) The black family and its children: The survival of humaneness, *Black Books Bulletin* 6: 7–14.

Okoth-Ogendo, H (1989) The effect of migration on family structures in sub-Saharan Africa, *International Migration* 27: 309–317.

Parsons, T (1951) *The social system*. New York: MacMillan.

Pauw, BA (1963) *Second generation: A study of the family among urbanised Bantu in East London*. Cape Town: OUP.

Russell, M (1994) Do blacks live in nuclear family households? An appraisal of Steyn's work on urban family structure in South Africa, *South African Sociological Review* 6: 56–67.

Schapera, I (1967) *Western civilisation and the natives of South Africa*. London: Routledge and Kegan Paul.

Schumpeter, JA (1976) *Capitalism, socialism and democracy*. New York: Allen and Unwin.

Simkins, C & Dlamini, T (1992) The problem of children born out of wedlock, in S Burman & E Preston-Whyte (eds.) *Questionable issue: Illegitimacy in South Africa*. Cape Town: OUP.

Siqwana-Ndulo, N (1998) Rural African family structure in the Eastern Cape Province, South Africa, *Journal of Comparative Family Studies* 29: 407–417.

Steyn, A (1991) The changing family in South Africa, *South African Journal of Sociology* 22(1): 23–30.

Steyn, A (1993a) *Gesinslewe in die RSA*. Kooperatiewe Navorsingsprogram oor die Huweliks- en Gesinslewe, RGN Verslag HG/MF-4.

Steyn, A (1993b) Stedelike gesinstrukture in die Republiek van Suid-Afrika, *South African Journal of Sociology* 24.

Steyn, A, Strijdom, H, Viljoen, S & Bosman, F (eds.) (1987) *Marriage and family life in South Africa: Research priorities*. Pretoria: HSRC.

Thompson, L (1990) *A history of South Africa*. New Haven, Connecticut: Yale University Press.

Turner, L (2002) Book review. Anthony Giddens, Runaway world: How globalisation is reshaping our lives (2000). New York: Routledge, *Transcultural Psychiatry* 39: 394–415.

Walker, C (2002) *Ensuring women's land access: Moderator's comments*. Regional workshop on land issues in Africa and the Middle East. Kampala, Uganda: 29.04–02.05.

Ziehl, SC (1994) Social class variation in household structure: The case of a small South African city, *South African Journal of Sociology* 25: 25–34.

Ziehl, SC (2001) Documenting changing family patterns in South Africa: Are census data of any value? *African Sociological Review* 5(2): 36–62.

The state of curriculum reform in South Africa: The issue of Curriculum 2005

Linda Chisholm

Introduction

One of the most controversial issues in education in the recent past has been the process of development and implementation of Curriculum 2005 (C2005). Curriculum 2005 is significant both because of the enormity of the practical and symbolic legacy that it attempts to address as well as the weight that is attached to what it can achieve. Not only is it expected to overcome centuries-old educational practices, social inequalities linked to educational difference, and apartheid-based social values, it is also expected to place South Africa on the path to competitive participation in a global economy. For many, curriculum carries the burden of transformation and change in education.

The process of curriculum change has been a slow one. Curriculum 2005 has its roots and precedents in the struggles of social movements around education and curriculum in the pre-apartheid period, but it is also a 'mutation' of those struggles born in a context of social compromise (Motala & Vally 2002: 180; see also Cross, Mngadi & Rouhani 2002) Negotiations between the then-apartheid government and civil society in the National Education and Training Forum in 1993 was followed by a process of curriculum 'cleansing' immediately after the first Minister of Education of a democratic South Africa took office. When C2005 was introduced in 1997, it was premised on three critical elements: the introduction of eight new learning areas suffused with the values of democracy, non-racialism and non-sexism; outcomes-based education (OBE) and the provision of a foundation in general education up to and including the 9th Grade (Kraak 2002; see Hindle 1996 on 1994/95 curriculum revision processes; see also Seleti 1997).

This chapter is written from the perspective of one who has been simultaneously outsider and insider in the development of Curriculum 2005. Insider accounts by outsiders can be given in different ways: as a need to explain and rationalise participation in unpopular policies (Hartshorne 1992), as a revelation of internal struggles in order to set the record straight (Dolny 2001), as a battle over meaning and identity (Rensburg 2001), as a story about organisational change (Fleisch 2002) or as an analysis of the tensions that inevitably arise between scholars in state-led processes (Cherry, Daniel & Fullard 2002).

This paper will describe recent changes and explore some of the issues and tensions that arose in the course of the review and revision of the curriculum through a periodised and contextual account of the unfolding of the curriculum story between 1990 and 2001. In the process it will attempt to provide an understanding of the current state of the nation of curriculum for schools.

The apartheid legacy and outcomes-based education (1990–1997)

When Sibusiso Bhengu became Minister of Education in 1994, he inherited a complex and collapsed system of education. High levels of adult and matriculant illiteracy, dysfunctional schools and universities, discredited curricula and illegitimate structures of governance were the most immediate challenges. The school curriculum was seen as reinforcing racial injustice and inequality; its transformation a necessity for the promotion of 'unity and the common citizenship and destiny of all South Africans irrespective of race, class, gender or ethnic background' (ANC 1994: 68).

The transitional politics of 1990–1994 had given Bhengu new policies for the reconstruction of the finance, governance and curriculum of the system. Both the NP and ANC think-tanks had produced prescriptions for the reorganisation of education crafted in the light of both local social, economic and political needs as well as new global competitiveness imperatives. But what was needed, above all, was a new philosophy of education which would sweep away all remnants of apartheid policy and practice, be comprehensive and neutral enough to be acceptable to wide social layers, and provide the basis around which the system could be legitimately reconstructed. Such a philosophy was found in the National Qualifications Framework (NQF). It provided the basis for the vision of a core national curriculum which would integrate academic and vocational skills. Forged in the 1990–1994 period by business and Cosatu, and taken up by the ANC, it took legislative force through the *National Education Policy Act* (No. 27 of 1996).

The NQF provided the 'curriculum' for the reconstruction of the destroyed apartheid education system: a re-visioning of how the system could be changed such that it would become the virtual opposite of everything signi-fied by apartheid education. Curriculum 2005 came a year later. Integral to both the NQF and C2005 is an outcomes-based educational philosophy. In the official version, 'outcomes' derive from the Constitution, are both broad and narrow and thus serve a metaphorical purpose: they define the kind of citizen that the education system should produce and, in so doing, the kind of citizen a post-apartheid society would like to see created. As the ultimate goal of education, outcomes are seen as having to shape teaching and learning in the curriculum. Spelt out in the *South African Qualifications Act* (No. 58 of 1995) (SAQA), the critical and developmental outcomes occupy an iconic sta-tus in relation to curriculum and assessment.

Outcomes-based education as a philosophy has been differently interpreted by different writers in the context of the unfolding debate over outcomes-based education. There are few educationists in South Africa who have not taken a stance either for or against outcomes-based education. Writers such as Mohamed (1998), Malcolm (1999) and Odora-Hoppers (2002) have defended OBE, where others such as Kraak (2001) have been moderately critical, and yet others such as Jansen (1997; 1998; 1999, 2001a and b), Jansen and Christie (1999), Muller (1998; n.d., circa 2001), Muller and Taylor (1995) and Unterhalter (1998b) have questioned its foundations. The nature of the debate has also shifted over time. The debate has polarised people who, to all intents and purposes, all see themselves as, in one way or another, 'educational pro-gressives'. Thus, it has been possible for some to see OBE as a narrowing and de-radicalisation of educational goals, and for others to see it as expanding and revolutionising them; for some to see it as permitting the play of differ-ence, and allowing local, hidden knowledges to surface; for others to see it as yet another form of universal knowledge which stamps upon these; for some to see its learner-centred focus as allowing greater possibilities to the poor and others to see it as an educational romanticism which has the effect of denying the poor real learning opportunities (see above).

Its effect in international and comparative context has also been seen, in some cases, as integral to competency-driven, marketised forms of knowledge, and in others as promoting forms of knowing which contest these. For some, OBE has worked; in others, it has not. Its relationship to the NQF has been debated less often. Early on, however, the NQF was identified as constraining educa-tional goals to serve narrowly economic ends (Samson & Vally 1996;

Unterhalter 1998b; Muller 1998), rather than, as claimed, integrating education and training.

Outcomes-based education is thus the ultimate 'floating signifier', meaning different things to different people, who invest it with diametrically opposed qualities. As a construct of social possibility and/or limitation, it speaks to public and private desires and relationships to the emerging social order. But seeing it as this purely symbolic social construct also militates against an understanding of the material effects of the multiple social dynamics, processes and struggles of which it is a part and in which it is finely imbricated. It is towards an understanding of the asymmetrical relationship between the two, understanding that the symbolic can be material and the material deeply symbolic, that an examination of the unfolding of the curriculum story in post-apartheid South Africa pushes.

The critical and developmental outcomes provide the symbolic glue holding together the different versions and revisions of C2005 (see *SAQA* 1995; DoE 2002a). The critical outcomes envisage learners who will be able to:
- Identify and solve problems and make decisions using critical and creative thinking.
- Work effectively with others as members of a team, group, organisation and community.
- Organise and manage themselves and their activities responsibly and effectively.
- Collect, analyse, organise and critically evaluate information.
- Communicate effectively using visual, symbolic and/or language skills in various modes.
- Use science and technology effectively and critically showing responsibility towards the environment and the health of others.
- Demonstrate an understanding of the world as a set of related systems by recognising that problem-solving contexts do not exist in isolation.

The developmental outcomes envisage learners who are able to:
- Reflect on and explore a variety of strategies to learn more effectively.
- Participate as responsible citizens in the life of local, national, and global communities.
- Be culturally and aesthetically sensitive across a range of social contexts.
- Explore education and career opportunities.
- Develop entrepreneurial opportunities.

These critical and developmental outcomes formed the basis for the further development of specific outcomes for each phase and learning area in Curriculum 2005. These came to be known as the 66 specific outcomes. It was intended that teachers would use these outcomes to organise learning and resources in such a way that the emphasis would fall on the process of learning. Instead of teaching to the test, teachers would facilitate learning according to the pace and interests of each learner. Learners' participation in classroom processes rather than passive absorption and memorisation of pre-determined 'facts' formed a driving force for the new approach.

The structure and organisation of the curriculum became increasingly determined by the introduction of features which would allow integration across learning areas. The emphasis now fell less on subject content and values and more on the use of curriculum design tools such as 'phase organisers', 'programme organisers', 'range statements', 'performance indicators', 'expected levels of performance' and 'assessment criteria'. From early on, critics lambasted this dimension of the curriculum for being unnecessarily complex and jargonised (see later).

Context of curriculum change (1997–2000)

Curriculum 2005 came into being in 1997 in the immediate post-apartheid context of negotiated transition and belt-tightening economic policy.

In a wider context of national reconciliation based on a historic compromise achieved between old and new ruling elites, the curriculum represented a compromise between old and new forces. New values to which all could subscribe were articulated, the social content of the curriculum was underplayed, and its design and development decentralised. While there were new elements in the curriculum, there were also continuities with curriculum policy proposals made by the pre-1994 national Department of Education (DoE) in its 1992 *Curriculum Model for a New South Africa* (see also Kraak 2002).

Even as social expectations were high for radical change in a number of spheres, there were clear signs that South Africa was embarking on a form of self-imposed structural adjustment (Chisholm, Soudien, Vally & Gilmour 1999; Hart 2002). Fiscal discipline and constraint were the watchwords of the day as the new government adopted Gear. Strict monetarist policies took precedence over more expansionist and welfarist visions. In this context, equity became a function of the achievement of efficiency; effective schools were those which could balance their budgets and produce sound learning outcomes. The purposes of schooling at this time were framed in terms primarily of its economic functions and ability to meet larger economic needs. Human capital theory and school effectiveness approaches featured prominently in official thinking about education.[1] While the education budget was restructured to achieve greater racial equity, it was not expanded. The *South African Schools Act* (1996) effectively decentralised authority to struggling provincial administrations and highly unequally-endowed school governing bodies. The latter were given a range of powers including those of raising funds and setting fees.

When it was launched in 1997, C2005 gave hope once more. The principles on which C2005 was based represented a dramatic departure from those which underpinned apartheid education. They included commitments to human-resource development, learner-centredness, relevance, integration, differentiation, redress and learner support, nation-building and non-discrimination, creative and critical thinking, flexibility, progression, credibility and quality assurance (cited in Lubisi, Wedekind, Parker & Gultig 1997). Around these a degree of synergy and common purpose began to be built. In addition, the results-oriented focus drew attention away from learning content and to learning process. This meshed well with new understandings of learning in the 'knowledge society.'

But what rapidly began to create difficulties were the assumptions about teachers and classrooms as well as the conception of curriculum design that informed the new model. At the same time as critics such as Jansen found their critical views on 'why OBE will fail' taken up with remarkable speed across the country, evidence was beginning to emerge that not only schools and teachers, but also informed commentators such as those in Education Policy Units, were struggling with the terminology involved in mastering the new curriculum (Greenstein 1998; Jansen 1999). A complex new terminology – the design tools for a curriculum which essentially left the content of curriculum building to teachers – began to characterise and stand for the curriculum. Teachers also experienced difficulties in operationalising new modes of assessment. Debates raged across the country, with the South African Democratic Teachers' Union (Sadtu) nailing its colours firmly to the mast of OBE as it found expression in the NQF and Curriculum 2005 and major education reporters, such as Philippa Garson of the left-leaning *Mail and Guardian*, revealing in remarkable prose, on a week-by-week basis, just exactly what was wrong with Curriculum 2005.

In 1999, three things happened which were to have a decisive effect on the curriculum: the first was the accession of Professor Kader Asmal as Minister of Education, the second was the connection made between South Africa's poor learner achievements and school curricula and the third was increasing departmentally-based evidence that implementation was not going as planned.

A shrewd politician with a sharp mind and forceful, no-nonsense approach, Asmal immediately embarked on a 'listening campaign'. Out of this and internal departmental processes, flowed the 'Call to Action' and Tirisano framework of principles and strategies for achieving the educational goals of the Department. In his 'Call to Action' on 27 July 1999, Asmal gave OBE a specific content. He said that he:

> recognises the damage done over the decades by an approach to education that was essentially authoritarian and allowed little or no room for the development of critical capacity or the power of independent thought and inquiry. OBE is an approach that embraces the capacity of learners to think for themselves, to learn from the environment, and to respond to wise guidance by teachers who value creativity and self-motivated learning. (Asmal 1999)

But he also distanced himself from the version of OBE that had become practice. The Department, he said:

> resists over-zealous attempts from any quarter to convert OBE into a new orthodoxy with scriptural authority. There will be no mystification of an approach to learning and teaching that is essentially liberatory and creative.

Asmal was also keenly interested in the fate of history teaching and values underlying the new educational system and would soon initiate a working group on values in education under Wilmot James, who subsequently brokered a number of interventions around values in education (DoE 2000a).

At the same time as this shift was occurring in official thinking, research findings were mounting that South Africa's learner achievement remained exceptionally poor despite curriculum changes. Research conducted in schools for the President's Education Initiative (PEI), under the auspices of the DoE, were widely publicised. The PEI Report (Taylor & Vinjevold 1999) linked performance and curriculum, arguing that curriculum and the teaching and learning process were crucial to performance. In this context, it was highly critical of C2005 and all its associated dimensions, particularly the proscription against the use of textbooks and the nature of outcomes-based assessment methods. These were described as unworkable. The message of the PEI Report was that C2005 was not improving the capacity for learner achievement, but further damaging it.

A number of studies conducted at the same time and after have come to similar conclusions. For example, the Third International Mathematics and Science Repeat Study (TIMMS-R), which was conducted in 1998 in countries which included Australia, Bulgaria, Cyprus, Finland, Indonesia, Thailand, Jordan, Lithuania, Tunisia, England, Hungary, Singapore and Turkey, placed South Africa well below the international and continental mean for mathematics and science. The study was based on 225 schools selected from all nine provinces. South Africa achieved an 85 per cent response rate and the national sample was considered representative for the country as a whole. Only the most proficient mathematics learners in South Africa attained the level of the average learners from Singapore. Science results were not significantly better. The TIMMS-R report noted a number of contributing factors. As far as curriculum was concerned, it drew attention to the fact that while the interim C2005 curricula for maths and science in South Africa:

> revealed several similarities with curricula internationally ... one
> of the exceptions was the lack of major emphasis in science on
> knowing basic science facts and understanding science concepts.
> While most countries placed a major emphasis on this in the cur-
> ricula documents, South Africa did not. (Howie 2001: 39)

The more recent DoE's *Education for All (Assessment)* (2000b) was based on data from the 1999 South Africa Monitoring Learning Achievement (MLA) Survey, the 1997 Education Management Information System (EMIS) dataset, the 1996 South African Population Census and the 1996 Schools Register of Needs dataset. It confirmed the overall picture presented by the TIMMS-R study. It found that the average score of Grade 4 learners was below 50 per cent in the literacy, numeracy and lifeskills tasks for which they were tested. Literacy and numeracy thus remain poorly developed within primary schools.

At a theoretical level, Taylor elaborated a critique in the PEI Report that he and Muller were developing of the constructivist approach to knowledge that underlay the construction of Curriculum 2005. According to the PEI Report, a constructivist approach wrongly valorises 'everyday knowledge' as against 'school knowledge' in the school context, sees the teacher as a facilitator of learning rather than someone with specialised knowledge and the textbook as a hindrance to rather than a support for learning (Taylor & Vinjevold 1999: 105–131).

Drawing on a range of critiques of progressivist theory and practice of education, often from left-wing sources, Muller and Taylor linked poor educational results to approaches advocated through C2005, which emphasise process and everyday knowledge at the expense of conceptual and content knowledge (see Muller n.d., circa 2001). A progressive approach, Muller argues, is one which, like Gramsci's, the Italian communist of the 1930s, sees the job of the school as being to 'accustom (the students) to reason, to think abstractly and schematically' by weaning them from folklore and teaching them facts. The problem with progressive education reform, for Gramsci (cited by Muller), is that it tackles the wrong object, 'the form of the curriculum instead of its content' (n.d., circa 2001: 66–7) This was a direct attack on existing curriculum policy. But it was not enough to provoke a review.

Research conducted both within the DoE and by academics in different parts of the country was also showing that policy, the curriculum framework, and aspects of implementation were facing severe difficulties (see Fleisch 2002; Jansen 1999; Khumalo, Papo, Mabitla & Jansen 1999; Marnewieck & Spreen 1999; Proudfoot Consulting 1999; Vinjevold & Roberts 1999).

After considerable deliberation with the DoE, the Minister appointed a committee to review C2005 in February 2000. It consisted of people who had both been involved in the development of C2005 and were pro-OBE, individuals closely associated with the PEI Report, and others who were critical in their individual capacities but not associated with either the pro- or against-lobbies. I belonged to the latter category.

C2005 Review Committee (2000)

The appointment of the Review Committee was extremely controversial. It provoked the ire of those, such as Sadtu, which supported the basic thrust of

C2005 but were not represented on the Review Committee. There were also intense debates within the ANC and unease in the Department of Education. The new NQF, the basis of the curriculum, had just begun to be implemented and a critical report was interpreted as going against the tenor of transformation. The report presented to the Minister in May 2000 was an independent report. It broke upon the South African public in media reports, which erroneously claimed that OBE had been thrown out. The fall-out amongst sections of the ANC, Sadtu and middle-level departmental bureaucrats was significant.

To this day, the DoE has not yet published the report. The version which has found its way into libraries and bookshelves was produced by the Review Committee. Nonetheless, it made a significant impact. In part, the Review Committee report made the impact it did because there was a pre-existing movement towards the reform of the curriculum; the report ratified this movement (see Lagemann 2000). Its recommendations for revision were effected between 2000 and 2002/3 in the *Revised National Curriculum Statements* for the General Education and Training (GET) and Further Education and Training (FET) bands.

The recommendations of the Review Committee were simple. The Minister of Education had tasked the Review Committee on C2005 to investigate the structure and design of the curriculum, the level of understanding of the curriculum, how implementation could be strengthened, and what needed to be done about implementation envisaged for 2001. The area of focus was what was known as the General Education and Training band, Grades R–9. The report was prepared within three months of intensive work on the basis of a review of existing research reports and papers, interviews with teachers, principals, managers, trainers, publishers and departmental officials, as well as public submissions made by a range of individuals, organisations and institutions.

Instead of reasserting the dominant human capital theory and school effectiveness approaches within which education was being cast, the report consciously promoted and reaffirmed the less dominant social goals of social justice, equity and development. It emphasised that 'the values of a society striving towards social justice, equity and development through the development of creative, critical and problem-solving individuals lie at the heart of this curriculum.' It stressed the anti-discriminatory and human rights-based orientation of the curriculum (Chisholm, Ndhlovu, Potenza, Mohamed, Muller, Lubisi, Vinjevold, Ngozi, Malan & Mphahlele 2000: vi–viii).

The report showed that while there was overwhelming support for the principles of OBE and C2005, which had generated a new focus on teaching and learning, implementation had been confounded by a number of issues. These included a skewed curriculum structure and design, lack of alignment between curriculum and assessment policy, inadequate orientation, training and development of teachers, learning support materials that were variable in quality, often unavailable and not sufficiently used in classrooms, policy overload and limited transfer of learning into classrooms, shortages of personnel and resources to implement and support C2005, and inadequate recognition of curriculum as the core business of education departments.

In order to address these issues the Review Committee proposed the introduction of a revised curriculum structure supported by changes in teacher orientation and training, learning-support materials and the organisation, resourcing and staffing of curriculum structures and functions in national and provincial education departments.

In order to address overcrowding of the curriculum in GET, it proposed that learning areas in this band be reduced from eight to six and that more time be allocated to languages and mathematics. The two learning areas that were so affected were technology and economic and management sciences whose substance could be absorbed into other learning areas. These rationalised learning areas should include languages, mathematics, science and technology, social sciences (history and geography), arts and culture and life orientation.

In order to address problems related to the complexity of the curriculum design and terminology, the Review Committee proposed that a revised, streamlined National Curriculum Statement be produced for Early Childhood Development, GET, FET and Adult Basic Education and Training (ABET).

In the immediate aftermath of the release of the Report, a lobby with a commercial interest in the technology learning area mobilised against the recommendations that this learning area should be integrated into the natural sciences. The report was taken to both the Council of Education Ministers and Cabinet in June and July 2000. All the recommendations were accepted by both bodies, except for those recommending the integration of the technology and economic management sciences into other learning areas. Perhaps for largely symbolic reasons, and the view that held sway that schools have a direct role to play in preparing learners for the labour market, Cabinet did not accept the view that these should be integrated into other aspects of the curriculum but decided that they should remain as separate learning areas.

The report further recommended that the proposed National Curriculum Statement should retain some design features and drop the majority: it should keep the 12 critical outcomes but drop the 66 specific outcomes, assessment criteria, phase and programme organisers, range statements, performance indicators, and expected levels of performance (Chishom et al. 2000: vii).

In addition, the report argued for more time for languages and mathematics, that history and geography should form the core of a social sciences learning area, and that arts and culture should have a place in the curriculum.

If the design of the curriculum needed overhaul, then so did implementation processes. These, in the view of the Review Committee, required not only a 'revised and streamlined outcomes-based curriculum framework which promotes integration and conceptual coherence within a human rights approach which pays special attention to anti-discriminatory, anti-racist, anti-sexist and special needs issues' (2000: 21), but also a national teacher education strategy which locates teacher preparation and development for the new curriculum in higher education and identifies, selects and trains a special cadre of regional and district curriculum trainers working with NGOs and higher education for short-term orientation; the production of learner support materials – especially textbooks – which should become the responsibility of publishers and dedicated units or institutes as proposed in the *White Paper on Education and Training* (1995); ring-fenced budgeting for the curriculum; reorganisation and reinforcement of curriculum functions both in the DoE and in the provinces; relaxation of the pace of implementation; a managed process of phasing out the current C2005 and phasing in of the revised curriculum and the establishment of a task team to manage the phase out and phase in process.

The naïvete of the Review Committee lay perhaps not so much in its critique as in its estimation of departmental capacity to address each and every one of these issues. These recommendations, as with all other commission and/or committee recommendations, do not fall onto a blank slate, but into a context where processes are underway, budgets committed and capacities are limited.

High-level decisions can be taken immediately, but follow-up and monitoring are crucial. When agendas are already full and responses to the recommendations are anyway ambivalent and divided, systematic follow-up is unlikely to be the case. In this respect, the role of a committee or commission is in part to play a symbolic and political role (Jansen 2001a).

Post-Review Committee: The Revised National Curriculum Statement and the NQF Review (2000–2002)

Between October 2000 and 2002, ministerial Project Committees were established to revise the curriculum for first Grades R–9 and then, when this was completed in April 2002, for Grades 10–12. A study team was also established to make recommendations on the implementation of the National Qualifications Framework. Its report appeared in April 2002.

These major curriculum revision exercises occurred against the backdrop of a dramatically changing regional and national economic, political and social landscape. While South Africa took steps to enhance its political and economic influence on the continent of Africa as well as regionally, the strategic significance of the region and regional balance of forces also shifted. A growing political role on the continent was matched by new economic developments. The Rand weakened, exports boomed, bringing in always much-needed foreign exchange, and balance-of-payments crises were temporarily averted.

New social policies came into being, but overall macroeconomic success was not reflected in changing conditions of poverty. Job losses continued relentlessly in key industries such as mining and farming. Cultivation declined in rural areas and micro-industries struggled to survive. New jobs in financial and services sectors declined. Conditions for the urban and rural poor worsened. The ability of men to secure a livelihood, linked to a sense of manhood, eroded marriage prospects and with marriage, a sense of citizenship. Stresses on families increased as women shouldered more authority and the HIV/AIDS pandemic bit even deeper (Cross 1999). In November 2002, Statistics South Africa (Stats SA) estimated that while there had been an increase in jobs from 1995 to 2000, there had also been an increase in unemployment. The average annual income of South African households had effectively declined in this period. The consequence of job loss, unemployment, declining livelihood and increased poverty was increased domestic violence, rape, child abuse and generalised crime.

These developments all had an impact on the general context of schooling which shape the experience of what goes on inside schools. Statistics South Africa reported in November 2002 that, while 94 per cent of all children between the ages of seven and 15 attend school, children seem to be struggling to complete school and actual educational attainment is low. This picture reinforces the work of van der Bergh who has shown that while fiscal transfers may have become more equitable since 1994, this has not translated into improved learning achievement. He suggests that the problem may well be the management of resources rather than the absence of resources (van der Bergh 2001; van der Bergh, Wood & Le Roux 2002).

Resources in the school context related to curriculum include books and stationery, libraries and laboratories, as well as actual curriculum guides. Despite dramatic increases in spending on learning support materials from 1998 to 2001, their availability, quality and use in schools remain variable (DoE 2002b). The recommendations made by a departmental *Review of the Financing, Resourcing and Costs of Education in Schools*, released for comment in 2003 (DoE 2003), to lower the price of textbooks are promising, but will take some time to be realised in practice.

A simplified C2005, the *Draft Revised National Curriculum Statement for Grades R–9 (Schools)*, was developed by a combination of departmental officials and non-departmental participants in the shape of teacher educators, NGOs, representatives of teacher unions, and others. Apart from the working groups for each learning area, special attention was paid to implementation, human rights and inclusivity in the curriculum, as well as how the environment and indigenous knowledge could be addressed across the curriculum. Building on the principles contained in the critical and developmental outcomes, the *Draft Revised National Curriculum Statement* stressed a rights-based approach to citizenship and nation-building alongside clarity and accessibility of the curriculum (see DoE 2002a).

During this phase of production of the curriculum, major issues and debates centred on language, the way in which economic and management sciences should be approached, and the role of 'content'. The *Revised National Curriculum Statement* was ultimately made available in all 11 official languages. The key debate, however, was not so much respecting these constitutional obligations to recognition of all languages, as over the more symbolic dimensions of language. What to some was the renaming necessary to signify new approaches and habits of thinking consonant with democracy, appeared to others as jargon. How to outline an economic and management sciences curriculum that problematised approaches to economic and social development was the key challenge here. The debate about content cut across all learning areas but emerged most strongly around history. Here there were three approaches: there should be no content, there should be some content, whatever content there is should create the basis for challenging racism and sexism in new and creative ways through being embedded in skills and values.

In time, those voices opposed to history in primary school became less vociferous. This was partly due to the Minister's determination to see history in the curriculum, partly due to the emerging actual approach to and content of the new history curriculum, and partly to the weight given to the issue by the mobilised history community through the publication of the *History and Archaeology Report* (DoE 2000c) and the subsequent establishment of the South African History Project.

The *Draft Revised National Curriculum Statement* was released for public comment at the end of June 2001. Substantial comment was received from universities, NGOs, teachers and their unions, and provincial education departments. But there was also a public campaign from a fundamentalist Christian constituency that considered the Africanist and humanist content of the history curriculum to be anathema to their beliefs and values. This constituency combined a loose alliance of a home schooling movement led by a former University of Pretoria educationist, an evangelical Christian movement, the African Christian Democratic Party and NNP (see Chisholm 2002 and Chidester 2002 for further analysis, and Apple 2001 for an account in the United States context of similar groupings). It in effect sought a return to Christian National Education with the Bible as the basis of all teaching and learning.

The campaign of the Christian right focused not only on history but also the teaching of evolution, sexual responsibility, values and the approach to education about religion. In accordance with the Department's *Manifesto on Values, Education and Democracy* (Gevisser & Morris 2002) and policy on religion education produced in the course of the revision of the curriculum, the curriculum sought to teach children about the diversity of South Africa's religions and, in so doing, promote greater knowledge and understanding of this diversity. As Chidester remarks, the primary educational objective of religion education in the Revised National Curriculum is framed within a constitutional and human rights framework (2002: 94). As such, it provoked a substantial controversy amongst those who were not comfortable with this framework. In response, the Minister and Department of Education called a public hearing on the issue on 13 November. Hereafter, public comments were synthesised and the 'Draft Revised National Curriculum Statement' was revised. In April 2002 it became policy.

In this context it is useful to highlight the role of the teacher unions. Whereas all three major teacher unions distanced themselves from this right-wing campaign and associated themselves with the values and broad goals that the curriculum sought to achieve, they were active participants on different sides in key debates. Whereas the Suid Afrikaanse Onderwysers Unie and National Association of Professional Teachers Organisations of South Africa were on the whole concerned about creating a workable curriculum for the classroom, Sadtu was mainly concerned about teachers' roles in curriculum development and implementation.

In April 2002, two significant developments reinforced the revision of the curriculum: the revision of the FET curriculum (Grades 8–10) began on the same basis as that for GET (Grades R–9) and the *Report of the Study Team on the Implementation of the National Qualifications Framework* was published jointly by the DoE and Department of Labour. Within six months of starting, the draft curriculum for FET (schools) was available for public comment. There were a number of differences between this revision process and that for Grades R–9, not least the fact that the Review Committee report was essentially a review of the curriculum and its implementation in Grades R–9 and not Grades 8–10. During the months that this curriculum was revised, reports were published that the closure of teacher education colleges and incorporation into universities had led to major reductions in the number of especially black student teachers, even as young qualifying teachers were being recruited to teach abroad in increasing numbers (*Sowetan* 08.11.2002; *Citizen* 07.11.2002).

When the draft curriculum for FET published its recommendations for a reduction in the range of subjects and introduction of new subjects such as mathematical literacy, teacher unions reacted, foreseeing job losses if massive retraining was not undertaken (*Citizen* 03.11.2002; *Star* 03.11.2002). The *Mail and Guardian* (09.11.02) launched a swinging attack on the Department for not making timeous preparations or planning adequately in light of the envisaged implementation date of 2004. A subsequent meeting of the Council of Education Ministers in late February 2003 fixed the date of implementation of the curriculum in Grades 10–12 as 2006.

The overall direction of policy was now clear. The *Revised National Curriculum Statement for Grades R–9* would be implemented in 2004 in the foundation phase, and for Grades 10–12 in 2006. Changed teacher education policy had ensured that universities would be responsible for teacher education. Short-term training on the cascade model, such as that undertaken for C2005, was not the answer to the long-term professional and educational needs of teachers. A wide-ranging solution however needed to be found for multiple questions related to teacher orientation to the new curriculum, as well as teacher recruitment and retention.

The curriculum revision process was perceived by many to be a direct challenge to the way in which policy in education had unfolded since 1995. First, it departed from a unit-standards-based process to determining curriculum and then it also had the apparent effect, through its concentration on a curriculum for schools alone, of undermining the NQF, which sought the integration of education and training through a unit-standards and competency-based framework.

Discussions for a review of the NQF were initiated in early 2001, when the curriculum revision process was underway. The sensitivity of this NQF review is evident in the way it was kept out of the public eye, as well as in a reading of the background to the report and the report itself (DoE/DoL 2002). Chaired by Professor Jayram Reddy, the review was initiated in the light of 'mounting concern about the early bureaucratisation of the NQF' and 'a broad malaise of discontent with SAQA and the NQF' that had taken hold 'some time last year' (2002: 143). The Minister of Education and the DoE cited the fact that specific constituencies had raised concerns, amongst them, the higher education sector, employers concerned at the standards-setting process, unions, community bodies and 'a more general concern about the complexity of the systems…' (2002: 144).

Like the review committee on C2005, the study team on the NQF reaffirmed basic policy, but called for surgery of the bureaucratic language and excesses. In this regard, the review committee report was probably more radical. But the NQF review did recommend the dis-establishment of national standards bodies set up with policy-making authority, and it recognised the role of the DoE in setting standards for schooling, technical colleges and ABET non-vocational standards and qualifications. The role of the Department of Labour was recognised as the standards-setting body for generic vocational standards. Amidst a host of other recommendations, a new funding model was also proposed for a streamlined SAQA. The implications of this review are still to be seen as the two departments grapple with one another over its inter-pretation.

Conclusion

A final assessment of the state of the nation in this area cannot be a simple one. At both the practical and symbolic level, there have been achievements, but challenges remain. The goals and values of education, as manifested in C2005 and the *Revised National Curriculum Statement*, have changed dramat-ically within the space of less than ten years. As a consolidated, simplified and strengthened version of C2005, the *Revised National Curriculum Statement*, for better or worse, represents democratic South Africa's first national cur-riculum for schools. It is a product of history and the myriad struggles at multiple levels that have shaped South African education and curriculum. Its implementation will likewise not be a smooth translation into practice; the search for such a translation is a futile exercise. But it is likely that schoolbooks will be printed and teacher education revamped in terms of images of its intentions. Interpretations of the curriculum, its representation, will also con-tinue to be struggled over.

At the practical and material level, spending on education has improved, infrastructural provision has expanded, pupil:teacher ratios have narrowed and enrolments and participation of children in schooling have increased. Numerous programmes have been initiated across all areas that could make a difference to educational achievement. And yet much still remains to be done: resources remain unequally spread, the quality of education remains compro-mised by intractable legacies of the past and learning achievements remain poor, especially amongst the poor in those provinces that have incorporated the former bantustans. These are the harsh realities of contemporary South African education.

Note

1   Human capital theory rests on the assumption that education and skills lead to increased productivity, which in turn results in higher wages. School-effectiveness approaches in turn are based on the assumption that schooling outputs can be improved through correct calibration of the inputs.

References

ANC Education Department (1994) *A Policy Framework for Education and Training.* Braamfontein: ANC.

Apple, M (1990) *Ideology and curriculum,* 2nd edition. New York: Routledge.

Apple, M (2000) *Official knowledge: Democratic education in a conservative age,* 2nd edition. New York: Routledge.

Apple, M (2001) *Educating the 'right' way: Markets, standards, God and inequality.* London: Routledge.

Asmal, K (1999) *Call to action: Mobilising citizens to build a South African education and training system for the 21st century,* 27.07.99. Available at http://education.pwv.gov.za/Media/Speeches1999/July.

Cherry, J, Daniel, J & Fullard, M (2002) Researching the 'truth': A view from inside the Truth and Reconciliation Commission, in D Posel & G Simpson (eds.) *Commissioning the past: Understanding South Africa's Truth and Reconciliation Commission.* Johannesburg: Witwatersrand University Press.

Chidester, D (2002) Christianity and evolution, in W James & L Wilson (eds.) *The architect and the scaffold: Evolution and education in South Africa.* Cape Town: HSRC/NAE.

Chisholm, L (2002) Religion, science and evolution in South Africa: The politics and con-struction of the Revised National Curriculum Statement for Schools (Grades R–9), in W James & L Wilson (eds.) *The architect and the scaffold: Evolution and education in South Africa.* Cape Town: HSRC/NAE.

Chisholm, L, Soudien, C, Vally, S & Gilmour D (1999) Teachers and structural adjustment in South Africa, *Educational Policy* 13 (4): 386–401.

Chisholm, L, Volmink, J, Ndhlovu, T, Potenza, E, Mohamed, H, Muller, J, Lubisi, C, Vinjevold, P, Ngozi, L, Malan, B & Mphahlele, M (2000) *A South African curriculum for the twenty first century: Report of the Review Committee on Curriculum 2005.* Presented to the Minister of Education, Professor Kader Asmal, Pretoria, 31 May.

Cross, C (1999) Women and land in the rural crisis, *Agenda: A Quarterly Journal of Gender Studies,* Special Issue on Land and Housing 42: 12–28.

Cross, M, Mngadi, R & Rouhani, S (2002) From policy to practice: Curriculum reform in South African Education, *Comparative Education* 38 (20): 171–187.

DoE (Department of Education) (2000a) *Report of the Working Group on Values in Education: Values, Education and Democracy.* Pretoria.

DoE (2000b) *Education for All (Assessment)*. Pretoria.

DoE (2000c) *History and Archaeology Report*. Pretoria.

DoE (2002a) *Revised National Curriculum Statement Grades R–9 (Schools)*. Pretoria.

DoE (2002b) *Draft Education for All Status Report 2002 South Africa Incorporating Country Plan for 2002 to 2015*. Pretoria

DoE (2002) *Report of the Study Team on the Implementation of the National Qualifications Framework*. Pretoria

DoE (2003) *Review of the financing, resourcing and costs of education in schools*. Pretoria.

Dolny, H (2001) *Banking on change*. London: Penguin.

Fleisch, B (2002) *Managing educational change: The state and school reform in South Africa*. Cape Town: Heinemann

Gevisser, M & Morris, M (2002) Manifesto on values, democracy and education, in K Asmal & W James (eds.) *Spirit of the nation: Reflections on South Africa's educational ethos*. Cape Town: NAE/HSRC/DoE.

Greenstein, R (1997) New policies and the challenges of budgetary constraints, *EPU Quarterly Review of Education and Training in South Africa* 4(4): 1–17.

Hart, G (2002) *Disabling globalization: Places of power in post-apartheid South Africa*. Pietermaritzburg: University of Natal Press.

Hartshorne, K (1992) *Crisis and challenge: Black education in South Africa 1910–1990*. Cape Town: OUP.

Hindle, D (1996) A review of curriculum development structures and processes in South Africa, 1994–1995. *EPU Working Paper* No. 6, Education Policy Unit, University of Natal, Durban.

Howie, S (2001) *Third International Mathematics and Science Study Repeat (TIMMS-R) Executive Summary*. Pretoria: HSRC.

Jansen, J (1997) 'Essential alterations?' A critical analysis of the states syllabus revision process, *Perspectives in Education* 17 (2): 1–11.

Jansen, J (1998) Curriculum reform in South Africa: A critical assessment of outcomes-based education, *Cambridge Journal of Education* 28 (3): 321–331.

Jansen, J (1999) 'A very noise OBE': The implementation of OBE in Grade 1 classrooms, in J Jansen & P Christie (eds.) *Changing the curriculum: Studies on outcomes-based education in South Africa*. Cape Town: Juta.

Jansen, J (2001a) Rethinking education policy: Symbols of change, signals of conflict, in A Kraak & M Young (eds.) *Education policy implementation in South Africa*. Pretoria: HSRC.

Jansen, J (2001b) The race for education policy after apartheid, in Y Sayed & J Jansen (eds.) *Implementing education policies: The South African experience*. Cape Town: UCT Press.

Jansen, JD & Christie, P (eds.) (1999) *Changing curriculum: Studies on outcomes-based education in South Africa*. Cape Town: Juta.

Khumalo, LP, Papo, WD, Mabitla, AM & Jansen, JD (1999) *A baseline survey of OBE in Grade 1 classrooms in the Northern Province.* Centre for Education Research Evaluation and Policy, University of Durban-Westville.

Kraak, A (2001) Policy ambiguity and slippage: Higher education under the new state, 1994–2001' in, A Kraak & M Young (eds.) *Education policy implementation in South Africa.* Pretoria: HSRC.

Kraak, A (2002) Discursive shifts and structural continuities in South African vocational education and training: 1981–1999, in P Kallaway (ed.) *The history of education under apartheid, 1948–1994: The doors of learning and culture shall be opened.* Cape Town: Maskew Miller Longman.

Lagemann, EC (2000) *An elusive science: The troubling history of education research.* Chicago: University of Chicago Press; *Report of the President: Lessons learned,* Spencer Foundation Annual Report 2002.

Lubisi, C, Wedekind, V, Parker, B & Gultig, J (eds.) (1997) *Understanding outcomes-based education: Knowledge, curriculum and assessment in South Africa.* South African Institute of Distance Education (SAIDE) & DoE.

Malcolm, C (1999) Outcomes-based education has different forms, in J Jansen & P Christie (eds.) *Changing curriculum: Studies on outcomes-based education in South Africa.* Cape Town: Juta.

Marneweck, L & Spreen, CA (1999) *Dancing with the monster: Mastering the steps of OBE in the Northern Province.* Mimeo.

Mohamed, H (1998) The implementation of OBET in South Africa: Pathway to success or recipe for failure, *Education Practice* 1: 3–16.

Motala, S & Vally, S (2002) People's education: From people's power to Tirisano, in P Kallaway (ed.) *The history of education under apartheid: The doors of learning and culture shall be opened.* Cape Town: Maskew Miller Longman.

Muller, J (1998) NQF and outcomes-based education: Pedagogic models and hard choices, in Centre for Education Policy Development (eds.) *Reconstruction, development and the National Qualifications Framework: Conference proceedings.* Johannesburg: CEPD.

Muller, J (n.d., circa 2001) Progressivism redux: Ethos, policy, pathos, in A Kraak & M Young (eds.) *Education in retrospect: Policy and implementation since 1990.* HSRC & Institute of Education, University of London.

Muller, J & Taylor, N (1995) Schooling and everyday life: Knowledges sacred and profane, *Social Epistemology* 9: 257–275.

Odora-Hoppers, C (2002) *Higher education, sustainable development and the imperative of social responsiveness.* Mimeo, University of Pretoria.

Proudfoot Consulting (1999) *Interim Report on the Provision of Learner Support Materials: Business Reviews.* Prepared for the Department of Education.

Rensburg, I (2001) Reflections from the inside: Key policy assumptions and how they have shaped policy making and implementation in South Africa, 1994–2000, in A Kraak & M Young (eds.) *Education in retrospect: Policy and implementation since 1990*. HSRC & Institute of Education, University of London.

Samson, M & Vally, S (1996) Snakes and ladders: Promises and potential pitfalls of the NQF, *South African Labour Bulletin* 20(4): 7–14.

Seleti, Y (1997) *From history and human and social sciences: The new curriculum framework and the end of history for the General Education and Training level*. EPU Working Paper No. 14, Education Policy Unit, University of Natal, Durban.

Taylor, N (1999) Curriculum 2005: Finding a balance between school and everyday knowledges, in N Taylor & P Vinjevold (eds.) *Getting learning right: Report of the President's Education Initiative*. Johannesburg: Joint Education Trust.

Taylor, N & Vinjevold, P (1999) *Getting learning right: Report of the President's Education Initiative*. Johannesburg: Joint Education Trust.

Unterhalter, E (1998a) Citizenship, difference and education: Reflections on the South African transition, in P Werbner & N Yuval-Davis (eds.) *Women, citizenship and difference*. London: Zed.

Unterhalter, E (1998b) Economic rationality or social justice? Gender, the National Qualifications Framework and educational reform, in South Africa 1989–1996, *Cambridge Journal of Education* 28(3).

Van der Berg, S (2001) Resource shifts in South African schools after the political transition, *Development Southern Africa* 18(4): 405–421.

Van der Bergh, S, Wood, L & Le Roux, N (2002) Differentiation in black education, *Development Southern Africa* 19(2): 289–306.

Vinjevold, P & Roberts, J (1999) *External evaluation report: Provision of learning materials Grade 7 pilot project*. Johannesburg: Joint Education Trust.

The state of higher education in South Africa: From massification to mergers

Jonathan Jansen

Introduction

The policy ambitions of the South African government for higher education can be distinguished by two landmarks: the optimism of massification in the mid-1990s, and the reality of mergers almost ten years later. Whereas massification signalled a possible expansion of higher education opportunities, mergers mean a contraction of higher education institutions. While massification assumed greater student demand on the 36 public institutions of higher education, mergers represent (in part) a response to the unexpected and rapid decline in qualifying students from the school sector. And while massification left institutional identities relatively unscathed, mergers were deployed as a direct intervention to recast institutional landscapes. To understand the state of higher education in 2003, it is important to trace briefly the origins of massification and then to discuss in more detail the evolution of merger thinking in South Africa.

Higher education during the 1990s: the problems and the promises

The post-apartheid government inherited a deeply divided higher education system. A developing nation of slightly more than 40 million people had a stunning array of post-school institutions: 21 universities, 15 technikons, 150 technical colleges, 120 colleges of education – alongside a large number of police, nursing and agricultural colleges, among others. The 36 public institutions of higher education divided into 21 universities and 15 technikons. This set of 36 institutions could – at least in terms of origins – be divided into 11 white universities and ten black universities, and eight white technikons and seven black technikons. Another division would yield seven white Afrikaans universities and four white English universities.[1] And while there has been a slow but inevitable deracialisation of former white institutions, principally in the distribution of students, higher education remains visibly marked by racially skewed staffing patterns, resource disparities, differential research productivity, gross differences in student pass and progression rates, and resilient symbols of dominance and traditions of exclusion (see DoE 2001a; Government of South Africa 2002; Mabokela 2000; Mabokela & King 2001; Cloete et al. 2002).

How would this legacy be confronted? A 'programme of transformation' was announced through *Education White Paper 3* that would develop specific strategies for equity and redress, democratisation, development (including the building of human capacity), quality, effectiveness and efficiency, academic freedom, institutional autonomy and public accountability (DoE 1997). From an institutional point of view, the interpretation of these principles and commitments was generous:

> Much was expected to change in the academic profession in South Africa following the election of a black government in 1994. Staff equity profiles suggested that the number of black and women academics would increase significantly. Everyone expected that black institutions would receive redress funding to compensate [them] for decades of underdevelopment. Academics anticipated that salary levels and working conditions would improve. Others expected improvements in research output. (Koen 2002: 405)

Such expectations were not without foundation since policy promised 'earmarked funds for institutional redress ... that would redress inequities and deficiencies experienced in particular by historically disadvantaged institutions' (DoE 1997: 28).

Yet very little changed in terms of these indicators of higher education transformation in South Africa, despite the heady optimism of the *White Paper on Higher Education* and its institutional interpreters; and there was no large-scale bail-out funding for historically disadvantaged institutions. It is important to realise, though, that the optimism of the early to mid-1990s was based on the expectation of dramatic growth in student demand for higher education i.e., massification. It is important to understand also the collapse of this national development ambition and its displacement over time with an all-pervasive discourse of mergers.

Great expectations I: massification

In a remarkably short period of operation (1995–96), the National Commission on Higher Education (NCHE) produced a report that laid the groundwork for higher education policy in South Africa. According to one of its key authors:

> The central proposal of the NCHE was that South African higher education should be massified. Massification was the first proposal that attempted to resolve the equity-development tension since increased participation was supposed to provide greater opportunity for access (equity) while also producing more high-level skills that were necessary for economic growth. (Cloete et al. 2002: 97)

Definitionally, massification assumed an absolute growth in student enrolments as well as a more egalitarian distribution of students in higher education – one that reflected the race and gender profile of the nation. This would mean, in essence, a shift from higher education as an elite system to higher education as a mass-based system.

In response, the emphasis in both the *Green Paper on Higher Education Transformation* (1996) – which makes no reference at all to mergers – and *Education White Paper 3* (1997) falls on the *expansion* of higher education opportunities, especially to those disadvantaged under the apartheid system. In the anxious wording of the *Green Paper*:

> Greater numbers of students will have to be accommodated ... Such 'massification' of South African higher education will necessarily involve different patterns of teaching and learning ... In a situation of financial constraints, planning and negotiations will have to ensure wider participation is affordable and sustainable. (DoE 1996: 15)

The subsequent *White Paper* rode the tide of expectation – with some degree of financial caution: 'There is a clear case for the expansion of the higher education system if it is to meet the imperatives of equity, redress and development' (DoE 1997: 9).

But massification did not really happen. Where it did, it was restricted to a small number of historically white institutions capable of expanding their market share in the mid-1990s at the same time that overall higher education enrolments spiralled downwards (Cloete & Bunting 1999). This does not mean that the absolute number of students in higher education did not gradually increase after the late 1980s (Cooper & Subotsky 2001);[2] what matters for the purpose of this analysis is that the expectation of massive demand by students and, in particular, non-traditional students (black), did not happen. The NCHE predictions of student growth and massification were completely off target (see Figures 13.1, 13.2 and 13.3).

Figure 13.1 *Head-count university plus technikon enrolment projections, 1995–2002 (000's)*

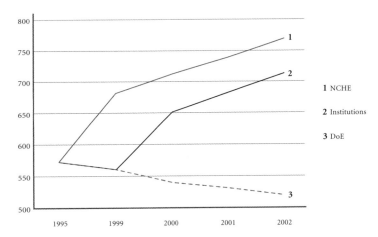

Source: Cloete & Bunting (1999)

In 1997 there were 21 000 fewer students enrolled in higher education than predicted in the NCHE report, and about 140 000 fewer than predicted by 1999 for the sector as a whole. What is much more striking, though, is the differential impact of the national decline in enrolments, with historically black universities severely affected by the decline, even as enrolments increased in former white universities and technikons. It is this dramatic drop in enrolments in black universities (among other factors) that lies at the root of the institutional decay and instability in these institutions in the mid- to late-1990s.

The decline of massification as a national development project eventually gave way to the emergence of merger thinking as a dominant project of the post-apartheid state. But the history of merger thinking has to be carefully traced since it was by no means mutually exclusive to the massification project; it did, however, signal a difference of emphasis in the policy and planning initiatives of the post-apartheid government.

Figure 13.2 *School-leavers obtaining full matriculation exemption ('000s)*

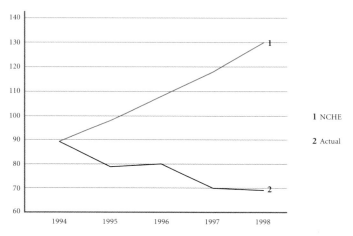

1 NCHE

2 Actual

Source: Cloete & Bunting (1999)

Figure 13.3 *Gross participation rates, based on age group 20–24*

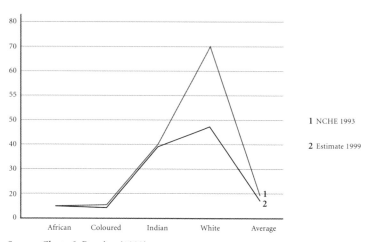

1 NCHE 1993

2 Estimate 1999

Source: Cloete & Bunting (1999)

Great expectations II: mergers

The founding policy document on higher education after apartheid is the report of the *National Commission on Higher Education: A Framework for Transformation*, produced by 13 commissioners whose terms of reference included advising the Minister on 'the *shape* of the higher education system … in terms of the types of institutions' and 'what the *size* of the higher education system should be' (NCHE 1996: 266).[3] In other words, the language of size and shape already had its origins in this base document.

However, the NCHE was careful to defer any specific proposals on institutional restructuring, holding that over a period of time the number of institutional types required would become clearer. The emphasis in the NCHE was on institutional differentiation that would, in the aspirations of the Commission, be attained through governmental requirements for institutional missions, 'programme mix' and the regulatory authority of the new national qualifications framework. In addition, faith was expressed in statutory regional structures that could be 'consulted on the planning needs of the region, mergers [and] rationalisation …' (1996: 198). In short, against the background of a predicted expansion of enrolments, an expressed faith in the authority of regulatory means for achieving institutional differentiation, and a clear commitment to voluntarism through regional collaboration among institutions, the NCHE's approach to the subject of mergers is rather underplayed – almost invisible – in the more than 400 pages submitted to President Mandela in July 1996.

Where the subject of mergers does feature in the NCHE report it is in the context of the colleges, a focus no doubt inspired by the earlier release of the National Teacher Education Audit in 1996, which suggested high levels of inefficiency and low levels of quality in the college sector (Hofmeyr & Hall 1996). According to the NCHE, the authorities should determine which colleges are needed and it contemplated the possibility of merging several colleges to constitute a new university or technikon, with the proviso that 'the merger should be multi-disciplinary, involving colleges from more than one field…' (NCHE 1996: 156). If anything, the NCHE report allowed for the possibility of more rather than fewer universities, with merger activities restricted to the college sector. But it is safe to claim that the overwhelming emphasis of this substantial document was not on mergers, and certainly not on university mergers. The tone was set, rather, for institutional differentiation.

Perhaps unsurprisingly, therefore, the subject of mergers did not enjoy prominence in the subsequent *White Paper on Higher Education*. The paper contains an isolated reference to the possibility that '...planning [which] may lead to institutional mergers and closures' (DoE 1997: 2.45) and the promise that:

> Incentive funding will be available on a selective basis to support the costs involved in regional collaboration among institutions which aim to consolidate, merge, share or otherwise collectively improve the efficient use of their facilities and resources for teaching, research or community service. (4.59)

The first substantial reference to an imminent institutional restructuring process only emerged in July 1999, following the appointment of Prof. Kader Asmal as the second post-apartheid Minister of Education. In his *Call to Action*, the Minister announced that:

> The shape and size of the higher education system cannot be left to chance if we are to realise the vision of a rational, seamless higher education system ... The institutional landscape of higher education will be reviewed as a matter of urgency in collaboration with the Council on Higher Education. This landscape was largely dictated by the geo-political imagination of apartheid planners. (DoE 1999)

The Council on Higher Education (CHE), a statutory body that advises the Minister, was approached to provide advice on the reconfiguration of the higher education system. In December 1999 the CHE responded with a memorandum to the Minister, *Towards a Framework and Strategy for Reconfiguring the Higher Education System in South Africa*, in which a task team was proposed to deliver on this reconfiguration exercise. In January 2000 the Minister bluntly spelt out the brief of the task team:

> a set of concrete proposals on the shape and size of the higher education system and not a set of general principles which serve as guidelines for restructuring. I cannot over-emphasise the importance of this point. Until and unless we reach finality on institutional restructuring, we cannot take action and put in place the steps necessary to ensure the long-term affordability and sustainability of the higher education system. (CHE 2000: 2)

The task team was constituted in February 2000 and on 7 April of that year it produced a discussion document that offered a differentiated system of higher education based on institutional types, distinguished by various levels, types and durations of qualifications offered, eg. two-year qualifications offered in one kind of institution and four-year bachelors' degrees offered in other kinds of institutions. Strikingly, there is no reference in this document to institutional mergers but, rather, to institutional differentiation. Nevertheless, in a May 2000 press statement, the Minister made the point that the task team exercise was not 'targeted at closing institutions ... On the contrary, the reconfiguration exercise is key to preventing closure of those institutions that are experiencing serious difficulties' (CHE 2000: 8).

In July 2000 the CHE task team presented its report. In the final chapter on 'National Steering and Planning', the task team:

> advances a number of recommendations on the size of the system in relation to the number of institutions, closures, combinations and funding [and] provides examples of possible combinations that could create a more rational and coherent higher education landscape. (CHE 2000: 51)

Here, for the first time, the spectre of 'combinations' of institutions is explicitly discussed and elaborated beyond the hitherto more vague terms such as 'restructuring' or 'reconfiguration'. But what did the task team mean by 'combination'? It is unclear, but at the time it did not appear to be synonymous with mergers, as the following extract from the report suggests:

> Institutional combination must not be viewed as a threat but as an opportunity to reorient and revitalise higher education in pursuit of important social and educational goals. However, *the combination of institutions – whether through mergers or other mechanisms* – will be demanding processes. (CHE 2000: 55, emphases added)

At the same time, a literal reading of the CHE report instructs that *combinations* are intended to reduce the number of institutions without closing them. The wording is slippery: '... the task team recommends reducing the absolute number of higher education institutions. This does not necessarily imply closing institutions' (CHE 2000: 56). But it goes on to say that:

> although Section 25 of the *Higher Education Act* [of 1997] makes provision for closure of institutions, the task team recommends

that there should be no closures. The task team recommends reducing the present number of institutions through combining institutions. (CHE 2000: 56–7)

The task team then took the bold step of listing 'examples of possible combinations' (2000: 60), warning that 'these are not meant to be exhaustive. They must not preclude the Minister identifying other possible combinations' (2000: 63) that could achieve the national goals for higher education.

In response to the CHE report, the Minister released a *National Plan for Higher Education* on 5 March 2001 that essentially agreed with their recommendations, but with two amplifications:

> The CHE's notion of combination may, however, be conceived too narrowly to refer specifically to mergers of institution. The Ministry's view is that the notion of combination must be broadened to include a variety of arrangements, including not only mergers but also programme and infrastructural collaboration. (DoE 2001a: 86)

And that:

> the number of public higher education institutions in South Africa could and should be reduced. However, reducing the number of institutions does not imply that some institutions would be closed and discontinue offering higher education programmes. (2001a: 87)

The Minister also hinted at yet another investigation, this time:

> to investigate the feasibility of reducing the number of institutions and establishing new institutional and organisational forms through a more rational arrangement for consolidating the provision of higher education on a regional basis. It is important to emphasise that the focus of the investigation would not be on whether the number of institutions can or should be reduced, but how they can be reduced and the form restructured institutions should take. (2001a: 89)

Later in March 2001, the Minister appointed a National Working Group (NWG) consisting of 11 persons from business, labour, higher education and government 'to advise on the appropriate arrangements for restructuring the provision of higher education ... including institutional mergers...' (DoE 2001b: 4). In December 2001 the NWG released its report, *The Restructuring of the Higher Education System in South Africa*, and recommended the reduction of higher education institutions from 36 to 21 through the specific mechanism of mergers, listing the specific institutions in various provinces to be targeted for merging. To achieve these specific merger goals, the NWG drew attention to the critical ingredients of political will on the part of government, additional financial resources – 'including the removal of current debt burdens' – institutional commitment, clear targets and time-frames, and a 'social plan' to deal with the inevitable human resource implications (DoE 2001b: 9).

In late April 2002 the Minister finalised his own proposals, based on the technical report of the NWG, and took these to the Cabinet for approval, with the focus on implementation of the final merger recommendations. With a few modifications on the Minister's proposals, the Cabinet approved the following mergers and incorporations (Asmal 2002):

o   The University of Natal and the University of Durban-Westville.
o   The University of the North-West and Potchefstroom University.
o   The Technikon Pretoria, the Technikon Northern Gauteng and the Technikon North West.
o   The University of Fort Hare and the East London campus of Rhodes University.
o   The incorporation of Vista University campuses into specified universities and technikons in the region where each campus was located, eg. the incorporation of the Mamelodi campus into the University of Pretoria.
o   The University of Port Elizabeth and the Port Elizabeth Technikon.
o   The University of the North and the Medical University of South Africa.
o   The University of the Transkei, the Border Technikon and the Eastern Cape Technikon.
o   The Rand Afrikaans University and the Technikon Witwatersrand.
o   The Cape Technikon and the Peninsula Technikon.

But there was another development in higher education that paralleled the general emergence of policy-thinking on mergers in higher education; this parallel process (already mentioned briefly) concerned the colleges of nursing, agriculture and education. While the first two (nursing and agriculture) are ongoing processes of merger deliberations, the colleges of education have enjoyed a fairly long and arduous journey to their current incorporation status. This line of development has to be traced separately from the general narrative, in part because three of the case studies involved colleges of education being incorporated into universities, and in part because the college narrative sheds light on the incoherence of policy and planning in the early years of transition.

Since 1910 at least, the jurisdiction of colleges has been contested between central government and the four provinces, a contest that was eventually settled by housing colleges in racially segregated provincial authorities under apartheid (Hofmeyr & Hall 1996). It was left to the post-apartheid *Constitution of the Republic of South Africa Act* (No. 108 of 1996, Schedule 4) to make all tertiary education a 'national competence'. The legal implication for colleges in terms of the *White Paper* (1997) and the *Higher Education Act* (No. 101 of 1997, Section 21.2) was that colleges could either be established as autonomous institutions or as subdivisions that would be incorporated into an existing university or technikon.

This status for colleges was not anticipated, however, in the first National Teacher Education Audit released in 1996 (Hofmeyr & Hall 1996). The audit made three points about college governance. First, that the status of colleges must be resolved, noting that 'the dominant view in the college sector is that colleges should be national institutions of higher education' (1996: 84). Second, that appropriate autonomy should be devolved to colleges, which would then establish their own councils and senates. And third, that colleges should break their isolation through strategies that include 'affiliation by colleges to universities through schemes of association' (1996: 85).

It was left to the first Minister's NCHE (1996) to contemplate the incorporation or reorganisation of colleges into existing universities and technikons, a recommendation that was acted on through policy (the *White Paper* of 1997) and the law (the Act of 1997), as indicated earlier.

The implementation of these provisions was left to a departmental Technical Committee appointed in September 1997, which in 1998 delivered a document called *The Incorporation of Colleges of Education into the Higher Education Sector: A Framework for Implementation*. It is this committee that recommended the option of incorporation or autonomy for colleges with the proviso that 'an autonomous college … to be financially viable [it] would require a minimum enrolment of 2 000 students' (DoE 1998: 15). For the purposes of this study, the anticipated organisational arrangements are most interesting:

> There are different structural arrangements possible within the option of incorporation into an existing higher education institution. The college may lose its identity completely and either become a faculty or be absorbed into an existing faculty of the higher education institution. Alternately, the college, while being juristically and administratively part of the higher education institution, retains by agreement, rights and powers beyond those of the usual academic components of a higher education institution, and is recognised as a special case among such components ... The Act ... does not require uniformity in intra-institutional structural arrangements. (DoE 1998: 15)

The provincial reaction to the so-called 'framework document' was swift. By the start of 2000, the number of colleges had been cut from 120 (80 000 students) to 50 (15 000 students) (CHE 2000/2001). By the end of the year that number had been reduced to 25 'contact institutions' holding 10 000 students (and 1 000 staff). Another 5 000 students were registered in two distance learning colleges (with 500 staff) – the South African College for Teacher Education (Sacte) and the South African College for Open Learning (Sacol).[4]

The next step was the publication of a Government Notice (No. 1383, 15 December 2000), which served as a Ministerial Declaration of Colleges of Education as Subdivisions of Universities and Technikons. This notice provided a *Schedule* that specified for each province the college of education and the receiving institution of which it would be a subdivision.

Almost simultaneously, the DoE and the employee bodies of college staff signed the *Framework for the Management of Personnel in the Process of Incorporation of Teacher Education into Higher Education* (Public Service Co-ordinating Bargaining Council Resolution 2000). This agreement held that all college employees 'shall be absorbed by the relevant provincial Education Department' (Public Service Bargaining Council 2000: 3) and that all new posts created by the receiving higher education institution would first be advertised on a vacancy list 'restricted to personnel currently or formerly appointed or seconded by the Department to a College of Education ...' (2000: xx).

Earlier, at the negotiations of the Public Service Co-ordinating Bargaining Council, the employee parties had apparently requested an independent body, the Joint Education Trust (JET), to facilitate the implementation of this agreement with respect to personnel employment conditions and data generation on students, programmes, property, plant and finances. In August 2000, the College Fund, a United States Agency for International Development (USAID) contractor, funded JET on behalf of the Department of Education to play the role of external agent to facilitate the incorporation of colleges of education into the higher education system. In September 2000, JET produced *A Guiding Manual for The Incorporation of Designated Colleges of Education in Higher Education*, which spelt out tasks to be undertaken by JET in facilitating the process of incorporation.

In January 2001, after the framework document had been signed, the JET wrote to college rectors with the promise of facilitation and a checklist of responsibilities to be completed 'towards the finalisation of the incorporation process'. The subsequent progress on incorporation during 2001 and into 2002 assumed very different pathways, and unfolded at very different speeds and with markedly different effects in the various college-into-university incorporations. It is these uneven processes, and their effects, that this study seeks to explain. In doing so, the case studies yield less buoyant findings than declared by the most recent investigation into higher education: 'The National Working Group has further noted that colleges of education were rationalised and *successfully incorporated* into the higher education system with effect from January 2001' (DoE 2001b: 18; emphasis added).

This is how a more or less literal and official narrative of events relating to mergers in higher education – from the *White Paper* of 1997 through to the NWG Report of 2002 – reads. As a narrative it is conscious of its limits in capturing the intense and influential contestations that lay behind and between the move from one report to another, or from one moment in the restructuring process to the next; and of Throgmorton's (1993) 'tropes' – those rhetorical devices in a policy document that propose explanations, inspire public visions and recommend actions – that give policy 'its contingent meaning, and thus its power, from a particular audience, time, place and articulation' (Fischer & Forester 1993: 11).

Unscrambling the rationale for mergers

Staying with the official narrative for the moment, a critical question is why these mergers were contemplated in the first place? The CHE task team, the Ministry's National Plan and the NWG all hold to the same basic motivation, which is repeated in the National Plan as 'the basis for assessing combinations of institutions' (DoE 2001a: 89). Put directly, a merger can be deemed as successful if, among other things:

o it enhances access and equity goals for both staff and students;
o it enables economies of scale through the creation of larger multi-purpose institutions with more efficient uses of buildings, facilities and human resources;
o it overcomes the threat to institutional viability in terms of student numbers, income and expenditure patterns, and management capacities;
o it creates new institutions with new identities and cultures that transcend their past racial and ethnic institutional histories and contribute to their deracialisation.

The official rationale for mergers was not shared by all stakeholders in higher education. To some, like the Association of Vice Chancellors of Historically Disadvantaged Institutions (ASAHDI), the mergers represented a deliberate attack on historically black universities, on poor and rural students, and on the cultural and intellectual legacy of the historically black universities.

The South African University Vice Chancellors Association (SAUVCA), while noting common aspirations for mergers (like equity), offered a very different rationale for institutional mergers (Kotecha & Harman 2001). To SAUVCA, the official rationale for mergers sought to:

o resolve the high maintenance costs per student of some institutions;
o remove differences in perception of quality among higher education institutions;
o prevent closure of institutions that are not financially viable;
o redress the dilemma of low management capacity in some institutions.

The organisation also had the impression that the rationale had been written to justify decisions that had already been made rather than to explain them. The perceptual divide is significant. For one set of actors the mergers seek to deal with dysfunctional institutions which, it so happens, are the historically black institutions carrying the disadvantage of apartheid (*Business Day* 07.03.02). For another group of persons, the mergers represent one of the key strategies for creating 'the new system of South African institutions and not a collection of disparate historically white or black institutions' (Asmal 2002).

The problem partly with these readings of policy is that they are based on a literal reading of official documents on the one hand, and with a preferred interpretation of emphases on the other hand. Critics of mergers stress the national development commitments of the *White Paper on Higher Education* and, indeed, its commitment to redressing the plight of the historically disadvantaged institutions. Little attention is assigned to the symbolic meanings of policy as distinct from its implementation logic within educational contexts. What the final section of this chapter offers, therefore, is a set of explanations as to why the current strategy for restructuring – mergers – is in fact consistent with a more balanced reading of higher education policy.

Explaining the trajectory of higher education restructuring

The restructuring of higher education has been driven by the twin goals of global competitiveness and national development. It is very clear from a succession of policy documents that the task of positioning South Africa for technological and economic competitiveness was a crucial goal of the new government. In this process, universities play a crucial role as sites of new knowledge production and technological innovation. Recent affirmation of these goals, already elucidated in the *White Paper on Higher Education Transformation* (1997) and the *White Paper on Science and Technology* (1996), came on the occasion of the announcement of South Africa's research and development strategy:

> Critical in this regard (wealth creation in the context of globalisation) is the matter of *human resource development*. We have to exert maximum effort to train the necessary numbers of our people in all the fields required for the development, running and management of modern economies … we must also identify and develop the lead sectors that will help us further to expand the base for creation of wealth and give us the possibility to *compete successfully within the dynamic world economy*. (Mbeki 2002: 3, emphases added)

In this regard, the Department of Arts, Culture, Science and Technology argues that:

> Our approach to human resource development is rooted in the need, on the one hand, to radically increase the number of women and people from disadvantaged communities entering the sciences and remaining there and, on the other hand, a strategy to maximise the pursuit of excellence in global terms. (DACST 1996: 16)

It is equally clear that universities are not only being called on to play a strategic role in meeting national development goals such as human resource capacity, but also to train this new cadre of scientists and technologists to enable global competitiveness. This dual focus on building capacity and increasing competitiveness fits perfectly, of course, with global demands on higher education in the third world (see World Bank 2002).

The strategy for pursuing these goals was the reconfiguration of the higher education landscape, *not* the retention of institutions that were inefficient (in terms of the utilisation of state resources) or ineffective (in terms of delivery on national development goals). What propelled the state in actively pursuing this relatively dormant agenda[5] were two critical factors that threatened to undermine this ambition for global competitiveness and national development.

The first factor was the dramatic decline in student enrolments in higher education. This decline impacted directly on the already vulnerable historically black institutions, struggling with financial deficits, high failure rates, managerial ineffectiveness and poor students unable to pay for higher education (Habib 2001; Jansen 2002a). If the absolute decline in high-school graduates was a reality for all institutions, it was a disaster for black universities in that, increasingly, middle-class and above-average black students were drawn to the former white institutions. The net effect of this shift was to place already weak and fragile black universities in a precarious position in terms of funding and, as it turns out, future survival.

The second factor was the dramatic incline in institutional instability during the mid- to late-1990s. Black institutions were embroiled in a vortex of student revolt, staffing conflicts, managerial ineptitude, unstable councils and senates, and a general failure of the leadership of universities and technikons to effectively manage this instability (Durand 1999a, 1999b; Nhlapo 2000; Saunders 1999; Skweyiya 1998). In the meantime, deficits soared and education quality nosedived even further. Under a post-apartheid government this was not only a political embarrassment but a development crisis (Habib 2001). This led to a rapid rewriting of legislation allowing government to not only launch several commissions of inquiry but also to appoint a series of administrators for the interim management of these unstable institutions.

The focus of this governmental strategy, from an institutional point of view, was race-blind, in that the aim was to deracialise all institutions and to create a smaller number of high-quality, non-racial institutions. This is what critics of restructuring fail to understand: that the recasting of the institutional land-scape was never about retaining pockets of black institutions on the one hand, and islands of white institutions on the other. In this respect, the decision not to merge Fort Hare was a reluctant compromise on the part of government, given the intense opposition from leading politicians within the ruling party, based on the historic and symbolic role of the University of Fort Hare in the previous century. Rather than nourish black institutions simply because of their racial and historical status, the focus of government was on opening up and accelerating access of black students and staff into high-quality institu-tions. For this reason the unrelenting pressure from activist groups – like ASAHDI – on the sentimental issue of what one of its leaders calls 'native issues',[6] is unlikely to alter the path of institutional restructuring. This will not be easy, though, since the emotional rhetoric around the preservation of black institutions and the black working classes strike a sensitive chord among pow-erful figures in the ruling elite.[7]

But this focus was not only averse to nurturing inefficient black institutions, it was also committed to retaining efficient white institutions; this logic was already established within *White Paper* 3, without (understandably) racial referents:

> Despite the negative consequences of the apartheid legacy, some higher education institutions have developed *internationally com-petitive research and teaching capacities.* Their academic expertise and infrastructure are national assets. It would be detrimental to the national interest and the future provision of quality higher education if the valuable features and achievements of the existing system were not identified, *retained* and used in the restructuring process. (DoE 1997: paragraph 1.5, emphases added)

The path chosen for higher education restructuring enables one to explain a number of recent events. It explains why recent language policy for higher edu-cation finally deflated expectations of designated Afrikaans-exclusive institu-tions – at least one in the north, presumably the University of Potchefstroom, and one in the south, presumably Stellenbosch University. Acting against these key recommendations of the Gerwel Report,[8] the Cabinet decided that no uni-versity would be able to offer instruction in the exclusive medium of Afrikaans, given the negative implications for access of black students (and staff) and, of course, the deracialisation of white institutions. It also explains why none of the inefficient rural institutions (mainly black universities) were earmarked for merger with highly efficient urban institutions (mainly the former white universities). The reasoning of government and its advisory body, the CHE, was not to destabilise already efficient institutions, except to require some minimal adjustments to counter the political charge of leaving white institutions untouched. Such small adjustments include, for example, the former white universities losing specific programmes (like dentistry at Stellenbosch University going to the University of the Western Cape) or incorporating small entities (like the University of Pretoria being required to incorporate the small college campus of Vista University in Mamelodi, Pretoria).

Finally, this standpoint explains why the highly inefficient colleges of education were closed (and the few effective ones incorporated into universities), effectively removing 80 000 student teachers from the system; and why 150 technical colleges were merged, literally overnight,[9] into only 50 new institutions to deal with the high costs of generally inefficient technical schools.

In sum, the idea was to strengthen the competitive position of the urban and former white institutions while at the same time dealing with the inefficiencies of rural and black institutions through closure, merger or incorporation.

Implications for the nation

What does this mean for the nation? First, it means that South Africa will have a smaller number of institutions with a much narrower quality range than in the past. These institutions will be mainly the former white universities and technikons that are dominant in the urban areas and which will become deracialised in terms of staffing, students and culture so that over time their racial birthmarks will be eroded. What remains in question is the pace of this transformation in former white institutions; this will depend on the quality of leadership, in terms of commitment and strategy, within such institutions. This is especially true with respect to changes in staffing and institutional cultures. What also remains in question is whether this transformation will yield on the issue of academic standards or managerial efficiencies, and whether strategies will be pursued to enhance overall institutional standing and competitiveness.[10] It could go either way.

Second, what this also means is that the class character of these institutions will change as more and more middle-class black and white students begin to populate these urban, former white institutions.[11] These students in general will be academically better prepared than their rural, poor counterparts, especially as the urban white school system becomes more and more deracialised with respect to learner enrolments. This also means that institutional efficiencies will not suffer any significant setbacks – in terms of student pass and progression rates – because of the class and quality of the deracialised student body.

Third, it means that there will be fewer access routes open to rural students wishing to pursue university education *unless* meaningful alternatives are instituted, nurtured and sustained. The closure of inefficient technical colleges and colleges of education, the effective closure of certain universities (like the University of the Transkei), and the merger of black universities (like the University of Durban-Westville) with former white institutions, effectively means that poor, under-performing students who often scraped through higher education, will in effect have fewer opportunities for such access because of the tuition structure of the more competitive institutions and the higher levels set for admission to such institutions. It will be crucial to the credibility of restructuring efforts (and the legitimacy of government itself) that quality access institutions and programmes be set in place (without creating any new ones) to enable rural black students eventually to enter higher education well prepared for the task. In this scenario, the quasi-welfare status of many historically black universities and the pretence of offering university-level education to the struggling graduates of a dysfunctional school system will eventually be terminated. In the long run, there is no alternative but to improve dramatically the quality of school education so that more and better-prepared high-school graduates, especially from rural areas, are delivered to the higher education system.

Notes

1   The distance education institutions, the University of South Africa and Technikon South Africa, were controlled by the white administration of the so-called House of Assembly during the apartheid days, even though they could enrol black students outside of the permit regulations, given that the students were off-campus.

2   These three illustrations are drawn directly from Cloete & Bunting (1999).

3   This section of the paper borrows liberally from the introductory chapter to a recent book that I edited, *Mergers in Higher Education: Lessons learned in transitional contexts* (Jansen 2002a).

4   All student numbers are cited as full time equivalent (FTE) students, i.e. the subsidy value of a student determined on the basis of courses and contact time. This is typically less than a straightforward head-count enrolment of students. So, for example, SACTE and SACOL had 20 000 students in the late 1990s but this actually comes to about 5 000 FTE students because of factors like the registration for single courses by individual students under flexible registration requirements.

5   'Dormant' in the sense that while institutional reconfiguration was prefigured in the 1997 *White Paper on Higher Education*, it was not elevated to the level of policy and planning action until 2000. I hold that the combination of an activist Minister and a set of black universities in crisis, propelled the second Minister of Education in the post-apartheid government to act on these 'landscape issues'.

6   Professor Itumeleng Mosala, at the October 2002 Conference on Mergers at the University of South Africa, made the provocative point that 'the native question' had not been addressed in the merger proposals of government.

7   Among others, the Premier of the Eastern Cape directly challenged the merits of the merger proposals coming from his senior colleagues in the Ministry of Education; this was striking because of the lack of public dissent within the ranks of senior members of the ANC and through the public media.

8   The Gerwel Report was the product of an investigation into the role of Afrikaans in higher education institutions, commissioned by the Minister of Education, Prof. Kader Asmal, and led by Prof. Jakes Gerwel, retired Vice Chancellor of the University of the Western Cape. See *Report to the Minister of Education AK Asmal by the Informal Committee Convened to Advise on the Position of Afrikaans in the University System*. Available at http://education.pwv.gov.za/DoE_Sites/Higher_Education/ Higher_Education_ Index.html.

9   The fact that colleges of education and technical colleges were closed, incorporated or merged with little resistance, is largely because of the lack of political muscle and institutional status of this component of the post-secondary education sector.

10 I have made the point repeatedly in other forums that while former white institutions have generally maintained a high standard of managerial efficiency (especially the universities) and a reasonable standard of academic quality (although this is highly uneven across academic departments), it is by no means world class.

11 I am grateful to Mandisa Mbali from the University of Natal for reminding me of this important trend.

References

Asmal, K (2002) *Press statement by the Minister of Education, Professor Kader Asmal, on the Transformation and Reconstruction of the Higher Education System*, 09.12.02. Pretoria.

CHE (2000) *Towards a New Higher Education Landscape: Meeting the Equity, Quality and Social Development Imperatives of South Africa in the 21st Century*. Pretoria.

Cloete, N, Maasen, P, Moja, T, Perold, H, Gibbon, T & Fehnel, R (eds.) (2002) *Transformation in higher education: Global pressures and local realities in South Africa.* Cape Town: Juta.

Cloete, N & Bunting, I (1999) *Higher education transformation: Assessing performance in South Africa.* Pretoria: Centre for Higher Education Transformation.

Cooper, D & Subotsky, G (2001) *The skewed revolution: Trends in South African higher education, 1988–1998.* Cape Town: UWC, Education Policy Unit.

DACST (1996) *White Paper on Science and Technology: Preparing for the 21st Century.* Pretoria: Department of Arts, Culture, Science & Technology.

DoE (Department of Education) (1996) *Green Paper on Higher Education Transformation.* Pretoria: Department of Education.

DoE (1997) *Education White Paper 3: A Programme for the Transformation of Higher Education.* Pretoria: Department of Education.

DoE (1998) *The Incorporation of Colleges of Education into the Higher Education Sector: A framework for implementation.* Pretoria: Department of Education.

DoE (1999). *Call to Action: Mobilising Citizens to Build a South African Education and Training System for the 21st Century.* Pretoria: Department of Education.

DoE (2001a). *National Plan for Higher Education.* Pretoria: Department of Education.

DoE (2001b). *The Restructuring of the Higher Education System in South Africa – Report of the National Working Group to the Minister of Education.* Pretoria: Department of Education.

Durand, JJF (1999a) Investigation of the situation of the Vaal Triangle by the independent assessor, *Government Gazette* No. 19239 (11 September). Pretoria: Government Printer.

Durand, JJF (1999b) Report of the independent assessor to the Minister of Education on Mangosuthu Technikon, *Government Gazette* No. 20485 (17 September). Pretoria: Government Printer.

Fischer, F & Forester, J (eds.) (1993) *The argumentative turn in policy analysis and planning.* Durham, North Carolina, and London: Duke University Press.

Government of South Africa (2002) *The National Plan for Research and Development.* Pretoria.

Habib, A (2001) The institutional crisis of the University of the Transkei, *Politikon* 28(2): 157–179.

Hofmeyr, J & Hall, G (1996). *The national teacher audit: Synthesis report.* Pretoria: Department of Education.

Jansen, JD (ed.) (2002a) *Mergers in higher education: Lessons learned in transitional contexts.* Pretoria: UNISA Press.

Jansen, JD (2002b) Political symbolism as policy craft: Explaining non-reform in South African education after apartheid, *Journal of Education Policy* 17(2): 199–215.

Koen, C (2002) Challenges and pressures facing the academic profession in South Africa in P Altbach (ed.) (2002) *The decline of the guru: The academic profession in developing and middle-income countries.*

Kotecha, P & Harman, G (2001) *Exploring institutional collaboration and mergers in higher education.* Pretoria: SAUVCA.

Mabokela, RO (2000) *Voices of conflict: Desegregating South African universities.* New York: Routledge.

Mabokela, RO & King, KL (eds.) (2001) *Apartheid no more: Case studies of southern African universities in the process of transformation.* London: Bergin & Garvey.

Mbeki, T (2002) The context for the national R&D strategy, in *South Africa's National Research and Development Strategy: 3.* Pretoria: Government of South Africa.

NCHE (1996). *National Commission on Higher Education Report: A Framework for Transformation.* Cape Town: NCHE.

Nhlapo, T (2000) Investigation into the affairs of the University of the North by the independent assessor, *Government Gazette* No. 21654, (16 October). Pretoria: Government Printer.

Public Service Bargaining Council (2000) *Resolution 12: Framework for the Management of Personnel in the Process of Incorporation of Teacher Education into Higher Education.* Pretoria.

Saunders, SJ (1999) Report of the independent assessor to the Minister of Education to investigate the affairs at the University of Fort Hare, *Government Gazette* No. 19842 (12 March). Pretoria: Government Printer.

Skweyiya, TL (1998) Investigation into the situation at the University of the Transkei by the independent assessor, *Government Gazette* No. 19501 (20 November). Pretoria: Government Printer.

Throgmorton, JA (1993) Survey research as rhetorical Tropes: Electric power planning arguments in Chicago, in F Fischer & J Forester (eds.) *The argumentative turn in policy analysis and planning.* Durham, North Carolina, and London: Duke University Press.

World Bank (2002) *Constructing knowledge societies: New challenges for tertiary education.* Washington DC: International Bank for Reconstruction and Development, the World Bank.

HIV/AIDS policy-making in post-apartheid South Africa

Mandisa Mbali

Introduction

Recent post-apartheid Acquired Immune Deficiency Syndrome (AIDS) policy-making in South Africa has been contested terrain, where civil society organisations like the Treatment Action Campaign (TAC) and the Government have assumed radically differing positions over what appropriate government responses to the pandemic ought to be. Central to the conflict over policy are two inter-related issues: President Mbeki's advocacy of a denialist[1] position on AIDS and the dispute over the provision of anti-retroviral drugs in the state sector.

AIDS infection in post-apartheid South Africa represents a fundamental crisis for the country. A recent national survey concluded that 11,4 per cent of South Africans are HIV-positive (Shisana et al. 2002). According to the Department of Health (DoH 2001), the number of HIV-infected persons in South Africa has topped four million. This gives South Africa the dubious distinction of being the country with, if not the highest, certainly one of the highest rates of HIV infection in the world. Among numerous indications of the scale of the crisis are the increasing number of press reports to the effect that in heavily-affected areas in KwaZulu-Natal, for example, cemeteries are running out of burial space (*Daily News* 10.02.03). Others are warning of an AIDS-orphans crisis, with estimates that by 2001 there will be three million such orphans (Dorrington & Johnson 2002). At the household level, the death of breadwinners and primary care-givers is contributing to the deepening of the poverty experienced by the poorest children and families (Gow, Desmond & Ewing 2002).

AIDS is also impacting heavily upon the productivity of workers, with rising morbidity and mortality leading to increases in employee absenteeism as well as sickness and death amongst workers. One study has estimated that AIDS shaved at least 0,3 percent off South Africa's GDP in 2001 alone (Quattek cited in Barnett & Whiteside 2002).

AIDS has also had other important impacts on, for example, the status of women and children in South Africa. The so-called 'virgin-cleansing myth' has led to an upsurge in incidents of rape and female child abuse, while in masculine-dominated and conservative circles women are increasingly stigmatised and blamed for the spread of AIDS (Leclerc Madlala 1996, 2002). To top this, it does seem that in South Africa women are more vulnerable to HIV infection due to a range of biological, socio-economic and cultural factors related to gender inequality (Abdool Karim, Soldan & Zondi 1995; Strebel 1992).

Increasingly, this escalating national crisis over AIDS in post-apartheid South Africa has led to calls from civil society and the media for firm policy and planning responses to the crisis by the government. However, the response has been uneven and insufficient for a range of reasons.

Early post-apartheid AIDS policy-making: the Mandela era

In the early1980s, the ANC-in-exile spoke boldly of the architecture of a post-apartheid health system. Speaking at a WHO conference on apartheid and health, Secretary General Alfred Nzo declared that the ANC aimed for a 'health revolution in service of our people' where '… a preventative health scheme shall be run by the state; free medical care and hospitalisation shall be provided for all, with special care for mothers and young children; the aged, the orphans, the disabled and the sick shall be cared for by the state' (Nzo 1981: 12).

The ANC won an overwhelming majority in the first democratic elections in 1994. This was due in no small part to the developmentalist agenda espoused in the RDP, in which promises of 'health for all' mirrored the buoyant promises of jobs, houses, water and electricity for all South Africans. The ANC's *National Health Plan for South Africa* (1994) strongly asserted the right to health for all and the responsibility of the state to provide health services. These pledges placed specific emphasis on maternal and child health, and recognised that conservative economic policies could adversely affect the provision of health and social services.

In the early post-apartheid period, the challenges posed to the health sector by the apartheid legacy were enormous. There were many key priorities in health policy, including integrating nine bantustan health departments into one national and nine provincial departments; co-ordinating policy at local, provincial and national levels; finding an appropriate balance between spending on health and other budgetary priorities and ensuring equitable access to health care (Price & van den Heever 1995).

None of this has proved to be easy. Schneider and Stein (2001) have argued that the difficulties of co-ordinating health policies at local, provincial and national levels of government has complicated the AIDS policy-implementation process. Schneider (1998) has also argued elsewhere that in regard to the provincial allocations, the provinces have shown differing levels of commitment to the issue of AIDS, causing uneven implementation of spending and policy recommendations.

The current alienation of civil society groups and medical and scientific researchers from the government over AIDS policy dates back to early in the post-apartheid period, pre-dating the emergence of both President Mbeki's denialism and the TAC's campaign for anti-retroviral therapy. However, as will be demonstrated in this chapter, the tense relations of the Mandela era have in the present frayed to the point of breakdown through the President's (and his Health Minister's) denialism and the long-running conflict over anti-retroviral policy. Even so, it is worth reminding ourselves that the scandal of South Africa's current AIDS policy was preceded by some bizarre scandals in the Mandela presidency.

Sarafina and Virodene

The first of these was the so-called 'Sarafina II' scandal. It hinged around less than opaque tendering procedures and a grant in excess of R14 million to the prominent director, Mbongeni Ngema, for an AIDS-awareness musical. Sarafina II attracted criticism from civil society organisations, opposition parties, and even some members of the ANC, who felt that the play's budget was excessive and that there had been a lack of transparency in tendering and financing for the project. Critics pointed out that much less money could have been better spent on funding a number of community-based drama groups, while the fact that the funds came from the European Union (EU) also soured the relationship between the EU and the Government (*Mail & Guardian* 09.02.96).

With the Sarafina debacle receding, Government's policy on AIDS took another baffling turn when in 1997 it began to champion a new experimental drug, Virodene, as an 'AIDS cure'. Developed by three scientists attached to the

University of Pretoria, Government went to the extraordinary lengths of giving the three a hearing before Cabinet in which they appealed for government funding for their research (*Mail & Guardian* 24.01.97). The media fanfare created by what became billed as the 'miracle AIDS cure' was accentuated by apparent support for further human trials to research the drug by then Health Minister Nkosasana Zuma and Deputy President Thabo Mbeki (*Mail & Guardian* 28.02.97).

The farce was brought to an end when the Medicines Control Council (MCC) cast doubt on the safety and efficacy of the drug and banned any further clinical trials of the drug. It also turned out that the researchers had not submitted their findings to peer review by the scientific community, while the tests upon which the researchers had made their claim to having found an 'AIDS cure', turned out to be only a phase-one trial. This is insufficient grounds upon which to claim conclusive proof of the safety and efficacy of a drug (*Mail & Guardian* 24.01.97). Ultimately it was established that Virodene was little more chemically than an industrial solvent, which was blocked for human use in South Africa and elsewhere internationally due to its dangerous side-effects (*Mail & Guardian* 19.03.99). Indeed, some research by virologists went so far as to suggest that the main chemical component of Virodene may even activate HIV and prompt the more efficient replication of the virus (*Mail & Guardian* 20.03.98).

This late 1990s clash between the Health Minister and the then Deputy President and the MCC set a precedent of high-profile South African government figures taking on recognised medical authorities in the AIDS policy arena while also coming out in support of unorthodox dissident scientists in disputes over science.

AIDS policy in the Mbeki era

The state's current AIDS policy is articulated in the *2000–2005 HIV/AIDS/STD Strategic Plan for South Africa* (DoH 2000). Despite its controversial features, not all aspects of the policy are deemed as failures. Indeed, AIDS policy analysts note successes in such areas as the increased provision of male condoms; the widespread training of secondary school teachers in HIV/AIDS awareness; the continuation of the annual antenatal survey of HIV and syphilis prevalence; and the DoH's AIDS Directorate's establishment of a moderately successful Beyond Awareness Campaign (Dorrington & Johnson 2002; Whiteside & Sunter 2000).

Before analysing the AIDS policy debacles over Mbeki's AIDS denialism and access to anti-retroviral drugs in the public sector, it is worth considering government AIDS policy in more general terms in three key policy areas.

Prevention

Prevention is still the key focus of government AIDS policy (Tshabalala-Msimang 2002b) and there is some evidence that efforts to promote HIV prevention may be bearing some fruit. The recent Nelson Mandela Foundation/HSRC study has shown that more people are using condoms in the early 2000s compared to the late 1990s. It also shows that this is due to fear of contracting HIV, indicating that knowledge of the epidemic may be translating into behaviour change (Shisana et al. 2002).

On the other hand, there have been problems with the ways in which condoms are distributed and the numbers which government distributes. Critics of government's AIDS policy, such as the TAC, have pointed out that in 2002 Government only distributed 200 million condoms. This is on average sufficient for sexually-active South Africans to have sex using a condom 20 times per annum (TAC 2003a). There is also criticism of state policy on the provision of condoms in prisons which are currently provided by health professionals, as part of AIDS counselling and not in a more discreet manner that is, without requiring face-to-face interaction (Goyer 2003).

AIDS orphans and the social security system

Child-support and foster-parent grants have been made available to caregivers of AIDS orphans. However, there have been numerous problems with the poor administration and uptake of these grants, including lack of transport and money for orphans and their care-givers to get to Department of Social Welfare and Department of Home Affairs' offices; applicants lacking relevant documents such as birth certificates and identity documents and potential applicants lacking information about the availability of grants (Streak 2002). On the other hand, the 2003 budget made provision for the phased extension of the child-support grant to 14 years of age.

Prevention of Mother to Child Transmission (MTCT)

The long-running dispute between civil society and the Government over the efficacy, affordability and safety of anti-retroviral drugs can be traced back to 1998. This was when the National Association of People Living with HIV/AIDS (NAPWA) began to demand that the anti-retroviral AZT be made available to HIV-positive pregnant women to prevent them passing the virus to their children. It was this campaign that led to the formation of the TAC (Schneider 2001).

Rapidly developing into a nationwide social movement, TAC's mobilisation of thousands in demonstrations and its pursuit of court action against the state seemed to have borne fruit in the Cabinet's April 2002 statement. In it, the government relaxed its opposition to the provision of anti-retrovirals to survivors of sexual assault and their babies. Prior to this, the government had only been committed to researching the use of anti-retrovirals for post-exposure prophylaxis in the case of rape, and to review, revise and monitor policy in line with research on MTCT.

Many at the time interpreted the statement as an official repudiation of Mbeki's AIDS denialism. And indeed it was partially so. Nonetheless, the government remained opposed to providing anti-retrovirals in the public sector in the form of Highly Active Anti-Retroviral Therapy (HAART – also referred to as 'triple therapy'). HAART is a combination/cocktail of anti-retroviral drugs prescribed to HIV-positive people for life, which can dramatically extend the lifespan and health of HIV-positive people by suppressing HIV and thereby preventing opportunistic infections. Government's position against triple-therapy provision in the public sector rested on arguments about the drugs' expense, side-effects and lack of a sufficient health infrastructure to provide them. These arguments were reiterated in the Health Minister's address on 9 October 2002 and her 2002 World AIDS Day address (Tshabalala-Msimang 2002a, b).

In the light of government's overall capitulation over the provision of anti-retrovirals to prevent HIV transmission in the case of rape and from mothers to infants during and following birth, the major remaining disagreement between the state and the TAC is over the TAC's demand that the government provide HAART in the state sector.

The TAC and its allies, like Cosatu and the South African Medical Association (Sama), favour the provision of triple therapy in the public sector. This position has been framed in the language of socio-economic rights and the courts have been used to force the state to provide anti-retrovirals to prevent MTCT (Annas 2003). Their stance on anti-retrovirals has implied a firm faith in the latest orthodox medical views on how best to treat HIV and to prevent new infections. Their campaign is deeply rooted in mainstream western bio-medical understandings of the disease and epidemic. This has placed it on a direct collision course with that handful of powerfully-placed government figures who have publicly supported AIDS denialism. The result has been a paralysis in serious policy-making engagement between the TAC and its allies and senior government officials over AIDS policy.

The origins of AIDS denialism and its relevance to government policy-making on AIDS

It is now widely recognised that decisive leadership on AIDS policy by heads of state can be crucial in turning the tide of the epidemic, especially in developing countries. Thailand and Uganda are often cited as cases in point, where infection levels have either stopped rising, or have actually declined, and where the government's leadership has assumed a high profile in their prevention campaigns (Barnett & Whiteside 2002).

However, in South Africa the coherence and effectiveness of official state anti-AIDS programmes has been undermined by the highly public articulation of AIDS-denialist positions by President Thabo Mbeki and Health Minister Manto Tshabalala-Msimang. At the core of this position is a denial of the viral causation of AIDS, as well as of the extent of the infection and the efficacy and safety of anti-retroviral therapy. Until the adoption by the President of these views, AIDS denialists (or AIDS 'dissident' scientists as they like to refer to themselves) were virtual unknowns in South Africa. Nor did anyone take seriously the claims of the likes of Peter Duesberg and David Rassnick, who argued that HIV was not the cause of AIDS, that HIV tests were inaccurate and that anti-retrovirals were poisonous to the extent of causing AIDS deaths themselves (see Schüklenck 2002). These ideas were fringe notions circulating on remote internet sites like Virusmyth.com. President Mbeki has changed all that, and these ideas, which fall outside mainstream biomedical understandings of the disease, have seriously impacted on AIDS policy-making since the late 1990s.

While he had given hints earlier on in the Mandela era that he was partial to unorthodox views on the causes of HIV/AIDS, the extent to which the new President was prepared to identify himself with denialism only became clear in 2000 when he convened a Presidential Advisory Panel on AIDS and included on it such dissident scientists as Duesburg and Rassnick, along with other medical and scientific researchers holding orthodox views on AIDS. Their brief was to debate the basic tenets underpinning mainstream medical and scientific approaches to AIDS, explore the accuracy of HIV tests and the issue of whether HIV caused AIDS.

International controversy over his views grew when, at the 2000 International AIDS Conference in Durban, President Mbeki used this global forum to reiterate his dissidence. He claimed that not everything could be 'blamed on a single virus' and that poverty killed more people around the world than AIDS (Mbeki 2000: 4). The link between poverty and inequality and AIDS had been made before and might not have been so controversial had it not been for the President's questioning in the speech of 'the reliability of and the information communicated by our current HIV tests' (Mbeki 2000: 5). Soon thereafter in an interview with *Time* magazine (11.09.02), and again during parliamentary question time, Mbeki claimed that HIV could not cause AIDS on the grounds that a virus could not cause an immune-deficiency syndrome (see Schücklenk 2002).

Further evidence of the extent to which denialism had penetrated the ANC's thinking came in the form of an article posted on the organisation's online newsletter *ANC Today* in 2001. Almost certainly written by the President, it again expressed doubt as to the cause of AIDS and questioned the accuracy of HIV tests, stating that:

> Scientists have been grappling with these questions for 20 years, and yet there are still some disputes on these issues. The first relates to the virus itself. The questions to be answered are:
> - Does an infectious agent exist? If it does, is it a virus? Is this virus then the main cause of the immune-suppression seen in patients who have tested HIV-positive?
> - Are the tests that we use to detect the virus reliable?
> - Do the tests measure HIV? (ANC 2001: 7)

Consistent with this thinking, the DoH in the same year began circulating pamphlets to clinics promoting denialist views.[2] These were views which the

President repeated time and again, until in the face of growing public alarm and national and international ridicule, he decided to withdraw from the public debate on AIDS in April 2002.

AIDS and racism

In one key respect the AIDS denialism of President Mbeki and those in the ANC who subscribe to his views differs from the international variant of AIDS dissidence, and that is that it exhibits a preoccupation with racialised notions of the epidemic. This can be linked, in terms of intellectual history, to the historical legacy of certain racist public health responses to the epidemic in South Africa and internationally. The question, therefore, of what has led to such beliefs holding sway in the corridors of power can be answered at least partially by analysing AIDS denialism in historical context and as a reaction to the legacy of apartheid and colonial discourse around Africans, medicine and disease.

Speaking at Fort Hare University in October 2001, Mbeki argued that mainstream scientific views on AIDS were racist:

> Thus does it happen that others who consider themselves to be our leaders take to the streets carrying their placards to demand that because we [black people] are germ carriers, and human beings of a lower order that cannot subject its [sic] passions to reason, we must perforce adopt strange opinions, to save a depraved and diseased people from perishing from self-inflicted disease ... convinced that we are but natural-born promiscuous carriers of germs ... they proclaim that our continent is doomed to an inevitable mortal end because of our devotion to the sin of lust.

This theme was echoed in a pamphlet allegedly authored by Peter Mokaba (2002), an ANC MP and confidante of the President, which presented conspiratorial arguments that an 'omnipotent apparatus' of AIDS doctors, scientists, activists and the pharmaceutical companies aimed to kill black people in South Africa by prescribing 'toxic' anti-retrovirals.[3]

President Mbeki was not the first prominent African to make the link between AIDS causation and racism. In 1989, Richard and Rosalind Chirimuuta, Zimbabwean tropical health specialists at the London School of Hygiene and Tropical Medicine, published an AIDS denialist text entitled *AIDS, Africa and*

Racism. In what they considered a defence of African sexuality and humanity, they pushed many of the lines later espoused by Mbeki – that HIV did not cause AIDS, that AIDS did not originate in Africa, and that anti-retrovirals were 'poison' (Chirimuuta & Chirimuuta 1989). They also argued that the extent of the epidemic was exaggerated as part of a racist plot to discredit African culture and sexuality. They cited early medical journal articles that made insulting and culturally inaccurate speculations about African sexuality. For instance, they criticised researchers who claimed that HIV passed from monkeys to Africans through bizarre sexual practices involving monkey blood, that Africans engaged in anal intercourse more frequently than other race groups, and that in general they were 'excessively' promiscuous.

It was not only African intellectuals who ascribed to this latter view at the time. African health ministers and leaders were at the time contesting the HIV prevalence statistics being presented by the World Health Organization and medical researchers from the US and Europe (Garrett 1994). At the same time, articulations by South African health authorities (primarily white) and many white South African doctors as to what was driving the epidemic relied heavily on racist and sexist stereotypes of a diseased African sexuality (Mbali 2001).

In this regard, they were espousing a view that went far back into colonial and apartheid medicine. As the noted Africanist scholar, Megan Vaughan (1991), has shown, colonial medical discourse about Africans was highly sexualised, especially in regard to programmes designed to manage the transmission of sexual diseases. It portrayed Africans as sexually primitive and lacking in control in regard to their 'excessive' sexual appetites. In similar vein, Gillman has shown how in western post-enlightenment culture and science 'the black' was represented as 'an icon for deviant sexuality in general' and the female black 'an icon for black sexuality' (1985: 79, 83).

The impact of denialism on state policy

Given that it is official state policy that HIV causes AIDS, the question arises as to whether denialism still has any impact on AIDS policy. The answer must be that it does. First, it must be a contributory factor to the high levels of public scepticism about the sincerity and degree of commitment of the DoH to its policies, given the continuing stewardship of the Department by Minister Tshabalala-Msimang. Second, it offers in large part an explanation for the snail's pace at which the DoH has moved to implement the court-ordered roll-out of anti-retroviral therapy for prevention of MTCT in some provinces (especially Mpumalanga). Third, given the national shortage of skilled personnel, how else can one explain the many punitive measures directed at doctors and nurses who have pushed beyond the limits of official state policy in regard to HIVAIDS, and in particular its policy on anti-retroviral provision? The case of Dr Thuys Von Mollendorf stands out here. Disciplinary proceedings were instituted against him in 2002 for allowing an NGO providing anti-retrovirals to sexual assault survivors as post-exposure prophylaxis to operate within the premises of a large state hospital in Mpumalanga where he was superintendent (Landman et al. 2002).

Overall, the denialists have overly prolonged a national debate which has undoubtedly diverted government resources and the attention of government officials from the main policy tasks at hand: using the latest mainstream medical and scientific research to prevent new infections and provide the best standards of treatment and care for HIV-infected persons and AIDS orphans.

The TAC position

From its origins in 1998 as a campaign by HIV-positive AIDS activists for anti-retrovirals to be provided to prevent MTCT, the TAC has expanded into a broad-based nationwide civil society campaign which has lobbied for multinational pharmaceuticals to lower costs of anti-retrovirals and for government to roll out anti-retrovirals in the public sector for post-exposure prophylaxis in the case of sexual assault, prevention of MTCT and triple therapy.

According to its February 2003 submission to the Parliamentary Portfolio Committee on Health, the TAC has eight objectives. They are to:
- Campaign for affordable treatment for all people with HIV/AIDS.
- Campaign and support the prevention and elimination of all HIV infections.
- Promote and sponsor legislation to ensure equal access and equal treatment of all people with HIV/AIDS.
- Challenge by means of litigation, lobbying, advocacy and all forms of legitimate social mobilisation any type of discrimination relating to the treatment of AIDS in the public sector.
- Educate, promote and develop an understanding and commitment within communities of developments in HIV/AIDS treatment and care.

○ Campaign for affordable and quality access to health care for all people in South Africa.
○ Train and develop a representative and effective leadership of people living with HIV/AIDS in the basis of equality.
○ Campaign for an effective regional and global network comprising organisations with similar aims and objectives. (TAC 2003c: 1)

In action, the TAC has campaigned on two fronts. One has been directed at the pharmaceutical industry using patent monopolies to retain high profits on AIDS drugs, which inflates their price. The second has been directed at the Government to provide access to anti-retrovirals in the public sector. This latter fact has not prevented the TAC and Government from operating in harmony at times, as in the case of the TAC's support of the Government in its defence of the *Medicines Act* in 2000, against the Pharmaceutical Manufacturers' Association's (PMA) attempt to strike it down in a court case.

Over 40 multinational pharmaceutical companies took the South African government to court in 2001 to prevent the *Medicines Act* of 1997 becoming law. That particular piece of legislation was controversial as it allowed for the generic production of drugs and their parallel importation, and it would have forced pharmaceutical industry into more transparent pricing mechanisms, all of which would have reduced the price of pharmaceutical drugs in South Africa.

The TAC's support of the Government's defence of the Act took the form of it becoming a 'friend of the court' in the case. It also mobilised thousands to demonstrate against the drug companies' stance both in South Africa and overseas. The TAC also successfully built links with international civil society organisations such as the Health Gap Coalition, Oxfam and Doctors without Borders (*Medicins sans Frontiers*), which, in turn, lobbied and demonstrated around the issue in Europe and the US.

Within South Africa, large and frequent demonstrations increased the pressure on pharmaceutical companies. A march by over 500 staff and students from the University of Durban-Westville on the offices of Merck pharmaceuticals (one of the protagonists in the case) influenced the company to drop out of the case within 24 hours of the protest. In a televised public debate with Miryana Deeb, the representative of the Pharmaceutical Manufacturers Association, Zackie Achmat, the chairperson of the TAC, provided a devastating repudiation of Deeb's argument that the industry used significant proportions of the vast profits generated by patents for research and development. In large part due to this local and global public pressure, the court case was dropped in April 2001. It was also due to the fact that the negative publicity generated by the case was impacting negatively on the whole image of the pharmaceutical industry.

Mother to child transmission and AIDS denialism

With the PMA court case settled, the TAC turned its attention to the issue of MTCT and the need for cheaper anti-retrovirals. In government circles, however, articulations of AIDS denialism resurfaced with almost daily accounts of high-profile government officials pronouncing negatively on the affordability and efficacy of anti-retrovirals. On this score, the short-lived unity between the TAC and government dissipated. They once again became adversaries, facing off in the Pretoria High Court and then the Consitutional Court over the issue of a roll-out of anti-retrovirals to prevent MTCT. In July 2001, government opted for a pilot study in the public sphere on the use of Nevirapine for the prevention of MTCT by establishing two pilot sites in each province where the drug could be administered. At all other public sites, doctors and nurses were prohibited from prescribing the drug.

In its arguments in both courts for a public sector roll-out of Nevirapine, the TAC argued that the government was breaching the rights of mothers and newborns to healthcare and life by failing to provide the drug for prevention of MTCT (Annas 2003). By contrast, the Government argued that the infrastructural costs of providing the drug would be prohibitive, and that its safety had not been proven (Annas 2003). In its widely distributed fact sheets and pamphlets, the TAC also repeated the claim that Government had overestimated the cost of preventing MTCT, a claim based on research by economists based at the University of Cape Town. The TAC contended that a MTCT-prevention programme would cost R80 million per year as opposed to the R800 million lost per annum by failing to prevent babies from contracting HIV from their mothers: the Government could not afford *not* to roll out a MTCT prevention programme (TAC 2001; Nattrass cited in HEARD 2001).

The Constitutional Court found in favour of the TAC and the Government has begun, albeit reluctantly and unevenly, to comply with the court decision. Not least of all in its April 2002 Cabinet statement, the Government proceeded with the roll-out of Nevirapine for MTCT prevention. At the time of writing, the TAC was of the view that the roll-out of the programmes was proceeding well in most provinces, with the singular exception of Mpumalanga. It also expressed the view that Finance Minister Trevor Manual's 2003 budgetary provision for the MTCT roll-out was sufficient.

Triple therapy, Nedlac and civil disobedience

For the TAC, the last remaining area of AIDS policy contestation has become the provision of triple therapy in the public sector. There is little doubt that the challenge of providing triple therapy in the public sector is immense. Both Government and the TAC have acknowledged this. However, whereas Government has represented the infrastructural and budgetary challenges as insurmountable, the TAC has consistently argued that ways and means can be found to overcome these obstacles.

On the back of its success in the court challenge over MTCT, at a special congress in Durban in July 2002 the TAC discussed an extensive 'National Treatment and Prevention Plan.' The plan contained several key points including expansion of voluntary counselling and testing, including education on safer sex; expanded condom distribution; the expansion of MTCT prevention; improvements in management of sexually-transmitted infections; and most crucially, access to HAART (triple therapy). According to research commissioned by the TAC from actuarial scientists at the University of Cape Town, the plan could:

o Reduce by nearly three million the number of HIV-related deaths between 2002–2015.
o Halve the number of children that will otherwise be orphaned by the HIV epidemic by 2015.
o Produce an average life expectancy in South Africa of approximately 50 years of age as opposed to 40 years in the absence of such interventions. (TAC 2003c: 11–13)

By contrast, the Government argues that it would cost R7 billion per annum to provide triple therapy to one million HIV-positive individuals and that the healthcare system will need to be drastically overhauled in order to provide the drugs. The TAC's view is that in the first year of implementation at current generic prices, triple therapy would cost less than R500 million, rising to R7 billion in the fifth year, and peaking at R20 billion in 2015 (TAC 2003c).

Armed with this plan, the TAC decided to negotiate with business, labour and government through Nedlac. It has been a slow and bumpy process. In September 2002, the Nedlac management committee responded to TAC and Cosatu's request for Nedlac to be used as a forum to negotiate for a national treatment plan by establishing an HIV/AIDS task team. By late November, the various sectors had developed a 'framework agreement'. Government's withdrawal from the Nedlac agreement, coupled with the Health Minister's recent championing of AIDS denialist Robert Giraldo's claims that AIDS can only be treated with nutrional supplements such as garlic, olive oil and sweet potato, fanned the flames of the TAC's discontent (*The Mercury* 20.01.03).

At the time of writing, the TAC has launched a campaign of civil disobedience in support of the agreement. At the 2003 opening of Parliament, over 10 000 demonstrators marched on parliament in support of the campaign. This, along with the Nelson Mandela Foundation/HSRC finding that 95 per cent of respondents agreed that anti-retroviral therapy should be provided in the public sector, has added grist to the mill of the TAC's stance. It suggests that the government's delay of a roll-out of triple therapy runs counter to the tide of public opinion (Shisana et al 2002). With an election looming in 2004 this is something the vote-conscious ANC government cannot afford to ignore

Conclusion

The development of a national AIDS treatment policy has been a long and tortuous process. Denialism has deep roots in the upper echelons of the current ANC government and even though it may now be on the wane, it has since its high point in 2000–01, in some vital respects paralysed post-apartheid AIDS policy with lethal consequences for HIV-positive South Africans. It has also revealed disturbing indications of an authoritarian tendency in the government. This has been reflected in its unwillingness to defer to accepted scientific expertise, its foot-dragging in regard to implementation of court rulings, and its reluctance to engage in a serious policy dialogue with civil society.

It has above all, in my view, led to a serious lessening of the moral authority of the post-apartheid state. Unless the government finally repudiates AIDS denialism and rolls out anti-retroviral triple therapy in the public health sector, it is likely that Mbeki's denialism will eradicate from historical memory many of the positive aspects of his tenure in office.

Notes

1   Mbeki publicly distanced himself dramatically from this viewpoint in April 2002. This still does not reduce it as a policy influencing, historically interesting phenomenon. About the term itself: Mbeki's 'denialism' is a neologism that has been coined by AIDS activists in South Africa. To use the more neutral term 'scepticism' would tend to imply that it is a fruitful philosophical endeavour in the western philosophical tradition. On the other hand, Mbeki and his followers have denied the scientific facts. The reason why I am using the more loaded term 'denialism' is to indicate my own disagreement with this viewpoint. It is also to indicate that his denial is made up of a complex set of political and philosophical beliefs, which can be placed in a historical context: in a true sense it is a new ideological '-ism' in South Africa.

2   I saw one such pamphlet in the Campus Clinic at University of Natal, Durban in 2001.

3   It has been claimed that the author of this document is Mbeki himself. However, in the absence of a claim of authorship by Mbeki it is better to work on the assumption that Mokaba wrote the document, as he claimed (*Mail & Guardian* 14.06.02; *Cape Times* 02.04.02).

References

Abdool Karim, Q, Abdool Karim, S, Soldan, K & Zondi, M (1995) Reducing the risk of HIV infection among South African sex workers: Socio-economic and gender barriers, *American Journal of Public Health* 85 (11): 1512–1525.

African National Congress (1994) *A national health plan for South Africa*. Johannesburg: ANC.

African National Congress (2001) HIV/AIDS in South Africa: Challenges, obstacles and responses, *ANC Today Briefing Document 30.11.01*. Available at www.anc.org.za/anc-docs/anctoday/2001/at04.htm.

Annas, GJ (2003) The right to health and the Nevirapine case in South Africa, *New England Journal of Medicine* 348: 750–754.

Barnett, T & Whiteside, A (2002) *AIDS in the twenty-first century: Disease and globalisation*. London & New York: Palgrave.

Chirimuuta, R & Chirimuuta, R (1989) *AIDS, Africa and racism*. London: Free Association Books.

DoH (Department of Health) (2000) *2000–2005 HIV/AIDS/STD Strategic Plan for South Africa*. Pretoria: Department of Health. Available at www.doh.gov.za.

DoH (2001) *National HIV and Syphilis Sero-Prevalence Survey in South Africa*. Pretoria: DoH. Available at: www.doh.gov.za.

Dorrington, R & Johnson, L (2002) Impacts epidemiological and demographic, in J Gow & C Desmond (eds.) *Impacts and interventions: The HIV/AIDS epidemic and the children of South Africa*. Pietermaritzburg: University of Natal Press and UNICEF.

Garrett, L (1994) *The coming plague: Newly emerging diseases in a world out of balance.* Harmondsworth: Penguin.

Gillman, SL (1985) *Difference and pathology: Stereotypes of sexuality, race and madness.* Ithaca & London: Cornell University Press.

Gow, J, Desmond, C & Ewing, D (2002) Children and HIV/AIDS, in J Gow & C Desmond (eds.) *Impacts and Interventions: The HIV/AIDS epidemic and the children of South Africa.* Pietermaritzburg: University of Natal Press and UNICEF.

Goyer, KC (2003) *HIV/AIDS in prisons: Problems, policies and potential.* Institute for Security Studies Monograph 79. Pretoria: ISS.

HEARD (Health Economics & HIV/AIDS Research Division) (2001) *The cost of HIV/AIDS care in South Africa: A literature review.* Durban: HEARD, University of Natal.

Landman, W, Schuklenk, U, Cleaton Jones, P, van Niekerk, A, Benatar, S, Chetty, A, Naude, P, Ngwena, C, Dhai, A, Moodley, J, Howarth, G & Jenkins, T (2001) Statement by academics on sacking of Dr Thys von Mollendorf, *TAC e-newsletter* 18.03.02.

Leclerc Madlala, S (1996) *Demonising women in the era of AIDS: An analysis of the gendered construction of HIV/AIDS in KwaZulu-Natal.* PhD thesis, Anthopology Department, University of Natal, Durban.

Lecerc Madlala, S (2002) On the virgin-cleansing myth: Gendered bodies, AIDS and ethno-medicine, *African Journal of AIDS Research* 1: 87–95.

Mbali, M (2001) *A long illness: Towards history of NGO, government and medical discourse around AIDS policy-making in South Africa.* Honours dissertation, Historical Studies Department, University of Natal, Durban. Available at www.nu.ac.za/ccs.

Mbali, M (2002) 'One step forward two steps back': The AIDS policy impasse and HIV treatment in South Africa, *Journal of the KwaZulu-Natal Institute for Architecture* 2: 3.

Mbeki, T (2000) Speech of the President of South Africa at the Opening Session of the 13th International AIDSA Conference, Durban.

Mokaba, P (2002) *Castro Hlongwane, caravans, cats, geese, foot & mouth and statistics: HIV/AIDS and the struggle for the humanisation of the African.* Available at www.mg.co.za/mokabadoc/.

Nzo, A (1981) Address by Alfred Nzo, Secretary General of the African National Congress read at the International Conference on Health and Apartheid at Brazzaville, in S Marks & N Andresson (eds.) *Apartheid and Health.* Geneva: World Health Organization.

Price, M & van den Heever, A (1995) *Strategic health policy issues for the Reconstruction and Development Programme.* Johannesburg: Development Bank of Southern Africa.

Schneider, H (1998) The politics behind AIDS: The case of South Africa, in R Rosenbrock (ed.) *Politics behind AIDS policies: Case studies from India, Russia and South Africa.* Berlin: Wissenschaftszentrum Berlin fur Sozialforschung.

Schneider, H (2001) *The AIDS impasse in South Africa as a struggle for symbolic power.* Presented at the AIDS in Context History Workshop 04–07.04.01. Johannesburg: Centre for Health Policy, University of Witwatersrand.

Schneider, H & Stein, J (2001) Implementing AIDS policy in post-apartheid South Africa, *Social Science and Medicine* 52: 723–731.

Schüklenk, U (2002) Professional responsibilities of biomedical scientists in public discourse. Unpublished.

Shisana, O et al. (2002) *Nelson Mandela/HSRC study of HIV/AIDS: South African national HIV prevalence, behavioural risks and mass media household survey 2002: Executive Summary.* Pretoria: HSRC/Nelson Mandela Foundation.

South African Cabinet (2002) *Statement of Cabinet on HIV/AIDS, April 17th 2002.* Pretoria: Government Communications (GCIS).

Streak, J (2002) Mitigating the impacts with a focus on government responses, in J Gow & C Desmond (eds.) *Impacts and interventions: The HIV/AIDS epidemic and the children of South Africa.* Pietermaritzburg: University of Natal Press and UNICEF.

Strebel, A (1992) 'There's absolutely nothing I can do just believe in God': South Africa women with AIDS, *Agenda: A Journal About Women and Gender* 12: 50–62.

TAC (Treatment Action Campaign) (2001) *Mother to Child Transmission Prevention (MTCTP)* . Pamphlet: Durban: KwaZulu-Natal Provincial Office, TAC.

TAC (2002) Support legal action against GlaxoSmith Kline and Boehringer Ingelheim. Poster, available at www.tac.org.za.

TAC (2003a) *We can save millions of lives! Let us work together for an HIV/AIDS treatment plan!* Pamphlet. Durban: KwaZulu-Natal Provincial Office, TAC.

TAC (2003b) *TAC response to Budget.* TAC News Service news @tac. org.

Treatment Action Campaign (2003c) *Putting the record straight – what really happened at Nedlac.* Submission to Parliament. TAC News Service news@tac.org.

Tshabalala-Msimang, ME (2002a) *Lend a hand in the campaign of hope against HIV/AIDS!: An update on Cabinet's statement of 17 April 2002 on fighting HIV/AIDS.* Pretoria: DoH. Available at www.doh.gov.za/ediaroom/index.html.

Tshabalala-Msimang, ME (2002b) *Address by the Minister of Health, Dr ME Tshabalala-Msimang on the 2002 World AIDS Day.* Pretoria: DoH. Available at www.doh.gov.za/ediaroom/index.html.

Vaughan, M (1991) *Curing their ills: Colonial power and African illness.* Cambridge & Oxford: Polity Press.

Whiteside, A & Sunter, C (2000) *AIDS: The challenge for South Africa.* Cape Town: Human and Rousseau Tafelberg.

The land question in contemporary South Africa

Michael Aliber and Reuben Mokoena

Introduction

Historically, land has been a source of conflict and contention in South Africa. Colonial and apartheid policies dispossessed millions of black South Africans of their land and moved them into overcrowded and impoverished reserves, homelands and townships. It has been estimated that 3,5 million people were forcibly removed from their land between 1960 and 1982 alone (SPP 1983). These racially-based land policies were a cause of landlessness, insecurity, poverty and great hurt amongst black people, and also resulted in inefficient urban and rural land use patterns and a fragmented system of land administration. On the eve of the 1994 elections, whites controlled about 84 per cent of non-public land, while blacks controlled only about 16 per cent, predominantly in the 'homelands' and 'coloured reserves'. [1]

Not surprisingly, land reform was held to be part and parcel of the transformation process ushered in by the new democratic dispensation. As made clear in the 1993 framework document for the ANC's Reconstruction and Development Programme (ANC 1994) and in the ANC's 1994 election manifesto, land reform encompassed both economic and social objectives, and both of these in turn were important in and of themselves as well as being part of the overall process of historical redress. The RDP framework document therefore spelled out the main elements of that land reform. These elements, which were later provided for in the Constitution, are and remain:

- Land redistribution, through which citizens can apply for grants with which to purchase land for farming and/or settlement.
- Land restitution, involving the restoration of land or cash compensation to victims of forced removals.
- Tenure reform, which seeks to improve the clarity and robustness of tenure rights, mainly for residents of former homeland areas.

The RDP framework document furthermore asserted that within five years 30 per cent of the land would have been redistributed through redistribution and restitution. The target date was therefore 1999 and as the record shows, was not even remotely attained.

Since 1994, only around 1,5 to two per cent of the land has been reallocated to Africans and coloureds through redistribution and restitution. Of the almost 80 000 validated restitution claims received by the Commission on the Restitution of Land Rights, 36 488 have been settled (Didiza 2003), but these have been disproportionately urban claims settled through cash compensation (Walker 2003), whereas many of the large, complex rural land claims remain unresolved. Success with redistribution has been even more limited, not only in terms of the number of people helped or amount of land involved, but in the quality and nature of redistribution projects through which land is accessed. Tenure reform has largely entailed a slow, halting process of legislative reform, with the key piece of draft legislation, the *Communal Land Rights Bill*, finally on the verge of being presented to Cabinet after hanging in the balance for the past four years.

The purpose of this chapter is to offer a critical perspective on the government's record on land reform since 1994, and point to the chief challenges that remain unresolved.

Land redistribution

The Department of Land Affairs' (DLA) land redistribution programme is now in its second phase. The first phase, which lasted from 1994 to early 2000, ceased soon after Thoko Didiza took over from Derek Hanekom as Minister of Agriculture and Land Affairs. What Hanekom was trying to do in terms of redistribution, whether and why it was unsuccessful, and whether Didiza's approach represents a change in the right direction, remain highly contentious issues.

In late 1994 and early 1995, the DLA initiated its redistribution programme with a number of pilot projects spread throughout the country. Notwithstanding the difficulties experienced by a number of these projects – not least that some of them were pervaded by a strong 'restitution ethos' that could not be easily accommodated through the redistribution process – the pilots formed the basis for the redistribution programme that was to follow. The main elements of the programme were that:

○   Households could apply for grants, up to a maximum of R15 000 per household, to be used for land acquisition and land development.
○   Households could form groups and apply for grants collectively.
○   Beneficiary groups could purchase and own land together, usually in terms of a legal entity called a communal property association.[2]
○   Land acquisition was through the open market, i.e. the 'willing-buyer/willing-seller approach'.

The grant, known as the Settlement and Land Acquisition Grant (or SLAG), was linked to the housing grant, both in that the maximum amount was the same as for the housing grant, and in the sense that a given household could not access both grants in full measure, though it could in principle access a certain amount from each totalling not more than R15 000. The enabling legislation for the SLAG was the *Provision of Land and Assistance Act* (No. 126 of 1993), which provides for the making of financial grants for settlement and production purposes in order to assist historically disadvantaged people. The SLAG was complemented by a planning grant to be used to engage the services of facilitators and/or consultants to conduct feasibility studies, prepare business plans, conduct valuations, and meet certain transfer costs.

The numerical delivery record of redistribution in this first 'SLAG phase' is shown in Table 15.1. What is striking is, first, the rapid upswing over the first four years, corresponding to the DLA's increase in staff capacity and refinement of delivery procedures; and second, the downturn in the last two years, owing to the moratorium placed on new redistribution projects by then newly-appointed Minister Didiza in 1999 pending her review of the programme. Even in the absence of the moratorium, however, and assuming the DLA had been able to maintain the pace of delivery it attained in 1998/99, it would still have taken over a hundred years to attain the 30 per cent target stated in the RDP framework document. Instead, the total hectarage transferred through the SLAG-based projects was less than one per cent of the total commercial farmland in the country.

The qualitative record of delivery is more difficult to summarise. There was and is a widely-shared view, both inside and outside of the DLA, that the SLAG-based redistribution projects tended to be highly problematic. Some critiques could be heard across the board: the beneficiary groups were too large; they could not manage complex agricultural enterprises; there was inadequate post-transfer support. Other critiques were more typical of the 'commercial farmer lobby', within which one must include the University of

Pretoria and, for the most part, the National African Farmers Union: the level of financial support from Government was insufficient; only applicants with agricultural skills should be assisted, and/or there had to be more emphasis on pre-transfer training. And still other critiques were distinct to – and perhaps symbolic of – the 'left', eg. the land rights NGOs and left-leaning academics: the willing-buyer/willing-seller approach to redistribution was paralysing delivery, and beneficiaries ended up on marginal land.

Table 15.1 *SLAG-based land redistribution projects, 1994–2000*

Year	Number of projects	Number of households	Redistributed hectares
1994/95	3	394	4 984
1995/96	16	3 223	23 200
1996/97	41	4 809	91 319
1997/98	140	22 354	148 161
1998/99	121	25 674	196 734
1999/00	120	17 538	181 668
2000/01	72	12 946	86 828
Total	513	86 938	732 894

Source: DLA (2000).

While most of the critiques had some degree of validity, there was a curious lack of convincing evaluation informing them. The DLA itself commissioned only one rigorous evaluation of redistribution in the first five years, and this report was largely ignored.[3] Policy makers and observers at large tended to subscribe to what very quickly congealed into the conventional wisdom, namely, that the small size of the grant forced people into large groups to be able to purchase farms, and these large groups proved unmanageable.[4] (The conventional wisdom on the left is that this was all the more so because government was shelling out too much for the land, which in any event was not held legitimately.)

Although this view, even in its amended form, is not without merit, we offer a different perspective on what went wrong during the first phase of redistribution by looking at the elements of typical redistribution projects during that time. By 'typical projects' we mean those that had become the norm by 1996–1997. Although more impressionistic than objective, we maintain that there was a rapid convergence of projects around the following three characteristics. First, project business plans commonly assumed that the goal of a project was to provide the maximum cash income to each of its members, if not a full 'job-equivalent income' to each of them. Second, the usual strategy for seeking to accomplish this was to promote the idea that the group should continue with the farm activity that was undertaken by the previous owner. Often this was embellished with new activities that promised to add even more income (or, more accurately, to compensate for the fact that the existing farm enterprise was insufficient to support all the beneficiaries), for example, broileries, piggeries, 'knitting groups', and so on. And third, the implication was that the group would run the farm as a group. To compensate for the group's lack of management and/or farming experience, the plan often called for the group to hire a manager, perhaps on a temporary basis.

Projects formulated along these lines – and many if not most fit this description – struggled and limped along, and largely failed relative to the ambitions stated in their business plans. The ensuing failure was seen as presenting a picture perfectly in keeping with the conventional wisdom. We feel, however, that an alternative interpretation needs to be considered. Our view is that the fundamental error was not inadequate resources, but rather the assumption (pretence?) that land could substitute for jobs on any significant scale. Oddly, despite some early, well-meant rhetoric recognising the multi-faceted value of land redistribution, eg. in enhancing rural livelihoods and the psychic benefits of secure tenure,[5] there was at Land Affairs a mounting sense of worry that land reform might actually aggravate poverty unless one could ensure significant cash incomes from farming. Into this breach were invited legions of consultants to assist applicant groups prepare their business plans and applications. Many of these assumed the role of assuaging the fears of government officials (and thus getting their projects approved with relative ease) by offering rosy cash-flow projections that commonly even the consultants did not believe.[6] One rather curious consequence of the emphasis on profit maximisation was that many business plans called for projects to make scarce use of the one factor of which most SLAG beneficiaries had a copious supply, namely their own labour. The majority of beneficiaries were thus superfluous right from the outset. Since the project plan called for only a few people to be actively involved on a full-time basis, the rest were 'passive shareholders'.

The argument here is that the typical redistribution project was based on the wrong assumptions in pursuit of the wrong goal. Had there been less exaggerated expectations, perhaps a great deal more would have been achieved. Because of the almost universal assumption of group production, there was generally no consideration of tenure options other than group ownership. A few notable exceptions were undertaken in the southern Cape, where formal subdivision was undertaken and each beneficiary household ended up owning a small plot in terms of freehold. These exceptions proved the rule – perhaps because it was so expensive to undertake subdivision, in effect absorbing a large share of the grant, it was rarely considered. Initiatives to reduce subdivision costs or investigate forms of virtual/informal subdivision were pursued with little vigour, if at all.

In early 2000, phase one ended and the present phase began. Cancelling the moratorium on new redistribution projects in August 2001, Minister Didiza unveiled the new redistribution flagship initiative, 'Land Redistribution for Agricultural Development', or LRAD. LRAD was largely inspired by staff of the World Bank, drawing on their recent experiences in Brazil and Columbia, and then adapted by officials of the National Department of Agriculture and consultants from academia.

One of the primary differences from the old programme is that the LRAD grant is available in a range from R20 000 up to R100 000 per adult individual, depending on an own contribution which rises disproportionately according to the grant level (that is, from R5 000 to R400 000). Despite Didiza's occasional public broadsides against white commercial farmers for either impeding or exploiting the redistribution programme, and rumblings about making greater use of expropriation in the future, the new programme is decidedly market-friendly, fully embracing the willing-buyer/willing-seller approach that was adopted in 1994. Organised agriculture is more vocally supportive of the new programme than of the old, mostly because it has sympathy with its dominant focus – to provide opportunities for blacks to farm on a commercial scale – but also because it addresses white farmers' fears of having groups of blacks moving in next to them as opposed to individuals.

One thing is for certain: the larger size of the grant has facilitated project delivery, most especially land purchase. Between August 2001 and December 2002, 624 LRAD projects have been approved, and about 11 000 people have been awarded LRAD grants with which they will be able to acquire some

250 000 hectares of land (about 0,3 per cent of all commercial farmland) (DLA 2003a). However, based on discussions with numerous officials working on LRAD, an order-of-magnitude estimate is that the average grant per beneficiary is R35 000, and that there are five beneficiary members belonging to the same household/family.[7] This implies a total grant captured by the same household of R175 000, effectively more than ten times the old SLAG. This, in turn, implies that, under its present capital budget, Land Affairs can only afford to assist 1 600 to 2 500 different households a year, a figure that remains tiny even if one quadruples it. This is an example of what we might call 'arithmetic failure' – the inability to see that the present scale of redistribution is not remotely commensurate with the size of the rural economic problem, eg. landlessness in the neighbourhood of 675 000 households, and rural unemployment experienced by 3,2 million Africans and coloureds.[8]

Research by the HSRC reveals that there are two main types of projects under LRAD: family-farm projects, which typically involve local elites who see LRAD as an opportunity to diversify their interests to complement their existing business activities (taxi owners, bottle store owners, etc.); and farm-worker projects, wherein a group of farm workers use LRAD to acquire the farm where they have been working, often at the impetus of the seller (HSRC 2003). The former have a good chance of succeeding as farms, but one must question what is truly being accomplished. The latter are in many respects very much like the old SLAG-based projects, and it is likely only a matter of time before we start to observe the familiar problems with group-based farming. Moreover, the old SLAG-based programme and LRAD share another flaw, namely, that they are fundamentally ill-suited to decongesting the former homelands, which is where the bulk of poor and effectively landless households still reside.[9]

Given that LRAD is still relatively new, and given the sense among DLA officials that for the first time in years redistribution is going well (not least in terms of being able to spend the budget), it is hard to imagine that the DLA will soon be open to a searching re-examination of its approach to redistribution. However, there is a real possibility that as LRAD makes more and more progress in terms of its own goals, its overall inadequacy will become more obvious, especially the fact that its overall impact is nearly imperceptible. Its inadequacy in this respect is already drawing fire from the most vocal grassroots constituency, namely the Landless People's Movement (LPM). Modelling itself on Brazil's influential Landless Workers' Movement, and drawing inspiration from Zimbabwe's 'fast track' land reform, the LPM's motto is 'Landlessness = Racism. End Racism! Give Us Our Land Now!' The LPM has two main messages: that land reform is imperative for redressing past injustices, and that land reform should benefit the poor masses rather than the fortunate few. Clearly LRAD is out of sync with these views. The question is, what constituency is LRAD trying to please?

Land restitution

The goal of restitution is to restore land and, where this is not practicable, provide other remedies to people who have been dispossessed of land due to racially discriminatory legislation. The *Restitution of Land Rights Act* of 1994 provides for the restitution of rights in land to persons or communities dispossessed of such rights after 19 June 1913 as a result of past racially discriminatory laws or practices. According to the overriding principles of fairness and equity, each restitution claim must be treated on its merits. In the case of a valid restitution claim, the claimant has the constitutional right to participate in the formulation of a restitution package specific to that claim.

In order to give effect to these principles, the Act established two institutions, the Commission on the Restitution of Land Rights and the Land Claims Court. Apart from the Chief Land Claims Commissioner, the Commission consists of six Regional Land Claims Commissioners responsible for overseeing the overall restitution process in the various regions, i.e. KwaZulu-Natal, Western Cape, Eastern Cape, Free State and Northern Cape, Gauteng and North West, and Mpumalanga and Limpopo. The Land Claims Court was constituted in 1996, and has since been reconfigured as a special division of the High Court.

Some 63 455 restitution claims had been lodged with the Commission as of the 31 December 1998 cut-off date. The validation process, which was effectively completed in early 2003, has led to the recognition that many of the claim forms submitted in fact represented more than one claim, thus excluding 439 claims that have been dismissed as invalid or duplicates, the total number of claims received is 79 687. Of these, approximately three-quarters are claims for urban property, however, whereas an urban claim tends to be for a single household, rural claims typically encompass groups of households, sometimes even whole communities.

The process of settling claims is similar in both instances. First, a preliminary investigation is undertaken to 'validate' that a dispossession has indeed taken place and, where necessary, to 'verify' the link between the claimants and those who were dispossessed (i.e. where the claimants are the descendants of the latter). Second, the existence of the claim is formally made public through being gazetted and all directly affected parties are informed. Third, the claim is subjected to a more thorough investigation, following which the claim is settled through negotiation, or failing that, through the Land Claims Court. If the success of the claim calls for land to be restored, land development and settlement support are provided. The DLA carries the cost of buying out the land. Expropriation has in no case been used to settle restitution claims, though it is provided for under the Constitution and could, in principle, be used, subject to compensation to the expropriatee as prescribed by the so-called 'property clause', i.e. section 25(3).

The pace at which claims are settled has increased significantly since the first few years. In part, this relates to the fact that the full process of settling a claim may take well over a year, thus many of the claims being finalised now are those on which the Commission started working in the mid- and late-1990s. However, policy changes along the way have also made a difference. A ministerial review under Derek Hanekom identified several areas where the process could be expedited and improved, the most significant change being a shift from a court-driven approach to more administrative process. The policy of seeking to apply a 'standard settlement offer', i.e. a cash settlement based on rudimentary information about the property that was dispossessed, has sped up the pace at which urban claims are settled in particular, which is not to say that all urban claims are settled in this manner.

Of the 36 488 claims that had been settled as of April 2003, almost 80 per cent were urban (Walker 2003), and the majority of these involved cash compensation rather than restoration of property. These settled claims have to date encompassed fewer than 90 000 households, which suggests that the claims that remain to be settled are the larger and generally more complex ones. Indeed, a concern that has been raised about restitution is that Government is opting more and more for cash compensation, in some instances even for rural claims, as an easier way out.[10] No one doubts that the actual restoration of land is an extremely complex undertaking, but whether sufficient human resources are being devoted to it is an open question. On the other side of the coin, a major concern raised regarding the restoration of rural land is the economic and social viability of relocated communities, not least because of the challenges of co-ordinating delivery from diverse government structures to ensure access to services and amenities to what in the present day are often remote settlements. Some of the earlier, large rural restitution projects, eg. Riemvasmaak in the Northern Cape, have become emblematic of the hardships sometimes caused by good intentions, as well as of the serious internal squabbles that can impede larger groups from moving forward despite these challenges.

Notwithstanding these concerns, government's restitution programme is arguably the most successful part of the broader land reform initiative. Having said that, restitution as an idea or a value extends well beyond the restitution programme, a significant point that is often lost. Recalling the RDP's 30 per cent target, it is notable that the restitution programme *per se* has the potential to only account for less than one-third of this.[11] Thus, although on the face of it the restitution programme is different from the redistribution programme by virtue of its unambiguous focus on redressing past injustices, and by contrast redistribution would appear to be more of a purely economic proposition, in fact the greater share of the task of redressing past injustices must fall to redistribution.

The 30 per cent target is revealing in another way. Unlike the redress of *specific* injustices, as catered for through the restitution programme, the 30 per cent target bespeaks an intention to redress collective grievances owing to South Africa's long history of land dispossession. In fact, only redistribution can do this. Whereas restitution requires proof on a case-by-case basis, eligibility for redistribution requires only that one is a black South African.[12] Very likely, this element of redressing the collective injustice is what accounts for the persistence of the 30 per cent target in the public sphere, even though it was in the first place a purely arbitrary figure with no intrinsic significance. It very likely also accounts for the popular appeal among many black South Africans of Mugabe's 'fast-track land reform'.[13] And very likely as well for the rejection by the LPM, the PAC, and others, of the whole willing-buyer/willing-seller concept, which confers on white farmers generally the power to decide what land will and will not be made available to blacks. The implication is that the restitution programme may be relatively successful in relation to its specific objectives, but that the larger project of redressing past injustices falls outside its ambit. To the extent Government construes redistribution to be mainly about creating a cadre of economically successful black commercial farmers, as evidenced by the enormous increase in the size of grants for which people can apply, it is missing one of the main points about redistribution, even as it continues to cite the 30 per cent target which it is so ill-equipped to achieve.

Land tenure reform and land rights

Until the 1990s, it was the government's policy that black people should not own land or have land registered in their own names. Black people were relegated to occupy land in townships, homelands, and coloured reserves. Land occupation in the homelands in particular was mainly in terms of temporary permits to land that was held in trust by the government for residents' use, frequently under a fragmented and chaotic system of land administration. Tenure reform is therefore about improving the terms and conditions through which people hold, use, occupy and access land. Tenure reform as such is complemented by specific measures to address the insecure land rights of blacks living in rural 'white South Africa', in particular labour tenants and others whose homes are on commercial farms.

The focus of Government's work on tenure reform and land rights since the early 1990s has been on introducing legislation to protect those with insecure land rights, notably through the *Land Titles Adjustment Act* of 1993; the *Interim Protection of Informal Land Rights Act* of 1996 (IPILRA); *Land Reform (Labour Tenants) Act* of 1996; and the *Extension of Security of Tenure Act* of 1997. The major challenge has, however, remained unresolved, namely, whether and how to reconfigure tenure in the former homeland areas. Since the mid-1990s, work has been underway to draft a further, much more ambitious and important piece of legislation – previously known as the *Land Rights Bill*, and now the *Communal Land Rights Bill* – but the process has been slow and halting. The reason is that, although there is unanimity that the tenure situation in the former homelands remains highly problematic, there is no consensus as to what tenure in former homelands should look like, and just as little agreement as to how any new tenure regime should be put into practice.

The core issue has been the complex question of ownership. When work on the *Land Rights Bill* began in the mid-1990s, many in South Africa perceived the goal of tenure reform to be the correction of the inferior tenure status of Africans in the former homelands through the expansion of ownership as it had historically been available to whites – i.e. individual, freehold ownership. Making ownership available to those to whom it had traditionally been denied was therefore, in part, motivated by redressing the historical injustices created by separate development. For a while, the vision of those contemplating the new tenure legislation coincided happily with a largely separate lobby, namely, those who felt that private ownership was a necessary ingredient to agricultural development in the former homelands. According to this view, 'communal tenure' was both undevelopmental and largely responsible for the environmental degradation observed in former homeland areas, never mind the extreme population densities there caused by separate development. The deficits of communal tenure were, for example, cited in the 1995 submission of the National Department of Agriculture to the then separate Ministry of Land Affairs, which argued that only private, individual ownership provided the right conditions to inspire investment and higher productivity.[14]

What appeared to be an emerging consensus, however, fell apart. Those whose concern was especially with rights (as opposed to productivity), came to appreciate the uncertainties associated with rapid, radical tenure change, and in particular, the danger of introducing forces in former homeland areas that would benefit some people at the cost of further marginalising others. Under the guidance of a specially appointed task team to investigate the development of a new *Land Rights Bill*, a gradual shift took place. Most significant in this process was the active attention to other examples from Africa: at the one end of the spectrum, the example of Kenya, with its tenuous gains – in terms of security, equity, and productivity – earned from the continent's most ambitious and sweeping attempt to replace customary tenure with a statutory tenure system based on individualised ownership; and at the other extreme, Botswana, which became a beacon of innovation and good sense by devising a gradualist approach to redefining tenure rights, in which a modern land administration infrastructure was created that explicitly took heed of indigenous tenure institutions.

To the authors of the *Land Rights Bill*, it seemed South Africa could learn a great deal from Africa. The near-final version of the Bill produced by late 1999 revealed an attempt to balance the need to allow gradual, self-determined change on the one hand, and a practicable institutional framework to facilitate that change, on the other. However, the draft Bill was not without its detractors, and foremost among these were traditional leaders who perceived the Bill to be usurping their powers in respect of land. Upon taking over the land portfolio, Minister Didiza shelved the draft Bill. After a long lapse, work on it resumed, at one stage ceding to the wishes of traditional leaders almost entirely, but later coming back to resemble the original Bill, albeit with major differences. What is now called the *Communal Land Rights Bill* will likely be presented to Cabinet in 2003, but enactment of this legislation is so overdue that it is difficult to predict what will happen. The fact that the present draft still attracts a fair amount of criticism from all quarters may be one indication that it is approximately aimed in the right direction. Among those who lament the failure to pass the pre-Didiza draft, the main concern is that the administrative system provided for under the current draft appears weak. It may be that whether or not the draft *Communal Land Rights Bill* is enacted any time soon, tenure reform, which potentially has an impact on far more lives than either redistribution or restitution, will remain the most unfulfilled aspect of land reform.

Conclusion

Beyond the details around the specific land reform initiatives, there is an abiding puzzle about land reform in South Africa. On the one hand, the media is flooded with shrill warnings that unless land reform is sped up in South Africa, the same violent land grab that passes for land reform in Zimbabwe could start to happen here.[15] The ANC meanwhile has chosen to collude with Zanu-PF in propelling the fiction that land reform in Zimbabwe is a national priority, even though, in the months just prior to the invasion there, an Afrobarometer survey showed that only 1,1 per cent of Zimbabwean respondents listed land among the top three problems with which the government should concern itself.[16] On the other hand, land reform is clearly not a priority for either the South African government or for the average South African. Altogether less than one per cent of the government budget goes to land reform, far less than goes to, say, agriculture or water infrastructure. According to the same Afrobarometer survey, land was listed among people's top three concerns for only 1,3 per cent of South African respondents.

Perhaps the gulf in perceptions about the importance of land reform owes to the fact that there is no national consensus as to whether and why it is worth pursuing. The negative motivation of ensuring that South Africa 'does not go the way of Zimbabwe' appears to be much more of concern in the media and some particular lobby groups than for the government as a whole, and this is right: notwithstanding the nature of South Africa's land hunger – about which we know very little – South Africa's leadership is generally responsible rather than opportunistic, and the likelihood of state-sponsored land grabbing is remote. However, even if the land question in South Africa does not exactly represent a ticking time-bomb, it does remain problematic. Above and beyond the specific concerns about South Africa's land reform raised above, the most critical problem at present is the same one that obtained in 1994, namely lack of a clear vision about what land reform can and should achieve, both by way of redressing past wrongs and of promoting economic empowerment. Or perhaps the biggest problem is in imagining we have answered this question when in fact we have not.

Notes

1   Non-public land excludes land designated for 'public use', such as national parks, road reserves and military bases. Prior to 1994, the black-white dichotomy in land owner-ship was typically described as 87 per cent versus 13 per cent, where all public land was included as part of 'white land', presumably on the grounds that it fell under the con-trol of the minority white government. The so-called 'homelands', or 'African reserves', were created with the *Natives Land Act* of 1913, which, along with prohibiting Africans from buying land in areas designated for white farmers also forbade them from share-cropping. The 23 so-called 'coloured reserves', which were and are much less populous than the homelands, have a more diverse history, including those that started as mis-sion stations created to give refuge to Khoi-Khoi peoples forced out of the southern Cape by colonial expansion. The former 'coloured reserves' are located largely in Northern Cape but also in Western Cape, Eastern Cape, and Free State.

2   These were provided for under new legislation that had been created with exactly this purpose in mind, namely the *Communal Property Association Act* of 1996 (No. 28 of 1996).

3   See May et al. (2000). Among the concluding comments: 'This report has shown that that there are projects that have managed to generate significant profits, as well as indi-vidual households that are successfully engaging in agricultural production … . The fact that the economically viable projects still constitute only a small share of the total, points to the fact that economic success is not the only objective currently pursued under the land reform programme. The analysis suggests that there would be many advantages from a policy decision on the relative importance of "livelihood" as com-pared to productive projects.'

4   This is the view expounded for example in the only review conducted under the aus-pices of the Ministry of Agriculture and Land Affairs following the appointment of Thoko Didiza as the new minister. The review, undertaken by one of the Minister's advisors, resulted in a memorandum entitled 'Preliminary Report on the Review of the Settlement/Land Acquisition Grant – Work in Progress' (1999).

5 'The purpose of the land redistribution programme is to provide the poor with access to land for residential and productive uses, in order to improve their income and quality of life. ... Although the scale of the proposed redistribution is not yet quantifiable, it must achieve the following outputs: a more equitable distribution of land and therefore contribute to national reconciliation and stability; substantially reduce land-related conflict in areas where land disputes are endemic; help solve the problem of landlessness and pave the way for an improvement in settlement conditions in urban and rural areas; enhance household income security, employment and economic growth throughout the country' (DLA 1997: 38).

6 An irony is duly acknowledged: the term does not necessarily exclude some of the authors of this chapter. However, another irony of note was more emblematic of the contradictions within redistribution, namely that a number of the consultants engaged to help plan redistribution projects were the same wretched firms that a generation or two earlier had been lucratively commissioned to design group-based commercial farming enterprises in the homelands, the failed legacy of which is largely still with us.

7 Since it is now adult individuals rather than households who pool their grants together, the DLA has no real basis for reporting the number of distinct 'beneficiary households', thus this must be inferred.

8 The number of landless households is calculated from Stats SA's 1997 *Rural Survey*, while the unemployment figure is calculated from Stats SA's February 2002 *Labour Force Survey*.

9 There are however some exceptions to this, for example, adjacent to former QwaQwa and former Transkei, where LRAD has enabled larger stockowners to purchase their own land outside the communal areas and relocate themselves and their stock there. In some cases, such stock owners are deliberately targeted by provincial DLA staff.

10 As of end of March 2003, the cumulative expenditure via the restitution programme on land acquisition was R442 million, versus R1,3 billion for cash compensation (DLA 2003b).

11 This is based on a rough extrapolation taking into account the amount of land restored thus far relative to the number of outstanding rural claims.

12 It used to require also that one was poor.

13 According to a 2001 survey of 3 700 individuals conducted by the Institute for Justice and Reconciliation, 85 per cent of black respondents agreed with the statement, 'Most land in South Africa was taken unfairly by white settlers, and they therefore have no right to the land today', while 68 per cent agreed that 'Land must be returned to blacks in South Africa, no matter what the consequences are for the current owners and for political stability in the country.'

14 'Tenure reform by promotion of individual ownership of land is of the utmost importance for the sustainable utilisation of agricultural resources' (Department of Agriculture 1995: 2). Ironically, several years after the NP had withdrawn from the GNU and the agriculture portfolio had passed over to the ANC, senior leadership in

the Department of Agriculture still espoused much the same view. As revealed by early drafts of the LRAD policy produced by the National Department of Agriculture and its consultants, LRAD would have been designed so as to enable individuals to access government grants with which to purchase land within the former homelands and make their private property. These proposals were subsequently dropped due to objections raised by those working on the new tenure legislation.

15 See for example, 'Zimbabwe crisis early warning for SA' (*The Star* April 2000); 'Grondkrisis kan oorspoel na res van Suider-Afrika' (*Die Burger* April 2000); 'We need to heed warning signs' (*The Star* April 2000) and 'Land reform: SA's white farmers better get cracking' (*The Star* September 2002); 'More money needed to avoid Zim-like land grab' (*The Daily Dispatch* September 2002).

16 See Mattes *et al.* (2000). The exact wording of the question was, 'What are the most important problems facing this country that the government should address?'

References

African National Congress (1994) *The Reconstruction and Development Programme: A Policy Framework*. Johannesburg: ANC.

Department of Agriculture (1995) *Official submission to 'the drafting team' of the 'land reform policy document' at the Ministry of Land Affairs*, 26 June.

DLA (Department of Land Affairs) (1997). *White Paper on South African Land Policy*. Pretoria.

DLA (2000). *Critical Project Database*. Electronic data.

DLA (2003a) *Statistics on LRAD projects*. Unpublished document, Monitoring and Evaluation Directorate. Pretoria.

DLA (2003b) *Settled Restitution Claims: National Statistics* (http://land.pwv.gov.za/restitution/updated%20stats.htm).

Didiza, T (2003) *Budget Speech Address by Minister for Agriculture and Land Affairs at the Budget Vote of the Department of Land Affairs*, 1 April.

HSRC (2003) *Evaluation of DLA's Programme 'Land Reform for Agricultural Development': Preliminary First-Year Findings*. Unpublished report.

Mattes, R, Davids, Y & Africa, C (2000) Views of democracy in South Africa and the region: Trends and comparisons, *Afrobarometer* Paper No. 8.

May, J, Roberts, B, Govender, J & Gayadeen, P (2000) *Monitoring and evaluating the quality of life of land reform beneficiaries, 1998/1999: Technical report prepared for the Department of Land Affairs*. Unpublished report.

Ministry of Agriculture and Land Affairs (1999) *Preliminary Report on the Review of the Settlement/Land Acquisition Grant – Work in Progress*. Unpublished report.

Ministry of Agriculture and Land Affairs (2001) *Land Redistribution for Agricultural Development: A sub-programme of the Land Redistribution Programme*. Pretoria.

Surplus Peoples Project (1983) *Forced removals in South Africa. The SPP Reports. Volume 1, General Overview.* Cape Town: Surplus People Project.

Walker, C (2003) *Urban restitution: Seminar on urban land challenges in South Africa.* Paper presented to the Department for International Development, Pretoria, 3 April.

Part IV: South Africa in Africa and the world

South Africa as an emerging middle power: 1994–2003

Maxi Schoeman

Introduction

Despite the existence of an anarchical international state system, there is a clear hierarchy of states with roles and functions being adopted by, or thrust upon states, depending on their position within this hierarchy.[1] Although the term 'international division of labour' has traditionally been used in international political economy to denote the global production structure, this term is also applicable to international politics. One of the characteristics of this division of labour is the emergence of middle powers in the developing world. South Africa is now often labeled an emerging power, apparently referring to its position as a regional leader and its position in the broader or global political system as a possible middle power. The term 'emerging regional power' is also used to describe South Africa, as well as countries such as Brazil and India. The concept 'middle power' is not new and has been applied to countries such as Canada, the Netherlands, the Scandinavian states and New Zealand for a long time. However, when applied to South Africa it is considered to be 'emerging' (it has not, therefore, reached the status yet), it is part of the developing world (explaining the use of 'emerging', to go with 'developing') and it would seem to have a role somewhat different from established, developed middle powers.

This chapter examines the term 'emerging middle power' (see van der Westhuizen 1998) and the ambiguities surrounding it, pointing to the differences between these countries and the developed middle powers. First, it is argued that the term 'emerging power' or 'emerging middle power' should be treated and applied in such a way that it draws a clear distinction between an emerging power as a middle power in the international arena, and an emerging power as a regional power. Second, this chapter provides an analysis of the extent to which South Africa, after nine years of multi-party democracy and transformation, can be classified as an 'emerging middle power', distinguishing between its role in the broad international system and its regional position. Although the emphasis in this chapter is on broad security issues, a number of other concerns that inform the country's foreign policy objectives and activities are also discussed.

Middle powers, emerging middle powers and muddled powers[2]

The term 'middle power' – without the word 'emerging' attached to it – does not necessarily have a geographical connotation, or one referring to a level of development. Traditional middle powers, as defined in the literature, would seem to exclude the regional position of a state aspiring to or enjoying the status of being a middle power. Another interpretation would be that a middle power is defined vis-à-vis the existence of a major power(s) and is therefore not seen as a major power writ small in its own region – the examples of Canada, the Netherlands, New Zealand and Sweden support this interpretation. Cox notes that middle powers had no 'special place in regional blocs' (1996: 245) during the Cold War era and Wight (1979) distinguishes between regional powers and middle powers, the former having a geographically more restricted range.

In this article, the term 'middle power' is used first, in reference to a position within the broad or universal state system, based on an assumption that there is some hierarchical order of states, no matter the theoretical notion of the idea of anarchy and the equality of all states (the latter as, for instance, in the UN Charter) (see Bull 1977; Klein 1974; Wight 1979).

Second, it refers to their size and rank which places them in an international division of labour in which they have the opportunity of exerting a type of moral influence on the international system, a role they accept and actively seek to play. Although their position or rank is determined by the structure of the international system, their role and functions are not. Structure gives them the room or opportunity to take up a certain role. Against the Cold War background of superpower rivalry, the United Nations (UN) Security Council often came to depend on the good offices and intervention of these middle powers. During this period, middle powers had a valuable role within the international system, specifically in the development of UN peacekeeping operations.

Third, as Cox (1996) stresses, middle powers are closely linked to international organisation as a process. According to Cox, a middle power supports the process of international organisation because of its interest in a stable and orderly environment, and not because it seeks to impose 'an ideologically pre-conceived vision of an ideal world order' (1996: 243). Because it is a middle power and cannot impose its own vision of such an ideal world in the pres-ence of big or superpowers, it chooses, almost logically, to exert influence at the multilateral level where it can build consensus around certain issues. By implication, therefore, a middle power is one active in international organisa-tions, supporting the objectives of international peace and security, also as one of its defined 'national interests'. In other words, a sense of 'global responsibil-ity' and 'global citizenship' is clearly present in the case of a middle power. The Scandinavian countries and Canada,[3] in particular, contributed towards con-flict resolution through their own foreign policy emphasis on human rights and democracy.

The end of the Cold War and the eruption of various conflicts and civil wars in the former Second and Third worlds seems to have wrought a change in the definition, role and functions of some middle powers. This change has been captured in the term 'emerging middle power'. One of the most important changes is the fact that 'emerging' middle powers are part of the developing world. This explains why the term is also applied to India and Brazil. Emerging middle powers are, furthermore, regional powers: in their own regions, they are considered powerful, irrespective of whether they represent regional relationships of enmity or amity. But, a more pressing change or aspect of the status of being an emerging middle power, concerns the role and function of these powers. Traditional middle powers played their roles on a world scale. Yet, they were always subordinate to or in the direct presence of the superpowers and as interlocutors bridging the space between the power-ful and powerless in the international system.

Emerging middle powers seem to play or are expected to play the role of regional peacemakers and police; they have the responsibility for keeping their backyard neat and orderly with a measure of support from the big powers. These powers, at the regional level, seem to be expected to support and pro-mote acceptable rules and norms in terms of which international politics and relations are conducted. A broader role is also expected in their 'moral posi-tion' or status. Sometimes they are called upon to exert an influence in specific cases where big power influence does not seem to be sufficient to find solu-tions to problems. Again, during the first two decades after its independence,

India was called upon to play this role.[4] South Africa, more specifically in the person of former President Mandela, was asked to assist in finding a solution to the Haitian crisis in 1995 and was again approached in 1999 to intervene in the Kosovo crisis, while also being involved in the Palestinian question and in East Timor.

However, the emphasis of emerging powers also seems to be focused on regional leadership. The question then, is whether the term 'middle power' can be applied to these states, or whether they are regional great powers rather than middle powers? A second question, closely related to the first, is to what extent such an 'emerging middle power' determines its own role and to what extent this role is assigned to it by the major powers; in short – who confers this status and why?

If a middle power is cast as a regional great power it may in effect have to bear responsibility for regional peace and security and carry the blame for failure. Similarly, if a middle power assumes the mantle of regional responsibility and serves as the interlocutor between the region and the major powers, it may undermine one of the cardinal principles of the UN as a collective security system: that peace is indivisible and all states have a responsibility to avert a threat to peace anywhere in the system. Such a division of labour would or could turn emerging middle powers into regional hegemons (whether reluctantly or voluntarily), detracting from the broader (and original) role of middle powers and inherently changing the moral foundation of the UN which is based on the principle of collective security.

Le Pere quotes Kennedy, Chase and Hill (1996) on the American notion of 'pivotal states' in order to define the role and functions of an emerging power:

> A pivotal state is so important regionally that its collapse would
> spell trans-boundary mayhem ... A pivotal state's economic
> progress and stability, on the other hand, would bolster its region's
> economic vitality and political soundness ... (Le Pere 1998: 1)

Defined as such, the importance of an emerging power as a regional great power to maintain regional security becomes clear – regional security is, of course, in itself a form of international security. It could be said that it does not really matter whether the regional power voluntarily assumes this role, or whether it is thrust upon it, or expected of it – what is important is that this power should fulfil this role in support of international stability.

But to fulfil this role, a number of conditions have to be met:

- The internal dynamics of such a state should allow it to play a stabilising and leading role in its region. The implosion of the former Zaïre (now DRC) in the late 1990s illustrates the notion of a pivotal power whose disintegration not only reverberates across its boundaries to affect other states, but also the extent to which a lack of internal cohesion and stability can change or destroy a potential regional power's ability to fulfil such a role.
- The emerging power should indicate and demonstrate its willingness, and of course also its capacity or ability, to assume the role of regional leader, stabiliser and, if not peacekeeper, at least peacemaker.[5]
- The emerging power should be acceptable to its neighbours – the members of the security complex in which it operates – as a leader responsible for regional security. A broader, or extra-regional acceptance is perhaps a necessary condition, but not sufficient, even if supported and promoted by big powers.

Given the above, this seems a far cry from the original role and functions of a middle power. It is interesting to note that at least two of the so-called emerging powers in the developing world – Brazil and India – have traditionally attempted to play a middle power role, rather than a regional power role. Such an opportunity came through its sheer size and economic capabilities in the case of Brazil, and through southern leadership roles, for example, in the Non-Aligned Movement (NAM) and the Commonwealth, for India.[6] In the case of Brazil, its focus on regional relations, starting in the early 1970s, was based on a perception that its earlier policy of 'regional neglect' was, in fact, 'thoroughly counter-productive' (Hurrell 1992: 30) to its goal of a broader international role.

It would seem that emerging powers face and exhibit a dual role. On the one hand, due either to their economic size, military power or geopolitical importance, the role of regional leader seems to be specific, if not special, and they are supported by the major powers. On the other hand, because moral standing may be a defining characteristic of their power status, as in the case of India and South Africa, emerging powers would also seem, in turn, to strive for broader roles in the global system. This may be a quest for moral leadership or a pursuit of more tangible and immediate national interests (for example, Brazil). This role is more in line with that of a traditional middle power and is often pursued through international organisations and multilateral diplomacy. As with regional powers, this role is also sometimes supported and encouraged by major powers, though at times it is deeply resented, actively opposed, openly criticised and even subjected to threats of punishment. This happened in the case of India's nuclear testing in May 1998, and in the case of South Africa's relations with countries such as Cuba and Libya.

South Africa as a middle power

There are various examples of the high expectations of South Africa's role in the international system after 1994. Former United States ambassador to South Africa, Princeton Lyman, talked about 'South Africa's promise' (Lyman 1996) and Warren Christopher remarked during an official visit to the country: 'When I look around the world, I see very few countries with greater potential to help shape the 21st century than the new South Africa' (Christopher 1996). South Africa also seems to be accepting of a 'special' role, with former Director General of Foreign Affairs Jackie Selebi pointing to the fact that 'South Africa has experienced time and again how countries, organisations and people have looked to us to provide leadership, new ideas and break-throughs in deadlocked situations' (Selebi 1999).

In its role as traditional middle power, though, it is somewhat difficult to identify the exact expectations that the big powers have of South Africa, as well as to assess the extent to which South Africa is given free reign in its search for such a role. The country's scope for action and maneuverability seems to vary according to issue area, with perhaps the widest scope being offered in the field of arms control and disarmament and through multilateral institutions and co-operation. In this regard, it is necessary to explore some specific issues and events as examples of South Africa's role as a middle power in the domain of international security.

South Africa seems to prefer the use of multilateral forums rather than bi-lateral diplomacy as a vehicle for exerting influence. In the tradition of middle powers, the objective of multilateral diplomacy is to strengthen 'a rules-based system which limits the possibility of unilateral actions by major powers', while the practical advantage is to provide the opportunity for smaller states to 'participate on an equal footing on the world stage' (Nzo 1999). South Africa is driving its initiatives in the field of arms control, non-proliferation and disarmament through a variety of multilateral agencies and organisations and with the clear objective of 'playing a leading role internationally'(Department of

Foreign Affairs 1998). The NAM, the Geneva-based Conference on Disarmament (CD), and various international agencies and UN committees dealing with arms issues and the development or review of international arms conventions are the focus points of South Africa's participation in the field of promoting international peace and security.

Most prominent in the country's achievements[7] in this field since 1994 have been the following:

○ South Africa decided in the early 1990s to destroy its nuclear arsenal. By trading its status as a 'minor nuclear power' (Clough 1996) for that of being the first 'denuclearised' state, it gained significant moral influence within international institutions seeking to promote non-proliferation and disarmament.

○ During the Non-Proliferation Treaty (NPT) Review and Extension Conference in 1995, South Africa was instrumental in brokering an agreement between the so-called 'minimalist' and 'maximalist' groupings. It succeeded in getting the conference to adopt an indefinite extension of the treaty, tied to two other decisions concerning the strengthening of the review process of the treaty and a set of objectives and principles (non-binding) on nuclear nonproliferation and disarmament (see Masiza & Landsberg 1996). South Africa was initially criticised for bowing to Western pressure or, alternatively, to be pro-West in its stance. However, the South African position and its role in finding a compromise during the review conference, and its success in ensuring the survival of the NPT, clearly reflects a leadership role for South Africa, and one that was accepted by both camps in the debate.

○ South Africa played a major role in the negotiations on the international convention on the banning of anti-personnel landmines, chairing the Oslo negotiations dealing with the final text of the treaty. Again, South Africa's perceived credibility as a leader could be ascribed to the fact that it had been one of the first countries to enact a unilateral ban on landmines (Boulden 1998).

○ South Africa also took a leading role in the development of the Kimberley process aimed at halting the international trade in illegal diamonds, a process started in 2000.

Apart from playing an active role internationally in issues related to the international security agenda, South Africa has also, particularly since the start of the Mbeki presidency, forcefully articulated critical standpoints on both the

issue of international debt[8] and on the new round of multilateral trade negotiations in the World Trade Organisation (WTO).[9] In both instances one finds
evidence of a seemingly increasingly confident South Africa taking up a leadership position in and on behalf of the global South, but always with
particular emphasis on the needs of Africa.

There is also a middle ground, or area of overlap, between the roles of major
powers and regional powers, as pointed out earlier. South Africa's security
policies are obviously directed towards its neighbourhood and then further
afield on the African continent. Though the main justification for these policies has been regional needs, the decisions often reflect a broader influence.
Two examples of South Africa's role as a middle power illustrate the point:

○ In order to combat the international proliferation of small arms, the
   National Conventional Arms Control Committee (NCACC) decided to
   destroy rather than sell surplus stocks of small arms, a decision which
   elicited widespread international praise, and also again put South Africa in
   a leadership position with its example (Eavis 1999).

○ Problems related to increased mercenary activity and the privatisation of
   security world-wide, led to South Africa adopting the *Foreign Military
   Assistance Act* in 1998. This legislation is considered to be the most complete on the topic in the world (see Mills & Stremlau 1999), and a number
   of countries have already shown an interest in emulating the South African
   position.

South Africa's role as a middle power in the security domain, focusing on
issues of arms control and disarmament and the promotion of peace and stability, is one that seems to be approved of and encouraged by the big powers.
It is obviously considered to be useful in bridging the gap between North and
South, (consider, for example, South Africa's attempts to act as spokesperson
for debt relief for Africa's poorest countries). What is more problematic is its
attempts at establishing and maintaining relations with so-called rogue states
or terrorist states in the eyes of many Western powers. South Africa has been
severely criticised and condemned by the US, in particular, for its relations
with Libya, (*Business Day* 20.10.97) Syria and Cuba. In turn, South Africa
made it clear that it would not abandon solidarity politics (Batchelor 1998;
Olivier & Geldenhuys 1997). More recently, South Africa's vocal opposition to
the 2003 war against Iraq and its clear and outright criticism of the actions of
the US[10] resulted in expectations of punishment by the US, with South Africa
steadfastly defending its critical position.

On the other hand, South Africa's role as an emerging power has at times been actively encouraged and even solicited by the major powers when they needed such assistance and support. Indeed, during his official visit to South Africa in January 1999, Britain's Tony Blair discussed the Lockerbie issue with Mandela. Britain's approval of South Africa's relations with Libya only became clear when Mandela was able to strike a deal with the Libyan leader on the extradition of the Lockerbie suspects. The suspects were subsequently extradited to the Netherlands in April 1999, raising South Africa's stature as a mediator and illustrating the success of its continued conviction that, in the words of Deputy Foreign Affairs Minister, Aziz Pahad, 'political differences cannot, and should not, be solved by force' (Foreign Affairs Budget Debate, 25.03.03).

An area in which South Africa finds it rather difficult to reconcile its role as an emerging middle power with its objective of the creation of wealth is that of arms sales. This is one of the most contentious and complex issues for South Africa in both its foreign and its economic and trade policy (see Batchelor 1998; Battersby 1997; Suttner 1997). It is difficult to reconcile the image of international peacemaker and champion of arms control and disarmament with that of international arms producer and dealer. Arms deals and transfers are subject to a stringent list of criteria that has been described as representing 'the most sincere ... attempt by any country in the world to balance strategic, economic and national interests with moral and human rights considerations' (Battersby 1998: 251). However, South Africa has been severely criticised for a number of arms deals by a variety of critics, ranging from governments such as the US to domestic NGOs promoting human rights. These deals included sales to or arrangements with Rwanda, Algeria, Turkey, Syria, Indonesia and, most recently, China. In a number of cases, opposition was so strong that agreements were cancelled, suspended or only partially fulfilled.

South Africa as a regional big power

The international donor community has made it clear that its support to South Africa was largely influenced by its potential to become a major player in Africa. During his official visit to the country in February 1999, then Austrian Chancellor, Viktor Klima, referred to the important role of South Africa in the region and to South Africa's participation in finding a negotiated solution to regional conflicts. The extent to which South Africa is considered and expected to be an 'emerging power' has become clear. It has a role in stabilising and securing the international system and environment, and in supporting the US as superpower in attempts to control problems such as international crime and drugs and small-arms proliferation.

South Africa is widely touted as an example and model to other countries in transition. Its continued existence as a democratic and stable society supports the dominant global value system based on democracy and a free market economy. This interpretation of South Africa having an almost logical, if not predestined leadership role, especially on the African continent, rests firmly on a hierarchical understanding of politics, as pointed out by Vale and Maseko (1998). In politics, though, logic does not support ambition. Any analysis of South Africa's role as an emerging power with a specific role and function in and towards Africa, concerns the extent to which South Africa is accepted as a leader by its neighbours.

Extra-regionally, South Africa is encouraged in its role as emerging power with the emphasis on regional leadership and supported to this end by the donor community. In as far as responsibility for regional peace and security is concerned, South Africa is, for instance, one of the African countries targeted by the US (and also by the United Kingdom and France)[11] to accept Western support for building peacekeeping capabilities to be used in African crises. This effort, though, is viewed with scepticism by most African countries, including South Africa, and feared to be an indication of what Berman and Sams (1998) refer to as 'constructive disengagement'.

Western encouragement of South Africa as an emerging power results, inevitably, in South Africa being characterised as having a Western orientation in its foreign policy. South Africa's experience of the criticism of being the 'lackey of the West' has resulted in punishment by its African neighbours by means of ostracism. This is best illustrated in the aftermath of its criticism of Nigeria after the execution of Sara-Wiwo and eight other political activists in November 1995 (van Aardt 1996). The same criticism was leveled at South Africa after the NPT conference referred to earlier. It becomes serious when such criticism means that the country's credibility is questioned or undermined and it is prevented from playing a positive or leading role in managing conflict or pursuing international peace and security. So, for instance, when the civil war in the DRC broke out in 1998, President Mugabe did not invite either President Mandela or Deputy President Mbeki to the Victoria Falls meeting of the SADC in August of that year, and African countries also 'punished' South Africa by withholding their support for the country's bid to host the Olympic Games in 2004 (Mbeki 1998: 215).

South Africa's quest for a leadership role in Africa and beyond finds its clearest expression in what was originally known as the Mbeki doctrine embodied in the idea of an African Renaissance, since finding expression in the New Partnership for Africa's Development (Nepad). What is interesting about this doctrine is the fact that South African leadership in an African revival or rebirth is implied (and very cautiously so), rather than explicitly stated. This may be due to the care South Africa has to take in projecting itself as a leader for fear of rejection by its African peers. Mbeki and other policy-makers, in their public references to an African Renaissance and to Nepad, seem to take care always to use 'we' and 'us' or the passive form of reference in such a way that it can imply either South Africa, or the whole of the African continent. Perhaps the clearest indication of a South African leadership role in this renewal process, was an early remark by an Mbeki aide that '[a]s South Africa assumes the presidency of the NAM, we need to ask ourselves a question: in what way can the NAM enhance the drive towards the restructuring of the world order and the project of the African Renaissance?'(Mavimbela 1998: 33)

That South Africa is perhaps slowly gaining recognition as a leader on the continent is illustrated by its role in the establishment and development of the African Union (AU) of which it became the first chair of the new organisation in July 2002. By late 2002 the country officially offered to host the AU's Pan-African Parliament and since the inception of the organisation South Africa has also actively canvassed support for the ratification of the AU treaty establishing the organisation's Peace and Security Council. This organ is structured in such a way that it offers a strong possibility that South Africa (and a number of other big powers on the continent) will remain a permanent member of this council.

South Africa's reluctance to become involved in peacekeeping efforts beyond aspects such as mediation, fact-finding or facilitating negotiations, may in fact backfire on the country when it comes to the issue of restructuring the UN Security Council and the possibility of a permanent seat on this body. Increasingly, it would seem, South Africa is considering making a bid for such a position, despite the (then) OAU decision that any seat(s) that might be allocated to Africa, would be rotated. In his 1999 budget address to parliament, the late Alfred Nzo, Foreign Minister at the time, remarked that '[i]n 1997 I raised the question of South Africa having to consider whether it is prepared to serve as a permanent member of the Security Council ... It is imperative that we have that debate.' In an interview in late 1998, Selebi said that, '[s]ince South Africa's main foreign policy concern is to be part of shaping the global agenda, we would want to become a permanent member of the Security Council' (1998: 15, 41).

Yet, compared with Nigeria, one of the main African contenders for a permanent seat, South Africa has little, if any, experience in maintaining peace, security and stability on the continent. As Clough warns:

> Because of its size and past leadership role in Africa, the novelty of its recent return to democracy, and the international contacts and reputation of President Obasanjo, Nigeria could begin to supplant South Africa on many lists of "emerging powers". (1996: 8)

It is doubtful whether South Africa has shown sufficient proof of its willingness to shoulder regional and continental responsibilities in a bid to become a regional big power to the extent that permanent membership of the Security Council would imply. Its contribution of troops to the UN peacekeeping force for the DRC may indicate a new level of commitment and involvement, but does not compare with other African states. It should also be noted that South Africa has since 1999 been active in a number of other peace support operations, amongst them the UN Mission for Ethiopia/Eritrea and the AU's Conference on Security, Stability, Development and Co-operation in Africa (Henwood & Vickers 2002). Whether true or not, the country is perceived to be able to play a bigger role, but that it is reluctant to do so. In March 1999, the Zimbabwean Minister of Defence, for instance, publicly stated that the war in the DRC could be brought to a quick end if South Africa would use its political muscle to press Uganda and Rwanda to pull out of the DRC (*The Sunday Independent* 21.03.99).

On the other hand, it is not always clear that South Africa would be welcomed as a regional or continental big power. The role of a regional big power may be one pursued by the country in question, it may be (and is increasingly) encouraged by the larger powers and it may even be an almost 'natural' or obvious role due to its geographic, economic and political size and position within a region. The West may have expectations of South Africa as a regional peacekeeper and may want to make it responsible for peace and security in its backyard, but that does not necessarily give South Africa the authority, capacity or inclination, to do so.

There is at times a deep-seated suspicion among some countries about South Africa's intentions and 'real' role. Its legitimacy and credibility as an impartial leader, bent on doing what is right just out of concern and benevolence, are often questioned. This was the case during 'Operation Boleas' in September 1998 in Lesotho, and also previously after mediation between the Angolan government and Unita, when (the late) Jonas Savimbi was received by President Mandela at Tuynhuis (Cleary 1998). South Africa's subsequent reiteration of its support for Security Council resolutions on the Angolan civil war and public condemnation of Unita did not do much to heal the breach.

Fermenting its neighbours' distrust is the apparent rivalry between South Africa and Zimbabwe for regional leadership. This rivalry is perhaps best illustrated by the problems encountered in the SADC Organ on Politics, Defence and Security (Malan 1998; van Aardt 1997), but one that has had some serious ramifications in the conflicts in Lesotho and the DRC, also clouding relations between South Africa and other SADC members. This divide between the two countries has since been bridged, even if only in a very formal way, but South Africa's continued refusal to condemn the human rights and other abuses of the Mugabe regime points to a dilemma on the part of South Africa: Zimbabwe is still considered to be a (if not *the*) political leader in the sub-region, drawing support for its policies from the majority of SADC members (with the exclusion of Botswana), making it apparently impossible for South Africa to adopt a critical position (except in the Commonwealth, and then also with some hesitancy).[12]

In the case of Lesotho, the South African intervention, regardless of the fact that it formed part of a so-called SADC operation, was deeply and bitterly condemned and resented in certain circles in Lesotho and was criticised for many reasons from many quarters, both in southern Africa and abroad. Without passing judgment on the wisdom of the decision and the way in which it was carried out, it can be argued that using force in this instance has nevertheless been consistent with South Africa's position on these matters. While emphasising its commitment to peaceful solutions, South Africa has also indicated that the one area in which it would not hesitate to use force in accordance with SADC principles, was in the face of a threat to a democratically-elected government. Not one of the other conflicts complies with this requirement. Arguably, South Africa is not so much lacking the conviction that it needs to act rather more assertively in the region, but rather that its conception of when to use force and when to refrain from it, no matter the nature and seriousness of the conflict, is based on a set of principles that considerably narrows down the possibility of South African involvement in peacekeeping or peacemaking operations.

The country's involvement in the peace processes in Burundi and the DRC (and to some extent in negotiations in the Comoros as AU-mandated Co-ordinator of the Countries of the Region)[13] provides ample proof of this commitment to the peaceful resolution of conflict. Although an arduous task with success not yet guaranteed[14] in either the Burundi or DRC processes, South Africa has remained committed to these negotiation processes. In Burundi, South Africa did contribute troops to an AU peacekeeping force after drawn-out negotiations in which former President Mandela and Deputy President Zuma played significant roles.[15] In the DRC, South Africa's position eventually saw the withdrawal of a number of countries' troops from the DRC, amongst them those of Zimbabwe, and the signing of the Final Act at Sun City in late March 2003, according to which a transitional government would be set up that will oversee democratic elections after two years.[16]

However, leadership does not only have connotations of dominance, but also involves taking responsibility for those in need of assistance. In this sense, South Africa has shown beyond doubt that its emphasis on the southern African region as its first and foremost foreign policy concern is sincere and tangible. It demonstrated that security is not only about military matters and threats of war. Rather, security is a broad concept, encompassing various dimensions, which should also be treated and implemented as such in practice. Juxtaposed with the Lesotho intervention of September 1998 is the peaceful intervention in the country in 1996 by Presidents Nelson Mandela, Quett Masire of Botswana and Robert Mugabe of Zimbabwe. South Africa has shown the strength of its commitment to security in the region through its involvement and practical disaster relief: to Tanzania after the ferryboat disaster of 1996; the heavy snowstorms and resulting food crisis experienced in Lesotho in the winter of 1996; its assistance to Mozambique after the heavy rains, flooding and damage to infrastructure in February 1999, and again (and on a much bigger scale) in early 2000 and food aid to the SADC region during the famine and drought of 2002/3.

Conclusion

South Africa has in many ways adopted a middle-power position in its foreign relations and policies. There is also evidence, particularly in the establishment and development of the AU and Nepad, that the country might slowly be gaining sufficient confidence to 'grow' into the role of being a regional big power, though also in this instance it seeks to do so in conjunction with other big powers in Africa, particularly with Nigeria. Typical of a traditional middle power, it emphasises the promotion of international peace and security and therefore highly values participation in international organisations, particularly those concerned with arms control and disarmament and with socio-economic issues. In its defiance of Western opinion and preferences in the realm of relationships with 'outcast' states, especially Libya and Cuba, and its criticism of the involvement of the US and the UK in the 2003 Iraq war, it has managed to create a space for independent foreign policy making, while putting these relations, in the case of Libya, to good use in promoting peaceful relations among states.

In its quest to represent and promote the interests of the global South, South Africa is strengthening its position as a bridge with the North. Yet, although it attempts to fulfil this role in conjunction with other Southern countries through organisations such as NAM, the development of a unified position on issues of international concern remains difficult. This was seen clearly in the 1995 NPT Review Conference. Perhaps its real test of 'middle powership' was during this conference where the rather tenuous South position all but disintegrated: South Africa then had to act not so much in concert with either North or South – minimalists or maximalists – but as a genuine mediator, trying to reconcile the two camps. Its success at the NPT seemed to have given it the confidence to act much more assertively in other forums dealing with arms control and disarmament, and the country is clearly moving into a leadership position in these rounds of negotiations, as well as negotiations around international debt and trade.

With regard to a role as regional big power, South Africa's position is more uncertain. On the one hand, it seems to be willing to push for a stronger role in regional and continental affairs, as seen from its signals regarding Security Council membership, but much more so in its quest to have Nepad accepted and implemented and in its very active role in the establishment of the AU. On the other hand, it is almost overcautious, at times, in its dealings with its neighbours and the rest of the continent, ever sensitive to possible accusations of domination or hegemony. Though the West has made it clear that it is in favour of a regional leadership role for South Africa and willing to support and encourage such a role, Africa itself sends mixed signals in this regard. Accusations of South Africa being too pro-West and not really serious and concerned about Africa and intracontinental-relations can be contrasted with calls by African states and politicians for South African involvement in peace-keeping efforts and other aspects of security on the continent. There is as yet no clarity on or consensus about South Africa's role and position in the region or in Africa at large, either on the part of South Africa or that of its fellow African states.

A two-fold explanation can be proffered for the difficulty South Africa expe-riences in finding its place and playing a leadership role on the continent. The first is that, due to the vested interests of other leaders and a measure of fear of being sidelined or overshadowed by South Africa, its leadership has not been generally welcomed, accepted, or solicited. A possible solution to this problem might be an even stronger focus on continental multilateralism, though it would seem that the smaller the scope of organisation (moving from universal to continental-regional to subregional), the more difficult leadership 'softened' by multilateralism becomes. The second explanation might lie in the fact that liberal democratic values are usually associated with the West. A commitment to these values on a continent with a rather flawed history of respect for democratic pluralism and human rights, combined with the vested interests mentioned above, would then almost inevitably elicit accusations of being un-African and pro-Western. In this regard, the only obvious solution seems to lie in encouraging the development of like-minded political cultures. South Africa could therefore be expected to work very closely (and is doing so) with newly-democratised Nigeria (through the AU, Nepad and the Commonwealth) on issues affecting the continent and broader international relations.

In one area there is, however, no doubt about South Africa's leadership role, both as a traditional middle power in the international arena and as a regional leader: in the country's position and conduct as an example to other countries in a number of ways. It is not only in the sphere of peaceful change and deal-ing with the arduous process of democratisation and the consolidation of democracy that South Africa serves this role. In many other aspects, it has also become a trendsetter for both North and South, as witnessed in its unilateral decisions to ban anti-personnel mines and to destroy surplus small arms, its decision to 'denuclearise', its progressive legislation on privatised security and its involvement in the Kimberley process. These accomplishments, in themselves, point to a middle-power role. To the extent that the 'moral capital' gained from these policies facilitates South Africa's potential for playing an increasingly important role internationally, the country seems to fit the description of being an 'emerging power'.

Notes

1   This chapter is a revised version of an article, 'South Africa as an emerging power', which appeared in *African Security Review*, 9 (3), 2000.

2   The term 'muddled powers' was coined by Peter Vale and used by Van der Westhuizen, 1998.

3   An interesting analysis, though brief, of Canada's role in the international system is given by the late Canadian author, Robertson Davies, 'Literature in a country without a mythology' in *The Merry Heart: Reflections on Reading, Writing, and the World of Books*, Penguin, New York, 1996: 40–63, particularly where he employs the theatrical concept of 'fifth business' and muses that perhaps Canada is 'Fifth business in the affairs of the world' (p.59), the one 'you cannot manage the plot without', which has 'a career that sometimes outslasts the golden voices' (p.60).

4   India, as leader of NAM, was called upon to assist in mediating and negotiating international conflicts in Korea, Indo-China (as it was known then), the Middle East and the Congo. See V Gill, 'India as a regional great power: in pursuit of Shakti', in I Neumann (ed), *Regional Great Powers in International Politics*, Macmillan, Houndmills, 1992: 52.

5   Brazil makes for an interesting case in this regard, but due to constraints of space, it will not be discussed. The reader is referred to an analysis of Brazil as a regional great power by A Hurrell, 'Brazil as a regional great power: a study in ambivalence', in Neumann, op. cit: 16–48.

6   Veena Gill notes that 'in the first two decades of independence, India acquired an importance in international politics out of proportion to its power capabilities ... Nonalignment provided it with an unusual form of power in international politics – moral influence; India as the spokesman and leader of oppressed mankind.' See Gill, op.cit: 49–69 (quote from p.52).

7   The examples discussed here are selective, due to constraints of space. The annual reports of the Multilateral Branch of the Department of Foreign Affairs contain more detailed discussions of South African involvement in various arms control and disarmament issues.

8   See 'The position of South Africa regarding debt relief', www.dfa.gov.za, accessed on 24 April 2003.

9 See 'A broad South African approach to new multilateral trade negotiations in the World Trade Organisation', http://www.dfa.gov.za, accessed on 24 April 2003.

10 See, for example, 'Speech by Deputy Minister Aziz Pahad in the National Assembly Foreign Affairs Budget Debate', 25 March 2003. www.dfa.gov.za/docs/paha030328.htm.

11 This was the so-called P–3 Initiative, an offer to African countries by these three countries of training, instruction and equipment related to peacekeeping.

12 For a detailed discussion of South Africa's foreign policy towards Zimbabwe, see M Schoeman, 'The hegemon that wasn't: South Africa's foreign policy towards Zimbabwe', *Strategic Review for Southern Africa*, May 2003.

13 www.dfa.gov.za, accessed on 24 April 2003.

14 This chapter was finalised in early May 2003.

15 www.dfa.gov.za, accessed on 11 April 2003.

16 www.dfa.gov.za, accessed on 4 April 2003.

References

Batchelor, P (1998) Arms and the ANC, *Bulletin of the Atomic Scientists* September/October: 57.

Battersby, J (1997) South Africa's arms sales, in *South African Yearbook of International Affairs 1997*. Johannesburg: South African Institute of International Affairs.

Berman, EG & Sams, KE (1998) *Constructive disengagement: Western efforts to develop African peacekeeping.* ISS Monograph 33. Halfway House: Institute for Security Studies.

Boulden, L (1998) Developments in the international landmine regime, in SAIIA (1998) *South African Yearbook of International Affairs 1998/9.* Johannesburg: SAIIA.

Bull, H (1977) *The anarchical society: A study of order in world politics.* London: Macmillan.

Christopher, W (1996) The US view of South Africa, *International Update* 19.

Cleary, S (1998) *Angola's unremitting agony: Time for a rethink.* Paper read at SAIIA, Johannesburg, 11.03.98.

Clough, M (1996) *Constructing a role for South Africa in the emerging world order.* Paper read at Centre for Policy Studies workshop on South Africa as an emerging power, Johannesburg, September.

Cox, R (1996) Middlepowermanship: Japan and the future of world order, in R Cox & T Sinclair (eds.) *Approaches to world order.* Cambridge: Cambridge University Press.

DFA (Department of Foreign Affairs) (1998) *Thematic review: Strategic plans.* Pretoria: DFA.

DFA (2003) *Speech by Deputy Minister Aziz Pahad in the National Assembly Foreign Affairs Budget Debate*, 25.03.03. www.dfa.gov.za/docs/ paha030328.htm.

Eavis, P (1999) Awash with light weapons, *The World Today*, 55(4): 19–21.

Henwood, R & Vickers, B (2002) South African foreign policy and international practice, in 2002 – an analysis, *South African Yearbook of International Law* 27.

Hurrell, A (1992) Brazil as a regional great power: A study in ambivalence, in I Neumann (ed.) *Regional great powers in international politics*. Houndmills: Macmillan.

Kennedy, P, Chase, RS & Hill, EB (1996) Pivotal states and US strategy, *Foreign Affairs* 75 (1): 33–51.

Klein, R (1974) *Sovereign equality among states: The history of an idea*. Toronto: Toronto University Press.

Le Pere, G (1998) South Africa – an emerging power? *Global Dialogue*, 3(1): 1–2.

Lyman, P (1996) South Africa's promise, *Foreign Policy* 102: 118.

Malan, M (1998) *SADC and subregional security: Unde venis et quo vadis?* ISS Monograph 19. Halfway House: Institute for Security Studies.

Masiza, Z & Landsberg, C (1996) *Fission for compliments: South Africa and the 1995 Extension of Nuclear Non-Proliferation*. Johannesburg: Centre for Policy Studies.

Mavimbela, V (1998) The African Renaissance: A workable dream, in P Vale & S Maseko *South Africa and Africa: Reflections on the African Renaissance*. Occasional Paper 17. Johannesburg: Foundation for Global Dialogue.

Mbeki, M (1998) The African Renaissance, in *The South African Yearbook of International Affairs 1998/9*. Johannesburg: SAIIA.

Mills, G & Stremlau, J (eds.) (1999) *The privatisation of security in Africa*. Johannesburg: SAIIA.

Nzo, A (1999) *Foreign Affairs Budget Vote: Address by Minister Alfred Nzo*. House of Assembly, 04.03.99.

Olivier, G & Geldenhuys, D (1997) South Africa's foreign policy: From idealism to pragmatism, *Business and the Contemporary World* 9 (2): 273.

Selebi, J (1998) Interview, *Global Dialogue* 3(3):15–41.

Selebi, J (1999) South African foreign policy: setting new goals and strategies. Excerpt from a speech, South African Institute of International Affairs, Johannesburg, 18.05.99.

Suttner, R (1997) South African foreign policy and the promotion of human rights, in *South African Yearbook of International Affairs*. Johannesburg: SAIIA.

Vale, P & Maseko, S (1998) *South Africa and Africa: Reflections on the African Renaissance*. Occasional Paper 17, Foundation for Global Dialogue, Johannesburg.

Van Aardt, M (1996) A foreign policy to die for: South Africa's response to the Nigerian crisis, *Africa Insight* 26 (2): 107–119.

Van Aardt, M (1997) The emerging security framework in Southern Africa: Regime or community? *Strategic Review for Southern Africa* 19(1): 1–30.

Van der Westhuizen, J (1998) South Africa as an emerging middle power, *Third World Quarterly* 19 (3): 435–455.

Wight, M (1979) *Power politics*. Harmondsworth: Penguin.

The South Africans have arrived: Post-apartheid corporate expansion into Africa

John Daniel, Varusha Naidoo and Sanusha Naidu

> Shaking off decades of apartheid-era isolation, South African executives, both black and white, are moving north to buy struggling banks, rebuild rundown railways, and bring first-world technology ... to an impoverished continent ... this explosion of trade and investment ... is one of the most vivid illustrations of South Africa's metamorphosis since apartheid ended in 1994. Once a pariah state, South Africa now seems poised to dominate the continent that once shunned its products and leaders. (*New York Times* 17.02.02)

> I ... assure our neighbours and the peoples of the rest of Africa that the government we lead has no great power pretensions. We claim no right to impose our will on any independent country. We will not force anything on anybody .... (President Thabo Mbeki speaking in Parliament 18.02.03)

> With returns routinely over 30% – in some cases 50%–60% – compared to the 16–20% of South Africa, Africa's allure can be irresistible. (*Financial Mail* 07.02.03)

Introduction

From its inception as an independent entity in 1910 to the end of the minority-rule era in South African politics in the 1990s, successive South African governments assumed a proprietorial and interventionist attitude towards the African hinterland.[1] This was particularly so in regard to the sub-continent, which was viewed by the regime in Pretoria as 'its backyard' or sphere of interest, an exploitable resource, a bottomless source of cheap labour and an easily penetrable market for its products. It was also seen as readily controllable through a range of economic linkages (road and rail outlets to the sea, almost all of which traversed South Africa) and pan-regional institutions like the Southern African Customs Union (Sacu). Formed in 1909, this arrangement effectively integrated the economies of the then High Commission Territories (HCTs) of Basutoland, Bechuanaland and Swaziland into that of South Africa's on highly unequal terms, transforming them in the process into little more than economic dependencies of Pretoria.

The initial forms of integration of both the HCTs and an outer periphery of states which included Nyasaland (Malawi), Northern and Southern Rhodesia (Zambia and Zimbabwe respectively) and Mozambique, was based on migrant labour and transport services. As a means of sourcing cheap, plentiful and socially-disorganised labour, in the late nineteenth century South African mining companies turned to the region. Through a range of recruiting networks and devices, a regional labour strategy emerged which in the course of the twentieth century siphoned millions of workers out of the region and into South Africa's mushrooming minerals sector.

By the 1950s the majority of South African mineworkers were foreign migrants, with the largest contingents being supplied by the poorest countries of the region, Nyasaland, Basutoland and Mozambique. In the case of Mozambique, the South African Chamber of Mines, which managed and monitored labour recruitment on behalf of its member companies, designated and referred to fully half the country (the area south of the Save river) as a 'labour reserve'. By the 1970s, some 110 000 Mozambicans were employed on South Africa's mines. This group constituted one-quarter of all Mozambican wage earners and their collective earnings exceeded 'total income from commercial agricultural production in the south of Mozambique' by 150 per cent, while their deferred earnings (one-third of their total wages) 'was three times as high as income from family farms' (Castel-Branco 2002: 3). All this gave the South African government considerable political leverage over Mozambican affairs, as well as considerable capacity to inflict damage on the Mozambican economy in the event of a political fallout, as in fact subsequently ensued in the 1970s and 1980s. As Castel-Branco put it: 'in addition to being the largest employer of wage labour in Mozambique, South African mines were also, by far, the most important source of income and finance for the agricultural sector in the South of Mozambique' (2002:3).

Even though its road and rail transport system fed into the only two deep-water harbours on Africa's south-eastern coastline not part of South African territory, Mozambique's transport and port system were thoroughly integrated into the South African economy and economically unviable without those functioning links. Its road and rail services primarily transported local workers to and from their places of work in South Africa, while the ports of Beira and Lourenco Marques (Maputo) derived the bulk of their income from charges levied on South African mineral exports. In fact, according to Castel-Branco, 'the transport system of the port of Maputo was also the largest source of foreign currency for Mozambique, and may have contributed as much as 40% of total export revenue for the country' (2002: 4).

It was through such labour and transport arrangements, and in the case of the HCTs the Sacu framework, that South Africa ensured its hegemony in the region up to the 1960s. Accompanying this fact of economic dominance was an ideological attitude of overlordship on the part of the government in Pretoria. This was reflected in the fact that South Africa administered South West Africa (Namibia) as a fifth province, according representation to its white voters in the Parliament in Cape Town, and ignoring UN and World Court rulings as to the illegality of its occupation. Its similarly proprietorial behaviour towards the HCTs was governed by a view that they would eventually become juridically part of South Africa, provision for which had been included in the *South Africa Act* of 1909 by which the British Parliament granted independence to South Africa. As late as 1960/61, Dr Verwoerd launched the last of several bids by Pretoria post-1910 to give effect to incorporation. It was only the rejection of the bid in 1963 that led to South Africa instituting border control and pass-port/visa requirements between South Africa and the HCT territories. Up to then it had operated an open-borders regime.

Two other examples of South Africa's 'our backyard' attitude to the region are worth mentioning. The first occurred soon after the NP came to power in 1948 when it publicly expressed to the British government its objection to the pending marriage of Seretse Khama, then heir to the paramount chieftancy of the Bamangwato in Bechuanaland, to a white woman. The marriage went ahead but for many years the British appeased Pretoria by refusing to allow the couple to live in Bechuanaland.

The second refers to the fact that right up until the 1990s, Rhodesian and after 1980, Zimbabwean sports teams participated in South Africa's domestic sports competitions and individual members of these teams were eligible for selection to the South African national ('Springbok') teams. In fact, in a rather bizarre case in 1960, a Northern Rhodesian resident, Andy MacDonald, who played rugby for Southern Rhodesia, captained South Africa in a rugby test.

In the 1960s, this attitude of ownership towards the region acquired a security dimension in response to the rise of African nationalism and the steady with-drawal from the continent of most of the European colonial powers. South Africa's security strategists now began to conceptualise the region, and particu-larly the colonial and minority-ruled states of Southern Rhodesia, South West Africa, Mozambique and Angola, as a *cordon sanitaire* or buffer between the white-controlled south and those forces beyond this periphery threatening to it. As the threat developed, so South Africa assumed an interventionist response sending police units into first South West Africa to confront the South West African Peoples' Organisation's launch of an armed struggle in 1965, and then into Southern Rhodesia in 1967 to fight alongside Rhodesian security forces in its counter-insurgency campaign against Zimbabwean guerrilla forces.

Less direct and interventionist was South Africa's response to the wars in Mozambique and Angola. Here covert military aid was given to the Portuguese military in the form of cash, weaponry, equipment including helicopters, joint commando training and intelligence, the latter provided in part by covert ele-ments introduced into the two countries. It was, however, too little, too late, and Portugal's African empire ended with the overthrow of the fascist dictator-ship in Portugal in April 1974 and the new government's unilateral declaration of a ceasefire in its African wars and declared willingness to negotiate transfers of power. With these developments, the eastern and western flanks of the buffer collapsed and those fighting for majority rule in Namibia, Zimbabwe and South Africa now had direct access to South African soil.

South Africa's response was the 'total strategy', which in regard to the region, amounted to an aggressive, interventionist strategy of clandestine counter-insurgency warfare involving the deployment in the region of South African conventional, surrogate and covert military and police units. Over a ten to twelve-year period from 1978, and coinciding with PW Botha's leadership of the NP, South Africa waged war or intervened militarily – directly and/or indi-rectly – in at least eight Southern African states. The upshot was a period of intense conflict in which, according to the final report of the TRC, between 500 000 and 700 000 Southern Africans died as a direct or indirect result of

South African military aggression. As the TRC put it, 'the majority of the victims of the South African government's attempts to maintain itself in power were outside of South Africa' (1998, Vol. 2 Ch. 2; 43).

The economic consequences for particularly the outer-periphery states were catastrophic – roads and railroads were destroyed and/or closed (such as the Benguela rail route linking Angola and Zambia), ports went into decline, schools and clinics were damaged or destroyed, numerous profitable mines were forced to cease operations, and land was rendered untillable because of the widespread laying of mines. In growth terms, the economies of Angola and Mozambique spiralled downwards, forfeiting much of their immediate post-independence economic gains. To make matters worse, South Africa sharply reduced its recruitment of foreign mine workers, targeting two of its most vehement ideological opponents, Mozambique and Lesotho. Numbers of Mozambican migrants declined from 118 000 in 1975 to 41 300 in 1977. This, along with other punitive economic measures imposed by South Africa, devastated the Mozambican economy.

But South Africa, too, paid an economic price. Destabilisation – along with the imposition of economic and other sanctions – produced a decade of economic stagnation from 1982 with GDP declining in all but two of those ten years. It also produced a reduction in the South African economic presence in all of Africa bar the SACU states, Namibia and Zimbabwe. There, conversely, South Africa's economic presence from the late 1960s had expanded to the point where in the SACU member states, for example, South African capital eclipsed British as the predominant force within the economy. Swaziland, with its diversified agro-industry (timber, sugar and citrus), and Botswana, with the opening up of its diamond sector, being particularly attractive to South African investors. Overall, however, the apartheid era ended with South African capital effectively shut out of the extra-southern African marketplace and with shrinking market prospects in the rest of the world. In structural terms, the South African economy in the early 1990s reflected a paradox of comparative regional strength and growing international weakness.

The post-apartheid era

That the ending of apartheid would open up the African market to South African capital was never in doubt; however, few predicted the rapidity with which it would seek to exploit its new market opportunity or the sheer volume of its flow into Africa. What interested analysts more at the time was how democratic South Africa would express its growing hegemony on the wider African stage. Would its new-found economic strength allied to its historic attitude of overlordship render the new regime even more interventionist and imperialist than its apartheid predecessor?

In a 1992 article, political economist Robert Davies laid out three possible scenarios for the Southern African region. He dubbed them the 'South Africa first' approach, in which state and capital blindly pursued its narrow economic interests irrespective of the damage it inflicted on the region. Amongst possible measures consistent with this scenario would be further limiting the number of legally employed migrants working in the domestic economy. The second scenario he called the 'integration under South African hegemony' approach, in terms of which South Africa would initiate 'a regional co-operation and integration project largely shaped by its own narrow interests and aspirations to regional hegemony' (1992: 67). Favouring some subordinate states over others, South Africa would initiate a series of 'power-house' projects along the lines of the Lesotho hydro-electric power scheme 'tilted towards its interests' (1992: 68), exacerbating in the process both regional inequities as well as regional tensions and resentments. The third scenario – 'non-hegemonic regional co-operation and integration' – was favoured by Davies, but seen as the least likely to be pursued. This was because it would require South African capital to sacrifice maximal accumulation for long-term regeneration.

In this article, we attempt both to map the extent of South Africa's post-apartheid expansion into the African economy as well as to assess how South Africa's hegemony has been and is being expressed. Which, if any, of the above scenarios is being realised and if none, then how can South African-African relations be conceptualised? To these latter questions we will return in the conclusion to the paper. At this point our focus is on the former issue.

Before moving to this issue, however, it is important to note that it was not simply the fact of South Africa's political transition to democracy and international respectability that fuelled its economic penetration of the African market. There were other catalysts or 'push' factors, the major ones being the fact that the transition coincided with the end of the Cold War, the concomitant demise of the state-directed commandist economic model and the triumph of its neoliberal alternative. This latter prescribed a liberal political dispensation accompanied by a deregulated market economy with minimal state/government intervention as the norm for countries intent on engaging with the global economy. This discourse – captured in the International Monetary Fund and World Bank's 'Washington Consensus' – emphasised privatisation, open capital markets and trade liberalisation, market-based pricing, deregulated and flexible labour markets, and integration into the global economy as the most effective means to achieve economic development.

Governments worldwide, and especially in eastern Europe and Africa, now found themselves having to restructure their politico-economic regimes in accordance with a new international order. In terms of it, barriers to trade and investment were relaxed or eliminated altogether, state corporations and parastatals were put up for sale and/or opened up to foreign parties who were also sought for the rehabilitation and modernisation of Africa's outdated and/or disintegrating transport and utilities infrastructures.

With the rest of the world disillusioned with and losing interest in Africa and turning instead to the potentially more lucrative eastern European market, South African capital was well placed to take advantage of these new trade and investment opportunities. Having been frozen out of much of the world for the best part of a decade and a half, South African corporates had a surplus of investible capital available and were keen to take advantage of the weakness of the economies to the north of it. In short, to paraphrase Ahwireng-Obeng and McGowan (1998a, 1998b), it was the character of the South African transition and its relation to the ascendancy of the neoliberal economic paradigm which enabled South African business to capture, and in some cases, monopolise, the opportunities presented by a global economic regime that prompted and encouraged market penetration.

To understand the full extent of South Africa's post-transition expansion into the African economy two sets of economic indicators need to examined. The first pertains to Africa as an export destination for South African products, while the second relates to more direct involvement by way of mergers, acquisitions, joint ventures and new 'greenleaf' investments.

Africa as an export market

As Table 17.1 indicates, South Africa's export trade with Africa has grown significantly in the transition period. Africa is now by region South Africa's fourth largest export market and there are good reasons to believe that the volume of export traffic will increase sharply in the immediate future – peace in Angola and the prospects of peace in the DRC are two promising pointers – and that Africa's share of overall export trade will continue to climb. Having said that, in volume terms the EU, North American Free Trade Area (NAFTA) and the China-Japan-Malaysia-Singapore axis remain very much more important than the African market. The African market is tiny in consumer terms, limited by its overall poverty and comparatively small population. By contrast, the other three regions are massive in human consumer terms and by African standards, unimaginably wealthy. Furthermore, the increased trade opportunities spawned by the special trade arrangement with the EU and the United States's *Africa Growth and Opportunity Act* (AGOA) will ensure that these two regions remain more lucrative than the African market in the foreseeable future.

Table 17.1 *South African export destinations by region (percentages)*

Region	1991	2001
Africa	4	12
North America	0*	0
South America	8	4
NAFTA	0	17**
EU	15	22
Far East	57	40
Middle East	14	4
Others	2	1

*   Trade between South Africa and US was restricted at the time following the imposition of sanctions in terms of the 1986 *Comprehensive Anti-Apartheid Act*.

**   NAFTA embraces USA, Canada and Mexico and came into being in 1992.

Source: *Engineering News* 03–09.05.02 (www.engineeringnews.co.za/)

What these statistics do not reveal is the imbalance in the South African-African trade relationship and the extent to which South Africa dominates the African economy. With each of its African trade partners South Africa enjoys a surplus. For example, of South Africa's R20,3 billion trade with the member states of SADC in 1999, R17,7 billion were exports to the region. This is an imbalance of almost 7:1. According to Loxton, this imbalance rose to 8:1 in 2000 and 9:1 in 2001 (*Business Report* 19.06.02). These aggregate statistics also mask huge variations in the imbalances between South Africa and individual countries within the SADC bloc. For example, the balance in favour of South Africa in its growing trade with Angola stood at some 22:1 in 2002. In 2002 South African exports totaled R2,784 billion, while imports amounted to only R127 million. This gap can only increase as South Africa reaps the benefits of peace in Angola. According to Dasnois, South African business views Angola as a huge construction site strewn with lucrative contracts to be signed – some 20 000 km of roads damaged by war and by use to be rehabilitated; 350 bridges repaired; 1 650 km of power lines fixed; airports, harbours and railways rebuilt and industry modernised (*Business Report* 12.08.02). The paradox, of course, is that much of this destruction was inflicted by the South African military, or by a guerrilla grouping armed and funded by the apartheid regime, yet it will be South Africans who will make huge profits from rebuilding what they destroyed and by lifting the mines they themselves laid – a perverse manifestation of the expression 'reaping what one sows'.

The balance of trade between South Africa and the rest of the continent is also weighted in South Africa's favour. According to *Business Day* (17.04.02), total trade with Africa in 2001, excluding SACU, amounted to $856 million in imports and $3,7 billion in exports, an imbalance of nearly 5:1. Given this favourable balance for South Africa, it is little wonder that Africa features prominently in South Africa's trade and investment strategy. This is evidenced by the establishment since 1994 of trade offices in Angola, Egypt, Ethiopia, Ivory Coast, Kenya, Tanzania, and Zimbabwe. More such offices are planned, according to the Department of Trade and Industry (DTI).

Acquisitions, mergers, joint ventures and 'greenfield' investments

A fuller picture of the 'South Africanisation' of the African economy is provided by corporate South Africa's post-apartheid record of taking over and or joining up with existing African operations, as well as a new 'greenfield' investor in the Africa market. A cursory glance at the literature shows South African businesses running the national railroad in Cameroon, the national electricity company in Tanzania, and managing the airports located in or near seven African capitals. They have controlling shares in Telecom Lesotho and are the leading providers of cellphone services in Nigeria, Uganda, Swaziland,

Tanzania, Rwanda and Cameroon. South African corporates are also managing power plants in Zimbabwe, Zambia and Mali, building roads and bridges in Malawi and Mozambique, and a gas pipeline between offshore Mozambique and South Africa. They control banks, breweries, supermarkets and hotels throughout the continent (see box below re. Shoprite) and provide TV programming to over half of all Africa's states. The Shoprite case also illustrates the link between investing in Africa and the stimulation to South Africa's export sector, with the example of its 72 stores sourcing from South African producers goods to the value of R429 million.

Leading SA grocery retailer the Shoprite Group has taken a further step to becoming a player in the rest of Africa by acquiring the Champion supermarket group in Madagascar for an undisclosed amount.

Shoprite, which has retail outlets across the continent, has now taken control of the five supermarkets and one distribution centre on the Indian Ocean island with effect from October 28. The group said the acquisition was in line with its regional expansion programme outside of SA's borders. The group operates 72 Shoprite outlets in 13 African countries.

Shoprite MD Whitey Basson said the group hoped to be operating in most sub-Saharan countries by 2005. He said Shoprite had already bought land in Ghana, and was set to start operating in Angola next year. He said Gabon and Nigeria were also being looked at. In the Angolan capital Luanda, the group has begun construction on a R113m combined Shoprite and Megasave distribution centre. The stores in Madagascar, of which four are based in Antananarivo and one in Tamatave, will trade under the Shoprite brand.

The group said its expansion programme in Africa had also resulted in the creation of an export market for SA producers and manufactures. During the year, Shoprite exported stock to its outlets trading outside this country to the value of more than R429m. (*Business Day* 19.11.02)

Table 17.2 presents details by sector of the major South African corporates operative in Africa. What it reveals is an across-the-board involvement by every sector of the South African economy in the wider African market. Statistics are not available that distinguish between these different types of ventures, but the probability is that the bulk of the new activity in Africa has come about through mergers, take-overs and joint ventures rather than by new 'greenfield' investments generating new business operations. It is not, however, that this does not happen, as the case of Shoprite buying land and building new supermarkets in Ghana and Angola illustrates.

Nonetheless, what seems more common is for a South African operative to take over a local business and then to invest new capital in refurbishing and expanding it. This is clearly visible in the nurturing of infrastructure development across the continent, where investors from key sectors such as transport, construction, telecommunications, finance, manufacturing and mining have entered into joint partnerships in order to expand business opportunities and operations in the region. South African Airways (SAA), Murray and Roberts, Vodacom, De Beers and AngloGold, Stanbic and Absa have all favoured joint-venture arrangements with African partners, as has Shoprite in the case of its Madagascan operation. Lack of resources and capacity within the region make joint ventures, in particular, popular choices. Not only do these forms of partnership help assuage the resource/capacity void in African countries, it also assists in dispelling the notion of an ascendant and influential South African dominance. It is also the case that international financiers prefer to have an African bank on board when they launch projects on the continent, something on which the stronger South African banks like Standard, Absa and Rand Merchant have capitalised. They provide, as *Business Day* (16.07.02) put it, 'a level of comfort' for these backers.

Table 17.2 *Major South African corporates in Africa by sector*

Sector	Corporates	Located
Aviation and airport services	Airports Company of South Africa (ACSA)	In nine countries
Airlines	South African Airways (SAA)	Three joint ventures
Banking and financial services	Stanbic Absa Stanlib (joint venture between Standard Bank and Liberty Bank) Alexander Forbes	In 18 countries In four countries In nine countries In 11 countries
Construction	Murray and Roberts Group 5	Permanent offices in three countries and 13 country contracts 12 country contracts
Energy	Sasol Petro SA	Three country contracts Three country contracts
Manufacturing	Nampak Sappi	In 10 countries In three countries
Media and broadcasting	Multichoice TV Africa	TV and subscriber services in 21 countries Supplies programmes to 33 countries (includes the Cricket World Cup)
Mining	De Beers Anglogold Goldfields	In three countries In three countries In three countries

Retail trade	Shoprite	89 stores in 14 countries
	Massmart (Makro, Game, Dion, Cash & Carry etc.)	Over 300 outlets in SACU states
	SAB Miller	13 beer breweries in ten countries and 35 sorghum breweries in five countries
Research and development	Industrial Development Corporation (IDC)	Financing projects in 20 countries
	CSIR	Conducting research projects in 17 countries
Telecommunications	MTN/M-Cell	Cellular-fixed line contracts in six countries
	Vodacom	Cellular contracts in five countries
	Eskom Enterprises Telecommunications	One fixed line- cellular contract
Transport	Transnet: nine divisions including Spoornet and its subsidiary Comazar	Eight country contracts
	Unitrans	Seven country contracts
Tourism and leisure services	Protea Hotels	Resorts in nine countries
	Southern Sun	Resorts in six countries
	Imperial Car Rental	110 locations in eight southern African countries
Utilities Power	Eskom Enterprises	Three utility management contracts, one joint venture and 28 country contracts
Water	Umgeni Water	Three country contracts
	Rand Water	Four country contracts

Source: Table constructed by authors from information in the Corporate Mapping data set

South Africa is the biggest foreign investor in southern Africa. According to the *Financial Mail* (07.02.03), in the period 1994–2000 South African foreign direct investment (FDI) into SADC amounted to $5,4 billion, a total more than British and United States FDI combined. According to an United Nations Conference on Trade and Development (UNCTAD) report released in late 2002, South Africa is now also the continent's largest source of new FDI, averaging $1 billion per year since 1994. The South African Reserve Bank disputes this figure, suggesting instead that it has been below this annual average, but concedes that the figure has been growing in volume annually in recent years. The Bank estimates that the value of South African assets in Africa stood at R23 billion in 2000. This reflected an increase of R3,3 billion over the 1999 figure which, in turn, reflected an even larger increase of R6,1 billion over the 1998 figure.

A feature of the investment drive into Africa has been the fact that the six primary sectors of South Africa's economy (mining, retail, construction/manufacturing, financial services, telecommunications, tourism/leisure) have worked hand-in-hand in securing South African investment throughout the continent. For example, financial services expansion has paralleled the growing presence of other businesses on the continent. The Standard Bank group (Stanbic) is represented in 17 African countries outside South Africa with strong retail banking operations in Namibia, Swaziland, Lesotho, and Zimbabwe, majority shareholdings in banking operations in Ghana, Nigeria, Uganda and Malawi, a representative office in Cote d' Ivoire and an offshore banking unit in Mauritius. It also has other African operations which focus on trade and commodity finance and corporate banking. These activities have increased its Africa-generated earnings from R180 million in 1997 to R350 million in 2001 (*Business Day* 19.12.01). Anticipated earnings from 2002 put the figure at about R500 million, a return on investment of some 30 per cent. Less visible but also present in Africa are other South African banks, notably Absa, Rand Merchant and Nedbank, as well as the South African insurer, Alexander Forbes.

The expansion of major retailers such as Shoprite, Woolworths, Truworths, Pep Stores, and Metro Cash and Carry, and food chains such as Nandos and Steers, across the continent has been mirrored by an accompanying movement of South African property developers who are building shopping centres to house these chains. Furthermore, the expansion of Multichoice and TV Africa across the continent represents a prime communication's medium for commercial activity in Africa. In addition, burgeoning business travel stemming from trade and investment from South African groups such as MTN, M-Net, Shoprite, Absa and the mining conglomerates, coupled with the growth of regional tourism, holds a number of opportunities for hotel groups. For example, Protea Hotels has expanded a line of hotels from the east coast, including Kenya, Tanzania, Malawi, Zambia, Mozambique, and Swaziland, to the west coast of Africa including Ghana, Nigeria and Angola.

Another feature of South Africa's penetration of the African economy has been the promotional role played by the state through such entities as the Industrial Development Corporation (IDC), which not only provides funding but also shares the risk by taking a direct stake in some projects. For example, the IDC has a 25 per cent interest in the Mozal project in Mozambique. The IDC's portfolio of African projects under implementation or consideration currently includes 60 projects in 21 countries, spanning from Egypt and Algeria in the north to Nigeria and Senegal in the west, Sudan, Uganda, Kenya, Tanzania, Malawi and Swaziland in central, east and southern Africa (*Business Day* 26.09.02). By providing export finance, the corporation has facilitated the growing participation of South African industry in projects throughout the African continent. In 2002, the IDC focused on building up partnerships in Nigeria, Senegal, and Ghana. In Nigeria, for example, it has invested more than $1,4 billion, of which $75 million was in the telecommunications sector, $34 million in tourism and real estate, and $18 million in resources.

A further characteristic of the investment pattern has been the targeting of Africa's generally underdeveloped – or in some cases non-existent – infrastructure and it has proved to be a boon for South African contractors and parastatals. It is here that one finds the two truly 'big-league' South African players on the continent – Eskom Enterprises and Transnet, or more specifically in regard to the latter, its rail division, Spoornet, and subsidiary company, Comazar. Spoornet currently operates five contracts in Africa. The largest of these is the $78 million Ressano Garcia concession to operate the rail line between Komatipoort and Maputo harbour, as well as a further $10 million to rehabilitate the harbour itself. This rail link forms a key component of the even larger Maputo Development Corridor project linking the Witwatersrand industrial heartland and Mpumalanga's agro-industrial core to its export outlet in the port of Maputo.

Spoornet's activities, however, are dwarfed by those of Eskom. Capitalising on the business opportunities opening up to it in Africa, in 1999 Eskom established a wholly-owned subsidiary with a mandate to pursue ventures in Africa. Operating as Eskom Enterprises, its investment plan for 2000–2005 allocated $240 million to southern Africa, $445 million to West Africa, $86 million to North and Central Africa and $245 million to East Africa (*African Business* July/August 2002). By 2002, the company's African contracts reflected its pan-African ambitions. It was managing state electricity utilities in Rwanda, Malawi and Zanzibar, as well as in Libya as a joint venture with a Libyan utility; it was also managing power plants in Uganda, Zambia and Zimbabwe and hydro-electric schemes in Mali, Morocco and the DRC. The diagram below depicts the range of Eskom's activities in Africa.

Its flagship venture, however, is that of developing an energy grid across Africa. This is a project of awesome dimensions, as the diagrams below illustrate. It involves linking the Southern African Power Pool (a SADC project in

Figure 17.1 *Eskom's activities in Africa*

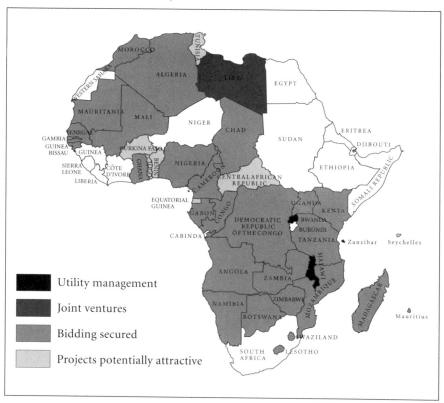

Source: www.mbendi.co.za/eskomenterprises/maps

which Eskom is the driving force) to a power-generation plant at Grand Inga Falls in the DRC. This, in turn, will lead to Eskom developing a transmission network from Grand Inga into Angola, Zambia, Tanzania, Kenya and Malawi, and then, finally, linking those to power grids straddling the rest of the continent. Chief Executive Officer of Eskom Enterprises, Jan de Beer, has decribed the project as 'a trans-African grid linking up all regions of the continent and it may only be as little as five years away, (*Business in Africa* April–May 2002).

The appalling state of fixed-line telephone and telecommunications' infrastructures in Africa has also generated lucrative opportunities for the South African

Figure 17.2 *Envisaged African transmission system*

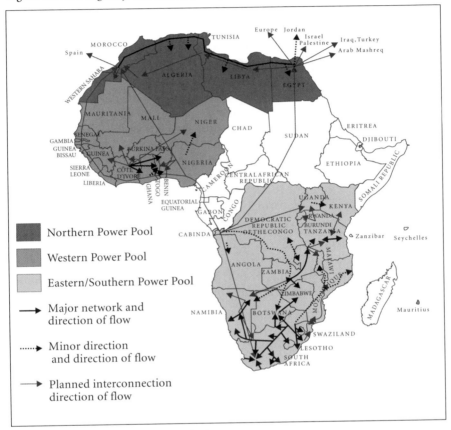

Source: www.mbendi.co.za/eskomenterprises/maps

telecommunications sector. So much so that Eskom Enterprises has entered the arena to compete with MTN and Vodacom, which between them have effectively cornered the African cellular market. Of the two, MTN is the larger and is currently operating in six African countries. Total revenue from its then five African operations in 2001 amounted to R2,97 billion, returning a profit of some R420 million. This was three years ahead of schedule as original MTN estimates had it that its African operations would be in the black only in 2004.

Mozambique: A case study in South African corporate penetration

The far-reaching changes which South African corporate expansion have wrought to the African political economy, and particularly to that of the southern African region, are well illustrated by the case of Mozambique. As a victim of a mix of Portuguese colonial exploitation and neglect and a decade-long anti-colonial war, Mozambique came to independence in 1975 as one of Africa's 'economic basket cases'. Its early economic gains post-independence were obliterated by South Africa's surrogate army, Renamo, which waged a nine-year long war of attrition in which it targeted civilians for killing and maiming, and their support facilities – schools, clinics, roads, bridges and power lines – for destruction. By the early 1990s, Mozambique had been reduced to the poorest performing economy in Africa and in terms of the UN's Human Development Index ranked amongst the most poverty-wracked and desperate countries on earth.

Yet, ten years later in 2001, Mozambique eclipsed Zimbabwe as South Africa's largest trading partner in the region. In that year, South Africa exported goods to the value of R5,72 billion to Mozambique, compared with R5,38 billion to Zimbabwe. At the same time, South Africa overtook the former colonial metropole, Portugal, as Mozambique's biggest foreign direct investor.

The largest of South Africa's investments in Mozambique is in the $1,3-billion Mozal I (now being expanded with Mozal II) aluminium smelter project near Maputo. The IDC, the state-owned South African national development corporation, holds 25 per cent of Mozal I shares alongside the 49 per cent held by BHP-Billiton, a mining multinational with partly South African roots. The IDC's involvement was significant in that it represented a whole new investment direction for the IDC, which had hitherto limited its funding operations to South Africa. The Mozal involvement was its first venture beyond national borders signifying, in a sense, South African capital's outward-looking orientation.

Since this first investment, the IDC has branched out into other ventures in Mozambique and beyond. For example, the IDC has arranged a ten-year loan of US$250 million to help Mozal II pay for imports of construction materials and services from about 150 South African companies. The construction of Mozal I, which started in May 1998, saw local companies bring home some R1,5 billion a year in exports of construction materials and services. It is estimated that the Mozal II expansion will generate some R530 million per year of exports from South Africa.

Outside of the Mozal project, South African companies have in recent years made a number of large investments into Mozambique. These include:

○ A $1,3 billion investment by Sasol in a gas pipeline in Sofala province.
○ A $50 million investment by South African Breweries (now SAB Miller) beer factories in Maputo and Beira.
○ A $63 million investment by Illovo Sugar in the Maragra sugar mill.
○ A $130,5 million investment by Eskom towards integrating a power line from South Africa via Swaziland to the Mozambican power utility, Montraco.
○ A $15,5 million investment by a South African property developer in construction of a large shopping mall outside of Maputo.
○ A $500 million investment by Southern Mining Corporation in the Corridor Sands project.
○ IDC involvement in a large-scale cotton farming and ginning project in Capo Delgado province, in the Maputo Iron and Steel project, and in a number of cashew, tea and coffee plantation operations.

In all, between 1997–2001, South African companies invested R9 billion in Mozambique and there are now over 250 South African companies operating in the country. Many of these are located within retail, tourism, telecommunications, financial services and the food and beverage industry. They include Shoprite, Nandos, Debonairs, Vodacom, Absa (which recently acquired a controlling share of Mozambique's Banco Austral) and Pep Stores. According to the *Financial Mail* (07.02.03), collectively these companies employ over 43 000 Mozambicans.

Not all a bed of roses

As the quote cited at the head of this paper suggests, South African corporates are on the whole doing well from their business ventures in Africa. MTN International's returns from its operations in Africa entered the profit column in 2002, a full two years ahead of schedule, while Stanbic's return on its investments in Africa were in excess of 30 per cent in 2002. Its overall contribution to group earnings was nine per cent. In similar vein, Eskom Enterprises, formed only three years ago, already contributes seven per cent to group turnover.

There is, however, a less positive side to this picture as involvement in the region has not been without its difficulties and setbacks, while some South

African corporates have been accused of some unsavoury practices. A 2002 UN report to the General Assembly named 12 South African companies in a list of firms accused of looting mineral resources in the DRC during its recent civil war. They included such 'blue-chip' names as Anglo American, Anglovaal Mining (Avmin), De Beers and Iscor.

Both Zimbabwe and Nigeria have also proved to be difficult operating environments for South African businesses. Shortages of various kinds – foreign exchange, fuel, electricity, spare parts, cement and so on – have caused South African firms in Zimbabwe either to close down or slow down their operations. The mining sector has been particularly hard hit. Other problems have been encountered in Nigeria. Despite its overall profit for 2002, MTN's expenditures have been far higher than anticipated as infrastructure costs are 2,5 times as much in Nigeria as in South Africa. In an earlier development in 2001, SAA halted flights on the route between Johannesburg, Lagos and New York after experiencing heavy financial losses (R54 million) in its joint venture with Nigerian Airways. In part, this loss came about as a result of Nigerian Airways' failure to meet its financial obligations.

A number of South African companies have experienced payment problems in several African countries. Murray & Roberts, for example, have had delayed contract payments problems over three of its road-construction projects in Benin, Mozambique and Uganda, while AngloVaal Mining has downscaled its copper and cobalt operations in Zambia for similar reasons. There are likewise tales of woe from South African investors in Zimbabwe.

These problems and setbacks notwithstanding, the African 'invasion' looks set to continue. For some South African companies seeking new markets, there is no choice. Too small to compete in the developed world, Africa is the one and only arena in which they find they have a comparative advantage. And there is the example of those who have experienced handsome returns, despite the difficulties of poor governance and corruption, of disease and poor health and transport infrastructures.

Conclusion: has the leopard changed its spots?

We return now to the issue raised earlier in this paper, namely, how the South African-African relationship is being expressed in this post-apartheid era. Is it merely more of the same with the aggressive interventionism of the past now further augmented by corporate South Africa's growing economic presence and influence on the continent? Or has it changed and if so, how? Earlier too, we made reference to Davies' three post-apartheid scenarios and the question is, do any of these reflect or approximate the nature of current South African-African state relations?

In looking at this issue, a distinction needs to be drawn between the behaviour of South Africa's corporates and its government. Like business anywhere, the South African business sector is driven by typical corporate interests – profit, market share, elimination of competition, the urge to dominate and or monopolise. As Absa Bank's Roger Pardoe has noted, Absa was 'not investing in Africa for altruism. We're investing in Africa to make some money' (*New York Times* 17.02.02). And in pursuit of profit South African capital has not always acted like angels. The opposite has sometimes been the case – witness the dubious and questionable practices of the 12 South African companies operating in the DRC which we cited earlier. Likewise, and despite the desperate need for new FDI in Africa, the South African investor has not always been welcome on the continent. Speaking in the Kenyan Parliament in 2001, an opposition legislator complained that 'if we continue doing this we'll end up owning nothing in Kenya ... they bulldoze their way around. It seems like they still have the old attitudes of the old South Africa' (*New York Times* 17.02.02).

How representative a view of South Africa's business executives this is amongst Africa's politicians we do not know. What we do feel certain about, however, is that it is not possible for Africa's politicians to make the same charge against those who represent South Africa's political interests in Africa. Here there has been a sea-change from the past. Since early in the post-1990 transition period, the ANC has articulated a very different position from that of the apartheid era. Its early policy documents spoke of the 'fate of democratic South Africa being inextricably bound up with what happens in the rest of the continent' (Mbeki 1991); that 'our foreign policy should reflect the interests of the continent of Africa' (Mbeki 1994) and that 'if we do not devote our energies to this continent, we too could fall victim to the forces that have brought ruin to its various parts ...' (ANC 1993).

A decade on, the ANC's position remains consistent with these early sentiments. The quote by Mbeki at the head of this paper was taken from the debate on his 2003 'State of the Nation' speech to Parliament. In it he argued that South Africa could conduct its international relations only within the context of international agreements approved by Parliament and the obligations imposed on the country by virtue of its membership of SADC, the AU, the NAM, the UN and the Commonwealth. 'Whatever we may think of ourselves, none of these give us the unilateral right to force anything on any other independent country' (*Business Day* 19.02.03).

With only one exception, South Africa has conducted its African relations within this ideological framework. That exception was the military intervention in Lesotho in 1998, which, though wrapped in a SADC cloak, was in reality a clumsy and apartheid-style case of South Africa flexing its muscles against the region's weakest member. The operation was widely condemned and criticised at the time and the exercise has not been repeated anywhere else on the continent. The irony, however, is that in retrospect, the 'occupation' can be said to have worked in that it eventually forced Lesotho's endemically hostile political factions into negotiating a long-overdue new electoral arrangement to replace the discredited first-past-the-post system. Since the intervention, Lesotho has enjoyed a period of unprecedented post-independence stability, during which a general election has been conducted without controversy, and, even more remarkably, without any challenge to the legitimacy of the outcome (Southall forthcoming).

With the benefit of nine years of hindsight, the Basotho case stands out as the exception to a general rule of non-coercive, non-hegemonic behaviour in Africa on the part of the new South African state. This is not to suggest for a moment that South Africa has been uninvolved in regional affairs. To the contrary, and particularly so in the Mbeki era, it has been exceptionally engaged but its approach to continental issues has been to operate within a regional cooperation framework, even when it has assumed a leading role. This is a position consistent with the themes which underpin both the notion of an African Renaissance and which informs the Nepad and AU policy frameworks.

This approach to African diplomacy has been clearly evident in the two African trouble spots which have most engaged the Department of Foreign Affairs in recent times – Burundi and the DRC. Years of painstaking and financially-costly negotiations rather than muscle-flexing has been the norm and the yield has been long in coming. In regard to Zimbabwe too, the South African approach has involved a mix of multilateralism involving the Commonwealth and SADC, and bilateralism. But the South African intent in both modes has been to avoid coercive measures in favour of what it has called 'quiet diplomacy'.

This is not to suggest, however, that we approve of South Africa's position over Zimbabwe, because we do not. While in general it is our view that states should in their relations with each other eschew power politics and coercion in favour of negotiation and persuasion, we do not believe that this norm is the be-all and end-all of diplomacy or an inflexible and absolute rule. While non-interventionism may foreclose acts of physical aggression or intrusion in the affairs of another state, it does not mean that nations also foreswear their rights to speak out or comment upon acts of moral outrage by fellow members of the international community. To speak out in such circumstances is, we believe, both a right and an obligation in the face of war crimes and crimes against humanity. In regard to Zimbabwe, where crimes against humanity have become commonplace, we feel South Africa has reneged on its obligation to condemn the atrocities being committed on its doorstep. Not only is it failing in its duties as a member of the international community but also its stance is at odds with our understanding of the African Renaissance or the good-governance principles of Nepad and the African Union. These are, as we have noted, central pillars in South Africa's approach to continental affairs, but it has failed at the first real test to apply them.

All that can be said is that South Africa's failure to act morally in the case of Zimbabwe has been consistent with its general eschewing of hegemony in its inter-state relations. Thus it would seem that that scenario which Davies (and others at the time) considered least likely – non-hegemonic co-operation – has in fact, been the option embraced by the post-apartheid South African state. The leopard has it seems changed its spots, but in so doing, it seems also to have lost its ability even to growl or scowl in regard to Zimbabwe.

Note

1   Much of the data presented in this paper is drawn from the database of the HSRC's South African Corporate Mapping project. Administered by Sanusha Naidu and John Daniel, the project collects data on South African corporate activity in Africa.

References

African National Congress (ANC) (1993) *Foreign policy in a new democratic South Africa: A discussion paper.* Johannesburg: Department of International Affairs.

Ahwireng-Obeng, F & McGowan, PJ (1998a) Partner or hegemon? South Africa in Africa, *Journal of Contemporary African Studies* 16 (1): 5–38.

Ahwireng-Obeng, F & McGowan, PJ (1998b) Partner or hegemon? South Africa in Africa, *Journal of Contemporary African Studies* 16 (2): 165–195.

Castel-Branco, CN (2002) *Economic linkages between South Africa and Mozambique*. Study for the Department for International Development of the British Government.

Davies, R (1992) Economic growth in a post-apartheid South Africa: Its significance for relations with other African countries, *Journal of Contemporary African Studies* 11 (1): 50–71.

Mbeki, T (1991) South Africa's international relations: Today and tomorrow, *South Africa International* 29 (4): 231–235.

Mbeki, T (1994) Foreign policy in a new democratic South Africa, in *International perspectives: Extracts from addresses by Thabo Mbeki, Salim Ahmed Salim, JD Barroso, Lord Carrington*. Johannesburg: South African Institute of International Affairs.

Southall, R (forthcoming) An unlikely success? South Africa and Lesotho's 2002 elections, *Journal of Modern African Studies*.

Truth and Reconciliation Commission (1998) *Truth and Reconciliation Commission of South Africa Report*. Pretoria: Government Printer.

United Nations (2002) *Final report of the panel of experts on the illegal exploitation of national resources and other forms of wealth of the Democratic Republic of Congo*. New York: UN.

Contributors

Michael Aliber
Chief Research Specialist,
Integrated Rural and Regional Development programme, HSRC

Miriam Altman
Executive Director,
Employment and Economic Policy Research programme, HSRC

Acheampong Yaw Amoateng
Research Director,
Child, Youth and Family Development programme, HSRC

Doreen Atkinson
Research Director,
Democracy and Governance programme, HSRC

Sakhela Buhlungu
Lecturer,
Sociology of Work programme, Department of Sociology,
University of the Witwatersrand

Linda Chisholm
Research Director,
Education Policy Research programme, HSRC

John Daniel
Director,
HSRC Publishing Department,
Democracy and Governance Research programme, HSRC

Madeleine Fullard
Researcher,
South African Development Education Trust

Jonathan Jansen
Dean of the Faculty of Education,
University of Pretoria

Adam Habib
Director,
Centre for Civil Society, University of Natal, Durban
Part-time researcher,
Democracy and Governance programme, HSRC

Xolela Mangcu
Director,
Steve Biko Foundation

Gerhard Maré
Professor of Sociology,
University of Natal, Durban

Mandisa Mbali
Research intern,
Centre for Civil Society,
University of Natal, Durban

Reuben Mokoena
Chief Research Specialist,
Integrated Rural and Regional Development programme, HSRC

Percy Moleke
Senior Research Specialist,
Employment and Economic Policy Research programme, HSRC

Varusha Naidoo
Lecturer in Political Science,
University of Natal, Pietermaritzburg

Sanusha Naidu
Chief Research Specialist,
Integrated Rural and Regional Development research programme, HSRC

Nicoli Nattrass
Professor of Economics,
University of Cape Town

Linda M Richter
Executive Director,
Child, Youth and Family Development programme, HSRC

Nicky Rousseau
Lecturer,
History Department, University of the Western Cape

Maxi Schoeman
Professor of Political Science,
University of Pretoria

Roger Southall
Executive Director,
Democracy and Governance programme, HSRC

Index

Page references in italics indicate figures and tables